CENTURY OF DIFFERENCE

CENTURY OF DIFFERENCE

How America Changed in the Last One Hundred Years

Claude S. Fischer and Michael Hout

Russell Sage Foundation ◆ New York

The Russell Sage Foundation

The Russell Sage Foundation, one of the oldest of America's general purpose foundations, was established in 1907 by Mrs. Margaret Olivia Sage for "the improvement of social and living conditions in the United States." The Foundation seeks to fulfill this mandate by fostering the development and dissemination of knowledge about the country's political, social, and economic problems. While the Foundation endeavors to assure the accuracy and objectivity of each book it publishes, the conclusions and interpretations in Russell Sage Foundation publications are those of the authors and not of the Foundation, its Trustees, or its staff. Publication by Russell Sage, therefore, does not imply Foundation endorsement.

Library of Congress Cataloging-in-Publication Data

Fischer, Claude S., 1948–
    Century of difference : how America changed in the last one hundred years
/ Claude S. Fischer and Michael Hout.
        p. cm.
    Includes bibliographical references and index.
    ISBN-10: 0-87154-352-4
    ISBN-13: 978-0-87154-352-3 (alk. paper)
    1. United States—History—20th century. 2. United States—Social conditions—
20th century. 3. National characteristics, American. 4. Social change—United
States—History—20th century. 5. Social conflict—United States—History—20th
century. 6. Social stratification—United States—History—20th century. 7. Pluralism (Social sciences)—United States—History—20th century. I. Hout, Michael. II.
Stiles, Jon. III. Title.

E741.F49 2006
306.0973'0904—dc22   2006021640

The paper used in this publication meets the minimum requirements of American National Standard for Information Sciences—Permanence of Paper for Printed Library Materials. ANSI Z39.48-1992.

Text design by Genna Patacsil.

RUSSELL SAGE FOUNDATION
112 East 64th Street, New York, New York 10021
10 9 8 7 6 5 4 3 2 1

CONTENTS

ABOUT THE AUTHORS

Claude S. Fischer is professor of sociology at the University of California, Berkeley.

Michael Hout is professor of sociology and faculty associate of the Survey Research Center at the University of California, Berkeley.

Aliya Saperstein is a Ph.D. candidate in sociology and demography at the University of California, Berkeley.

Jon Stiles is data archivist for U.C. Data Archive & Technical Assistance (UCDATA) at the University of California, Berkeley.

Jane Zavisca is assistant professor of sociology at the University of Arizona.

PREFACE

THE CONCERNS of the present, historians warn, often direct our views of the past. A couple of generations ago, in the middle of the twentieth century, learned observers worried that America had become a bland, uniform, conformist mass society; the specter of the Nuremberg rallies hovered in the background. They described an American history in which controlling and homogenizing forces from above—big government, big business, big media—had effaced local culture and individual distinctions. Other-directed conformists had replaced enterprising individualists. In our time, the public warnings instead are about too much division and difference, about a society that is crumbling into economic, cultural, and political fragments. Unsurprisingly, then, our effort to understand the vast social changes Americans experienced between 1900 and 2000 focuses on difference and diversity. However, what we end up seeing and reporting in this book are not greater divisions—in some ways, divisions narrowed over the years—but, more important, new patterns of division.

Drawing on a century's worth of censuses and seven decades of surveys, we describe how Americans changed demographically, economically, and culturally. We attend in particular to how the attributes that shaped Americans' lives in 1900 became less important and other attributes became more important. Region, race, and gender divided Americans much less in 2000 than they did in 1900. Other lines of division, most notably level of educational attainment, came to shape Americans' lives much more. America remained a divided society, but divided in modern ways. The critical dividing moments were less often birth and more often early adulthood—for example, gender less and graduation more. Also, divisions that touched on class tended to widen, while cultural differences, such as religion, nationality, and region, tended to narrow. Whether Americans form (or ought to form) a community of kindred souls or a nation of divergent groups has been under debate for generations. By drawing on these historical data, we hope to add some empirical material to the early twenty-first-century version of that discussion.

This project took seven years of planning and execution. The Russell Sage Foundation provided continuing financial and intellectual support, from inviting our proposal for the research to its final publication. We especially thank Eric Wanner for his engagement with the project and us. Berkeley's Survey Research Center and its data analysis and technical assistance staff also supported our work with local expertise, research facilities, and collegial environment. We are especially grateful to Director Henry Brady who always said "yes" whether we wanted to monopolize the conference room for a few days, use more staff time than we could pay for, or upgrade the computers with his money. The Integrated Public Use Microdata Series project of the University of Minnesota's Population Center provided one hundred years of census data in easy-to-use formats.

The Berkeley Sociology and Demography Departments offer an ideal environment for this kind of wide-ranging endeavor. We thank our colleagues who asked questions and offered suggestions at six colloquia where we presented draft chapters. And we took for granted and fully exploited the steady stream of unbelievable talent that flows through both graduate programs. First, we thank our collaborators and graduate student coauthors, Jon Stiles, Aliya Saperstein, Gretchen Stockmayer Donehower, and Jane Zavisca. Each was indispensable and instrumental to whatever success we have achieved. We also thank Christine Getz, Nancy Latham, Jenn Sherman, Stephanie Mudge, Melissa Wilde, Sara Nephew, Cid Martinez, Jianjun Zhang, Caroline Hanley, Emily Beller, and Shannon Gleeson for their assistance. They wrote detailed memos, crunched numbers, attended meetings, and enlivened the project in many ways.

Colleagues at Berkeley and around the country gave us help and comments at various points. We thank Mark Chaves, Sheldon Danziger, Reynolds Farley, Leo Goodman, Andrew Greeley, Kristen Harknett, Arne Kalleberg, Michael Katz, Ron Lee, Rob Mare, Adrian Raftery, Steve Ruggles, Christine Schwartz, Chuck Tilly, and John Wilmoth for their suggestions and advice.

Claude S. Fischer
Michael Hout

CHAPTER ONE

Introduction: The American Variations, 1900 to 2000

ON OCTOBER 12, 1900, as many as thirty thousand Italians paraded from Washington Square through lower Manhattan to celebrate Columbus's landing in America. They marched under a cloud of bad news: a state assembly resolution to prohibit the hiring of "alien Italian workers" for tunnel construction; a socialite's proud announcement to the press that she would ban Italian laborers from working on her estate, though it would cost her thousands of dollars; a brick-throwing brawl between Italian and Irish workmen ("Get out me way, yez Guineas," shouted teamster Thomas Conley at the hod carriers); an unannounced invasion on a Tuesday morning of homes in Harlem's Little Italy by police and sanitation workers, who liberally sprayed cellars with disinfectant (although, as chief inspector Feeney later admitted, they found few problems with uncleanliness); a request from the Italian government that those guilty of lynching five Italians in Louisiana in 1899 be punished; and the discovery in that summer of 1900 that Italians had been murdered in Mississippi.[1]

About a hundred years later, the Bronx Columbus Day parade, starting off on White Plains Road and heading to Pelham Parkway, featured local Italian-American businessmen and clergy, the New York City police band, Italian-, Irish-, Jewish-, and Puerto Rican–American politicians, a suburban drum-and-bugle corps, the "Dixie Dandies" traditional jazz performers, and a West Indian steel drum band. (In 2000, the parade also included a Chinese dragon.)[2] The great-grandchildren of 1900s Italian aliens had moved to the suburbs and found acceptance in America. More broadly, the multiculturalism of the Bronx parade and the whole genre of ethnic carnivàle in modern America signified a happy consensus that, now, at last, difference was wonderful. If only it were so easy.

The motto "e pluribus unum" inscribed on the Great Seal of the United States puts in Latin an American ideology. "From many, one" describes not only the union of many states into one federation, but also the faith that different kinds of people from many nations can coalesce. Yet every American generation has worried about that solidarity. At times, differences seem to overwhelm commonality.

The turn of the last century was one such time. The millions among the "huddled masses" and "wretched refuse" flooding from southern and eastern Europe to America's "golden door" seemed much more foreign than the earlier immigrants who had come from northern and western Europe—they were different "races." Gaps between newcomer and native, black and white, rich and poor, skewed the lottery of life: many Americans lived well and long, while many others lived grimly and briefly. Region still divided the native-born. Four of ten had been alive when Lincoln was shot, and most Americans still nurtured grievances from what the southerners called "the War Between the States." (The novelist Saul Bellow recalled a schoolteacher in the 1920s repeating tales of his father's Civil War battles.)[3] Regional contrasts were all too apparent in both the poverty and the distinctive lifestyle south of the Mason-Dixon Line. Reconstruction had ended a generation earlier after failing to remove the consequences of generations of slavery; subsequent years of Jim Crow had preserved many of its bitterest fruits.

The latest turn of century, in 2000, also had its divisions, the Bronx's ecumenical parade notwithstanding. The influx of Asian and Latin American immigrants worried many native-born Americans, just as the influx of Italians, Jews, and other swarthy people had worried earlier generations. And more than ethnicity split Americans. The economic gap between the rich and the rest was widening to a degree unseen for decades. Political lines had carved sprawling communities into small, competing fiefdoms. The Protestant uniformity of 1900 had given way to the denominational mélange of 2000, and secular and religious Americans contested society's moral ground rules.

The historian Thomas Bender has pointed out the persisting tension in American thought between, on the one side, a historic view that the nation requires commonality and consensus and, on the other side, a modern, cosmopolitan view that the nation is enriched by diversity.[4] This debate flared up in the seventeenth century when Puritans insisted on religious orthodoxy, and again in the nineteenth when Jeffersonians resisted the rise of industry and the laboring class it created. At the beginning of the twenty-first century, the debate has flared up around matters such as immigration restrictions, the role of government in leveling wealth, and multiculturalism. This enduring debate and efforts to synthesize the two impulses call Americans to understand their history of diversity and commonality.

In many respects, such as in their ethnic heritage and in the work they did, Americans clearly became more diverse over the twentieth century; in other ways, such as in basic living standards and childbearing, Americans clearly became less diverse; and in yet others, such as their incomes and some social values, differences widened in one era and narrowed in another. (Indeed, while commentators at both ends of the century focused on division, commentators in the middle of it, in the 1950s, dreaded too much uniformity.) There is no easy metric for determining whether America in 2000 was, in all such respects, more "pluribus" or more "unum" compared to America in 1900. We can see that *how* Americans differed and what kinds of differences *mattered* changed over the century. Gender, region, national origin, and even, in some matters, race became less consequential in shaping people's life chances and lifestyles (although the black experience remained distinct); age, income, and, notably, educational attainment became more consequential. This book describes how Americans differed from one another, even became divided against one another, over the twentieth century. It also describes ways in which Americans moved toward greater similarity and agreement over the century.

We are struck, in fact, by how often common values bridged American differences, especially by 2000. Americans prayed in a multitude of diverse churches and temples, but they did so in a relatively similar way (in weekly services led by a professional clergyman) and held much the same faith (in God and the afterlife). Americans descended from a global variety of cultures, but they valued much the same goals (self-reliance, free choice, true love, the single-family home, and a bedroom for each child). Americans lived in novel kinds of families, but they overwhelmingly agreed on the best family (a married couple with two children). Americans' financial assets ranged from billions of dollars to far below zero, but they shared similar tastes and owned similar goods (a car, a television, fashion clothing). This book tries to calculate the shifting balances of differences and similarities over the twentieth century.

The broadest change we describe concerns not the sum total of differences among Americans—did they become more or less alike?—but *how* they were different, the changing *axes of difference*. One of the most striking changes is that contrasts between people by place, race, and gender generally faded over the century but contrasts by education sharpened; at least since midcentury, education became a key sorter of Americans. How much schooling Americans got increasingly determined how they lived. The next chapter specifically describes the development of education and educational differences during the twentieth century.

Our approach thus sets aside the search for the mythic average American. To be sure, we describe what social scientists call "central tendencies." For example, Americans generally lived longer, made more money, moved to the suburbs, and more often endorsed racial and religious tolerance as the century unrolled. We dwell, however, on what social scientists call "variances." For example, variation among Americans in family size shrank, income differences narrowed and then widened, and divisions on family issues first widened and then narrowed. The reader can get an immediate sense of this distinction between a focus on central tendencies and a focus on variations by glancing ahead to figure 4.2 (64, this volume), which displays what happened to the life expectancy of women in the twentieth century. The average life span—more precisely, the *median* (fiftieth percentile) life span—increased about fourteen years, from about seventy-two for women born in 1900 to about eighty-six years for women born in 2000. More dramatically, the *range* of life spans shrank. Long-lived women born in the early 1900s lived about sixty-five years more than their short-lived sisters; long-lived women born around 2000, demographers project, will live about twenty years more than their short-lived sisters—so much did life spans at the low end increase. So Americans' longevity grew in the twentieth century, but *shared* longevity grew much more. It is this dimension of social change in the twentieth century—the history of variances, differences, and divisions—upon which we focus.

EVIDENCE AND ANALYSIS

Although this book rests on many numbers and on sometimes complex calculations, we have written it with general readers in mind, using, for example, simple graphs to convey the most essential findings. Motivated readers will find comprehensive discussions of the technical details—including a few methodological innovations we have developed—in the notes and appendices and on the book's website. Most readers can ignore these additions.

All readers should, however, understand the nature of the evidence underlining our discussion. The story of twentieth-century America has been told in various ways—for example, as personal biography, as the history of ideas, as political combat. We seek to describe the everyday diversity and commonality of ordinary Americans. This leads our search for evidence away from the journals, diaries, letters, and press accounts used in most histories to materials such as the decennial censuses. People sometimes doubt the accuracy of those censuses, wondering whether everyone is counted and whether people honestly tell the census-takers about their private lives. These concerns are well placed, and researchers have addressed them. We know, for example, that the census of 2000 missed perhaps as many as one in twelve African-American men. Undercounts were worse in earlier censuses, missing perhaps one in seven black men. We also know that census information on incomes is skewed by poorer people not reporting under-the-table income and even more by richer people underreporting their investment incomes. Similarly, marriage statistics are distorted when abandoned women report themselves as widowed and common-law couples say they are married. Nonetheless, the vast majority of Americans are forthcoming. Repeated examinations have confirmed that census data are quite accurate—and accurate enough for our purposes.[5] And finally, census data are the best and often the *only* evidence that can answer our questions. Where a problem is critical—such as the missing African-American men—we note and attend to it. Analyzing historical censuses has become practical thanks to the Integrated Public Use Microdata Series (IPUMS), which compiles, codes, and makes available the data on millions of past and present Americans.[6] In some places we draw as well on other Census Bureau data, especially the annual Current Population Survey (CPS) conducted in the last few decades of the century.

The census does not, however, ask Americans about everything we might wish to know. Censuses do not ask people about their faith, values, attitudes, or emotions. To track the history of Americans in these domains we use commercial and university-based national surveys. In particular, we draw on the many polls conducted by the Gallup organization from 1935 through 2000 and on the General Social Survey (GSS) for 1972 through 2000.

Popular skepticism about surveys probably exceeds that about censuses. And surveys do have faults. They sometimes undercount certain groups, such as people without telephones or workaholics who are never home, and some of the questions that interviewers ask are prone to distortion. Many people, for example, are reluctant to admit to racial prejudice. These are well-understood problems in the survey profession. Over the century the better polling organizations (and there are differences) have refined their techniques and provided accurate snapshots of Americans' views and experiences. A three-percentage-point error in predicting a close presidential election embarrasses a polling organization, but such small errors are much less important here. When the polls show, for example, that in the 1930s Americans overwhelmingly frowned on married women working and later polls show that in the 1990s Americans overwhelmingly approved of married women working, we can be confident that this difference indicates a real change in national views on gender. Similarly, when surveys show that after 1970 the gap between rich and poor Americans widened not only in income but also in how they felt about their incomes, we can be confident that there really was a growing divide in Americans' sense of economic security.

In the chapters that follow, we typically begin by describing Americans in

2000—how they formed households, their standards of living, their religious lives, and so on. We then put 2000 into historical perspective, tracing changes over the century—or as much of the century as the available data allow us to trace—and particularly changes in lines of division. How did diversity in family patterns or occupations or values change over time? When and to what extent did differences in, for example, wealth or religion or cultural values correspond to differences in race or region or education—to various axes of difference? In what ways did Americans divide or coalesce over the twentieth century?

OVERVIEW

We examine twentieth-century diversity and commonality in eight areas. In chapter 2, we describe the increase in Americans' educational attainment over the century, showing how women caught up with men, African Americans closed the gap with whites, and regional differences diminished. We also begin our discussion of how educational attainment increasingly shaped and distinguished Americans' fates and fortunes.

Chapter 3 examines diversity in the sense that most Americans hear the term: ethnicity and race. Ancestry was a controversial matter in the 1900s, when nativists openly testified in Congress about the influx of inferior European "races" such as Jews, Greeks, and those Italians who marched in lower Manhattan. The heterogeneity they feared became vastly greater in the final decade of the century with the arrival of millions of Asians and Latinos. Ironically, this diversity became less consequential as immigrants assimilated, intermarried, and increasingly gained acceptance from the native-born. The key exceptions to these homogenizing trends were African Americans, the descendants of America's "peculiar institution."

Chapter 4 treats the American family. Observers have warned that the households of married couples and children are "disappearing" as more and more Americans live as unwed couples, grow up in single-parent families, or even live alone. We describe a more complex story, one rooted in basic demographic shifts—longer lives and smaller families, in particular. In several ways, American family patterns did not change as much between 1900 and 2000 as many seem to believe, and much of the major change that did occur—such as increasing single-parenthood and one-person households—was specific to certain racial, educational, and age groups. The story is less one of increasing family diversity than of changing axes of diversity.

Chapter 5 describes the diversification of work in America, a consequence in part of the near-disappearance of farming, once Americans' main occupation, and in part of the invention of new jobs. The march of women into the labor force obliterated one of the biggest differences among Americans: that men worked for pay and married women did not. Education and age replaced gender and marital status in determining who worked, how many hours they worked, who had the best job, who got paid the most, and how people felt about their jobs.

In describing American inequality in living standards, chapter 6 moves beyond the usual discussion of recent trends in income differences to look, historically, back to the early twentieth century and, topically, to inequality in wealth and consumption as well. For most of the century, economic gaps narrowed, particularly as blacks and rural southerners caught up with the rest of the nation. After 1970, however, divisions of income and wealth widened again. In spending and consumption, America's cornucopia of productivity allowed poorer Americans to come closer to the standards of more affluent Americans; by 2000 few Americans really went hungry, and almost all Americans had color television sets. But even the equalization of consumption stalled or perhaps reversed over the last few decades. Material gaps between Americans generally became greater than they had been for much of the century—and polls showed that Americans sensed it.

Chapter 7 tracks the mass movement of Americans from countryside to suburbs over the century. One consequence of that movement was a shift in the geography of social differences. Where once South versus non-South and rural versus urban clearly coincided with differences of social class and ancestry, by 2000 suburb versus city was the more important axis of difference. Racial segregation, having intensified for much of the century, weakened inside American cities in the last decades. But at the same time, suburban boundaries stiffened, making the political geography of American metropolitan areas an increasingly important social divider of Americans.

Chapter 8 examines religious diversity and religiosity, a topic of much controversy in the early twenty-first century. Americans in the twentieth century largely retained their characteristic piety, experts' expectations of secularization notwithstanding. With the expansion of Catholicism and the emergence of Eastern traditions, Americans in the twentieth century became more diverse in their specific religious affiliations, but at the same time they seemed to become more alike in their actual beliefs, including many of the unchurched among them.

Chapter 9 confronts the end-of-the-millennium debates on whether Americans were becoming polarized or even fragmented on values issues, a thesis sometimes labeled "the culture wars." Taking a much longer view of Americans' attitudes—back to the 1930s—we see that the most polarized era was probably earlier, the 1950s and 1960s. We find that Americans were not "falling apart" culturally in the last decades of the century.

Chapter 10, the conclusion, reviews what we have learned about the twentieth-century course of diversity and unity, extracts a few implications for issues of concern to twenty-first-century Americans, and points to avenues of potentially fruitful research.

One such avenue of further work would be to explain *why* Americans became more or less divided in various ways. Our main task in this book is to *describe* historical trends, not explain them. Where there is a scholarly consensus on some trend, or a simple reason why it occurred, we note that. Where there is serious debate about explanations, we outline the controversy. At some points, we offer in passing what we believe to be a plausible reason for a development. We do not, however, thoroughly investigate and test theoretical explanations, as we would in a focused journal article. We do not, for example, try to resolve alternative explanations for the widening income gaps since 1970, or the convergence of Catholics' religious behavior with that of Protestants after about 1960.

SHIFTING LINES

The contrast between the Columbus Day celebrations in New York City, which bracketed the century, symbolizes the eventual assimilation of yesteryear's alien immigrants. It also illustrates more broadly how lines of division among Americans shifted over the century. The significance of European nationality clearly waned, and ancestry in general was far less a source of conflict in 2000 than in 1900; the marchers in 2000 even celebrated ethnic and racial diversity. But other differences among Americans, such as between living in the city or in the suburbs, between blue-collar and professional workers, and notably between the poorly and well-educated, shaped the lives of the great-grandchildren of the 1900 marchers much more than those immigrants parading out of Greenwich Village might have imagined.

CHAPTER TWO

How America Expanded Education and Why It Mattered

EDUCATION Is Good Business, a 1947 film short sponsored by the U.S. Chamber of Commerce, exhorted its audience to support investing more tax money into local schools. "Education is the basis of the genuine production of wealth . . . and the foundation of good business," the narrator insisted, and "tax investments return to the taxpayer." Clips displayed boys learning farm science, electrical work, and mechanics and showed girls typing and developing art appreciation. Better education would make young Americans better workers (and housewives); they would also earn more money and become better consumers. Ironically, during this era, the midtwentieth century, extra education made relatively little difference in the lives of individual Americans; its import would come later. Developments in the following decades overturned many of the film's presumptions: the occupations it touted dwindled, the high school graduation it celebrated became prosaic, the girls to whom it assigned supporting roles surpassed boys in schooling, and the college degree it never mentioned became the gateway to a better life—and, increasingly, the dividing line in American society.[1]

THE EXPANSION OF AMERICAN EDUCATION IN THE TWENTIETH CENTURY

Americans became much more educated over the course of the twentieth century. In 1900 people typically had only a primary school education, although more and more states and localities were mandating at least some high school. By 1920 high school graduation had become widespread; from 1960 onward, college followed for most high school graduates. As more Americans gained more schooling, education emerged as a key axis of difference in American society. The people who got the most schooling became increasingly distinct from those who dropped out as soon as the law allowed. Employers who once treated an employee's diploma as a bonus started to see it as a requirement. Life chances and lifestyles grew more distinct between the less- and the more-educated. Young people started to choose mates who had the same amount of education. Cultural trends, from new clothing styles to new gender roles, started with the college-educated and spread to the less-educated, with enough lag-time to create friction between "snobs" (with degrees) and ordinary "folks" (without degrees).

Education expanded not because of students' demand but because American public institutions supplied more of it and demanded it of workers. Cities and states built elementary and secondary schools, and then they required parents to enroll their children in them. Later, states vastly expanded the public colleges and universities and kept tuition below costs so as to fill them.[2] Private college and university enrollments grew only slightly faster than the eligible population did from 1940 to 1980, but enrollments at public colleges and universities soared. The University of Michigan enrolled twenty thousand students pursuing BA degrees in 1955 and forty-five thousand in 1975; enrollments at Ohio State exploded from fifteen thousand to sixty-two thousand in the same twenty-year period. California and New York built multicampus systems of community colleges, state universities, and research universities.

Telling the basic story of educational expansion from the individual point of view, figure 2.1 draws, as we will do throughout this book, from the national censuses as compiled and coded in the IPUMS. The population in any particular year blends people who are still in school, some who finished recently, and many who finished long ago—the grade school–educated septuagenarian along with the thirty-year-old holding an MA degree.[3] So for these purposes, we instead classify people by birth date according to the year they turned twenty-one; this gives us a better sense of the conditions at the time each person finished his or her schooling. We look only at native-born Americans here to focus on those whose exposure to schooling was solely in this country. The heavy line in figure 2.1 shows the median years of schooling that adult, native-born Americans attained from the first to the last decade of the twentieth century. We can see that average educational levels increased from a median of 7.4 years for birth cohorts whose members were old enough to be finishing high school in the first decade of the twentieth century to 13.8 years for the cohorts whose members finished their high school education in the last decade of the century.[4] The average American's schooling almost doubled over the ninety years.

Figure 2.1   Median Years of Schooling Completed and Number of Years Completed by the Least-Educated and Most-Educated 20 Percent of Adults, by Year of Twenty-First Birthday

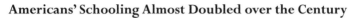

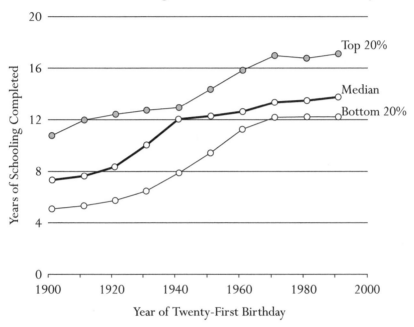

Americans' Schooling Almost Doubled over the Century

Source: IPUMS.

Figure 2.1 also shows us the variation in Americans' formal schooling by using a twenty-fifty-eighty percentile chart, first introduced in chapter 1. The most-educated fifth (the eightieth percentile) of 1901's native-born twenty-one-year-olds had completed at least 10.8 years of school; by the 1991 cohort, the most-educated had completed at least 17.1 years. The least-educated fifth (the twentieth percentile) had completed no more than 5.1 years in 1901 but had more than doubled that to 12.3 years in 1991. The gap between the top and bottom fifths of Americans shrank half a year over the century, from a spread of 5.7 years (10.8 minus 5.1 for 1901) to a spread of 5.2 years (17.1 minus 12.3 for 1991), indicating a bit more commonality among Americans in educational experience. This modest reduction in educational differences makes our later findings—

that the educational gaps became more consequential—all that more striking.

Earning a diploma or a degree is a more meaningful educational transition than passing from one grade to another. So we focus on trends in earning credentials. Figure 2.2 presents historical trends in high school and college graduation. The top left panel simply shows the diffusion of the high school diploma over the century. High school graduation rose from a privilege shared by just 19 percent of the American-born who came of age in the first decade of the twentieth century to an entitlement shared by 87 percent of those turning twenty-one from the 1970s onward. This revolution occurred largely because local communities made great efforts, particularly in the late nineteenth century, to construct high schools and, particularly in the early years of the twentieth century, to enforce school attendance. The motivations for trying to make public high school education universal were a mixture of a desire to corral and domesticate unruly youth, especially the children of immigrants, and a desire to train young workers for a changing economy (*Education Is Good Business*). The changing economy spurred attendance in two ways—first, by convincing some parents that their children's futures depended on getting a good education, and second, by eliminating the alternative jobs that uneducated children could take.[5] The widespread belief that education fostered good values while teaching practical skills generally increased public support for public schools, but trying to emphasize both goals did, from time to time, lead to conflicts over what to teach in public schools.[6]

The other panels of figure 2.2 show the spread of high school graduation by gender, region, and ancestry. Graduation rates topped out in the 1970s at 80 to 90 percent for both genders, all four ancestries, and all four regions. From about 1920, when high school graduation started its expansion, until near the end of the century, the South lagged behind the rest of the nation (lower left panel). African Americans, Latin Americans, and Native Americans (the latter two groups are classified as originating in the Americas; we explain these continent-of-origin categories in chapter 3) lagged far behind European and Asian Americans for most of the century (lower right panel), especially blacks in the South.[7] In the last decades, after significant struggle during the years of the civil rights movement, excluded categories of Americans were increasingly incorporated into high school. African Americans took advantage of new opportunities and closed the graduation gap, although test scores and spending in the schools that African Americans attended continued to lag behind those of other schools.[8]

In the latter half of the century, college graduation supplanted high school graduation as the educational watershed. Fewer than one person in twenty among the 1901 birth cohort earned a BA degree, but about one in four graduated from college among the 1971 to 1991 cohorts. The expansion of

Figure 2.2   High School Graduation Rates for All and by Gender, Region, and Racial Ancestry, by Year Person Turned Twenty-One

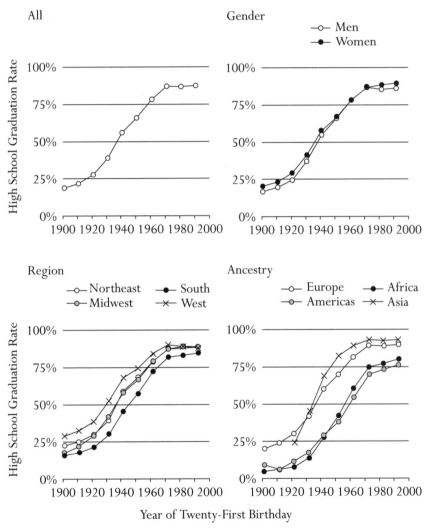

Americans of All Social Backgrounds Shared in the Dramatic Expansion of Secondary Education

Year of Twenty-First Birthday

Source: IPUMS.
Note: The data for the 1900 and 1910 cohorts contain too few Asian Americans to yield a reliable estimate.

postwar college education evident in figure 2.3 (top left) was the product of another burst of public commitment, this time in the form of state college-building programs and direct federal aid to students, first in the GI Bill and then later in grant and loan programs for low-income students.[9] The fastest-growing educational group since midcentury was that cohort of Americans who had some college and often had earned a two-year degree but no BA diploma; they formed one-third of the 1991 cohort. It is hard to explain why more young adults did not persist all the way to college graduation after 1970: the gap in earnings between high school and college graduates rose by 30 percent in those years, and getting just a couple of years of college education did not pay off well.[10]

Figure 2.3 replicates much of figure 2.2 for college graduation; it displays how differences in college graduation rates overlapped with other social distinctions. Unlike high school graduation, for which group differences narrowed, group differences in college graduation widened. The top left panel shows two views of college graduation rates. The black circles trace the trend for everyone, and the white circles show the trend just among high school graduates. The sharp increase in college graduation rates for high school graduates between 1940 and 1970 reveals that the expansion of higher education opportunities outpaced the growth in secondary education. The top right panel shows that men and women were about equally as likely to graduate from college when it was a rare thing for anyone to do. Men's graduation rates increased more rapidly than women's did at midcentury, peaking for the cohorts that came of age in the 1970s—the baby boom and Vietnam-draft cohorts. Men's rates then dropped noticeably after the 1971 cohort—for reasons that are unclear—while women charged ahead and passed men. Women also passed men in getting some college exposure short of a BA degree.[11]

The bottom-left panel shows regional differences (which, we should note, refer to where people were living when interviewed by the census, not necessarily where they were educated). Westerners exceeded people in all other regions throughout, although their advantage shrank a little after the 1971 cohort. More importantly, a gap in college graduation rates widened between the Northeast and the West, on the one hand, and the South and the Midwest, on the other: there was only a two-point difference between southerners and northeasterners before World War II, but the difference had widened to eight points by the 1991 cohort. The final panel shows college graduation rates by ancestry. Here too we observe a widening of differences, with European- and especially Asian-origin Americans moving ahead of African- and Western Hemisphere–origin Americans.

While the differences in college graduation rates by ancestry and region widened, differences in attending college at all narrowed after World War II, as did differences in high school graduation. Clearly, what we see here is the

Figure 2.3   College Graduation Rates for All, and by Gender, Region,
and Ancestry by Year of Twenty-First Birthday

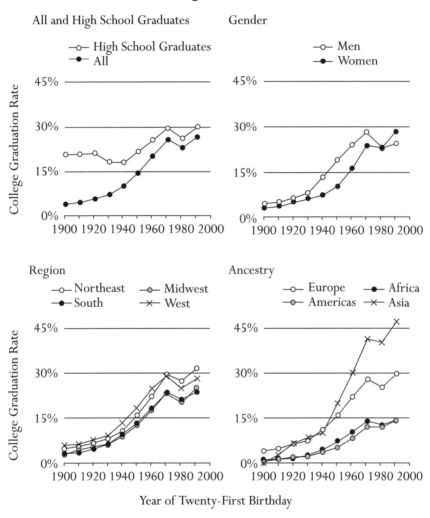

**Americans of All Social Backgrounds Shared in the Expansion of
College Education**

Source: IPUMS.
Note: The data for the 1900 and 1910 cohorts contain too few Asian Americans to yield a reliable estimate.

diffusion of education from higher-status to lower-status groups. As blacks and southerners (as well as rural residents, although we do not display those data) caught up with whites and nonsoutherners (and city folks) in high school graduation rates and then in achieving some college attendance, the advantaged groups moved further ahead by completing college. We might have anticipated that in due course—perhaps by the middle of the twenty-first century—the gaps in rates of earning a BA would narrow and perhaps the key differentiation would be having an advanced degree or not—except for the fact that the college graduation rates flattened out after the 1971 cohort. (We take up the growing importance of advanced degrees in chapter 5.) Perhaps this plateau was only a temporary break in the advance of education that preceded another public push for democratizing schooling, or perhaps the diffusion of education reached some social or cognitive limit in the late twentieth century.

The story displayed in figures 2.1 through 2.3, together with the growing weight of education in determining living standards and lifestyles, has profound implications. Secondary education became common for all but a small, disadvantaged subgroup of Americans. (We will see just how disadvantaged when, for example, we document in chapter 4 the increasingly difficult family lives of high school dropouts.) Immediately after World War II, common schooling and economic growth provided at least white, urban, and suburban northerners with relatively common living standards and lifestyles. But a new frontier of education and educational expectations emerged shortly afterwards. A bachelor's degree became the new entry pass; by the last quarter of the century, differences in living standards and lifestyles between those with and without it had widened greatly. Ironically, because college graduation became more closely tied to ethnicity and place of residence, it helped sustain some socioeconomic differences between racial groups and local communities even as race and residence otherwise faded in importance.

The connection between ancestry and education is sufficiently complex and controversial to warrant a closer look. Because gaps in high school graduation narrowed as gaps in college graduation widened (figures 2.2 and 2.3), trends in average years of schooling only modestly converged. European-origin Americans' schooling rose from an average of eight years among cohorts that finished their education before 1910 to fourteen years for those of 1970. African Americans stayed a year behind, their average schooling rising from seven to thirteen years between 1910 and 1970. Asian Americans surpassed European Americans in recent cohorts, rising from eight years in 1920 to nearly fifteen in 2000. Finally, native-born adults whose ancestors came from the Americas were similar to African Americans: average schooling rose from seven years in 1900 to about thirteen years in 2000. Persisting educational disparities between ancestry groups have received as much attention from social scientists as any other topic throughout the century. Early on, these analysts offered biological differences to explain why Italians, Poles, and Jews seemed so academically unpromising, an argument that prompted many to advocate immigration restriction. Later in the century researchers offered alternative explanations for the lagging performance of blacks and Latinos, such as institutional racism, family structure, wealth differentials, neighborhood conditions, school quality, and "stereotype threat" (the anxiety that undermines the performance of students whom the wider society expects to do poorly).[12]

The civil rights court decisions of the 1950s and the legislation of the 1960s took care of some minority disadvantages in education: the gap in average schooling between African- and European-origin Americans narrowed immediately afterwards, especially in high school graduation (figure 2.2). African Americans' deficit of nearly two and a half years of schooling for the cohort reaching adulthood in 1931 declined to under one year in the last cohort, and the educational deficit of those from the Americas narrowed by almost as much over roughly the same period. However, two aspects of life for African-American, Latino, and Native American youth continued to hold down their schooling through the end of the century (and explains their falling further behind in college graduation; see figure 2.3). First, family difficulties persisted in shaping the educations of later generations.[13] A legacy of discrimination and disadvantage cannot be wiped out even over a generation; it takes at least two generations, and maybe more, to overcome the handicaps linked to poverty and racial caste. Second, segregation persisted. As we document in chapter 7, segregation by municipality increased after 1960 even as segregation by neighborhood declined. The persistence of segregation had consequences for high schools, most of which were organized by municipality: they became more segregated in the latter part of the century.[14] These accounts do not, of course, explain the emerging educational superiority of Asian Americans, because the latter were somewhat disadvantaged compared to Europeans in other areas, such as parental education. Explanations of that gap will have to be found elsewhere.[15] Finally, we should not forget that there is great variation in educational attainment within continent-of-origin groups—between, for example, Koreans and Laotians, or between Cubans and Puerto Ricans.[16]

In 1980 William Julius Wilson introduced the notion of the "declining significance of race": class—education, we would suggest—was replacing discrimination as the major source of blacks' difficulties. He and others may have overstated the case (discrimination certainly persisted), but the claim is consistent with our findings: while race per se, like region, became a less important axis of difference over the century, the persisting connection between race and education, owing to the emergence of college graduation as the major hurdle, reinforced racial gaps among Americans.[17] We will see this played out over various topics in the chapters that follow.

The steep rise in Americans' average schooling (figure 2.1) suggests to some analysts that educational attainment became, like the American dollar, inflated. Perhaps a college degree at the end of the twentieth century was really "worth" only what a high school degree at the start of the century was worth; in both eras, only the best-educated quarter of young adults had the degree. One implication of this view is that researchers should not compare people by their years of schooling or by the degrees they have earned, but rather by their educational rank among their cohorts. Jon Stiles examines this question carefully. He compares the conclusions one would draw about historical changes in the effects of education when using each person's nominal educational attainment to the conclusions one would draw from instead using his or her rank in educational attainment—top, middle, or bottom quartile—relative to others in the birth cohort. Stiles finds that, for the great majority of research questions, the substantive conclusions are essentially the same either way. For example, divorce rates increased for thirty- to forty-four-year-old Americans after 1970, but they climbed much more for the less-educated than for the more-educated, so that by the end of the century the two groups differed substantially in propensity to divorce. Either measure of educational attainment, diploma or rank, reveals the same widening gap in divorce rates. Because the educational categories we use, like "high school dropout," "high school graduate," and so on, are material in their own right and also make intuitive sense, we stick with those.[18]

We will see in the chapters that follow that educational attainment increasingly shaped many aspects of Americans' lives, while for the most part gender, race, and region came to matter less and less. It is in this sense that we argue that education became a central, defining axis of social difference in American society. For all we know, luck, personality, looks, and personal connections might each also have created new divisions among Americans, but among the facets of life recorded in the census, none were more broadly consequential at the end of the twentieth century than education.

HOW AND WHY EDUCATION MATTERS

The chapters that follow document that after midcentury education became an increasingly crucial axis of difference among Americans. For example, the more- and the less-educated moved apart in income, wealth, and family life—who married, and to whom, who divorced, and what happened to the children.[19] It is beyond the scope of our inquiry to assess all the hows and whys of those changes. Yet we cannot leave the intriguing questions alone altogether either.

Scholars and writers before us have addressed the question of why education has become increasingly important. Among their answers, three in particular are relevant for us. First is the "human capital" metaphor for education.[20] Schools and colleges teach specific skills that employers look for, such as the typing or mechanical know-how that *Education Is Good Business* featured in 1947. That much is pretty obvious. Schools and colleges also provide their students with the opportunity to learn general math and language skills. Students who master them can gain further training and move into more specialized professional and technical fields. Finally, students acquire, in the process of going to school and doing homework, certain task and goal orientations, such as social poise and self-discipline, that can boost their earning potential. As the economy moved from the muscle power that led to success on the farm and in factories to the cognitive and "soft" skills useful in hospitals, offices, and schools themselves, education became increasingly important in the labor market. (We take up these economic changes in chapter 5.)

Second, while education was becoming more central in labor markets, it was also becoming more central to marriage.[21] Prior to World War II, education, especially college education, was more of a luxury than a necessity, especially for women. Marriages between college-educated men and women were an elite-family phenomenon. "Intermarriage," as it is called, was rare not only because college degrees were rare but also because there were social barriers that kept college-educated and less-educated people in different social circles. As college education became more widespread, the proportion of marriages across educational lines rose. But in the 1960s marriage partners started to sort themselves out by education again—that is, people with similar diplomas more often tended to marry one another. Also, beginning in the 1970s, the least-educated Americans started to become more socially isolated. Marriages between high school graduates and dropouts became less and less common as dropouts stayed unmarried. By the end of the century, exclusive marriages at the top of the educational pyramid and exclusion at the bottom of the pyramid had taken the overall degree of educational sorting in American marriage markets to levels as high or higher than before World War II.

Third and finally, a substantial body of research dating back to the 1950s shows that people with more education take a broader view of social relations. Educated people are more likely to view differences between themselves and others as positive instead of threatening, to participate in social institutions instead of staying on the sidelines, and to foster these kinds of values in their children. It was the blossoming of just such tendencies that educational reformers hoped to see in building the public schools. But the end-of-the-century ramifications included increasingly distinct ways of life demarcated by education—the college graduate way of having economic security, family stability, social engagement, church and community participation, and optimism; the high school dropout way of being warily subject to financial insecurity, family turmoil, and social withdrawal; and the high school graduate way of struggling to join the first social world but often slipping into the second.[22]

IS EDUCATION DIVIDING AMERICANS TOO MUCH?

In the 1990s scholars debated whether education was dividing Americans too much. On the one hand, educational haves and have-nots were moving further apart in the labor and marriage markets and in various cultural realms. On the other hand, education was widely available, seemed to be a more just way to apportion the good things in life than power, wealth, race, or region, and promoted a less xenophobic view of the social world. The debate cannot be resolved without distinguishing between two aspects of education (in America and elsewhere) that were first identified by Peter Blau and Otis Dudley Duncan in their classic book *The American Occupational Structure*: how education allows one generation to pass on its advantages to the next, and how education provides opportunities for moving up. Blau and Duncan found that Americans' family backgrounds (parents' education, father's occupation, number of siblings, and ancestry) partly determined how much education they got. Given that education provides great advancement in the labor market, that connection helps perpetuate advantage and disadvantage from one generation to the next. But—and this is the key finding—most of the variation in how much education people attained was independent of their family backgrounds. This finding implies that education serves to assist social mobility—moving up or down the economic ladder—more than it serves to pass on parents' positions; young people have experiences in school that separate them from their background.

Subsequent research discovered an added benefit of college education in the labor market. People who attain BA degrees are less affected in their further advancement by their parents' circumstances than people who do not complete college.[23] In other words, the expansion of higher education increased social mobility not only directly by giving students a career boost, but also indirectly by canceling the disadvantage of lower-class origins for those who completed college in spite of their family origins.

The balance between a greater or lesser impact of family background on schooling shifted historically. From as far back as good data stretch and up to the early 1980s, it appeared that family background, including class and ancestry, was mattering less and less and that a wider range of American youth were getting that ticket to the good life. After the early 1980s, the connection between family origins and educational attainment tightened, mostly because the cost of college went up.[24] Thus, access to a better life—signified not only by more money but also by better work, a better neighborhood, and a more stable family life—shrank even as college and postgraduate credentials became all the more critical. Education began to matter more as access to it expanded in the 1950s and 1960s; it mattered even more as access to it narrowed in the 1980s and 1990s.

In sum, while educational inequality contributes to labor market and other forms of inequality, higher education itself advances a number of important social goals. Among them are improved chances for upward mobility, cognitive skills, and a more open perspective on social relations. Blau and Duncan expressed it this way in 1967: "Superior status cannot any more be directly inherited but must be legitimated by actual achievements that are socially acknowledged."[25] And the key arena for those "actual achievements" and social acknowledgment is the educational system.

For these reasons, as well as for the sake of fostering democracy and good business, Americans pressed for more and more education—for their children and for others' children too. Yet one by-product was a widening social division by education. Late in the twentieth century, a person's educational attainment foretold his or her personal connections, opinions, and feelings more consistently than many prominent and historical distinctions such as gender and geography.[26] Even much earlier, many a novelist and memoirist had described the cultural barrier that advanced education creates between parent and child, between hometown and wandering son—such as Thomas Wolfe of Asheville, North Carolina, in *Look Homeward, Angel* (1929) and *You Can't Go Home Again* (1940).

CONCLUSION

Over the course of the twentieth century, the United States built one of the largest and most comprehensive public educational systems in the world. Americans took advantage of the opportunities that this social project offered them and raised their average level of learning from seven years of often interrupted and relatively primitive schooling to fourteen years of standardized, continuing, and relatively sophisticated education. First high school graduation, then college attendance, became common. In recent cohorts, 85 percent of native-born Americans graduated from high school, and most went on to some form of postsecondary education, typically college.

All this growth came without an increase in educational inequality; the spread in years of learning from the least-educated one-fifth to the top one-fifth was about as large in the last decade of the twentieth century as it had been in the first (see figure 2.1). The major inequalities among groups closed during this period. African Americans' educational levels, high school graduation rates, and college graduation rates grew faster than those of other Americans' in the twenty years from 1960 to 1980. Southerners closed the gap with other regions. Women caught and passed men.

Americans still wanted to expand education further. In the last years of the century, almost three out of four American adults told the General Social Survey that they thought the government spent too little on public education, up from half of adults in the 1970s.[27] Overwhelming support came from Americans of varying education, income, parenthood, region, and racial ancestry. (Self-defined liberals were, as one would expect, more likely than self-labeled conservatives to encourage education spending.) Part of the impetus to increase educational spending was the relatively poor showing American students usually made in international comparisons of educational achievement. For example, American eighth-graders in 1999 scored behind their counterparts from fourteen nations, including competitors like Japan and Russia as well as small countries like Singapore and Hong Kong.[28] More visibly, Americans could see great disparities between schools in some communities and those in others. Students who needed more support because their parents had less to give often actually got less in the way of qualified teachers, up-to-date facilities, and class size.[29] Finally, it was clear from the evidence of polls, ballots, and political pronouncements that Americans still had great faith, as they had in 1947, that education was not only good business but also the route to achieving personal success and making a better society—ironically, even as education became increasingly a social divider.

CHAPTER THREE

Where Americans Came From: Race, Immigration, and Ancestry*

IN SEPTEMBER 2000, *Newsweek* magazine set out to document "The New Face of Race" in the United States. "In every corner of America, we are redefining race as we know it," the magazine declared. "The old labels of black and white can't begin to capture the subtleties of blood and identity" (3). Looking only at the end of the twentieth century, it would be hard to disagree. In the spring of 2000, the U.S. census invited Americans for the first time to "check all that apply" when reporting race on the census questionnaires. With six major categories to choose from—white, black, American Indian or Alaskan Native, Asian, Native Hawaiian or Pacific Islander, and "other"—Americans could be any of sixty-three different racial combinations. The Census Bureau also asked whether the person being reported on was of Hispanic origin. When those replies were included with answers to the race question, the possible combinations of ancestries doubled to a mind-boggling 126. The resulting counts included, for example, 117,000 white-black-Hispanic Americans and 14,500 black-American Indian-Hispanic Americans.

In 1900 too, Americans thought they were a very diverse lot, even though seven out of eight were recorded by the Census Bureau as white. The historically unprecedented flow of immigrants pouring in between 1880 and 1920 transformed almost every state and all but the most isolated communities. English, German, and, especially, Irish immigrants, so numerous in the nineteenth century, were still arriving, but they were eclipsed in numbers by Italians, Poles, and Jews. Americans with northern European roots viewed these newest arrivals from elsewhere in Europe as inferior "races." In Janu-

---

*Coauthored by Aliya Saperstein.

ary 1900, a headline in the *New York Times* asked, "Are the Americans an Anglo-Saxon People?" The article's author, a doctor of medicine, declared emphatically, and proudly, that most Americans (60 percent by his calculations) could indeed claim membership in the "Anglo-Saxon race." He had determined that the rest of the white population was made up of "Continental Teutons" (23 percent), "Celts" (11 percent), and other "miscellaneous" groups (6 percent).[1]

The quarter-century that followed this declaration saw persistent struggles over whether to close the doors to the "Latin and Slavonic races" that made up those "miscellaneous groups"; as we recount in this chapter, the doors were effectively closed in 1924. A half-century later, they were reopened, and millions of far more culturally distinct newcomers arrived, mainly from non-European continents, sparking new debates about closing the doors. Meanwhile, one hundred years of mixing in schools, in workplaces, and, ultimately, in families had muted once seemingly immutable differences between varieties of European Americans and reduced their divisions from racial cleavages to "ethnic options"—the sociologist Mary Waters's term for whites' freedom to choose, or not, the ancestral identification they preferred.[2]

We report in this chapter on how this history of immigration, acculturation, and intermarriage changed not only the ethnic and racial profile of the American people but also the very ways in which Americans thought about ethnicity and race. Paradoxically, ancestry became a less critical axis of difference over the century even as Americans' ancestries became more varied. For example, differences between groups in learning English declined, and intermarriage across, first, national and, then, racial lines increased. Overt prejudice diminished, and in general Americans adopted more tolerant positions on controversial racial issues. The experience of African Americans at the close of the twentieth century is, however, an important exception to this story of convergence and change (as we will see again and again in the chapters that follow). Though the significance of race certainly declined, as William Julius Wilson argued in his controversial 1978 book, a profound gulf yet remained between black and nonblack Americans on many measures of well-being at century's end.[3]

Our first task is to describe Americans' ancestral diversity in 2000. Plenty of controversy surrounds what to call differences that stem from people's roots in different parts of the world. "Race" is only one of many options, and Americans' understanding of what "race" is has changed over the decades. Nevertheless, because the question that Americans answered on their 2000 census forms referred to "race," that is the term we start with.[4]

RACIAL DIVERSITY AT THE END OF THE CENTURY

In 2000 the Census Bureau asked Americans two key questions about each member of their households: "Is this person Spanish/Hispanic/Latino?" and "What is this person's race? . . . White; Black, African Am. or Negro; American Indian or Alaskan Native; [etc.]." (We discuss the history and meaning of such questions later.) Figure 3.1 shows the results: three-fourths of the American population was recorded as white: the 6 percent who were first checked "Hispanic" and then marked "white," plus the 69 percent who were first checked "not Hispanic" and then marked "white." Twelve percent of all Americans were coded black or African-American, 4 percent Asian or Pacific Islander, fewer than 1 percent American Indian or Alaska Native, 6 percent "some other race," and 2 percent two or more races. (And 823 individuals were marked as *all* of the above.) The Hispanic portions of all these racial groups summed to 13 percent of the total population.

Figure 3.1   Distribution of the Population, by Race and Hispanic
Origin, 2000

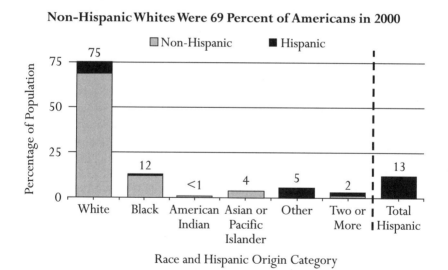

Source: U.S. Bureau of the Census, *Census 2000*, "Population by Race and Hispanic or Latino Origin," PHC-T-1.

Note: Darker shading indicates percent reporting a Hispanic origin within each racial group. Bar to the right of the vertical line sums the Hispanic origin percentages. Percentages to the left of the vertical line represent the entire U.S. population.

The proportion of Americans counted as nonwhite in 2000 was unprecedented.[5] In 1900 the census recorded one in eight residents as being of a race other than "white"; African Americans formed the great majority of the non-whites, although American Indians and immigrants of Japanese and Chinese origin also fit in that category then. In 2000 one in four was of a nonwhite race, twice the fraction a century earlier. If we add to these people Hispanics of whatever *racial* identification, then nearly one-third of Americans were of non-European origin in 2000.

Another way to demonstrate the increasing diversity of Americans is by using the "index of qualitative variation," a measure that quantifies the diversity within a population.[6] By that measure, racial diversity in the United States stood at .49 in 2000—double the level fifty years earlier. (The index ranges from 0 to 1, where 0 means the entire population is of the same race and 1 means the population is evenly distributed across racial categories.) However, some regions and communities were significantly more diverse than others in 2000. Figure 3.2 maps the racial diversity of the nation in 2000, county by county. The places with the greatest diversity were counties in California, Texas, and Florida, as well as the Chicago, Washington, D.C., and New York metropolitan areas. In general, these centers of heterogeneity were major ports of entry for new immigrants. Many also had large concentrations of African Americans. Other counties with great diversity were in the Southeast, where almost all residents were either black or white and the two groups were close to equal in size. Most counties in New England, the Midwest, and Appalachia, in sharp contrast, had diversity scores below .15.[7]

The primary source of America's racial diversity in 2000 was immigration, mostly from Asia and Latin America in the latter half of the twentieth century. As we see in figure 3.2, many of the most diverse places in the United States were located along the coasts or the border with Mexico. Another way to see the contribution of immigration to diversity is to calculate the proportion of each racial group that was born in a foreign country. More than two-thirds of Asian or Pacific Islanders, 46 percent of "others," 44 percent of Hispanics, and 27 percent of people described by "two or more races" were born outside the United States. More than 93 percent of whites, blacks, and American Indians, on the other hand, were born in the United States.[8]

Even if immigration were to stop completely tomorrow, racial diversity in the United States would almost certainly continue to increase. Elderly Americans are a relatively homogeneous group racially, and as they die they will be replaced by cohorts that are increasingly diverse. We calculated diversity scores for different age groups in 2000, using the same population diversity index that the Census Bureau used to make the map in figure 3.2. For Americans over eighty years old, the diversity score was .26; as age dropped, the score rose regularly, up to .66 for twenty- to twenty-four-

Figure 3.2   Diversity Index by County, 2000

Coastal and Southern Counties Were More Diverse Than the Interior

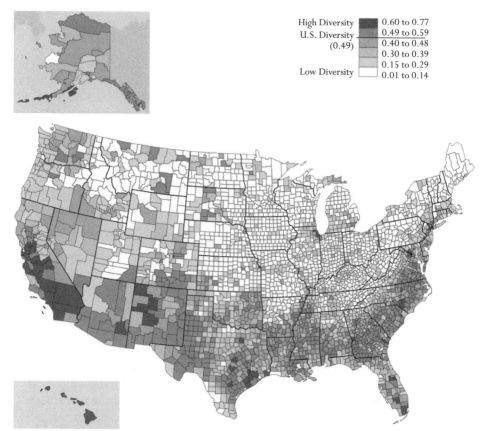

High Diversity	0.60 to 0.77
U.S. Diversity	0.49 to 0.59
(0.49)	0.40 to 0.48
	0.30 to 0.39
	0.15 to 0.29
Low Diversity	0.01 to 0.14

Source: U.S. Bureau of Census, *Mapping Census 2000.*

Notes: The diversity index reports the percentage of times two randomly selected people will differ by race-ethnicity. Working with percentages expressed as ratios (for example, 63 percent = 0.63), the index is calculated in three steps: (1) Square the percentage for each group; (2) sum the squares; (3) subtract the sum from 1.00.

Eight groups were used for the index: white, not Hispanic; black or African-American; American Indian and Alaska Native (AIAN); Asian; Native Hawaiian and other Pacific Islander (NHOPI); Two or more races, not Hispanic; Some other race, not Hispanic; and Hispanic or Latino. People indicating Hispanic origin who also indicated black, AIAN, Asian, or NHOPI were counted only in their race group (0.5 percent of the population). They were not included in the Hispanic group.

year-olds and .69 among children. It is these youngest Americans in the most diverse cohorts who will bear the children of the next generation. By one estimate, through continued immigration and cohort replacement, Hispanics and Asians could double their shares of the U.S. population, to 25 percent and 8 percent of total population, respectively, by the year 2050.[9]

Of course, diversity of ancestry is more than just diversity in racial identification. Given the centuries of European immigration to America, the people recorded as white on the census race question were a very heterogeneous group. Another census question taps this within-race diversity: "What is this person's ancestry or ethnic origin? For example: Italian, Jamaican, African Am., Cambodian, Cape Verdean, Norwegian, Dominican, French Canadian, Haitian, Korean, Lebanese, Polish, Nigerian, Mexican, Taiwanese, Ukrainian, and so on." Like the race question, the ancestry question allowed multiple responses. The most common combinations involved the biggest groups, the three possible pairings of German, British, and Irish. These combinations foretell our discussion about marriage across ancestral lines later in the chapter. For white adults, German was the most frequent single response given in 2000, followed by British (which includes English, Welsh, and Scottish) and Irish (see figure 3.3). Next in line was "American," an increasingly common answer for whites whose ancestors arrived many generations ago.[10] The tenth and twelfth most common responses were also noteworthy: 1.6 percent of whites were labeled as "white" on both the race and the ancestry question (more than twice the percentage as in 1990), and another 1.6 percent of whites were identified as having American Indian ancestry, though they were not labeled as American Indian on the race question. In addition, almost one-fifth of whites chose—or had chosen for them by the family member who filled out the census form—no national or ethnic origin. Those labeled "American" or "white" or nothing at all might be thought of as one of three kinds of non-ethnic Americans: those who recalled only their American roots; those who identified racially but not nationally or ethnically; and those for whom ancestry meant little. In 2000, 30 percent of white adults were one of these kinds of non-ethnic Americans.

Although the fraction of non-ethnic white Americans increased over the last decades of the twentieth century (at the same time that nonwhite racial diversity was accelerating), the phenomenon did not occur nationwide. Much like the regional differences in racial diversity depicted in figure 3.2, diversity in ethnic and national origins varied geographically as well. "Unhyphenated" or non-ethnic white Americans concentrated in the southern states. People most commonly identified as either "American" or "African American" in nearly all counties in southern states east of the Mississippi River, except the ones in Florida. "American" was also the most common ancestry among whites in Arkansas and the parts of Louisiana that have few Cajuns. Mexicans predominated in most of Texas and westward to California,

Figure 3.3   Top Fourteen Ancestry Responses and Percentages
Mentioning No Ancestry Among Whites Eighteen Years
Old and Over, 2000

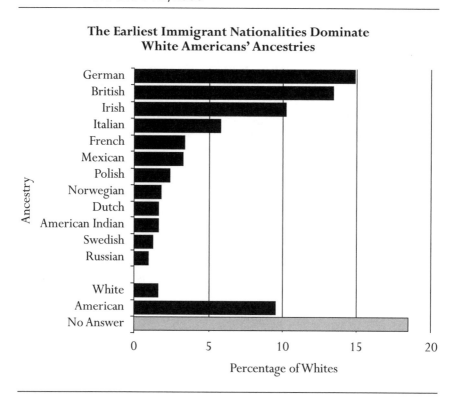

**The Earliest Immigrant Nationalities Dominate
White Americans' Ancestries**

Source: IPUMS.
Note: Darker shading shows the percentage who mentioned the ancestry named at left either first or second among whites who mentioned any ancestry. Lighter shading indicates those who mentioned no ancestry among all whites.

while Germans were the majority in most midwestern counties outside the major urban centers. In the Northeast, the Irish, English, and Italians each had pockets of concentration.

In sum, the United States of 2000 was a racially and ethnically diverse society. Some Americans celebrated that; others worried—much as some had done at the beginning of the century—that such diversity threatened cultural coherence and national purpose.[11] Our next task is to show how America arrived at this diversity. But before we can do that, we need to consider some tough questions about what we mean by race and ancestry and, more important, what Americans have meant by those terms over the twentieth century.

THE EVOLUTION OF RACIAL AND ETHNIC CATEGORIES

In America race is widely discussed, assigned, and counted, but that does not make it easy to study or explain. Most people assume race is an unchangeable attribute that is determined at birth and easily identified by observation, feeling, or deduction from family ancestry. Yet a glance at the U.S. census forms used during the twentieth century reveals just how complex a task it is to describe Americans' ancestries and how attempts to measure them changed. One challenge is posed by the complex political history that surrounds notions of "race." The racial categories that appeared in the census were a jumble of terms that referred to skin color, religion, geographical origin, and nationality, all of which defined "races" at one point or another. Another hurdle to assessing change is that the very measure of racial diversity keeps changing. In each decade of the twentieth century, the government altered the racial categories on the census form in one way or another (see figure 3.4 for three examples). How Americans routinely talked about race was no more consistent. Variations in the census question not only altered the numbers reported for each group but affected—even as they reflected—Americans' sense of who they were and what the term "race" meant.

Scholars trace the word "race" to the Spanish "la raza" and estimate that it was first used, in the way most twentieth-century Americans used it, around the time of the Spanish Inquisition. It connoted pure (or impure) bloodlines, and in the late 1400s it was Moors, Jews, and heretics who were deemed races apart from the rest of the Spanish population.[12] By the eighteenth century, Europeans commonly spoke about particular races as having distinct physical traits (such as skin color, skull shape, and hair type) but also characterological traits (such as laziness, criminality, and virility) that were passed down from generation to generation. According to the historian George Frederickson, these distinctions made race different from other social divisions such as religion or ethnicity: Catholics or Protestants were convertible, new languages and customs could be learned, but one's race—because it was seen as biological and inheritable—was permanent.[13] This notion of race fixed weaker groups into their inferior positions; it also rationalized enslaving Africans, displacing American Indians, and promoting colonialism across the globe.

In the late nineteenth century, claims of biological superiority or inferiority were buttressed by academics who asserted that "Caucasians" had the largest and most perfectly proportioned skulls, or that mulattoes, like

Figure 3.4   Excerpts From U.S. Census Forms, 1900, 1970, and 2000

The Census Race Question Is an Ever-Changing Measure of Diversity

1900 Form

Name	Relation	Personal Description								
of each person whose place of abode on June 1, 1900, was in this family Enter surname first, then the given name and middle initial, if any Include every person living on June 1, 1900 Other children born since June 1, 1900	Relationship of each person to the head of the family	Color or race	Age	Date of Birth		Age at last birthday	Whether single, married, widowed, or divorced	Number of years married	Mother of how many children	Number of these children living
				Month	Year					
3	4	5	6	7		8	9	10	11	12

[Instructions:] Column 5. Color or race. Write "W" for white; "B" for black (negro or negro descent); "Ch" for Chinese; "Jp" for Japanese; and "In" for Indian, as the case may be.

1970 Form

4. Color or Race

Fill one circle.

If "Indian (American)," also give tribe.

If "Other," also give race.

○ White
○ Negro or Black
○ Indian (Amer.) Print tribe →

○ Japanese
○ Chinese
○ Filipino

○ Hawaiian
○ Korean
○ Other–Print race

2000 Form

6 What is this person's race? Mark ☒ one or more races to indicate what this person considers himself/herself to be.

☐ White
☐ Black, African Am., or Negro
☐ American Indian or Alaska Native— Print name of enrolled or principal tribe.

☐ Asian Indian
☐ Chinese
☐ Filipino
☐ Japanese
☐ Korean
☐ Vietnamese
☐ Other Asian— Print race.

☐ Native Hawaiian
☐ Guamanian or Chamorro
☐ Samoan
☐ Other Pacific Islander— Print race.

☐ Some other race–Print race.

mules, were sterile and sickly and would eventually die out. This "scientific racism" had many vocal proponents in the United States, even though its claims were often based on anecdotal evidence, small samples, and other questionable methodology.[14] By the end of the century, genetic evidence had revealed that 99.9 percent of human genes are shared across groups and that there is more genetic variation within racial groups than between them. Most social scientists in 2000 agreed that centuries of disparate treatment, not biology, had left some ancestry groups behind others in educational attainment, income, wealth, and health.[15]

This history of categorizing and ranking groups by race left its mark on the U.S. census. Though ostensibly nonpartisan, the Census Bureau is not immune to the scientific and political climates of an era. In the late nineteenth and early twentieth centuries, the bureau often added racial categories to census forms for the purpose of "monitoring" the size and progress (or lack thereof) of different groups.[16] From 1970 on, the federal government used racial counting in order to monitor groups in a more benign way: to enforce various laws, such as affirmative action compliance and the Voting Rights Act, and to distribute funding for various federal programs. The bureau took those needs into account.

Americans were differentiated by race in the very first census in 1790 (and in many colonial laws long before that). That census used the categories of free whites, other free persons, and slaves. In the second half of the nineteenth century, census officials added (and later removed) categories for mulattoes, quadroons, and octoroons to try to describe the many Americans who had both black and white ancestors, and they started counting the Chinese, Japanese, and American Indians separately as well. Complications mounted. Early in the twentieth century census-takers were told to count Americans who came from India as "white," but from 1920 to 1940 the instruction was to count them as "Hindu," even though most Asian Indian immigrants at that time were Sikhs. A "Mexican" was anyone born in Mexico or whose parents were from Mexico and who was "definitely not white, Negro, Indian, Chinese or Japanese"—but only in 1930. In all other years, "Mexicans" were counted as "white" except when they were "definitely" something else. American Indians were always recorded as Indians—except if they were either "Negro" or accepted as "white" by the community in which they lived. The census has defined "blacks" or "Negroes" in all sorts of ways, from a person whose ancestry was three-quarters or more "black" to a person who was "evidently full blooded," to one with any "Negro blood—no matter how small the percentage."[17]

Complicating matters further, for much of the twentieth century the decision about what to write down for someone's "color" or "race" was up to official census enumerators; they presumably drew their own conclusions from the looks and accents of their respondents.[18] It was only in 1970 that

Americans began to fill out census forms themselves and could choose the category they felt best described themselves and their family members.[19] That change in procedure introduced its own discrepancies from one decade to the next. Counts for certain groups increased when the census form specifically gave them as options—for instance, by providing separate categories for Koreans or Vietnamese, or by listing "Argentinean" or "Dominican" as examples of Hispanic. Some respondents also crossed out terms they did not like, wrote in new or different terms, or simply wrote in phrases instead of checking the boxes.[20]

After the civil rights era, when the purpose of racial enumeration changed, many organizations with racial constituencies viewed the census as a means of achieving recognition of their groups' existence and their claims to rights and benefits. Hispanics and several Asian and Pacific Islander groups all lobbied to be counted separately in the census and gained that recognition in 1980.[21] Native Hawaiians (and other Pacific Islanders) got their own category in 2000 after seven thousand Hawaiians signed yellow postcards and sent them to Washington asking for that change.[22] Some groups also lobbied *not* to be listed as a separate category. Mexican spokesmen did so in the 1930s; their fear was that American authorities would use the tabulations to find and deport Mexican nationals from the Southwest. Arab Americans had asked for but been denied a separate category in the 2000 census; after September 11, 2001, they dropped their pleas, hoping to avoid the same kind of easy detection that had aided the roundup and internment of Japanese Americans during World War II.[23]

Across the century, the public also debated what certain groups should be called on the census form and in everyday speech. For example, on June 10, 1906, a banner headline in the *New York Daily Tribune* read: "What Is the Proper Name for the Black Man in America?" The query was prompted by a dispute in Congress over whether the wording of a bill designating seats on the Washington, D.C., board of education for members of "the colored races" was too vague and whether it would be impolite to use "Negroes" instead. One congressional representative wrote to Booker T. Washington, then president of the Tuskegee Institute, for his opinion. Washington's response—that he preferred "Negro" spelled with a capital *N*—touched off a national debate. The *Tribune* printed a full page of letters from prominent white and black judges, ministers, college presidents, newspaper editors, and the like weighing in on the question. Its informal poll found that 55 percent of the men in the category to be named said they preferred to be called "Negro," but many of the rest, according to the article, found the word "insulting, contemptuous and degrading" and variously preferred "Afro-American," "Negro-American," "colored," "black," or "anything but 'nigger.'"[24] On March 7, 1930, nearly a quarter-century later, the *New York Times* announced in an editorial that it was changing its style to always spell "Negro" with a capital *N*, in "an act of recognition of racial self-respect for those who have been for generations in 'the lower case.'"[25] In May 1969, two years after Stokely Carmichael first uttered the phrase "black power," a Gallup/ *Newsweek* poll asked a national sample of Negroes what they preferred to be called. The most popular answer was still "Negro" (38 percent), and "Colored" came in second (20 percent); *Newsweek* reported that "black" was gaining in popularity (19 percent), however, especially among young, northern adults.[26] In 1982, when the General Social Survey asked the same question, "black" had become the clear favorite (52 percent), with "Negro" and "Colored" combined being chosen by just 10 percent.[27] By 2000, 48 percent of adults polled by the National Survey of Black Workers preferred to be called "black," and 49 percent preferred to be called "African American" when they were given a choice between the two terms.[28] The changing category name on the U.S. census form reflected these evolving and revolving preferences: "Black" until 1930, "Negro" from 1930 to 1970, "Negro or Black" in 1970 and 1980, "Black or Negro" in 1990, and "Black, African Am. or Negro" in 2000. (In this book, we use both "black" and "African American.")

Similar naming debates occurred among Latinos after the Hispanic-origin item first appeared in the 1970 census.[29] Table 3.1 documents the evolution of the census question; in this case too inconsistency has been the rule. The new information provided by the Hispanic-origin item sharpened analysts' picture of the nation's diversity, but it further complicated the task of separating real changes in the composition of the population from changes in the census questions.

This history shows that the concept of race and its categories are far from physical realities. The question options varied over time, and the answers given varied by how the question was asked and who answered it—underlining historical accounts of the fluidity of racial categories, even the basic categories of black and white.[30] Clearly, no one name or category will ever describe every American's ancestry. This history also raises the danger of comparing apples to oranges, such as mulattoes in 1920 to Negroes in 1960, and to "Black, African Am. or Negro" in 2000.

Researchers interested in racial ancestry have to decide *what* they want to study and *why* to determine which categories and which labels best serve their purposes. Because we aim to describe changes across the entire twentieth century, we have chosen to assemble the various census categories into four broad ancestral groups. The divisions are not an attempt to describe "races" that share specific physical traits or supposedly immutable characters but to capture the diversity of Americans through their continental origins. To help us distinguish when America was the most or least diverse, we chose groupings that remained relatively consistent over the century, sidestepping the proliferation of racial categories. Later in this chapter, and throughout the book, these continental categories also will help us document whether ancestry-group differences in opportunities, lifestyles, and material well-

Table 3.1   Questions and Answers Used to Measure Hispanic Origins, 1970 to 2000

1970

13. Is this person's origin or descent (Fill one circle)

O Mexican
O Central or South American
O Puerto Rican
O Other Spanish
O Cuban
O No, none of these

1980

7. Is this person of Spanish/Hispanic origin or descent? Fill one circle.

O No (not Spanish/Hispanic)
O Yes, Mexican, Mexican-Amer., Chicano
O Yes, Puerto Rican
O Yes, Cuban
O Yes, other Spanish/Hispanic

"A person is of Spanish/Hispanic origin or descent if the person identifies his or her ancestry with one of the listed groups, that is, Mexican, Puerto Rican, etc. Origin or descent (ancestry) may be viewed as the nationality group, the lineage, or country in which the person or the person's parents or ancestors were born."

1990

7. Is this person of Spanish/Hispanic origin? Fill ONE circle for each person.

O No (not Spanish/Hispanic)
O Yes, Mexican, Mexican-Am., Chicano
O Yes, Puerto Rican
O Yes, Cuban
O Yes, other Spanish/Hispanic (Print one group, for example: Argentinean, Colombian, Dominican, Nicaraguan, Salvadoran, Spaniard, and so on.)

2000

5. Is this person Spanish/Hispanic/ Latino?

Mark [X] the "No" box if not Spanish/Hispanic/Latino.

□ No, not Spanish/Hispanic/ Latino
□ Yes, Mexican, Mexican Am., Chicano
□ Yes, Puerto Rican
□ Yes, Cuban
□ Yes, other Spanish/Hispanic/ Latino -Print group.

Source: U.S. Bureau of the Census, enumeration forms for the censuses of 1970–2000 (available at www.census.gov).

being have converged or diverged over the century—as in the educational differences we described in chapter 2.

The four ancestry categories we constructed are: (1) "Europe," which includes white Americans from Canada, Australia, and New Zealand on the supposition that almost all had other ancestors, further back, who came from Europe; (2) "Africa," which includes the black, Negro, and mulatto categories of previous censuses; (3) "America," which includes American Indians, Hispanics, and Central and South Americans, few of whose ancestors, we presume, came from Europe; and (4) "Asia," which includes people from most Asian nations but may include only East Asians under the rubric used in some censuses.[31]

Some detail is certainly lost in using just four categories to capture the diversity of American ancestries. As we noted earlier, in 1900 the category "European origin" included a wide range of national-origin groups, from well-established British and German Americans to marginalized Italian and Russian Americans, some of whom were considered and treated as "racially" inferior. (Recall from chapter 1 how much life had changed for the Italians marching in the 2000 Columbus Day parade.) Only later did all these European groups "become white" in a sociological sense as their differences in language, occupations, and living standards dwindled. Still, the categories we have deployed capture the larger, qualitative differences between continent-of-origin groups. Each arrived in America in different periods, through different means, and under vastly different political, social, and economic circumstances. Even in 1900 American society distinguished and treated very differently people of African origin, and this was true in the West for those of Asian, Hispanic, and Native American origin as well. Italians, Poles, and Jews were often treated as though they were "not quite white," but they were never denied citizenship nor separately enumerated in the census race question. However stigmatized some European immigrants were, they felt that they were a rung above the non-Europeans, and they were generally treated that way.[32]

THE FALL AND RISE OF CONTINENT-OF-ORIGIN DIVERSITY

Continent-of-origin diversity actually declined slightly from 1900 to 1930, when European Americans peaked at 88 percent of the population, their highest proportion in national history.[33] However, as figure 3.5 shows, by 2000 Europeans' 69 percent share was the smallest ever.[34] The percentage of Americans with African roots varied over a narrow range in the twentieth century; they were 12 percent of the population in 1900, 10 percent from 1920 to 1960, and then 12 percent again from 1980 onwards. The fraction from the Americas was no more than 1 percent until 1920, but Hispanic immigration after 1960 raised the Americas-origin group from third to second place at 13 percent. The Asia-origin population also used to be negligible, but it amounted to almost 4 percent by 2000.

Given the relative stability of the black and American Indian populations, the twentieth-century rise of America's continent-of-origin diversity is largely the history of immigration. We turn now to a fuller description of that history. Economic booms and busts channeled the most migrants, that is, the majority who moved for material reasons. Labor recruitment was one form of economic migration: agents enticed Chinese, Japanese, and Filipino workers to the Hawaiian sugar cane plantations and, under the bracero program, Mexicans to western fields. Political events also pushed migrants to

Figure 3.5   Continent-of-Origin Ancestry, by Year

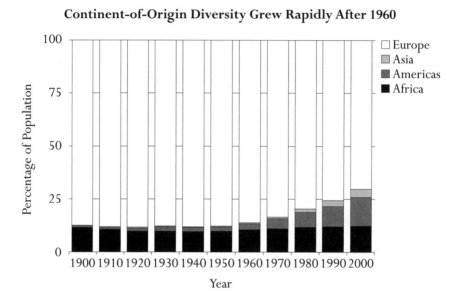

Continent-of-Origin Diversity Grew Rapidly After 1960

the United States. For example, U.S. military interventions in Korea, Vietnam, and Cuba all brought in people from those countries, and earlier imperial expansion stimulated immigration from the Philippines and Puerto Rico.[35] In the last decade of the century, immigration accounted for as much as half of the population growth in the United States, largely from regions outside of Europe.[36] Most of the immigrants officially admitted in the 1990s came from Mexico (2.25 million), the Philippines (500,000), the Soviet Union (460,000), China (420,000), and India (360,000).[37] Another perhaps 1.6 million "unauthorized" immigrants also arrived that decade.[38] The steady increase in the continent-of-origin diversity of America's immigrants, and thus the increasing diversity of the American population as a whole, dates to the mid-1940s (see figure 3.6). Before then, more than 85 percent of immigrants came from Europe or Canada, but by the last decade of the century fewer than 20 percent did. Diversity also increased within the continent-of-origin groups: the British, Irish, and Germans, who were most of the European-origin population in 1900, were shortly joined by an influx of Italians, Poles, and Russians; the Chinese and Japanese, who together were nearly all the Asian-origin immigrants in 1900, were joined by Koreans, Filipinos,

Figure 3.6   Immigration by Continent-of-Origin, by Decade

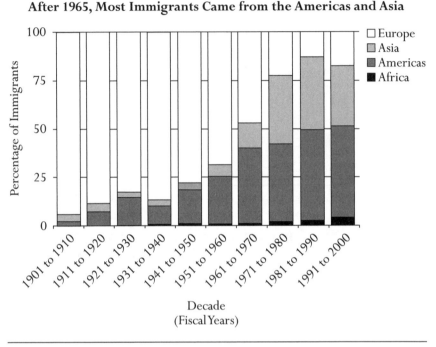

After 1965, Most Immigrants Came from the Americas and Asia

Source: INS, *2000 StatisticalYearbook of the Immigration and Naturalization Service*, table 2.

Asian Indians, and Vietnamese; and after the 1950s, American Indians and Mexicans were joined increasingly by Cubans, Puerto Ricans, and Central and South Americans.

These immigrations, often cited as a credit to the United States—symbolized by the Statue of Liberty's welcome to "huddled masses" and mythologized in "the melting pot"—were also a source of conflict, especially at both the beginning and the end of the century when many millions of people entered.[39] Nine million legal immigrants landed in the first decade of the century and about the same number in the last decade—more than arrived in all four decades between 1921 and 1960.[40] In the first quarter of the century, Americans on both sides of the political aisle—and for reasons as wide-ranging as wage fluctuations and scientific racism—sought to restrict which and how many immigrants could come. Concerns were rampant about acculturation and about how well immigrants and their children would adapt to American society: What jobs would they do? What language would they speak? How would they vote? Whom would they marry? In the last part of the century, the objects of native-born Americans' fears were different, but Hispanics and Asians stimulated similar concerns then as Italians, Jews, and Slavs had done in the early 1900s. In both periods, ethnic differences generated political divisions.

The First Quotas

When the twentieth century opened, nativists cried that Anglo-Saxon America was being overrun by the peasants of continental Europe and Asia. On September 28, 1900, a headline in the *New York Times* announced: "Immigration of Aliens, Northern Races Fall Off; Tendency of Inflows from S. European and Oriental Countries More Marked than Ever." According to the Immigration and Naturalization Service, the top five immigrant groups that year were Italians (82,000), "Hebrews" (45,000), Poles (25,000), Slovacs (25,000), and Irish (25,000). "Old-stock" immigrants from England, Scotland, and Wales had long since fallen out of the top ten. Even the Irish and Germans, who had topped immigration lists in the 1870s, were being replaced as the latest feared threat to the American social fabric. By 1902, southern and eastern Europeans accounted for 78 percent of all immigrants to the United States.[41] Around the same time, social Darwinism and eugenics had become in vogue among the European American elite,[42] and immigration restriction was being urged, no longer primarily by organized labor on the West Coast, seeking to bar Asian workers, but in blanket statements by the president of the United States. In his 1903 State of the Union address, Theodore Roosevelt declared: "We cannot have too much immigration of the right kind, and we should have none at all of the wrong kind."[43]

Eighteen years before Roosevelt's pronouncement, Chinese laborers had been the first to be officially excluded. Then the "Gentleman's Agreement" of 1907 barred Japanese workers too. (The Japanese government agreed to stop issuing passports to laborers bound for the United States in exchange for the city of San Francisco's agreement to reverse its policy of segregating Chinese and Japanese students in its public schools.) That year the United States officially admitted its highest number of immigrants to date, nearly 1.3 million, at the highest rate ever, 14.2 immigrants per 1,000 Americans.[44] Though the outbreak of World War I slowed the flow of immigrants considerably, the government added further restrictions.[45] And when immigration began to increase again after the war, Congress responded with a series of national quota laws intended to curtail entry from all countries outside northwestern Europe. By the mid-1920s, American policy restricted total immigration from beyond the Western Hemisphere to 150,000 a year, allotted quotas within that total to different nations in proportion to their representation among Americans in 1890, and kept out east Asians altogether.[46] Senator David A. Reed (R-Pa.), a sponsor of the central 1924 quota law, explained a key purpose behind all these moves: "The races of men who have been coming to us in recent years are wholly dissimilar to the native-born Americans . . . our incoming immigrants should hereafter be of the same races as those of us who are already here."[47]

Undoing National Quotas, 1946 to 1964

The Great Depression and World War II helped make quotas largely irrelevant between 1931 and 1946; no more than 100,000 immigrants (and as few as 23,000 in 1933) arrived each year.[48] Between 1921 and 1950, about one-third of all immigrants came from either Canada or Mexico. Starting in 1946, Asian exclusions were dismantled, one group at a time, in great measure because the Philippines, India, and China were U.S. allies in the war; moreover, some Filipinos, Asian Indians, and Chinese served in the American armed forces or married American servicemen. In 1952 the Immigration and Nationality Act completely eliminated race as a grounds for excluding an immigrant and for the first time since 1790 made all races eligible for naturalization.[49] The national-origins quota system came to an official end in 1965 with the passage of the Hart-Celler Act. The act still limited the number of immigrants, but nation of origin was no longer the criterion for granting admission. Instead, priority went to relatives of U.S. citizens and to immigrants with special occupational skills. Although the legislation was in part a bow to the civil rights spirit of the 1960s, lawmakers also expected that it would primarily increase immigration from Europe, because most Americans had originated there.[50]

Policy and Experience, 1965 to 2000

As it turned out, few Europeans took advantage of the family reunification provisions of the 1965 immigration reform.[51] Instead, Asians and Latin Americans filled the quotas and then some, to a number unimagined by the Congress. During the 1950s, one in twenty immigrants came from Asia; by the end of the century, the fraction had risen to about one in three. Some of the rapid increase was due to wars in Southeast Asia, which drove refugees to the United States. (All told, 2.3 million refugees from various regions of the world legally entered the country after 1970.) The growth in immigration from Mexico was the most dramatic and most controversial. The border between the two countries had long been vague. Exploitative "smoke and mirrors" policies designed to simultaneously attract cheap labor and bar costly dependents made illegal immigration an especially volatile issue.[52] Undocumented immigration, by definition, is hard to document. Comparisons between the enumeration of foreign-born persons in the census and other administrative data yielded an estimate of 8.5 million undocumented immigrants living in the United States in 2000.[53]

The relaxed quota system—particularly the ability of immediate family members to immigrate, outside the quota—took the number of all immigrants, authorized or not, to its highest point in American history: upwards of 11 million in the 1990s. However, the total American population was so large that the immigration *rate* did not increase commensurately. From 1901 to 1910, there were approximately ten immigrants for every one thousand people already living in the United States, and from 1991 to 2000, only three immigrants arrived for every one thousand Americans.[54] But the late-century immigrants came from parts of the world—Latin America and Asia—that had sent relatively few immigrants from 1900 to 1920. That raised a new round of questions about if, or how quickly, the immigrants would acculturate. We turn next to these controversial issues.

ANCESTRY, LANGUAGE, AND MARRIAGE

The question of whether the newest immigrants were fitting in, or even trying to fit in, roiled American politics in the last decades of the century. In California, for example, political fortunes were made and lost in the 1990s on campaigns to restrict services to undocumented immigrants. In the Southwest, there were numerous confrontations between self-appointed border guards and defenders of immigrant rights. Around the country, "English-only" drives sought to legislate the languages to be allowed in schools and government offices, reflecting the conviction of many that the new immigrants were unlike the early-century European immigrants: the newcomers were sticking stubbornly to their own cultures. Of course, this same debate had swirled around the "old" immigrants, such as the Greeks and Poles, who had seemed insular compared to the Irish and Germans who came before them.[55]

Most adult immigrants of whichever wave came to America seeking economic advancement, and most arrived with limited English proficiency and little formal schooling. Others came with advanced degrees or rare skills. Numerous American scientists, musicians, and sports heroes were born elsewhere, and the dot-com boom of the 1990s prompted computer companies to import engineers and programmers from overseas, universities to hire foreign faculty, and isolated towns to recruit foreign doctors. But the big debate focused on the larger group, the less-skilled workers. Immigration critics worried about "low-quality" immigrants who would be a drain on the national economy and culture.[56] In 2000 foreign-born Americans were as likely as native-born Americans to have a college degree (24 percent of each group), but the foreign-born were more than twice as likely to have failed to graduate from high school (38 percent versus 17 percent of the native-born).[57] This second contrast reinforced the end-of-the-century concern that the newest immigrants were relatively unassimilable.

Learning English

The immigration scholar Alejandro Portes wrote in 2002: "The surge of immigration into the United States during the past 30 years has brought a proliferation of foreign languages, and with it fears that the English language might lose its predominance and cultural unity may be undermined. . . . These fears are proving unfounded."[58] Our analysis sustains Portes's conclusion. In figure 3.7, we contrast the linguistic assimilation of early-twentieth-century immigrants with that of more recent immigrants. The lines represent the percentage of each immigrant cohort who spoke English at a given time after their arrival, from the first few years to more than two decades of residence in the United States. The lowest line (marked with open circles) displays the history of immigrants from all nations from 1900 to 1920; the highest line (marked with filled-in circles) tells the story of immigrants from all nations from 1980 to 2000; and the middle line isolates the experience of immigrants from the Spanish-speaking Americas from 1980 to 2000.[59]

Fewer than half—45 percent—of the "old" immigrants spoke English in their first five years in America. In their next five years, another 30 percent learned English, and that generation topped out at 90 percent proficiency for those in the country twenty years or more. In contrast, almost 80 percent of the "new" immigrants spoke English within their first five years. That is, the later immigrants had higher rates of English proficiency at their five-year anniversaries than the earlier immigrants had at their tenth. After twenty years, 96 percent of the recent immigrants reported that they spoke English. (We made similar calculations raising the linguistic threshold at the end of the century to speaking English "very well," and the conclusions are substantively the same.)[60]

The "low-quality immigrant" controversy focused mostly on Latino immigrants. So we repeated our calculations for immigrants from the Spanish-speaking nations of Mexico, the Caribbean, and Central and South America—the middle line in figure 3.7. Seventy-one percent of more recent immigrants from Latin America arrived with English proficiency or acquired it in the first five years after arrival, well ahead of the 45 percent proficiency of earlier, largely European immigrants. At each arrival anniversary, more late-century Latino immigrants spoke English than had been the case for the earlier immigrants. After twenty years in the United

Figure 3.7   Use of English Among Foreign-Born, by Years in the United States, 1900 to 1920 and 1980 to 2000

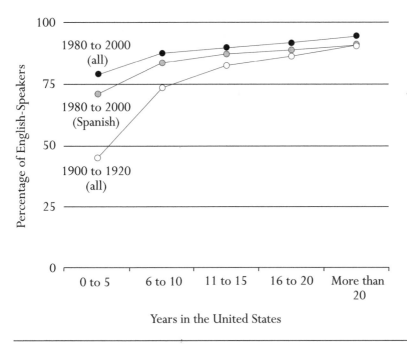

More of the "New" Immigrants Spoke English on Arrival in the United States

Source: IPUMS.

Note: The English-language question was asked about children ten years old and over and adults in 1900 to 1920; it was asked about children three years old and over and adults in 1980, and children five years old and over and adults in 1990 and 2000.

States, they were still one point ahead—91 versus 90 percent—of the earlier immigrants.

This finding may surprise some readers, but consider the many renowned ethnic neighborhoods in northeastern cities such as Little Warsaw, Little Sicily, Greektown, and the Lower East Side. They were renowned in great measure because as late as 1940 the languages of their streets, stores, places of worship, homes, and often schools were Polish, Sicilian, Greek, and Yiddish, respectively. The Koreatowns and barrios of 2000 were hardly new developments. In other ways too, late-century immigrants were roughly on track to assimilate as well as the earlier ones had.[61]

Convergence in Marriage

The ultimate convergence of ethnic or racial groups occurs when people from different groups marry one another. Repeated often enough, intermarriage both erases such ethnic lines and testifies to their erasure. Groups that either face being shunned by others or erect barriers to keep outsiders out tend to marry only within the lines. Sociologists use the rate of intermarriage between pairs of groups or the overall rate of out-marriage for each group to gauge their social distances. We do the same in figure 3.8.[62]

The figure shows the percentage of respondents to the GSS (and their spouses) who married someone outside their ethnic, national, or racial groups, by the year they married. In the last part of the century, Americans married "out" at rates that ranged from 28 percent to more than 70 percent—with one exception. Only 8 percent of African-American weddings between 1970 and 1994 involved a non-African-American partner. Most groups—especially the turn-of-the-twentieth-century immigrants, the Italians, Jews, and Poles—out-married more after 1970 than they had earlier. The out-marriage rate increased forty-three percentage points over the century for Italians (to 61 percent) and thirty-two percentage points for Jews (to 37 percent). In the last cohort, Poles out-married at a higher rate than any other group (72 percent). When Poles, Italians, and Jews did marry out of their group, they were most likely to marry Americans from larger ancestry groups that had first come to the United States in the eighteenth or nineteenth centuries, the Germans and the Irish. The huge numbers of Americans who were wholly or partly of German or Irish or British origin made them popular as marriage partners for every other group and for one another, even in 1900, and that explains why intermarriage rates for these three groups were relatively high throughout the twentieth century.[63] Also, the religious diversity of the Germans and the Irish (each group was about half Protestant and half Catholic) facilitated intermarriage with many groups, including the late-twentieth-century immigrants. In general, marriage partners were determined more by religion than by national origin.[64]

Intermarriage rates increased more slowly for native-born Mexicans—just twelve percentage points between mid- and late century. However, because the modest increase in out-marrying occurred in spite of the vast expansion of potential Mexican partners after 1965, it would seem that the underlying trend toward intermarriage for Mexicans was a strong one. (In fact, the expansion of partners for other Latinos—Cubans, Puerto Ricans, and so on [not shown]—explains the 23 percent drop in their out-marriage rate in the last marriage cohort.) We do not have sufficient numbers of Asian Americans in the GSS sample to display their data, but other studies document that they had high and rising rates of out-marriage in the late decades of the century. For example, according to the 2000 census, 44 percent of

Figure 3.8   Intermarriage by Ancestry and Marriage Cohort

Intermarriage Increased, Though African Americans Remained Separate

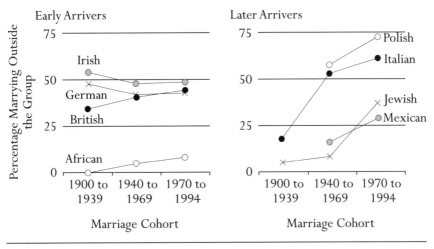

Source: IPUMS.
Note: Early-arriving groups had significant numbers already in the United States prior to the Civil War; late-arriving groups had significant immigration from 1880 to 1920 or later.

young, U.S.-born, Asian-American women who had married had married out. The marriage experiences of Asian and Latino Americans may not match those of the specific European nationalities, but they point nonetheless toward increasing rates of this most intimate form of assimilation.

African Americans, however, were distinct. Although their rate of outmarriage increased from essentially 0 to 5 percent around midcentury, it reached only 8 percent in the last period of our chart. This low rate of intermarriage for African Americans—added to their persisting economic disadvantages, segregation, and experiences of discrimination—has suggested to many scholars that the emerging racial divide in late-twentieth-century America was not white versus nonwhite, as it was in 1900, but black versus nonblack. (More precisely, given the recent experiences of foreign-born Africans and Caribbeans, the division may be between the descendants of American slaves and all others.)[65] Social scientists have described the American assimilation of the European "races," such as the Irish, Italians, and Jews, as a process of "whitening." That is, after some period of ambiguity, nativeborn, white, Protestant Americans came to view these groups—and they came to view themselves—as on the white side of the black-white divide. The prospect of the twenty-first century is that Asians and most Latinos will experience that same acceptance, and blacks will not.[66]

FROM PREJUDICE TO TOLERANCE

The depth of prejudice that ethnic and racial groups have toward one another and the thinking that supports such prejudice are hard to plumb with the polite questions social scientists ask; survey interviewers and respondents are often on their best behavior. We make extensive use of such questions here anyway, because they reveal one of the major developments of twentieth-century America: at the least, even mildly racist comments had become inappropriate, and at the most, prejudice had declined precipitously. We begin with a quote, not from an average survey respondent, but from a Virginia judge who expressed the following opinion at the trial that started the Loving v. Virginia case, which eventually led to the Supreme Court decision against antimiscegenation laws:[67]

> Almighty God created the races white, black, yellow, malay, and red, and He placed them on separate continents. And, but for the interference with His arrangement, there would be no cause for such marriage. The fact that He separated the races shows that He did not intend for the races to mix.

This view, mildly shocking in 1959, would almost certainly stir a furor if issued from a court today. It reflected the ideology of a disappearing racial order. (A shallower, if cruder, expression of such views cost Earl Butz his job as secretary of agriculture eighteen years later, and in 2003 praise of Senator Strom Thurmond's (R-S.C.) racist 1948 presidential campaign cost Trent Lott (R-Miss.) his position as Senate majority leader.) Evidence in this chapter, in other chapters, and throughout the broader social science literature makes it clear that Americans' prejudices have tempered over time.

Prejudice and xenophobia were not just black and white, of course. American history offers many examples of groups eager to close the nation's door behind them; having found a home in America, they wanted to keep others out. Nonetheless, and despite congressional restrictions on immigration passed in the 1920s, no evidence suggests that a majority of Americans ever held such nativist views in the twentieth century.

Racial attitudes are hard to quantify at any time, but the task of gauging how widespread prejudice was prior to the development of public opinion polls in the 1930s—the Gallup organization first began formal polling in 1935—is beyond us. Also complicating the effort to track Americans' feelings about touchy subjects such as race is the "ambulance-chasing" nature of most surveys. That is, pollsters typically ask questions about a topic only after it has become newsworthy. For example, nationwide surveys did not ask whites how they felt about sharing streetcars with blacks until laws segregating public transit were challenged. (Even then, the polls often did not ask blacks how they felt about sharing streetcars—or schools or neighbor-hoods—with whites.) Similarly, whether Americans liked or disliked Japa-nese people did not become a poll-worthy issue until after the attack on Pearl Harbor; five months later, 29 percent of the nearly three thousand people the Gallup poll surveyed answered "yes" to a question asking whether they "hated" the Japanese.[68] (More than fifty years later, Gallup again asked Americans about their feelings toward the Japanese, and just 9 percent an-swered that they felt "unfriendly.")[69]

Social scientists argue over whether answers to survey questions can ac-curately portray prejudice; the answers may not reflect what people really feel, much less what they actually do. Some suggest that the only thing pub-lic opinion surveys can measure is change in what is socially acceptable to say.[70] Still, the trends in these public expressions of prejudice, as revealed by polls taken over a span of time, are substantial, valid, and profound. Ameri-cans' stated tolerance for people of diverse ancestries increased over the last three-quarters of the twentieth century. The longest-running surveys that capture the widespread decline in prejudice are a series of "social distance" studies first conducted by the sociologist Emory S. Bogardus and later repli-cated by other scholars. They measure college students' acceptance of thirty different ancestral groups from 1926 to 1977.[71] In each study, researchers asked the students to rate each group on each of the following seven cate-gories of preferred social distance:

1. Would marry

2. Would have as regular friends

3. Would work with in same office

4. Would have as neighbors on the same street

5. Would have as citizens of same country

6. Would allow as visitors to the country

7. Would exclude from the country

The researchers averaged the respondents' ratings and presented the results as a scale that ranged from 1 to 7, with lower scores indicating willingness toward intimacy and higher scores indicating a preference for distance.

Each year (1926, 1946, 1956, 1966, and 1977) the average scores across all groups declined, and the range among the groups narrowed, evidence of generally growing acceptance of minority groups.[72] The trajectories for spe-cific groups varied, largely as a function of historical events. Rated social dis-tance for Japanese people increased dramatically between the 1926 and

1946 studies, but declined steadily afterward. Germans and Italians also registered World War II–era spikes in social distance, while groups from countries with Communist governments, such as Russians, Czechs, and the Chinese, did so in 1956. Despite such fluctuations and the overall decline in social distance, the rank order of the thirty ethnic groups changed little over the fifty years. The top ten groups were all of northern European or North American origin, with the addition of Italians in 1966. The middle ten groups were primarily southern and eastern Europeans, and the bottom ten groups included Mexicans, blacks, and, most often, those of Asian origin.

Other survey data also point to growing tolerance—or at the least, growing willingness of Americans to express tolerance—although typically surveys ask about only blacks and occasionally a few other groups. For example, survey researchers have regularly asked national samples whether they would vote for a Catholic, Jewish, or black person for president. We analyze these items closely in chapter 9, but we can report here that the proportion of Americans saying "yes" increased substantially over several decades. Similarly, the National Election Survey regularly asked respondents to rate various groups on a "feeling thermometer" from cold to warm. Between 1964 and 1992, feelings toward blacks, Jews, and Catholics grew slightly warmer; negative ratings fell from between 10 and 16 percent for each group to just 4 to 8 percent.[73]

Attitudes toward the general group "immigrants" did not show similar steady improvement over the last decades of the century; instead, Americans' opinions seemed to follow economic conditions. In 1965, at the start of the late-century increase in immigration, one-third of Americans said that fewer immigrants should be admitted. That percentage rose for thirty years as immigration increased rapidly; in 1995 almost two-thirds of Americans said that immigration should be decreased. But after 1995, fewer Americans endorsed the anti-immigrant position, which dropped down toward one-third again by 2000. The most likely reason for Americans' increased tolerance of immigration in the 1990s was the economic boom of those years, which softened the perceived threat posed by newcomers.[74]

Nuances aside, there is no doubt that in their publicly expressed opinions—and, to some extent, in their private feelings—Americans became more tolerant of racial and ethnic minorities over the century. The polling data on the growth of tolerance is reinforced by, among other material signs of changing behavior, increases in black-white residential integration (chapter 7), in the number of elected officials from racial minorities, in the visibility of such groups in the media, and in intermarriage for most. The hostilities that divided American ancestral groups softened, though they did not disappear.

Our next question is whether divisions in public opinion about ethnic and racial issues also narrowed; that is, we move from examining the general development of tolerance among Americans as a whole to examining differences among Americans in tolerance, by region, age, or education, for example. Later, in chapter 9, as part of our exploration of cultural fragmentation, we look at how Americans divided on the "vote for president" measures. Here we look closely at two particularly contentious issues that specifically involve African Americans.[75] Many questions about blacks, unlike other ancestry groups, were asked repeatedly and over many years. African Americans also present, as we have seen, the toughest case for assessing the development of tolerance in the United States. We examine two questions: "Do you think there should be laws against marriages between blacks and whites?" (yes or no), and "Here are some opinions some people have expressed in connection with black-white relations. Which statement on the card comes closest to how you feel? . . . Blacks shouldn't push themselves where they're not wanted." (The answers, shown to respondents on a response card, were "agree strongly," "agree slightly," "disagree slightly," "disagree strongly," and "no opinion.")

Describing Differences in Opinion

Before proceeding, we need to explain briefly our method for analyzing public opinion data, which we apply in most of the chapters that follow (see appendix A).[76] We have two aims: first, tracking changes in overall public opinion over as much of the twentieth century as possible; and second, tracking the diversity of public opinion—differences in views between races, social classes, regions, and so forth. To accomplish the first, we use as many polls on each topic as we could reasonably find, drawing often on just their published results. To accomplish the second, we analyze a subset of those polls. These second results concerning group differences in opinion appear as *deviations from the main trend*. They show how opinions changed over the years for, say, rural people compared to city people.

For any particular question, we take the basic results for each poll that was taken—for example, the percentage of respondents who said marriage between blacks and whites should not be banned—and plot them over time. To summarize the historical trend underlying these survey results, we use a smoothing technique that provides a "best-fitting" line. It is necessary to smooth such data because polls are taken episodically and are typically accurate only within a margin of plus or minus three to five percentage points overall; estimates for subgroups (for example, young and old, North and South) are even less precise. Also, respondents' answers can be influenced by several incidental conditions of any particular survey, such as the topic of the question asked immediately before. Smoothing helps extract the "signal" from the "noise" in the trends. For our analyses of public opinion, we use a statistical technique known as locally estimated regression ("loess," for short) to fit a line to all the national data points we found. This loess line represents the national trend.[77] Then, using only the surveys that contain details about the subgroups that concern us, we estimate how attitudes of Americans from those groups deviated from the national trend. The procedure is apparent in our first example, on whether Americans thought there should be laws banning intermarriage between blacks and whites.

Increasing Approval of Intermarriage

The intermarriage question was first asked in a national survey in 1963, repeated in 1967 and 1970, and then incorporated into the GSS. (When the Supreme Court ruled in 1967 that laws banning marriages between blacks and whites violated the Constitution, sixteen states still had such laws.) In 1963, 37 percent of (nonblack) American adults said "no"—marriages between blacks and whites should not be banned—while a strong majority, 63 percent, said "yes," there should be laws against black-white marriages. Opposition to the ban rose quickly; twelve years later, in 1975, the percentages were reversed: 63 percent said "no" to the ban and 37 percent said "yes." In figure 3.9, the thick gray line shows the national trend against intermarriage bans. The pace of change slowed slightly from 1975 until 1986, after which it quickened again. By 2000, 87 percent said they would not ban black-white marriages. The Gallup poll also regularly asked about the topic, but with a different question: "Do you generally approve or disapprove of marriage between blacks and whites?" In 1958, 4 percent of whites approved; by 1997, 61 percent of non-Hispanic whites approved (rising to 70 percent approval by 2003).[78] Remember, however, that while expressed opinions shifted radically, actual black-white marriages increased only minutely—from 4 to 8 percent of all marriages involving African Americans.

Returning to the question about laws against intermarriage, figure 3.9 divides the respondents by their years of birth and reveals that expressed hostility to intermarriage was literally dying out. The vast majority of Americans born before 1900 favored laws against intermarriage even after most Americans opposed the bans. But each successive cohort opposed the laws more; baby boomers, born between 1945 and 1959, and the post-1960 cohort opposed the bans by great majorities from the first time they were old enough to be included in the sample. Such "cohort replacement" accounts for almost half of the overall upward trend.[79] Its importance is represented in our figure by the slower pace of change *within* cohorts—the narrow lines—than we see when we consider all adults together. The gray line rises faster because it deletes people from the low lines as they die and adds people from the high lines as they become adults.[80] Real change occurred within cohorts too, except between 1976 and 1985. But there is little evidence of either convergence or divergence between birth cohorts

Figure 3.9   Opposition to Laws Banning Marriages Between Blacks and Whites, by Year and Year of Birth

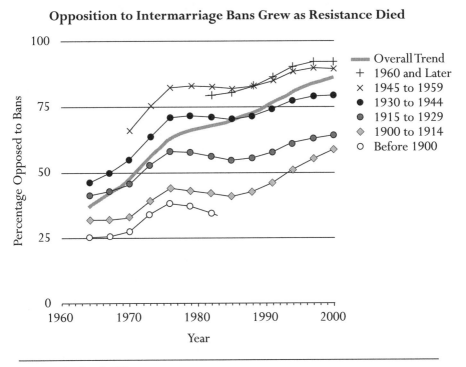

Opposition to Intermarriage Bans Grew as Resistance Died

Source: NORC and GSS.
Note: Excludes African-American respondents. Data smoothed using locally estimated (loess) regressions.

(except perhaps between the 1900 to 1914 cohort and the 1915 to 1929 cohort).

In other analyses, we found that there was significant convergence of opinions between regions, especially as southerners liberalized more quickly than Americans outside the South.[81] Southerners lagged far behind through 1985, when a bare majority of them, 54 percent, said that they opposed intermarriage bans. Southerners then joined the rest of the nation, increasing their opposition to the bans by thirty percentage points between 1985 and 2000. Other significant differences include a substantial gap by education: opposition to banning intermarriage was fifty-two percentage points higher among college-educated nonblacks than among nonblack high school dropouts in the mid-1970s. The education gap in opinions about laws against intermarriage closed as college graduates' opposition maxed out at 95 percent while high school dropouts' opposition continued rising from 40 percent up to 60 percent by the mid-1990s. This is a story of an emerging consensus that outlawing the marriage of a black and white couple is, at least in public conversation, unacceptable.

Declining Distaste for Black Mobilization

Alienation between blacks and whites lingered nonetheless. The chance for an individual to have a fulfilling private life was one thing, but group rights to equal opportunity in workplaces, schools, and the housing market remained contested. Affirmative action was particularly controversial. At the end of the century, a slim majority of whites (51 percent) told the Gallup poll that they would rather have minorities "help themselves" than have the federal government "make every possible effort" to improve their conditions (41 percent).[82] Many whites also felt, in the words of the second question we examine closely, that "blacks should not push where they are not wanted"; the majority said so as late as 1994. The "push" question seems especially sensitive to racial unrest, as we see in figure 3.10. Between 1967 and 1972, an era of riots and demonstrations, there is a slight dip in the overall trend toward disagreeing that blacks were pushing too hard.[83] Afterwards, the late-century impetus toward greater tolerance and acceptance reduced whites' sensitivity to black mobilization—but did not eliminate it. When we measured the trends for each ancestry group separately (not shown), we found that whites were most inclined to feel that blacks were pushing too hard, but many Asians and Latinos held this view too.[84]

Cohort replacement was an important part of the growing disagreement with the "should not push" item after 1972, just as we saw with the opposition to banning interracial marriage. The differences between Americans with more or less education and between regions were also similar. Again, a modest consensus was growing. In figure 3.10, we show the regional patterns along with the main trend. Here the exceptional trajectory of northeasterners is particularly noteworthy. Though increasing numbers of non-black Americans in the Northeast dismissed complaints about black militancy, the trend rose more slowly in the East after 1980 than in either the West or the Midwest. Andrew Greeley and Paul Sheatsley wrote in 1971 that the proportion of white northerners who supported integration at one point in time was "quite close" to what the total white population accepted five years later; that is, that northerners led the liberalizing trend.[85] But right after they made that observation, the pattern changed. The Northeast slipped behind. We suspect that the school busing controversies of that era, which were much more intense in the Northeast than elsewhere in the na-

Figure 3.10   Disagreement with Position That Blacks Should Not Push
Themselves Where They Are Not Wanted, by Year and
Region

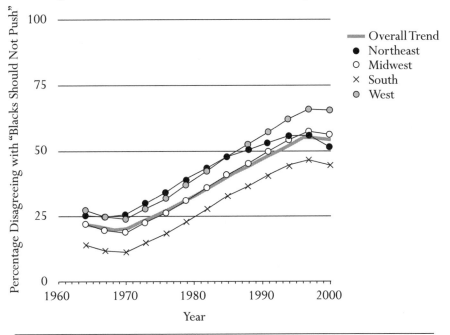

Acceptance of Black Mobilization Grew, Except in the Northeast

Source: NORC and GSS.
Note: Excludes African American respondents. Data smoothed using locally estimated (loess) regressions.

tion, tempered whites' support for black activism and prompted more of them to feel that blacks should stop pushing.[86]

In larger perspective, whatever reservations one might have about the accuracy of surveys on racial attitudes, Americans in the twentieth century increasingly set aside old prejudices and stereotypes. The racial violence that came to the North in the late 1960s and the influx of new immigrants shortly afterwards surely raised new tensions, but what seems remarkable is not the continuity of suspicion between ancestral groups—which seems almost universal among humans—but its muting.

CONCLUSION

The United States in 2000 was far more ethnically and racially diverse than it was in 1900. The late-century wave of immigration accelerated after 1985 and brought people from parts of the world that had not been well represented in the United States before 1980. Mexicans, Guatemalans, Salvadorans, Chinese, Filipinos, and Vietnamese diversified the nation as it had never been before. Though most came from countries in which English is rarely spoken, they knew some English upon arrival or quickly acquired it—and at a faster pace than the immigrants of the early twentieth century. Moreover, by 2000 Americans of Asian origin were attaining more education (chapter 2) and higher incomes than Americans of European origin.

Europeans were still the largest ancestral group in America in 2000. But in the nation's largest state, California, they were no longer the majority; no ancestral group formed over 50 percent of that state's population. Projections indicate that the same may be true of the country as a whole by 2030. Diversity by ancestry was the most visible source of difference in 2000 and can only become more so in years to come.

Such diversity need not, however, be divisive. The public suspicions, prejudices, and hatreds that were so common and so casual one hundred years ago had largely disappeared by 2000. Social distances between groups, as Bogardus and other midcentury sociologists thought of them, had declined as well. On a superficial level, Americans of all kinds ate spaghetti, bagels, and tacos—foods that had been seen as exotic even in the 1950s. On a deeper level, there were more Americans marrying partners outside their ancestral groups than Americans marrying inside them. Education contributed to Americans' greater appreciation of their differences and diminished prejudice. Still, even the college-educated of the 1950s were capable of a bigotry that is unthinkable among high school dropouts today.

Something else changed in the United States between the end of World War II and the turn of the century. We label it an appreciation of differences, but we have no direct measures of it beyond the survey questions we used to document its arrival. Something taught most Americans to value their differences—at least in public. By the end of the century, great majorities of Americans were telling poll-takers that racial and ethnic diversity strengthened their communities and was a major reason for America's success.[87] For some, these answers may have been "brotherhood" clichés, but far fewer would have repeated them a century earlier.

Take as illustration the case of Edward A. Ross. Ross was a prominent economist, sociologist, and public intellectual of a century ago. He was a progressive who supported organized labor and academic freedom—so much so as to get fired by Stanford University for objecting to the railroads' use of imported Chinese labor. Ross was also convinced that continental and national groups had deeply ingrained "racial" (albeit not necessarily biological) traits, such as energy, intellect, and emotionality, and he worried that white Americans faced the threat of "race suicide." In an address he delivered in 1901, Ross said that America's

> average of energy and character is lowered by the presence in the South of several millions of an inferior race [blacks]. . . . The last twenty years have diluted us with masses of fecund but beaten humanity from the hovels of far Lombardy and Galicia [Italian and Jewish immigrants]. . . . Our free land is gone and our opportunities will henceforth attract immigrants chiefly from the humbler strata of East European peoples.

Nonetheless, he concluded, on a largely wishful note, he had faith that the American race "is destined to play a brilliant and leading role on the stage of history."[88] Ross could hardly have imagined that in the ensuing one hundred years America would become so much more diverse, more melded, and more tolerant of "racial" mixing. Arguably, the United States became a superpower, not in spite of these trends, as Ross and other progressives of the early 1900s claimed, but in large measure because of its ability to incorporate those of "humbler strata."

Most of the differences between ancestry groups in language, family life, social class, and religion that had been so evident and so troubling to Americans like Ross in 1900 shrank greatly by 2000 (even, ironically, as the culture increasingly congratulated itself for cultural differences). The rest of this book explores those trends in greater detail. But these changes were also made more complex because of the special history of the descendants of America's slaves.

Twenty years ago, in closing his classic study of race and ethnicity in America, *A Piece of the Pie*, Stanley Lieberson wrote:

> The early living conditions of the new Europeans after their migration to the United States were extremely harsh, and their point of entry into the socioeconomic system was quite low. However, it is a *non-sequitur* to assume that the new Europeans had it as bad as did blacks or that the failure of blacks to move upward as rapidly reflected some ethnic deficiencies. . . . It is a serious mistake to underestimate how far the new Europeans have come in the nation and how hard it all was, but it is equally erroneous to assume that the obstacles were as great as those faced by blacks or that the starting point was the same.[89]

Our evidence echoes Lieberson's findings, and we echo his conclusions. African-origin Americans began the twentieth century locked in rural isolation, hemmed in by legal discrimination in the South, and held back by the legacies of slavery. At the same time, millions of new immigrants streamed into America's cities from Europe. Perceived as different races because they spoke English with accents (if they spoke English at all), they compounded their differences by practicing their Jewish or Catholic faith in what was an overwhelmingly Protestant country (see chapter 8). But in a generation or two, these foreign "races" had entered the American mainstream and been "whitened." African Americans were at least a generation behind. When they arrived in the same urban ports of entry, like New York, Chicago, and Detroit, their poverty was deeper, their lack of education and industrial skills more glaring, and the prejudice and discrimination they faced far more severe.

Following the civil rights movement, African Americans gained widespread admiration in popular culture, athletics, and politics. Public and private institutions no longer excluded African Americans (or Jews, Italians, Chinese, or any other ancestry group), as they had done in the first half of the century. Bigotry was no longer tolerated in public, as a few politicians discovered to their dismay. Yet, while the segregation of African Americans from other Americans receded somewhat, they were still more isolated than any other group in 2000. Intermarriage may have become increasingly common, but African Americans were largely left out. They had closed much of the gap in basic education but lagged far behind the descendants of the early-century immigrants in life, liberty, and happiness: African Americans had distinctively lower life expectancies, higher incarceration rates, and lower morale than other Americans.[90] There thus looms, as we mentioned earlier, the possibility of a twenty-first-century split along black-nonblack lines.

CHAPTER FOUR

How Americans Lived: Families and Life Courses in Flux*

WHEN THE Census Bureau released its findings from the 2000 census, newspapers and magazines featured articles on how "the American family" was disappearing. A dwindling proportion of households contained married couples with children, and a growing proportion of households contained only single individuals, unmarried partners, or one-parent families. "'Married with Children' Still Fading as a Model," read a *Los Angeles Times* headline on May 5, 2001. This familiar plaint about the family in decline lacks both analytical and historical perspective. Analytically, the statistics count *homes* rather than *people*; historically, it contrasts the contemporary family with that of the 1950s, an unusual era in American history. The full record, once closely examined, reveals some dramatic changes in American family life, but not necessarily the ones the media reports have focused on. Also, there was much continuity in family patterns over the century. Most important, there is no—and never was a—prototypical American family, only a mix of families and households. In this chapter, we describe how that mix changed over the century. The key findings are:

- Twentieth-century Americans predominantly lived in two-parent nuclear families, especially in the 1950s, though that was an unusual period. The greatest change over the century for Americans under forty-five years of age was that those living outside a nuclear family increasingly lived as single adults rather than in a larger, extended household.

---

*Coauthored by Jon Stiles.

- The greatest changes in family life happened to middle-aged and older Americans. They increasingly lived in empty-nest households—as a couple without children in the home—or as single persons.

- Americans traveled through the life course in increasingly similar ways as variations narrowed among them in how long they lived, how many children they had, and when they made key transitions.

- Nonetheless, substantial differences in family life opened up between African Americans and whites and between the less- and the more-educated. After 1960, the married-couple household became atypical for African Americans, and by 2000 it was atypical as well for white high school dropouts.

We begin by describing the diversity of family patterns at the end of the century.

AMERICANS IN HOUSEHOLDS IN 2000

Part of the popular confusion about family change arises from vagueness in delineating types of families. We defined six types of household arrangements to capture the major variations in how Americans lived, and we sorted all individuals into one of these types:[1]

1. *Primary-individual households*: In 2000, 12 percent of Americans were "primary individuals," meaning that they headed a household and lived without any adult relative or child. Although some had roommates or domestic partners—we will address the issue of cohabiting couples immediately—most lived alone.

2. *Single-parent households*: Eleven percent of Americans lived in a household of one parent and at least one child. Typically, these people were single mothers and their children, but some households included others, such as roommates and the unmarried partners of the single parent.

3. *Married-couple-with-no-children households*: Sixteen percent of Americans were in households of couples who had not yet had children or whose children had left home.

4. *Married-couple-with-child(ren) households*: Thirty-nine percent of Americans in 2000 lived in the "classic" nuclear family; they were married parents or the children of such parents. No other person shared the home.

5. *Extended-family households*: Fourteen percent of Americans lived in households that included a *relative*, other than the spouse or child, of the

household head; the relatives were typically his or her elderly parents, siblings, in-laws, or grandchildren.

6. *Shared-quarters households:* These households included two sorts of people: the 3 percent of Americans who lived in group settings, such as orphanages, dormitories, barracks, or assisted-living homes, and the 5 percent who were *nonrelatives* in the other five household arrangements—that is, the roommates, unmarried partners, boarders, or servants of the household head.[2]

Note that we count *people* and how they lived. Much of what has been written on the family sorts and counts *households*. The angle of vision makes a big difference. In 2000, for example, 26 percent of all *households* contained a single person, but only 13 percent of all *adults* lived alone. We prefer to count people rather than dwellings; it better describes Americans' experience.[3] It also helps us come to a better understanding of what shapes the formation of households.

One important complication is cohabitation. Only since 1990 has the census explicitly offered respondents the option of labeling adults in their homes as "unmarried partners"; before 1990, the census relied on crude estimates.[4] (In our scheme, the partner listed as the head of household is counted in category 1, the other partner in category 6. In our analysis, we check to see what distortions that might introduce.) Cohabiting was common in 2000; by one estimate, most young couples in 2000 had lived together before their wedding. Moreover, many divorced Americans cohabited rather than remarry. But cohabiting was usually brief, so that relatively few Americans were cohabiting on April 1, 2000—probably 4 to 5 percent of adults.[5] Cohabitation is, as many Americans can personally testify, a much vaguer arrangement than marriage. Some couples have deliberately planned and enduring partnerships that work much like marriages; others have casual and indefinite liaisons in which, for example, each person keeps a different official address. For these reasons, and also because only legal marriage was recognized in earlier censuses, we focus on the distinction between married and unmarried. But we note cohabitation when it is important to do so.

This typology is a useful tool for understanding family diversity, but to really make sense of household arrangements we need to distinguish people by age. (Children, for example, rarely live as primary individuals.) Figure 4.1 shows how Americans of different ages lived in 2000. Among the key points we draw from the figure are:

• About 62 percent of American children lived in nuclear family households—that is, with two parents or stepparents and perhaps siblings but no other relatives. Twenty percent lived in single-parent households, and 16 percent in extended households. (If we count cohabiting couples as married, the percentage of children who were living in two-parent families rises from 62 to 66 percent.)[6]

- Young adults age eighteen to twenty-nine lived in a wide variety of households—40 percent in a married-couple household (48 percent counting cohabiters), either as a child or a parent. Eight percent lived in group settings such as dorms, barracks, or prisons.

- About half of thirty- to forty-four-year-olds lived in a nuclear family of married parents and children.

- Over 60 percent of the forty-five- to sixty-four-year-olds lived in married couples, about half of those with children and half without children.

- Over 40 percent of the elderly were part of couples without children at home, and 30 percent lived alone (or with roommates). Fewer than 20 percent lived with their children or grandchildren, and 6 percent lived in a group setting of some sort.[7]

About half or more of each age group—except the eighteen- to twenty-nine-year-olds—lived in a household headed by a legally married couple.[8] Is this a lot or a little? We will see later when we explore how these figures changed over time.

Who Lived How?

Typical living arrangements differed not only by age but also by other axes of difference. Young women, for example, more often lived as single parents, and elderly women more often lived alone, than did men. Ancestry and education produced large contrasts. African-American children much more often lived with single parents than did children of other ancestries, as shown in table 4.1.[9]

The dramatically low 36 percent of black children who lived with two parents in a nuclear family resulted largely from the much higher percentage of black children who were born to unmarried mothers. In 2000, 62 percent of African-American women giving birth were unmarried, compared to 26 percent of non-Hispanic whites and 30 percent of Hispanics.[10] Adult African Americans and non-Hispanic whites also differed sharply in their household arrangements. Blacks were about twenty-five percentage points less likely to live in a married-couple household than were whites; they lived instead as single parents or in extended households. Black men were exceptionally likely to live in group quarters (14 percent of eighteen-

Figure 4.1   Types of Households in Which Americans Lived, by Age, 2000

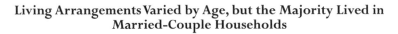

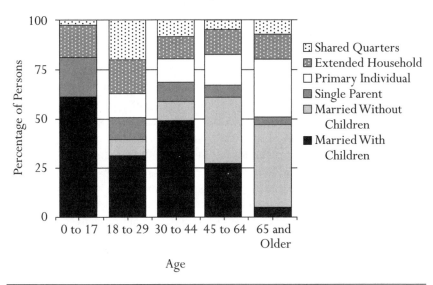

Source: IPUMS.

to forty-four-year-olds) notably in prisons.[11] The black-white contrast, we will see, grew over the century. Hispanics and Asians differed from non-Hispanic whites mainly in a much greater tendency to live in extended households, with grandparents or other kin.[12]

Table 4.1   Household Types in Which American Children Lived, by Ancestry, 2000

	Non-Hispanic White	African American	Hispanic	Other
Married with Children	77%	36%	53%	63%
Single Parent	12	33	13	11
Extended Household	9	28	31	24

Source: IPUMS.
Note: Other, minor categories are not included. All categories other than "Hispanic" are "non-Hispanic."

Table 4.2   Household Types in Which American Children Lived, by the Education of the Head of Household, 2000

	No High School	High School Graduate	Some College	College Graduate
Married with Children	42%	56%	63%	81%
Single Parent	22	24	22	11
Extended Household	34	18	13	8

Source: IPUMS.

Americans' living arrangements in 2000 also differed substantially by *educational* level. Take, again, the case of children, as shown in table 4.2.[13] The wide differences by education—the children of college graduates were about twice as likely as the children of high school dropouts to live in a nuclear household—also arose in part from differences in out-of-wedlock births: in 2000 only 9 percent of young, unmarried, college-graduate women were mothers, compared to a full 70 percent of young, unmarried high school dropouts and 53 percent of young, unmarried high school graduates.[14] The more educated adults were, the likelier they were to live in a married-couple household.[15] We can characterize the family differences by education this way: the more education Americans (or their parents) received, the more often they followed the "normal" life course of being raised by two parents, living as a single person, getting married, becoming a parent, and living in an empty nest. The less education they received, the more likely it was that Americans' life course would be "off-track"—that is, that they would be raised by a single parent, become a single parent themselves, live in an extended household, or be unmarried in middle age.[16]

Although most Americans in 2000 lived in nuclear, married-couple households, diversity marked American family patterns. To evaluate and understand that diversity, we must set it within its historical context and track its evolution. But before we can do that, we must understand the demographic changes of the century—in births, deaths, marriages, and marriage dissolutions—since those changes heavily determined Americans' options for family life.

THE CENTURY'S VITAL EVENTS

For much of the twentieth century, births and deaths, rather than preferences, largely determined Americans' living arrangements. And for much of the century, births and deaths were also out of their control. In 2000 planned births outnumbered unplanned births by more than five to one, but back in 1900 many fewer American couples pursued family planning, and even fewer attained it.[17] The ability to forestall death in this era of widespread infection and accidents was also limited; death rates were high. Most of the changes in family arrangements since 1900 resulted from curtailing childbearing and extending lifetimes. And in both regards, Americans became more similar to one another.

Longer Lives

The extension of Americans' lifetimes has been so great that it is hard to exaggerate its significance. Worldwide, life spans increased more between 1900 and 1980 than they had from prehistory to 1900.[18] Had the parents of a girl born in America in 1900 asked an expert about their newborn's prospects, they would have learned that she could expect to live to age forty-eight; a baby girl born in 2000 would have been expected to live to seventy-nine, an extra thirty-one years, thanks largely to a 90 percent drop in infant and child mortality.[19] One-fifth of Americans born in 1900 had died by their eighteenth birthday; the death rate of Americans born in 2000 will not reach one-fifth, demographers estimate, until their seventy-fifth birthdays—and that projection assumes no great medical breakthroughs in the meantime, such as curing cancer.[20]

Twentieth-century progress in longevity came in three phases. First, improved sanitation, especially municipal water and sewage treatment, and public health controls, such as meat and milk inspection, reduced the infections and diseases that targeted children. Second, inoculations and drugs like penicillin effectively eradicated smallpox, polio, measles, and deadly infections, again, largely extending children's survival. Third, toward the end of the century, new medical developments, such as improved therapies for heart disease and cancer, extended the lives of the middle-aged and the elderly.[21]

Figure 4.2 displays the century's change in women's life expectancy. The heavy line shows the age at which half of women born in the given year died or will die—that is, the average life span. The average rose from seventy-one and a half years for women born in 1900 to a forecast of eighty-six years for those born in 2000—an extra fifteen years. (The attentive reader will recall from a previous paragraph that the average baby girl born in 1900 would have been expected to live only forty-eight years. That *projection* was based on the death rates of infants, children, and adults in 1900. The typical woman born in 1900 actually lived to nearly seventy-two because of the health improvements that came along during her lifetime.) The lower line presents the trend for women who had short life spans, those at the twentieth percentile in life spans: 20 percent of the women born in 1900 died before their eighteenth birthday, but women born in 2000 will not see 20 per-

Figure 4.2   Observed and Projected Mortality of Women Born in the Twentieth Century, by Year of Birth

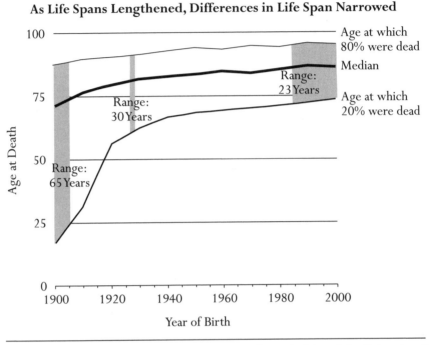

As Life Spans Lengthened, Differences in Life Span Narrowed

Source: National Center for Health Statistics (www.cdc.gov/nchs) and the University of California, Berkeley Human Mortality Database (demog.berkeley.edu).

cent of their cohort die until they reach their seventy-fifth birthday. The higher line in figure 4.2 traces the trend for long-lived women, those at the eightieth percentile in life spans. The 20 percent of women born in 1900 who lived the longest made it past age eighty-seven; the 20 percent of women born in 2000 who will live the longest will make it to at least age ninety-five.[22]

One further consequence of health improvements is the convergence in Americans' life expectancies displayed in figure 4.2. Long-lived women born early in the century had sixty-five more years of life than the short-lived. If the women born at the end of the century conform to demographers' predictions, the longest-lived among them will survive about twenty-three years more than their shortest-lived, cutting by two-thirds the variation among American women in life spans. Great disparities in health remain, notably by social class and race, and should temper any enthusiasm about this equalizing trend.[23] But on the most vital of vital statistics, the life span, Americans grew more alike over the twentieth century.

Less Fertility

In 1900 American women averaged between four and five childbirths in their lifetimes. This average is, however, misleading. Relatively few women gave birth exactly four or five times; more women either *never* gave birth or gave birth *seven or more times*.[24] Over the first part of the century, the average came down as fewer and fewer women bore seven or more children. By the depths of the Great Depression, ill health and even malnutrition had brought the average to a temporary bottom of just over two births per woman. The famous "baby boom" began in 1947 and peaked at an average of between three and four births per woman in the late 1950s. The subsequent "baby bust" brought fertility to an all-time low of one to two births per woman in 1976; then fertility bobbed back up to two births per woman in the 1980s—where it stayed through the end of the century.[25]

Fertility is a complicated mix of biology, choice, and happenstance. A nation's birth rate reflects millions of couples' decisions about the number of children they want and when they want them, accidental pregnancies, complications that prevent conception, and changes of partners through widowhood or divorce and remarriage. We can simplify the picture by looking at cohorts of women when they reached an age at which few would have yet another birth and calculating how many children they had had by that age ("cohort fertility"). Figure 4.3 presents the number of children a cohort of women bore in their entire lifetimes, charted by the year they turned thirty. We plugged in projections for those cohorts that were still having babies. (For technical reasons, the exact numbers in this figure differ from those given in the previous paragraph, but the trends are the same.)[26] The heavy line shows that women who had their children early in the twentieth century had an average of four births each. Average fertility then fell to nearly two births by 1940, rose to over three by 1961, and fell below two by 1979. The lower line shows the trend for women who had relatively few children. In 1900 women at the twentieth percentile of fertility averaged one child; in 1970 they averaged about two. The upper line shows the trend for women at the eightieth percentile: they averaged seven children in 1900, four in 1940, five in 1970, and fewer than four after 1990. Once again, American variability in a critical life event narrowed considerably. The difference between the most and least fertile women shrank from 6 to 2.4 children—mainly because large families became much less common.

This narrowing is depicted another way in figure 4.4, which compares four cohorts of women: the ones who were in the midst of their childbear-

Figure 4.3   Observed and Projected Fertility of Women Who Reached Childbearing Age in the Twentieth Century, by Year of Birth Plus Thirty

Birth Rates Dropped, Rose, and Dropped Again, but Kept Converging

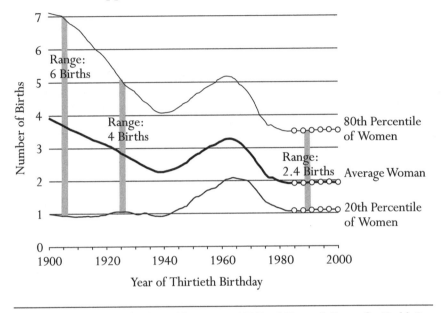

Year of Thirtieth Birthday

Source: Heuser, "Cohort Fertility Tables, 1917–1970," and National Center for Health Statistics, "Cohabitation, Marriage, Divorce, and Remarriage."
Note: For women born after 1955, we projected forward to when they finish their childbearing (projected fertility shown with circles on the lines).

ing in 1900, the ones who were around thirty years old during the Depression, the mothers of the baby boomers, and those who completed nearly all of their fertility by the end of the twentieth century. Within each cohort, we stack births up from zero to seven; the length of the bar indicates the percentage of women in that cohort who had that many live births. We also note the mean number of births for the cohort. At the turn of the twentieth century, far more thirty-year-old women had had either no children or seven children than had had the average of three or four. Depression-era women had much lower fertility, mainly because many fewer had large families and many more instead had one or two children. The next cohort, the mothers of baby boomers, had higher fertility because fewer women than ever remained childless and few stopped at one child. Then, with the baby bust, the

Figure 4.4   Number of Births over a Lifetime, by Year of Prime Childbearing Age

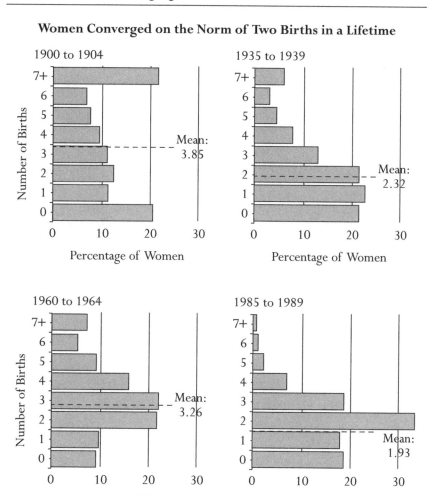

Women Converged on the Norm of Two Births in a Lifetime

variation contracted dramatically. Few women had more than three births, and one-third had exactly two births. The women born in the 1960s and 1970s appear headed to birth experiences much like the previous cohort. American fertility patterns remained stable for the last twenty-five years of the century—the only period of stable fertility in American history. (At a mean of 1.9 children, the U.S. population would begin to decline around 2045 or so were it not for immigration.) American women, in sum, have converged on two children as the norm.

An important detail in the story illustrated by figures 4.3 and 4.4 is childlessness. Early in the twentieth century, childlessness was as common as having large families. About one in five women who were thirty in 1900 had had no children. Then, in midcentury, childlessness was rare: during the 1960s fewer than one in ten women were childless. Finally, late in the century, childlessness was once again common; about one in five of the women who were thirty in 1990 will probably end up having no children. But the reasons for early- and late-century childlessness were quite different. In the first era, infections and other health problems made conceiving difficult, and miscarriages and stillbirths disheartened many who did conceive. In the later era, at least three-fourths of the childless women chose not to have children.[27]

Another key detail is the "baby boom." The explanation for the baby boom is still unclear to demographic historians, but some combination of catchup for delays during the Depression, improved nutrition after the war, medical advances ending barrenness, the changing trade-off between work and home, and certainly cultural fashion led Americans to marry younger and have children sooner and more often than the generations before or after them. The consequences of the baby boom have been enormous as the population bulge has worked itself through crowded schools, a tight job market, parenting, and, in 2000, anticipation of mass retirement.[28]

Thus, the history of American birth rates is partly one of changes in health early on and partly one of preferences, especially later on. Since the 1930s, the Gallup poll has asked people how many children they consider "ideal" for a family. The average number Americans gave dropped suddenly from three-plus to two or less around 1970 (a development we explore in detail later in this chapter). Americans decided, amid many dramatic social changes, that smaller was better. And the consensus that two was the right number increased.

Marriage

In the middle of the twentieth century, marriage was all but universal: only 5 percent of adults who came of age around 1950 never married. But that was not so earlier: over 10 percent of those who came of age between 1880 and 1900 never married. And it was not so afterwards: as many as 10 percent of recent cohorts will never marry.[29] The age at which Americans married also followed a cycle over the century, as shown in figure 4.5. The solid lines display the median age at first marriage for women (heavy line) and the ages at which the youngest-marrying 20 percent and oldest-marrying 20

Figure 4.5 Observed and Estimated Age at First Marriage and at First Union, by Year of Median Marriage

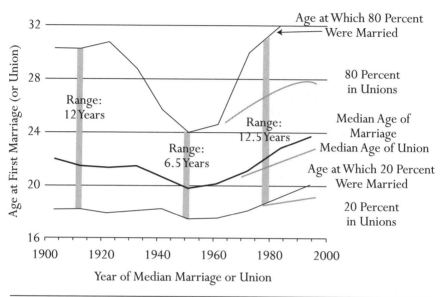

Women Married Two Years Earlier, Then Four Years Later

Source: Marriage: IPUMS and 1985 and 1995 CPS. "First union" is the first of either marriage or cohabitation, estimated from the 1988, 1995, and 2002 waves of the National Survey of Family Growth.

Note: Union percentiles are plotted for each cohort starting in the 1960s. Quadratic trend lines are added to smooth the point estimates derived from the NSFG. They are shown as gray curves.

percent of women (lighter lines) walked the aisle, sorted by the typical year of marriage for that cohort.[30] (Men, on average, married a few years later than women, but the difference shrank from three and a half years early in the century to under two years by 2000.) Early in the century, women married on average at age twenty-two. By midcentury, the median age had dropped such that the average bride was still a teenager by several weeks. Also, variation in age had narrowed; the late-marrying were now "late" by only a few years. By the end of the century, the median had soared to almost twenty-four, and the late-marrying were very late, perhaps not marrying until they were approaching forty. The gap between the late-marrying and the rest had widened back to its early-century dimension.[31]

But this conclusion about age at marriage needs to be severely qualified by considering cohabitation. In 1995 about one-third of women in their midtwenties who had not yet married had nonetheless lived with someone.[32] The gray lines on the right side of figure 4.5 estimate the ages at which women either first married *or first cohabited*—in other words, their age of "first union." By that standard, fin-de-siècle women were sharing a home with an official or unofficial spouse later than their mothers had, but not much later than their grandmothers or great-grandmothers had. Women forming a couple around 1995 did so typically at about age twenty-two and a half, a half-year later than women were married on average in 1905. Note also that the variability of women's ages at first union at the end of the century, while greater than that during the baby boom, was less than the variability in marriage age before the Depression.

The timing of marriage depends a lot on an income sufficient to start a household and plans for schooling. Historically, men delayed marrying until they inherited a farm or, more recently, got a job that paid a family-supporting wage. Once that became easier, especially after World War II, more people married, and married younger. In the later decades of the twentieth century, however, extended education for both spouses became a prerequisite for a middle-class income, and those who could advance in school put off marriage until they had graduated. At the same time, more of those who could not advance in school found themselves financially unable to marry.[33]

Divorce

Divorce replaced death as the prime reason marriages ended. The annual ratio of divorces granted to every one hundred marriages performed increased slowly but steadily (except for a major spike just after World War II), from thirteen in 1920 to thirty-three in 1970—when for the first time the number of divorces exceeded the number of marriages ended by deaths—and then soared to a peak of fifty-one in the early 1990s. About 25 percent of marriages formed around World War II had ended in divorce by the time the couples had reached age fifty-five, but 50 percent of marriages made in the 1970s ended by age fifty-five.[34] The divorce rate then declined slightly during the last few years of the century.[35]

Scholars explain the long-term rise in divorce mainly by the increasing employment of women (which may have given them more independence, exposed them to new ideas, or created marital strain) and by the stagnation in men's wages since the 1960s (which may have made marriage more difficult to sustain). That the divorce rate shot up rapidly between 1965 and 1975—from one divorce for every four marriages a year to one divorce for every two marriages a year—was surely tied to the spread of no-fault divorce during those years. The rising divorce rate may also have been part of the general cultural change of the 1960s. Divorce rates subsided in the

1990s, probably because Americans were marrying at older ages and were better educated.[36] About half of Americans divorced for the first time had not remarried within ten years, so the fraction of adults divorced at any one time continued to rise through the 1990s. Six percent of American women in 1970 were divorced, but 13 percent in 2000 were. (However, perhaps one-fifth of divorced Americans under sixty-five in 2000 were cohabiting.)[37]

Educational attainment increasingly determined who divorced and who remarried. Marriages formed in the early 1960s typically lasted just as long whatever the spouses' schooling, but the length of marriages of the 1980s depended on education: college-graduate women were much likelier to reach their tenth anniversary than other wives.[38] As we will see, the tightening connection between marriage and education is a critical feature of the later twentieth century.

Implications of Changing Demographics for American Households

Longer lives, fewer children, changing age at marriage, more divorce—these developments, abetted by increasing affluence, immigration, and changing tastes, shaped American families over the century. Gretchen Donehower's analysis of the historical data on living arrangements indicates that the long-term drop in birth rates most strongly determined living arrangements for most of the century. Fewer children meant fewer married-with-children households, more empty-nest households, and perhaps fewer of the elderly living with adult children.[39] Longer lives simplified living arrangements as fewer families had to take in widowed and orphaned relatives and as more grown-up children left home while their parents were still alive.[40] Household arrangements bend to the vital events of birth, death, marriage, and divorce.

The case of Cyrus, a coal miner from Mount Pleasant, Pennsylvania, illustrates how one death could change three families. Cyrus had married Catherine in 1882. They had ten children, three of whom died young. Late in 1901, Cyrus was struck and killed by a train at the mine, leaving Catherine with seven children and little means of support. The three boys moved in with Cyrus's younger brother, Jake, and his wife, who eventually had six children of their own. Catherine took the four girls back to her parents' home in Marianna, Pennsylvania. The children grew up, the grandparents died, and by 1919 only Sarah, the ninth child, still lived with Catherine in Marianna. That year, Sarah married Patrick, and the couple lived with Catherine. At the time of the 1900 census, then, there were three married-couple-with-children families: Cyrus's family, Jake's family, and Catherine's parents' family. Cyrus's death turned the three nuclear families into two extended families to be recorded in 1910: that of Jake plus his three nephews, and that of Catherine's parents, Catherine, another daughter, and four granddaughters. The 1920 census found a nuclear family—Jake's, now that Catherine's boys had moved out—and the shrunken extended family of Catherine, Sarah, and Patrick.

Large families and the caprices of early death created complicated households such as these early in the century. About one-fourth of mothers like Catherine, for example, were living apart from at least one of their young children.[41] By the middle decades of the century, the demographic trends of couples having fewer children and people living longer lives (and achieving greater economic security) had reduced some of this complexity. But with the emergence in the later decades of delayed marriage and more frequent divorce and remarriage, families became more complex again. This is the historical cycle we document in the next section. However, the end-of-the-century complexity was more often a matter of choice than of uncontrollable events like unplanned births, premature deaths, and financial destitution. When we say that births and deaths once altered Americans' living arrangements more than any conscious choices they made, the contrast between women like Catherine and her descendants are what we have in mind.

THE CHANGING PROFILE OF AMERICAN FAMILIES

A century of revolutionary changes in Americans' births, deaths, marriages, and divorces—together with other social changes like immigration, increasing wealth, and cultural shifts—produced the variety of living arrangements in 2000 depicted in figure 4.1. Figure 4.6 shows in all its complexity how American households changed—and in some important ways, did not change—from 1900 through 2000, focusing again on different age groups. Readers can glean many details from the graphs in figure 4.6; here we focus on only a handful.

The Under-Forty-fives

We turn first to those under age forty-five, for whom the net changes over the century were relatively modest. For the three youngest age groups, living arrangements at the end of the twentieth century were surprisingly similar to those at the beginning of the century; the middle decades were unusual. Throughout, the "modal," or typical, American under the age of forty-five lived in a household headed by two legally married adults with children (the dark circle lines in figure 4.6). White families were especially stable, as we see in more detail later. The proportion of young Americans in two-parent nuclear families peaked in the 1960s, when, for example, 78 percent of children lived in them—eight points higher than in 1900 and sixteen points higher than in 2000. The sixteen-point decline between 1960

Figure 4.6   Household Type, by Year and Age

Changes in Living Arrangements Were Greatest for People Forty-Five Years and Older

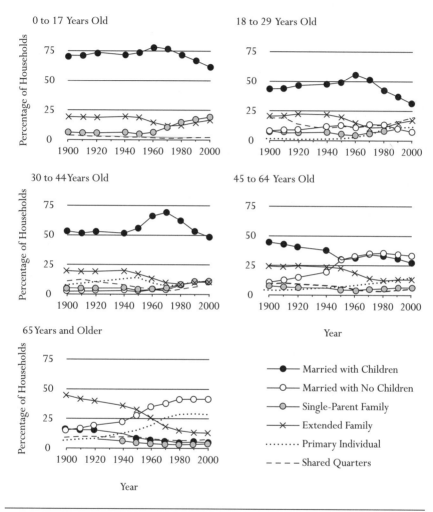

Source: IPUMS.

and 2000 is a ten-point decline when cohabiting couples are counted as married; we look at these numbers more closely later.

Although Americans typically lived in married-with-children households throughout the century, their second choices changed. Before midcentury, the most common second option for those under forty-five was to live in an extended household (the line with Xs in figure 4.6), the experience of the young widow Catherine being illustrative. After midcentury, the second option was increasingly either a single-parent household (shaded circles), for women especially, or a primary-individual household (pluses), for men especially. As late as 1960, only 6 percent of children lived with a single parent, but by 2000, 20 percent did (16 percent if we treat cohabitation as marriage).[42] The proportion of adults between the ages of thirty and forty-four living the single life—as primary individuals, single parents, roommates, or partners—declined substantially from 1900 to 1960, but increased greatly afterward (left-hand graph in middle row), no doubt because this age group married later and divorced more often than its predecessors had done in previous generations. We must also keep in mind that perhaps one-fourth to one-third of the apparent increase in single living reflects cohabitation.

The short story for Americans under forty-five was that their household situations were not much different or much more diverse around 2000 than just after 1900: a clear majority lived in a nuclear family. If we count cohabitating couples, whose numbers increased rapidly after 1970, then about the same proportion of under-forty-fives lived in two-parent nuclear households at the end of the century as at its beginning. Again, the midcentury was the distinctive era.[43]

These results help reframe the fin-de-siècle discussion about the fate of the family, a discussion largely posed as a debate between two alternatives. One view holds that the family *disintegrated* over the twentieth century, leaving more adults single, more children with one parent, fewer Americans committed to their families, and the family bonds frayed. The other view claims that the family *changed* in the twentieth century as Americans found alternative—and just as wholesome—forms of family life, each serving its members as well as, if not better than, the "traditional" form.[44] We can see in these data the special nature of the midcentury. Americans married young, set up independent households young, and had children sooner and more often than in the decades immediately before or after. They were able to do so because the postwar economic boom provided young men with well-paying jobs and because Social Security and private pensions reduced the need to house their elderly parents. These enabling economic and demographic trends were probably reinforced by a cultural uniformity that emerged around the uniformity of family experiences—the later-ridiculed "Ozzie and Harriet" way of life. Then came the 1960s, and American household patterns once again became diverse. Nonetheless, the major change for children and young adults was *not* that late-twentieth-century Americans abandoned the "traditional" nuclear family, but instead that when they were not in a nuclear family—when young singles left their parents' homes or when couples divorced—they turned to new alternatives. Rather than forming extended households, as was common before the war, Americans who found themselves in these circumstances lived in smaller-than-nuclear households—as single parents, as primary individuals with roommates, as partners—or they lived alone.

Thus, although the nuclear family continued to predominate and, in that sense, media descriptions of the family's demise were highly exaggerated, younger Americans clearly lived more independently at the end than at the start of the century. And thanks to the dropping birth rate, independent living by the elderly, and the decline of boarding and domestic service, even those in nuclear families lived in smaller households. One implication of the shrinking household is that parents had fewer hands to help care for the children, a smaller cadre of what Francis Goldscheider and her colleagues have called "co-moms."[45]

More broadly, younger adults increasingly determined their own living arrangements. As we have noted, they were freer of the arbitrariness of uncontrolled demographic and economic events. But they also grew freer of social constraints. Continuing a powerful social trend from the century before, people in their teens and twenties by degrees felt freer to leave their parents' homes rather than stay to work the farm or to assist with house chores. More women found the right and the power to avoid or abandon bad marriages and, when married, to demand equal voice on, say, further childbirth.[46] Women's exercise of these options helped shape the household patterns of the late twentieth century, notably spurring the rise of single-parent and remarried families. Although divorce in late-twentieth-century America resulted in great measure from the plight of poorly educated men, its rise through the earlier decades, most scholars agree, was in part a consequence of women's growing independence.[47] Individuals gained greater options for family life.

What did these developments mean for the *quality* of family life, particularly for the well-being of children? During the midcentury era of early marriage and high fertility, scholars worried that small nuclear families, stripped of grandparents, spinster aunts, older sisters, and nannies, were too fragile and psychologically intense for members' ultimate well-being.[48] More recently, scholars have debated whether the growing number of single-parent and stepparent families formed by divorce damage their members more than the intact nuclear families of miserably married couples do.[49]

Still, these changes, for all the well-placed concern, were largely at the margin. For most Americans—especially white, middle-class Americans—age forty-five or younger in 2000, the nuclear family remained about as central as it had been in 1900. This stability in living arrangements was not true for those forty-five and over.

The Forty-Five-Plus

As evident in figure 4.6, middle-aged and elderly Americans shifted radically to independent living, either as couples or as singles. Early in the twentieth century, three out of four forty-five- to sixty-four-year-olds lived in complex households with children and other relatives or both; only one in seven lived alone or with just a spouse. But in the last years of the century, half of the middle-aged lived in a childless couple or lived alone. The empty-nesters alone tripled from 11 to 34 percent of the middle-aged.[50] This increase was steady and undisturbed by the baby boom. Moreover, in 1900, 45 percent of Americans age sixty-five or older, especially women, lived in an extended household. This proportion declined steadily over one hundred years to only 13 percent in 2000, when the elderly lived either as empty-nest couples or alone. Because wives typically outlived husbands, 37 percent of elderly women in 2000 lived on their own, while only 18 percent of elderly men did.

Together, these changes describe the emergence over the century of a new and common life story for postwar middle-aged Americans: in their forties and fifties, married couples saw their children off and had the home to themselves; in their seventies and eighties, one spouse died, typically the husband, and the other continued by living alone. There are other scenarios—moving in with grown children, having an adult child linger at home, boarding or finding a roommate, going to an institution. Fewer and fewer mature Americans, however, lived those more complex story lines, which described the lives of eight of ten elderly persons in 1900 but only four of ten in 2000. Similarly, in 1900, 86 percent of forty-five- to sixty-four-year-olds lived in a complex household, but only 52 percent did in 2000 (and for half of these the complexity arose simply from late childbearing: a *minor* child was still at home). These findings echo our findings on the history of life events: Americans converged into common living patterns.[51]

Summary

For both younger and older Americans, the household shrank. In 1900 smaller households (those at the twentieth percentile in size) contained three people, the median household about five people, and the more crowded households (eightieth percentile) about seven. Except for a small bump during the 1950s, those numbers dropped steadily through 2000, when the range of household sizes were two at the low end, three in the middle, and five at the high end. American households also became less variable.[52] Three-fourths of Americans in 2000 lived alone or with one, two, or three other people; small-scale forms of living had replaced large-scale forms.

The overall changes in American living arrangements over the twentieth century were profound, but *not* of the sort on which much of the controversy has been focused (the "breakdown of the traditional family"), and the warning we started the chapter with bears repeating: the 1950s may be a poor benchmark for understanding the longer historical trends. Older folks' situations changed much more than younger folks' or children's. The two-parent household remained the predominant home for young adults and children. Simpler and smaller household arrangements became more common, but there was not the explosion of diversity that either the fans or the critics of the "traditional" family proclaimed.

AXES OF DIFFERENCE IN FAMILY LIFE

Over the course of the twentieth century, the American mix of family arrangements changed, as did the kinds of Americans who lived in the various kinds of households. The experiences, in particular, of black Americans and of less-educated white Americans took distinct tracks over the years. To describe these different tracks, we must simplify matters lest we get swamped by complexity. We simplify in two ways. First, we look at only three age groups: children, thirty- to forty-four-year olds, and those age sixty-five and older. Second, we collapse the six household types into three larger categories: married-couple households, with or without children; extended households that include relatives in addition to parent(s) and child(ren); and single-adult households headed by an unattached adult. People classified in this third category include lone adults, single parents and their children, nonrelative roommates, and people sharing group quarters. We note that some of these singles households contain cohabiting couples, and we track these as well.

Figure 4.7 presents these now-simplified trends. The solid lines count only legally married couples, and the dashed lines treat cohabiting couples as if they were married.[53] We see in the first panel that the living arrangements of children changed little until the post–World War II years, when nuclear family living became more common—at the expense of extended households—and then after 1960, when an increasing proportion lived with one parent. More and more Americans age thirty to forty-four lived as a married couple up to about 1970, and then fewer did; instead, single living became more common. The dashed line shows that, because of cohabitation, the 1970 to 2000 decline in *couples* was not as great as that in *married* couples, nor was the increase in singles as notable. And as we saw with the more detailed typology of figure 4.6, the dramatic change was among the elderly.

This, then, is the family history of Americans all pooled together; next we look at axes of difference.

Figure 4.7   Simplified Household Type for Three Age Groups, by Year

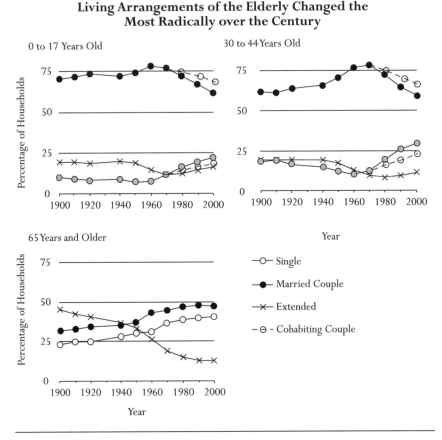

Living Arrangements of the Elderly Changed the Most Radically over the Century

Source: IPUMS.
Note: Dashed lines display values when cohabiting couples are counted as married.

The Widening Racial Divide

Earlier, we saw how strikingly different African-American and European-American households were in 2000. Just as striking is the fact that these differences *grew* substantially over the twentieth century. Figure 4.8 shows the patterns for children: the percentages of black children and white children living in two-parent, nuclear households and the percentages of black children and white children living in single-adult households.[54] The dashed lines

Figure 4.8   Simplified Household Type, by Year and Race

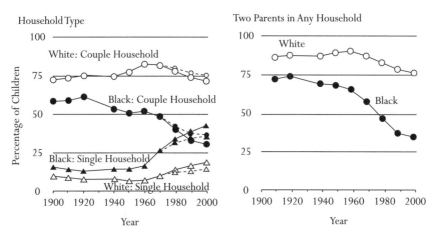

After 1940, the Family Experiences of Black and White Children Diverged

Source: IPUMS.

Note: Dashed lines display values when cohabiting couples are counted as married.

treat cohabiting couples as married. For ease of reading, the lines for extended households are not shown.

The left side of figure 4.8 shows that the proportion of black children who lived with two married adults in a nuclear household dropped rapidly over the century, from about six in ten to three in ten. In contrast, the proportions of white children who lived in such households were virtually the same, seven in ten, both in 1900 and 2000, albeit more often with remarried parents in 2000. The difference between black and white children tripled from fourteen to forty-one percentage points. Considering cohabitation does not change the story much.[55] The central question, however, may be not whether children lived in nuclear family households, but whether they lived with two parents in any kind of household. Some children lived with their parents and other relatives, such as grandparents. The right side of figure 4.8 displays the numbers that way, adding together children who lived with two parents whether independently in nuclear households or embedded in extended households.[56] Black and white still diverged sharply by just about as much. One conclusion does change a bit: In 1910, 87 percent of white children lived with two parents, while 76 percent did in 2000; all the net decline of eleven points occurred after 1960. This was not the sharp drop that occurred for black children (thirty-seven points), nor the kind that seems depicted in the media, but it is worth noting.

Widening racial divisions in living arrangements also occurred in other age groups. For example, in 1900 black and white men thirty to forty-four years old were relatively similar in their household patterns: 60 percent lived in couple households, 20 percent in extended households, and 20 percent in single arrangements. By 2000 black and white men's situations were very different: 60 percent of whites but only 40 percent of black men lived in married-couple households. Similarly, in 1900 most white and black women age thirty to forty-four were in married-couple households; in 2000 two-thirds of European-American women lived in married-couple households, but only one-third of African-American women did.

Racial differences in living arrangements arose from racial differences in marriage: at the beginning of the century, blacks were somewhat less often married than whites, but the gap widened greatly. Around 1940, age at marriage started rising rapidly for African-American women, and the percentage who never married also rose rapidly.[57] African Americans did not experience the marriage boom that whites did in the 1950s, and by the end of the century, their rates of marriage had plummeted. (Treating cohabitation as marriage reduces the contrast only modestly; black women increasingly lived outside of any union.) This divergence of black and white is especially striking because it happened while blacks narrowed their gaps with whites in health, longevity, educational attainment, and income. Indeed, this is one of the few ways in which racial gaps widened over the twentieth century.

Scholars have offered two general explanations for the distinctiveness of black marriage and household patterns. One explanation stresses traditions that originated in slavery or perhaps even in Africa, and nineteenth-century data do show a racial difference. But that racial difference widened, as we saw, in the middle of the twentieth century. Thus, most scholars focus on the second explanation, the deterioration of African-American men's economic circumstances during the century. The agricultural depression of the 1920s, the mechanization of southern farming, and the Great Depression hit African-American men hard; the millions who left the rural South became dependent on an unstable and discriminatory labor market in northern cities. Then, in the 1960s and beyond, the deindustrialization of major northern cities further undermined black men's employment chances. Unstable employment and low wages—which we explore in chapter 5—combined with high death and soaring imprisonment rates to further shrink the number of marriageable black men (that is, men who could reliably support a family). At the other end of the scale, the growing number of college-educated black women had a hard time finding comparably educated black men. With marriage difficult and becoming less common, the mother-headed household took on some cultural power of its own.[58] Whatever the explanation, the widening division of black and white in family experiences is a major story of the century.

Because the racial contrast is so great, it sways examination of other differences; therefore, in the rest of this section we look only at the *white* population. (Hispanics were overwhelmingly counted with non-Hispanic whites for most of the century; we distinguish them where needed.)

The Educated Family

Contrasts by education also widened after 1940 (the year the census first collected educational information). Figure 4.9 displays, as an example, the percentages of white Americans of different ages and educational attainments who were living in married-couple households. The lines represent those who did not graduate from high school, those who graduated from high school, those who attended some college, and those who graduated from college. For related minors, education refers to the educational attainment of the head of the household.[59] In 1940 there were few differences among the educational groups, but the gaps subsequently widened greatly; by 2000, the child of a college graduate had about a one-third better chance of living in a two-parent nuclear household than the child of a high school dropout, and about a one-fifth better chance than the child of a high school graduate. Counting cohabiting parents changes the story little. Smaller but similar differences emerged for the other age groups. Reciprocally, less-educated adults and the children of less-educated parents increasingly appeared in extended or single-parent households (not shown). Americans' family patterns came to depend heavily on educational attainment.

Other studies also point to this conclusion. We discussed earlier the growing influence of education in shaping women's chances of marrying and divorcing, but the role of education was even subtler and broader than that. For example, with women's advancement into higher education, Americans increasingly married someone of similar educational attainments. In the 1950s many business and professional men married their secretaries, nurses, or high school sweethearts; in the 1990s such men more often married business or professional women. Moreover, men began seeking spouses who were high earners, as women long had done, further accentuating the tendency for people of like schooling to marry one another.[60] Given the great growth in the proportion of Americans who finished high school and even of those who graduated from college, we might have expected the dilution of social differences along lines of schooling; instead, they sharpened.

Figure 4.9   Married-Couple Households, by Year, Education, and Age

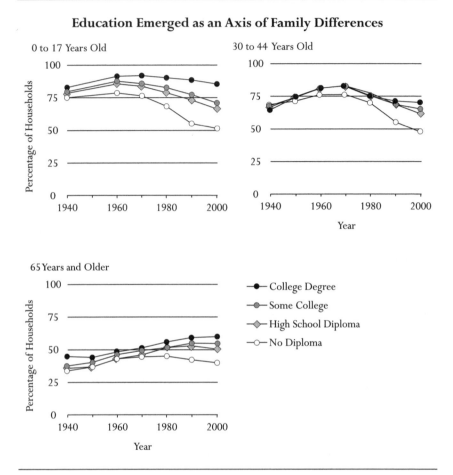

Education Emerged as an Axis of Family Differences

Source: IPUMS.
Note: The 1950 data are missing for children because the IPUMS sampling scheme precludes matching children to their parents.

Smaller Divides

The late-twentieth-century wave of immigration from Asia and Latin America introduced another dimension of difference, that between the native- and the foreign-born. Early in the century, European immigrants' household patterns were not much different from those of the native-born; their families were larger, but were Western in structure. After 1970, the foreign-born became over three times as likely to live in extended households as native-born Americans.[61] This emerging difference may reflect the particular "family strategies" of immigrant groups. European immigrants, for example, often boarded in a private home or lodged in a rooming house. In 1900 and 1910, about two in ten of the foreign-born lived in group quarters or as nonrelatives; in 1990 and 2000, fewer than one in ten did. One reason for the contrast, in addition to the cultural styles of the new immigrants, may be "family reunification" legislation, which increased the number of parents and siblings entering the country to join kin already here.[62]

On the other hand, family patterns became more similar across American regions.[63] We might also expect that urban-rural differences would have shrunk; instead, they changed axes. We pursue the complexities in chapter 7, but for present purposes, this gloss will suffice: in 1900 whites living in the countryside were more likely to live in nuclear households than were whites inside the cities; by 2000 that difference had *widened*. At the same time, the family patterns of white suburbanites (and their numbers swelled greatly over the century) shifted from similarity with those of city residents to similarity with those of rural residents—that is, they became heavily nuclear. Thus, contrast within urban areas sharpened: central cities increasingly housed single-person and, to a lesser degree, extended households, and suburbs increasingly housed nuclear family households.[64]

Summary

Americans' family arrangements generally depended on their race, class, and other social distinctions, but how much these distinctions mattered and how they mattered changed over the century. Region mattered less, as did urban or rural residence, while city versus suburb distinctions emerged. Nativity became more important as newcomers with distinctive strategies arrived after 1965. Most significantly, African Americans' family lives diverged sharply from those of whites: only a minority of African Americans were living in married-couple households by the end of the century. And a wide gap opened up between more- and less-educated white Americans; if we had included blacks in that comparison, the role of education would have been revealed as even greater.

A CLOSER LOOK: LIVING ALONE

Some observers have worried in particular about the increasing proportion of Americans living alone, a pattern that suggests isolation, longing, and pathology, although that suggestion may be based on a misconception.[65] The proportion of single-person households quintupled: only 5 percent of American homes contained a single person in 1900, but over 26 percent did in 2000.[66] But that comparison again counts housing units rather than peo-

Figure 4.10   Americans Who Live Alone, by Age and Gender

Americans, Especially Elderly Women, Increasingly Lived Alone

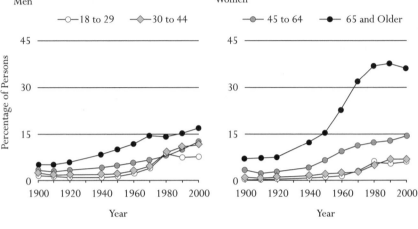

Source: IPUMS.

ple. We count people. So far in this chapter, the category of "singles" combines primary individuals, single parents, unrelated roommates, and residents of group quarters. In this section, we focus on Americans who lived completely alone.

Figure 4.10 shows the percentage of adult Americans who lived alone from 1900 through 2000 for different age groups, and separately for men and women. Rates of solo living rose substantially, especially for women and notably for older women. Elderly women were the only ones among whom at least 20 percent lived alone in any decade. Note also that the upward trend for living alone started among middle-aged and older Americans before World War II, but only after 1960 for younger Americans. We can get a better sense of what happened by looking closely at three specific groups of unmarried Americans: never-married young people, separated and divorced thirty- to forty-four-year-olds, and the widowed elderly.

No more than 3 percent of never-married eighteen- to twenty-nine-year-olds lived alone until 1960; then 11 percent did in 1980 and 10 percent in 2000. This post–baby boom tripling coincided with the increasing postponement of marriage and increasing affluence, both of which trends made moving out of parents' homes more reasonable.[67] Although living alone never exceeded 10 percent among these people, many went through that experience at least briefly. The experiences of divorced and separated thirty-to forty-four-year-olds took different turns for men and women starting in the 1950s. Divorced and separated men increasingly lived alone, reaching nearly 40 percent in 1980 and dropping to 31 percent in 2000; divorced and separated women living alone reached a high of 15 percent in 1990 (and 14 percent in 2000). The major reason ex-married men ended up living alone at more than double the rate of women was, of course, that formerly married mothers typically lived with their children while fathers typically did not. Early in the century, mothers without husbands often returned to their parents' homes; later in the century, they typically lived independently with their children.[68] Either way, divorced mothers were less likely than divorced fathers to live alone.

The most dramatic change in solitary living was among the widowed elderly. In 1900 it was a rare widow or widower who lived alone; only 10 percent did, even fewer than lived in shared quarters. In 2000 the great majority of the widowed elderly, 62 percent, lived alone. Many scholars have sought to explain what happened. A small part of the story seems to be demographic: as birth rates plunged, the elderly had fewer children who might be able and willing to house them.[69] A larger part of the story is economic. In the nineteenth century, American farm couples commonly had a grown son stay with them to help out until they grew too feeble to work the farm; then they handed the farm over to him and stayed in the house as his dependents until they died. The shift away from farming to industrial work in the twentieth century undercut that system. Then, with growing affluence, the institution of pensions, and especially the formation and expansion of Social Security and Medicare, elderly people increasingly had the resources (and health) to live alone. A third—and more debated—part of the story may be cultural: Americans increasingly valued independence. At least one scholar argues that American norms moved toward "uncompromising nuclearity," with all parties agreeing that the young should not have to live with the older generation.[70] Others, however, argue that the elderly always preferred independence for themselves; it was not until recently that they had the means to attain it. Still others argue that the elderly always preferred the opposite, coresidence, but in later decades children increasingly spurned their parents. Poll data from late in the century suggest that the elderly preferred independent living, but those polls cannot tell us whether this was a new development (for more on this point, see the analysis of the polls later in the chapter).[71]

In sum, the widespread concern over single-person households may be misplaced. Over 20 percent of Americans living alone in 2000 were elderly widows, even though they were only 3 percent of the population. Young never-marrieds who were briefly soloing during the transition from their parents' homes to couple households of their own formed another chunk of solitary residents. The singles probably of greatest concern are the separated and divorced thirty- to sixty-four-year-olds—about 5 percent of their age group—most of whom, research shows, would much rather be in a couple. Otherwise, the increased rates of living alone seem to be the result of increasing affluence and preference, not abandonment.

A CLOSER LOOK: A COMMON LIFE COURSE?

Delayed marriage, divorce, unwed parenthood, independent living, the entry of mothers into the labor force—these and other changes make it seem that family life and growing up became chaotic for many Americans. Yet we have already seen that in many ways their experiences became less, not more, disorderly. For example, early deaths became rare, and family sizes became more similar. Most family scholars would argue that Americans' life courses became, at least for most of the century, increasingly ordered, standardized, and predictable. More and more Americans finished school, left their parents' homes, married, bore children, and retired—in that order and on a common and predictable schedule.[72]

Changes in vital events made standardization easier, but social institutions formalized it. For example, the first school laws compelled only basic literacy training; then, early in the twentieth century, compulsory schooling expanded and children ended up in age-segregated classes. Similarly, states that had allowed fourteen- and fifteen-year-olds to marry pushed those ages upward, compressing age at marriage. Social Security and private pensions gave workers incentives to retire at sixty-five.

Another component of growing standardization is, paradoxically, greater choice. When people agree on what the good life is, variation in how they live usually reflects circumstances beyond their control, such as the early death of parents, unanticipated pregnancy, or economic busts. As the unpredictable became less frequent, Americans became freer to follow their preferences. Rather than generating more diversity, Americans' greater freedom from circumstance, historians such as John Modell argue, allowed them more freedom to conform to shared norms and to follow a standard life course.

Some research suggests that the standard life course became less standard again after 1970, perhaps as the consequence of a faltering economy or perhaps in response to diversifying preferences. Young Americans increasingly delayed marriage—see, again, in figure 4.5 the widening range of marriage ages—and delayed parenthood. More followed atypical sequences and found themselves in atypical situations, such as being unmarried in middle age or being an unmarried parent.[73]

David Stevens has presented some of the most persuasive evidence regarding the "orderliness" of the life cycle.[74] Using the 1900 through 1980 censuses, he calculated the variation in the ages at which Americans left home, married, had a first child, and so forth. Stevens found that the variation *narrowed* from 1900 to 1970; Americans increasingly took these steps at the same time in their lives. He also found that variation by region, race, and class shrank across the decades, suggesting, again, increasing similarity among Americans as they proceeded through the stages of life.

We pursue one aspect of the standardization issue to 2000, asking a simple question: did the connection between a person's age and the kind of household he or she lived in tighten or loosen over the century? If the connection grew stronger over the century—stronger in the sense that knowing a person's age more certainly allowed one to know what sort of household he or she lived in—then that is evidence that the living arrangements became more regularized. If the association grew weaker, that would suggest increasing disorderliness. We found a steady, roughly linear increase in the association between age and household type from 1900 to 2000.[75] The decline of the extended family household was the most important change behind this trend. Extended families mix generations, and therefore there is no direct connection between a person's age and living in an extended household. As extended household living declined, Americans became more concentrated in households typical of their age groups. Children lived with one or both parents, young adults with roommates or a spouse, middle-aged adults with their children, and seniors with a spouse or alone. Thus, we come back to the concerns that Modell raised. As demographic security and economic growth removed risks and offered choices, Americans "acted their age" in arranging their families. Almost everyone who wanted children had them, parents lived to see their offspring leave home, older couples chose the empty nest, and so on. Of course, divorce and out-of-wedlock births interfered with more people's plans as the century evolved, but even those developments occurred during narrow stages of life.[76]

As demographic and economic circumstances came under control, at least from 1900 to 1970, variation in how people lived increasingly arose when individuals chose to break from the general consensus—a woman would decide, for example, to have a child outside of marriage rather than have the father become an unwilling parent. It sometimes seems that the chaos of an earlier era was simpler. But the regularities that evolved over the last century suggest that the people who were exposed to complexities out of their control might have preferred the complexities we face that result from having more control.

FAMILY VALUES IN THE LATER CENTURY

We have seen that changes in living arrangements were driven by demographic shifts such as longer lives, economic changes such as greater affluence, and perhaps by changes in preferences—what we might term "family values." Disagreement about such values, whether about allowing divorce, deciding how to treat single mothers, or accepting gay marriage, is a recurrent source of national division. Family values changed substantially in the later part of the twentieth century, particularly during the 1960s and 1970s, and so did the way Americans divided on those values.

Here we explore the axes of difference on four specific value issues: the ideal number of children; the acceptability of premarital sex; leniency toward divorce; and where the aged should live. We chose these four issues because, among the topics covered in the archives of survey research, they represent a range of important family matters. (In chapter 9, we look at a related topic, attitudes toward the role of women.) Unlike census data, however, information on Americans' opinions typically covers only the last thirty to fifty years of the twentieth century. Nonetheless, substantial changes are evident even within one or two generations—changes in the views of average Americans and changes in who takes which side of these issues.

We apply the same technique introduced in chapter 3 and explained in appendix A to "smooth" the trends in the survey data and permit us to identify the lines of division on these topics. Also as in chapter 3, we combine polls conducted by both Gallup and the General Social Survey.

How Many Children Should We Have?

Excepting the baby boom, Americans had fewer children as the century progressed. Americans' preferred number of children—the answers respondents gave when asked, "What do you think is the ideal number of children for a family to have?"—also went down, dropping suddenly between the mid-1960s and mid-1970s.[77] Figure 4.11 shows the trend in the average number Americans gave when asked the question by Gallup polls taken since the 1930s and by the General Social Survey since 1972. The "ideal" line connecting the points traces the actual survey results. The "actual" line running below the trend in preferences represents the actual number of births that American women were having at the time.

The "ideal" line shows a precipitous change in Americans' ideal family size in less than a decade.[78] In 1967, 75 percent of Americans endorsed three or more children, and by 1976, a mere nine years later, only 39 percent did.[79] Note that Americans did not turn away from wanting children altogether; even at the end of the century, almost all adult Americans either had children or wanted to have children.[80] In no year did Americans' aspirations for children fall below the actual birth rates. Americans converged on a consensus that two children were ideal; in 1967, 25 percent of respondents answered the question with "two"; six years later, 51 percent did.[81]

Figure 4.11   Ideal and Actual Number of Births, by Year

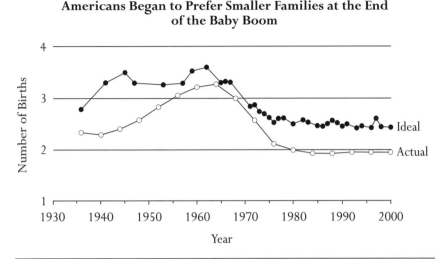

Americans Began to Prefer Smaller Families at the End of the Baby Boom

Sources: Ideal number of births (mean value): Gallup polls (1935 to 1997) and General Social Survey (1972 to 2000); actual number of births: see figure 4.3.

Note: Actual numbers of births are cohort total fertility rates dated to the year the cohort turned thirty years old.

By analyzing twenty-eight of the Gallup and GSS surveys from 1936 to 2000, focusing mainly on the volatile period of the 1960s and 1970s, we examined this convergence in more detail. During the 1950s, city residents preferred fewer children than rural residents, easterners and westerners fewer than southerners and midwesterners, men fewer than women, and Protestants fewer than Catholics, but these differences had narrowed by the 1980s as rural, heartland, female, and Catholic respondents increasingly gave smaller numbers.[82] For example, around 1950 southerners preferred, on average, 0.4 children more than northeasterners did; around 2000 the difference was well under 0.1 children.

Is Premarital Sex Acceptable?

More Americans had premarital sexual experiences and at younger ages as the century progressed. Two waves of sexual liberalization passed through twentieth-century America—one in the first couple of decades, which involved mostly "petting," and another in the 1960s, which included intercourse. Early in the century, girls typically married the boy they slept with, or at least married the boy who fathered their first child. Late-century pregnancies less often ended in a marriage. One survey found that 45 percent of people born around 1940 married their first sexual partner, but only 6 percent of those born after 1965 did. Demographers detected a leveling-off and perhaps a decline in premarital sexuality in the 1980s and 1990s, but generational change had sufficient inertia so that in the early 1990s, 53 percent of first-time mothers had conceived their children before marriage, compared to a mere 14 percent in the 1940s.[83] Younger sexual initiation, combined with delayed marriage, led to more single-parent households and more cohabiting households.

Americans' attitudes about premarital sex changed as well. Gallup has asked national samples, "Do you think it is wrong for a man and a woman to have sexual relations before marriage, or not?" In 1969, 21 percent said premarital sexual relations were "not wrong"; in 1973, 43 percent gave this answer—a doubling in merely four years.[84] The GSS, at which we shall look more closely, asked a similar question beginning in 1972: "If a man and woman have sex relations before marriage, do you think it is always wrong, almost always wrong, wrong only sometimes, or not wrong at all?" In 1972, 26 percent said "not wrong at all"; that percentage increased into the 1980s and then leveled off at 42 percent.[85] Note that, while Americans became more accepting of premarital sex, they became *less* accepting of *extramarital* sex—and that they accepted premarital sex for *adults*, not teens.[86]

Using these same data, David Harding and Christopher Jencks found that Americans substantially relaxed their views on adult premarital sex around 1970. After the mid-1980s, the liberal trend leveled off because of two roughly balanced processes. On the one hand, as people aged they became more sexually conservative.[87] On the other hand, as the years passed more conservative birth cohorts died out and liberal ones replaced them.[88]

After 1972 (the point at which we can start tracking opinions),[89] views on premarital sex converged across several dividing lines. Disagreement declined between age groups, between nonmetropolitan and metropolitan residents, and most sharply between the races as whites became more lax and blacks less so.[90] Differences in opinion by region and education did not change after 1972 because, we suspect, they had converged before 1972. Differences on premarital sex by gender remained wide: throughout the last three decades of the century, men were about eleven points likelier than women to see nothing wrong with premarital sex. But division on premarital sex widened sharply between Americans along one particular axis: religion. Figure 4.12 displays the patterns. Within the Christian groups, Catholics, mainline Protestants, and conservative Protestants began in 1972 with similar positions: 21 to 26 percent said premarital sex was "not wrong at all."[91] They then diverged, with conservative Protestants even reversing the liberalizing trend. In a similar fashion, beginning in the mid-1980s, fre-

Figure 4.12   Americans Who Said That Premarital Sex Is "Not Wrong at All," by Year and Religion

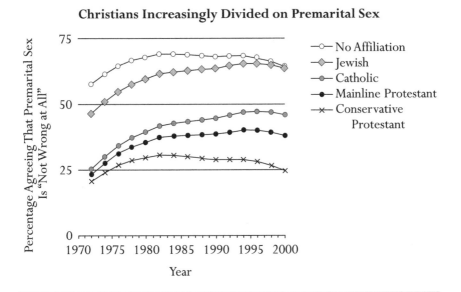

Christians Increasingly Divided on Premarital Sex

quent church attenders became conservative on the topic. The denominational divisions stand out in the context of convergence along other lines of division.

How Easy Should It Be to Get a Divorce?

Between 1960 and 1980, divorces zoomed up from nine to twenty-three per one thousand married women. Attitudes toward divorce also changed rapidly, as shown in answers to the question "Should divorce in this country be easier or more difficult to obtain than it is now?" "Easier" grew from 9 percent of responses in 1960 to 18 percent in 1966, to 32 percent in 1974.[92] Perhaps Americans were acknowledging the increasing reality of divorce, or perhaps they were responding to their rising expectations for a good marriage.[93] Then, after the 1970s, support for easing divorces dropped, going down to 24 percent in 2000. Support declined perhaps because no-fault divorce had in fact made it so much easier, and perhaps because of the escalation of divorce rates. Notably, the trend *against* easier divorce was led by the

Source: GSS.
Note: Data smoothed using locally estimated (loess) regression.

usually more liberal sectors of American society—the young, the urban, the less religious, and the better-educated.

In the 1970s, college-graduate Americans were considerably more liberal on divorce than the less-educated, but by 2000 they were more strict.[94] Steven Martin and Sangeeta Parashar have looked closely at this "education crossover" among younger Americans and consider it largely to be the product of increasingly unstable marriages—and thus, wariness—among the poorly educated.[95] And to be sure, divorce *had* become easier. Between 1970 and 1985, all the states had adopted no-fault divorce laws. Thus, the college-educated seemed to lead a modest movement recognizing that change and rejecting further easing. This reversal in attitudes also corresponded with the slight decline in divorce rates we noted before. As with premarital sex, the 1980s and 1990s saw modest moves in a conservative direction.

Where Should the Elderly Live?

So far, we have seen popular attitudes roughly parallel behavioral change (as cause, consequence, or coincidence, we cannot say). Not so on the issue of where the elderly should live. Over the twentieth century, more and more elderly Americans lived apart from their grown children (see figures 4.6, 4.7, and 4.10). However, Americans' attitudes on this issue moved, at least after 1957, in exactly the opposite direction. National samples have been asked, "As you know, many older people share a home with their grown children. Do you think this is generally a good idea or a bad idea?" In 1957 nearly two-thirds answered, "Bad idea"; at that time, about five in ten elderly Americans lived independently. But support for independent living then *dropped*, all the way down to one-third in 2000, even as by then more than seven in ten elderly Americans lived on their own.[96] The driving force was generational turnover: the later in the century people were born, the more they rejected the idea of the elderly living apart. On the other hand, older people, of whatever generation, were especially likely to endorse independent living. The shift against the elderly living apart—just like the move away from easy divorce—was led by the young and highly educated, as shown in figure 4.13.[97]

One possible explanation is nostalgia for the past. A younger, well-educated generation could express a costless romanticism, because it became less and less likely that Mom and Dad really *would* move in. Or perhaps they came to endorse coresidence because of their growing economic anxiety, increasing reliance on their parents for financial aid, and worries about their own "golden years."[98] Whatever the reason, Americans generally became *more*, not less, divided by age and education on this question.[99]

Figure 4.13   Americans Who Said That Elderly Parents Living with Their Adult Children Is a "Bad Idea," by Year and Education

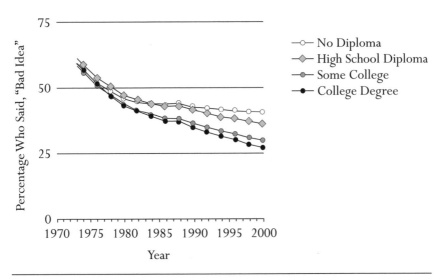

Fewer Americans Objected to the Elderly Living with Their Adult Children

Source: GSS.
Note: Data smoothed using locally estimated (loess) regression.

Summary

A few general points about Americans and their family values emerge from these details. Americans substantially changed their views on key family issues in the last half of the century, and even the last third. Between about 1965 and 1980, American preference moved rapidly toward smaller families, acceptance of premarital sex, and easier divorces. (In chapter 9, we will see shifts toward greater gender equality too.) After 1980, these trends stabilized or even reversed slightly. Though the story is different and more puzzling on the question of where the elderly should live, it is consistent with a conservative trend after the 1970s. Generally, different groups—regional, place, racial, gender—converged toward shared positions on these family issues. We saw a few noteworthy exceptions to the convergence: widening religious differences on premarital sex and widening differences by cohort and education on divorce and on where the elderly should live. There are suggestions here—as in the trends on actual living arrangements—that educational differences at least partly displaced racially and geographically based disagreements about family life.

CONCLUSION

Despite the politicized debate on whether the American family has splintered into various "broken" (the language of the right) or "alternative" (the language of the left) forms, the diversity of Americans' living arrangements was only modestly greater at the end than at the beginning of the twentieth century. The married-couple nuclear household remained the dominant form to about the same degree in 2000 as it had been in 1900, at least for nonblack, middle-class Americans. The century's middle years of many young and large nuclear families, the years that form the "once upon a time" of the political debates, were exceptional. Certainly, much changed over the century: people lived longer, started marriages later, had fewer children, and more often ended their marriages by divorce than death. Americans turned less often to extended households as the first alternative to the nuclear family and more often to single-adult households. In later decades, cohabiting households, though still a small percentage, became more common (or perhaps just more visible). But we are most struck by the relative stability—across more than three generations of profound changes in fertility, mortality, marriage, economics, and immigration—of younger Americans' living arrangements. And we are struck by the vast changes that occurred in the living arrangements of middle-aged and older Americans. Instead of having young children late into their lives or living in extended or other complex households, as they typically did at the beginning of the century, Americans over forty-five increasingly lived on their own as empty-nest couples or as singles. This change made the lifestyle of late-twentieth-century Americans during their middle and later years far different from what it had been for their grandparents and great-grandparents.

A full explanation for the changes in the mix of family patterns is beyond us here, but certainly demographic, economic, and cultural changes all played a part. The extension of lifetimes, for example, made the empty-nest and single households of older people possible. Rising wealth fueled the proliferation of one-adult households, whether for the young, the divorced, or the elderly. And new choices—for example, to have children but to have fewer of them and to have them later—facilitated several rearrangements of family life.

The image of greater family diversity is also challenged by the many ways in which Americans' family experiences became more similar over the century. Americans became more similar to one another in their life spans, in the number of children they had, and, at least into the 1970s if not beyond, in the life stages they passed through. To be sure, atypical family types—for example, the single-mother household, or the gay couple—became somewhat more common, but other living arrangements, such as the orphanage and the lodging house, nearly vanished. The nuclear household remained the standard for the great majority. Also, past family differences among Americans, especially differences by region and place, diminished.

Not all differences narrowed, however. Most critically, African Americans' families diverged sharply from those of other Americans as two-parent households became uncommon in the black community. Poorly educated whites' experiences diverged similarly from those of the better-educated. In the chapters that follow, we find such rearrangements of American diversity—such as the declining significance of region and the increasing significance of education—in other aspects of American life as well.

CHAPTER FIVE

How Americans Worked: New Workers, New Jobs, and New Differences

EVEN THE most visionary American living in 1900 could not have foreseen how Americans worked in 2000. Everything that is too familiar for us to notice—where we work, how we get there, what the workplace looks like, how long we work, what and who we work with, how much we are paid—changed. In 1900 most people worked at home, on their farms; most of the rest worked near home, walking to manual jobs at a mill or factory. They put in ten-hour days, often six or seven days a week. These men—and they were overwhelmingly men—typically worked with crops, animals, or objects like wood and steel for something around $4 an hour (in 2000 dollars). By the end of the twentieth century, typical American workers drove many miles to offices or sleek shops, put in about forty hours a week for upwards of $15 an hour, mixed with women as coworkers, customers, and clients (about half were themselves women), and spent their days working with information, people, or both.[1]

The world of work was transformed, and with the arrival of wives and the departure of older men, a new workforce emerged. Moreover, how Americans were divided at work and how work divided Americans changed over the century. The divisions Americans brought to work, such as gender and ancestry, lined up in 2000 in new ways with differences in work experiences. For example, who worked (for pay) changed. In 1900 gender and marital status heavily determined who worked: 88 percent of the employed were either men or unmarried women; in 2000 only 61 percent were.[2] Instead, age and education sorted out the working and nonworking segments of the population. Furthermore, the banning of child labor shrank the proportion of young workers, while retirement curtailed work at the other end of the life cycle.[3] A century ago, most men worked from childhood until death; by midcentury most could anticipate spending many years in retirement. (In 1880 about one-fifth of elderly men were retired, in 1950 half were, and in 2000 over 80 percent were.)[4] These changes combined to concentrate working in the ages between the late teens and the early sixties. In this respect, working Americans became a more homogenous group; gone were the scenes at mines, factories, or shipyards of small, smooth-faced boys mixing with hobbling, grizzled geezers.

But the changing character of the work itself created new differences. Over the century, employment moved from farm to factory to office, and jobs became increasingly specialized. Henry Ford and his imitators broke manufacturing down into an assembly line of many small, repetitive tasks. Major corporations also broke selling and services into finely grained assignments, each of which was performed by a specialist or a specialized subcontractor. Professionals continued to divide and subdivide themselves into specialties. The physicians, surgeons, and healers of 1900 gave way to medical specialists who focused on particular parts of the body and, increasingly, on specific diseases or conditions of that body part. New technologies and economic growth also reshaped the workforce. Occupations of note in 1900, such as farmer, collier, and blacksmith, dwindled or virtually disappeared; others, such as salesman and middle manager, expanded; and yet others sprang up. The Bureau of Labor Statistics in 2002 identified the following kinds of work as "major growth occupations" of the twenty-first century: administrative assistants, convention managers, environmental engineers, quality assurance directors, and volunteer coordinators—mainly new sorts of work requiring new sorts of training.[5] Most of the novel, growing occupations involved coordinating the work of others and analyzing abstract information. (The environmental engineers may focus on things, or at least on data about things.)[6] Farmers, colliers, and blacksmiths did not have to worry much about human relations; even coal-mine operators probably gave it little thought, although they probably should have. The increasing invention and subdivision of jobs created a diverse set of lifelong experiences for American workers.

Moreover, different kinds of jobs received different pay. Pay disparities narrowed from 1929 to about 1970 and then widened again.[7] In 1950 high earners, those at the eightieth percentile in earnings, made four times as much as low earners, those at the twentieth percentile. The ratio declined to three-to-one in 1970, but then rose back to four-to-one in 1990 and reached 4.35-to-1 in 2000.[8] How much workers earn depends on their job and their education; both increasingly influenced earnings after 1970. Pay also depends on a worker's gender, race, age, and region, but those differences became *less* important over the century.

For at least 150 years, social scientists have argued that differences in the work people do and in their pay for that work breed social and cultural differences among them.[9] Farmers, assembly-line mechanics, and financial analysts come from different places, but their jobs lead them further into yet more different places. Diversity in all aspects of employment grew over the century, giving fuel to the claim. We do not directly address the consequences of work here, although the issue invests our topic with greater weight. We return, however, to the idea that work diversity breeds other kinds of diversity in our final chapter.

In this chapter, we examine the questions of who worked in America in the twentieth century, what they did at work, how much they made at work, how many hours they worked, how many moved up at work, and how they felt about their work. We describe the patterns in 2000 and the historical development of work from 1900 to 2000.

WHO WORKED: LABOR FORCE PARTICIPATION

The American labor force is the sum of everyone who has a job and everyone who is looking for one. In 2000, 141 million people—75 million men and 66 million women—fit one of these definitions. Most of them had jobs. With an unemployment rate of 5.5 percent as the century closed—the rate typical of the late 1990s—7.4 million Americans were looking for work.

WHO PARTICIPATED IN 2000?

As we shall see later, the twentieth-century surge of women into paid employment nearly obliterated one of 1900's great distinctions between workers and nonworkers. In 2000 the percentage of women at work or seeking work was just thirteen points below that of men their same age. Unlike in earlier generations, most married women and mothers worked. Differences by age were far greater than those by gender. Most Americans began working, at least part-time, as a teenager, made work a major part of their life at some point in their twenties, changed jobs on occasion, but kept working until retirement in their fifties or sixties. In 2000, 85 percent of men and 73 percent of women between the ages of thirty and sixty, the peak years of employment, were active in the workforce. In contrast, just half of sixteen- to nineteen-year-olds and only one-eighth of people seventy years or older were in the labor force. The difference between the participation rates of men forty-five to fifty-four years old and men sixty-five to seventy-four years old was more than sixty points—85 percent versus 25 percent. (For women, there was about a fifty-point difference.) Age trumped gender in demarcating those who worked for pay.

Workers were distinctive in other ways as well, notably in education. The modern economy places a premium on education, so as traditional gaps between men and women and between mothers and other women closed, a new gap in working opened up between more- and less-educated men and women. Figure 5.1 shows the percentage of Americans, twenty-five to fifty-four years old, who were in the labor force according to their educational credentials, with separate lines for men and women and separate panels for people of different ancestry groups. The importance of education is evident. Even among European-American men (top left), there was about a thirteen-point difference in participation rates between high school dropouts and high school graduates, and then another five-point difference between high school graduates and college graduates. Educational attainment distinguished workers and nonworkers among women even more.

Ancestry also distinguished those in and out of the labor force. Men of Latin American heritage had the highest labor force participation rates, regardless of education: over 80 percent of them had a job or were looking for one.[10] African Americans had the lowest rates. Ancestry made the biggest difference in participation among men with little education and made the least difference among men with college diplomas.

Look more closely at the connection between education and work among women. Economists routinely refer to getting an education as "acquiring human capital," because it is like making an investment in oneself.[11] Logically, then, the more schooling people get, the more they want to work so as to get a "return" on their investment. (Also, most employers prefer educated workers. Thus, both sides of a job search give the advantage to the better-educated.)[12] The investment explanation for why labor force participation rises as education rises is, however, harder to apply to women.[13] In earlier generations at least, a major "payoff" for girls who stayed in school was not a good job but a good husband. Moreover, given gender discrimination in the job market, investing in school for job-hunting made less sense for women than it did for men. Educated women still faced some discrimination in 2000, but considerably less than in midcentury America.[14] Even in 2000 the burden of child care, cooking, and cleaning fell disproportionately on women.[15] For that and other reasons, many women with preschool children at home limited their labor force participation. Irrespective of her education, the more preschoolers a mother had, the less likely she was to work or look for work. Among college graduates, for example, 80 percent of women with no preschoolers, 70 percent of those with one, 60 percent of those with two, and 40 percent of those with three were in the labor force.[16] (The number of preschoolers made little difference to men's participation in the labor force.) The needs of children apparently persuaded many mothers to leave work. Also accounting for the children-work trade-off were the decisions by those women who most wanted to work to limit their fertility and, conversely, the decisions by those women who faced poor employment

Figure 5.1   Labor Force Participation of Twenty-Five- to Fifty-Four-
            Year-Olds, by Education, Gender, and Racial Ancestry, 2000

**Men and College Graduates Had the Highest Labor Force Participation
in 2000; Women and High School Dropouts Had the Lowest**

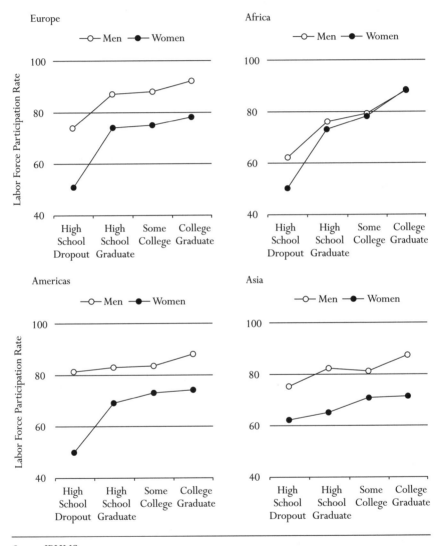

Source: IPUMS.

prospects to have more children or to have them sooner.[17] We focus on the connection between work and preschoolers because that is where the action was. Women with and without school-age children participated at virtually the same rates, and at rates almost as high as those of fathers.[18]

The most stunning finding from a historical perspective, however, is the proportion of mothers of preschoolers who worked outside the home. A century earlier, some black and poor women with young children worked because of dire poverty and, in some cases, abandonment. But in 2000 half of American women with even two preschoolers at home worked; only those mothers with three preschoolers tended to stay home. Also, very few mothers had three preschool-age children. That is another key finding about women and work: women controlled their fertility to the point that very few had more than one preschool-age child at a time; a major barrier to holding a job was thus reduced. After describing the growth of women's labor force participation, we return to the connections between career and fertility.

In 2000 Americans' educational attainment, age, ancestry, and, to a lesser degree, gender and parental status largely determined who worked or looked for work. Where they lived, by region or community size, where they were born, and whether they were married made little difference. And given that participation rates topped 80 percent for most groups of Americans, there was little room left for cultural or personality influences to shape the decision to work. The question "Who works?" had a notably different answer, however, earlier in the century.

Changes in Who Participated in the Labor Force, 1900 to 2000

In 1900, 24 million men and 5 million women made up the labor force of 29 million people age fourteen and older; it was one-fifth the size of the 2000 workforce. About 80 percent of adult men and 20 percent of adult women participated, as did 15 percent of ten- to fifteen-year-olds worked. By 2000 the American labor force topped 135 million, and the number of women approached the number of men (and, as far as we know, very few children under sixteen years old worked for pay).[19] Working had expanded: the number in the labor force grew 30 percent faster over the century than the population did because the women who joined the labor force more than made up for the children and older men who dropped out.[20] Figure 5.2 displays the growth of the labor force and women's share in it. The left-hand graph tracks the absolute numbers. (Note that the y-axis is in a ratio scale.) The total doubled between 1900 and 1940, and had doubled again by 1980; women's participation increased twelvefold, from 5 million in 1900 to 65 million in 2000. The right-hand graph shows the proportion of each gender

Figure 5.2 The Civilian Workforce and Labor Force Participation Rate, by Gender, 1900 to 2000

Women's Growing Labor Force Participation Increased the Size of the Labor Force and Narrowed the Gender Gap

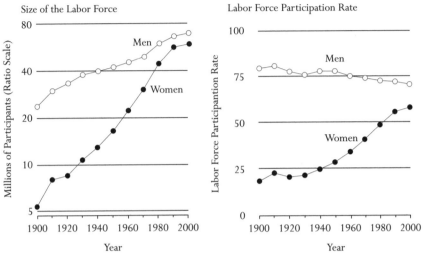

Source: IPUMS.

Note: Questions about employment status were not asked of persons under fourteen years old prior to 1940, nor of persons under sixteen years old from 1940 onwards.

who were working. Men were already participating at about 80 percent in 1900; their rates actually fell as retirement became important.

Meanwhile, men in their prime working ages, roughly twenty-five to fifty-nine, were just about as likely to be working in 2000 as in any year before, but men younger than twenty-five and older than sixty were much less likely to have a job or to want one. The expansion of secondary schooling in the first decades of the century and of higher education after 1940 kept ever more young men (and women) in school and out of the workforce. At the other end of the age spectrum, retirement became an option and, eventually, an entitlement for nearly all men. Early in the twentieth century, only about half of men even reached their sixty-fifth birthday, and only about half of those retired. In recent years—because of accumulated wealth, pensions, and Social Security—85 percent or more of men over sixty-five retire.

Although schooling and retirement also enticed more and more women away from work, stronger forces propelled women age twenty-five to fifty-nine into the labor force. Participation tripled from 20 percent of women age fourteen and older in 1900 to 60 percent of women age sixteen and older in 2000. (Note that our figures for the early part of the century are higher—but more accurate—than the official reports because we include farm and shopkeeper wives as workers in these estimates.)[21] Entering the twentieth century, working women were typically in service—as maids, laundresses, nannies, and such—or employed in a factory (which they much preferred), commonly in a textile mill, garment sweatshop, or tobacco factory. The better-educated started being hired as clerks and department store salesgirls.[22]

Three types of women pioneered the increase in women's labor force participation after World War I. The first of these was the "office girl" of the 1920s, who was typically a single woman under age twenty-five. The office girls generally ended their brief careers either when they married or when they had their first baby. (They were a minority of the earliest cohort, but their dropping out produced the dip in labor force participation after age twenty-five.) The next pioneer stepped forward in the 1940s: a mother whose youngest child had reached the teens. Chances were that she had worked in her youth and was returning to the sort of job she had left behind fifteen or twenty years earlier.[23] She probably liked the independence of working, and employers were pleased to have her back. Mothers of younger children were the third and final pioneers. In the 1970s and 1980s, they stayed on the job after they got pregnant and returned right away after they had their babies. By the end of the century, few women interrupted employment even while their children were young.

Each wave of pioneering women broke new ground by working at an age when women of previous generations had not. We can see that in figure 5.3 by following different cohorts of women from census to census as they aged from their twenties to their sixties.[24] Each line in the figure describes the employment history of a different cohort of women. More than one-third of women born from 1881 through 1890—the lowest line in figure 5.3—had paying jobs in their early twenties (and an equal proportion were already married with children). They tended to leave their jobs as they married and to never return. The next three cohorts—going up and to the right in the graph—also tended to drop out in their late twenties, but they subsequently returned to work. Each later cohort came back sooner than the one before had, and even worked at higher rates after turning twenty-five than they did in their early twenties (probably because a growing group spent their early twenties in school). The last cohort, late baby boomers born 1951 to 1960, basically stayed on the job throughout their prime working age.

Scholars have long sought an explanation for why married mothers increasingly went off to work and by that move radically transformed the American family and the American workplace. Both economic and cultural changes played a role early in the century. Jobs requiring literacy, detail

Figure 5.3   Labor Force Participation Rate of Women Age Twenty to
              Sixty-Four, by Year and Cohort, 1910 to 2000

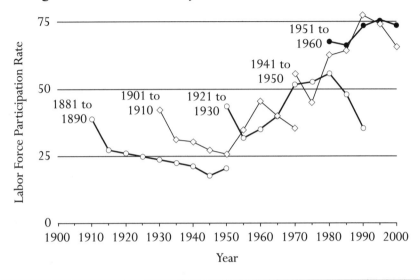

Source: IPUMS.
Note: The data points for census years are for women in the younger half of the cohort; the data points for years ending with "5" are the rates for women in the older half in the census year.

work, and people skills rather than simple brawn appeared, multiplied, and attracted women; new consumer goods made a second income attractive; having fewer children freed up time; and the liberalization of ideas about women's roles legitimated careers. During the Depression, many Americans objected to women taking "men's jobs," but the labor shortages of World War II reversed that trend. Women at that time did the sorts of muscle work, in shipyards and factories, that few women had done before.[25] For twenty years after the war, the economy and jobs grew at record rates, raising both standards of living and economic expectations. Most states expanded educational opportunities, and young women took advantage of them. By the early 1970s, a new wave of feminism demanded equal rights and the chance to compete for the top jobs that men monopolized. About the same time, economic uncertainty reappeared, and men's incomes stagnated. It was impossible to tell whether women were working to fulfill their aspirations, to assert their rights, to pay their bills, or all three. Family uncertainties, such as the high threat of divorce, increased too. By the end of the century, working was considered normal, even for married women with young children—a cultural revolution.[26] Thus, America arrived at 2000 to this diversity in work and family situations: a nation of working mothers and fathers who combined jobs and parenting; a small, childless minority who worked but forwent parenting; a smaller minority who went through life without marrying; and a once-dominant but dwindling minority of working fathers and stay-at-home mothers.

Retirement

Leaving the workforce was a luxury one hundred years ago, but by 1950 more men retired after their sixty-fifth birthday than did not. We estimate that 15 percent of elderly men were retired in 1900; that figure soared to 80 percent in 1970, where it stayed. Women in the labor force embraced retirement later. As late as 1970, only 20 percent of women over sixty-five years old were retired, but by 2000 two-thirds of them were retired. (The generations of women who kept house as their major work—or even as their "second shift"—rarely ever retired from *that* labor.) According to economic historians such as Dora Costa, the institution of retirement represents the intersection of longevity, affluence, and successful social policy. By 1930 almost one million people were living long enough to enjoy the benefits of retirement. Subsequent gains in life expectancy have swelled the senior ranks, as we saw in chapter 3. But to retire takes resources. The growth in affluence, personal savings, private pensions, and ultimately Social Security combined to make retirement economically feasible for most Americans.[27]

Figure 5.4 shows the strength of this development by charting men's employment rates over time for men in four different age groups. Men in all four age groups quit work younger in the later years of the century than their counterparts had earlier in the century. Men sixty-five to sixty-nine years old changed the most: over half of Americans that age in 1940 had jobs, while barely one-fourth of the same group had jobs in 1990 or 2000. Retirement altered the lives of sixty- to sixty-four-year-olds and seventy- to seventy-four-year-olds almost as much.

Ultimately, people stop working in one of two ways—either they retire or they die. By blending data on employment with data on longevity, we can estimate the trends for these two experiences. Eighty-five percent of the men (sixteen and older) who died in 1900 did so while still working; by 2000 only 36 percent of men died on the job. (For women, the percentage who died while employed stayed the same, at 20 percent, because during the same period the percentage who were working rose from 20 to 58 percent.)[28] As American men lived longer, they not only prolonged their working lives but gained a new leisure phase of life, retirement. A significant mi-

Figure 5.4   Employment Rate of Men Age Fifty-Five to Seventy-Four, by Year and Age Group

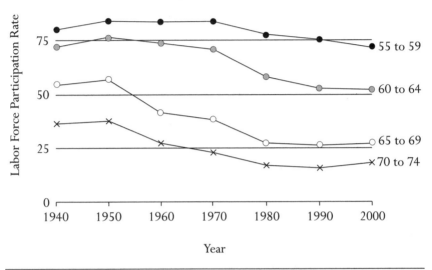

More Men Retired After 1950, and Men Retired at Younger Ages After 1970

Source: IPUMS.

nority, however, died in harness, usually because they did not reach sixty-five. Unlike many features of work life, retirement was not affected by either racial ancestry or education. In fact, age and gender were about the only major determinants of who retired. Education and occupation can affect *when* people retire but not the fact of retirement. In short, retirement emerged over the twentieth century as a benefit and a widely shared experience that eventually became available to just about everyone who lived long enough to claim it.

WHAT AMERICANS DID AT WORK

The variety and complexity of modern work can be astounding. The Department of Labor maintains information on over ten thousand different job titles. Some titles refer to ancient occupations such as farmer, miner, and laborer. The number of workers in these pursuits remained significant in

1900, but they had dwindled away by 2000. In 1900, 11 million Americans—one-third of the workforce—farmed their own land or worked on someone else's farm; in 2000 farmers and farmhands were barely 1 percent of the workforce. Coal mines employed 660,500 miners in 1900 and almost 1 million miners in 1920; by 2000 they were all but gone, down to 88,000.[29] Occupational turnover continues. We already noted that "major growth occupations" of the twenty-first century will require workers to supervise and coordinate the work of others or analyze data. Americans make fewer and fewer things at their jobs; instead, they boss, teach, and take care of one another (and they go out and buy things from elsewhere). In more formal terms, this "service economy" employs people to work with other people—in health care, education, food service, and the like—and to work with information in telecommunications, entertainment, research, financial services, insurance, and real estate. Over the century, manufacturing accounted for less and less of total economic activity. From 1935 to 1985, manufacturing grew, but services grew faster, overtaking manufacturing in 1970. In the last three recessions of the twentieth century, manufacturing employment declined in absolute as well as relative terms; it never recovered. By 2000 making things was a thing of the past.

Specialization and the Division of Labor

Dazzling technology and important innovations in how work and firms are organized diversified American occupations. Some jobs became much more specialized. The one-room schoolhouse had one teacher; a large consolidated high school might have dozens, each teaching a different subject. In some schools, different English teachers instruct students who grew up speaking English and students for whom English is a foreign language; neither group would imagine teaching French or history. Even what seem to be narrowly defined occupations have subspecialties—commercial jet pilots, for example. Aircraft differ in the number of hours of flight required for certification; as a result, most pilots have just one or two up-to-date certifications. One may fly only the Boeing 737, while another flies only the Airbus A-319.[30] The growth of the professions also increased specialization. As knowledge and power expanded in law, medicine, and the sciences, the occupations in those fields narrowed and multiplied.[31] The 1900 census category of "physicians and healers" turned into separate lines for oncologists, cardiologists, obstetricians, gynecologists, orthopedists, pediatricians, and on and on.

To move beyond the specific cases and track overall occupational complexity through the economy and the century, we used Theil's index of diversity (labeled "E"), a measure of the variation across complex classifica-

Figure 5.5   Occupational Diversity, by Year, for All and for Nonfarm
Occupations

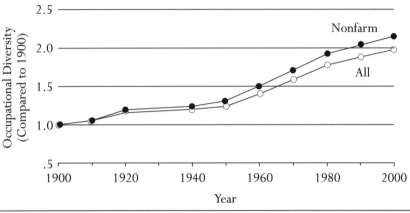

Americans' Jobs Became Much More Specialized over the Century

Source: IPUMS.
Note: Data refer to the Thiel index of qualitative diversity relative to its value in 1900.

tions such as the occupational categories that the census uses. We calculated
the E index across the occupational categories of 1900 and set it—for purposes of easier exposition—at 1.0.[32] Figure 5.5 displays what happened afterwards—an uninterrupted and nearly linear upward progression to much
greater diversity in occupations right through the end of the century, when
E stood at 196 percent of its initial value. The decline of farming was an important part of the trend from 1900 to 1970, so we took the farmers out of
the calculation and recomputed. With the farmers set aside, we see that
complexity outside the farm sector grew even faster; the Theil index in 2000
was at 216 percent of 1900.

As the degree of specialization in work doubled, the mix of work changed
as well. We have already mentioned the eclipse of farming, but we can follow other changes through the categories tracked in figure 5.6. We sorted
occupations into eight broad groups, displayed across four charts for ease of
reading: professionals (25 percent of Americans age twenty-five to sixty-
four in the labor force in 2000); other white-collar workers, such as clerks
and salespeople (23 percent); managers (11 percent); proprietors (2 percent); skilled manual workers (12 percent); unskilled and service workers (25
percent); farmers (.5 percent); and farm laborers (.5 percent).

In the top-left graph, we see the precipitous decline of farming (parallel-
ing the shrinkage of rural living displayed in figure 7.2). The top-right graph

Figure 5.6   Occupational Distribution of the Economically Active
Population: Persons Age Twenty-Five to Sixty-Four

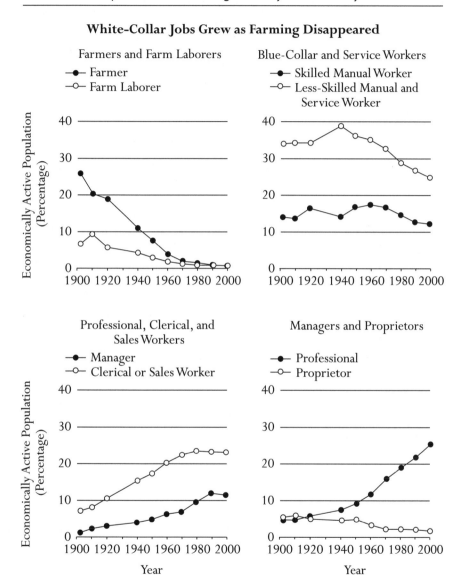

Source: IPUMS.

reflects the history of manufacturing. In the nineteenth century, the establishment of large factories had expanded the share of workers who did blue-collar work, from sewing to casting iron, but manufacturing slowed, stalled, and then declined in the twentieth century.[33] The clerical and manager lines in the bottom-left chart reflect how the consolidation, expansion, and vertical integration of businesses into large corporations in the late nineteenth and early twentieth centuries created new kinds of work: middle managers who could keep track of materials and money as they flowed through the company, on-site supervisors in far-flung mines and factories, and sales and marketing staff to sell the products.[34] By 1910, almost thirty thousand company "reps," as they were called, worked from coast to coast promoting their companies' goods.[35] National headquarters and regional offices employed a new cadre of clerks who produced and filed the paperwork that were the physical means of national coordination. The 1950 census tabulated over 1 million sales workers in manufacturing, nearly 8 million clerical workers (up from under 1 million in 1900), and 1.7 million typists and secretaries (up from 130,000 in 1900).[36] The world of work was starting to change in ways that demanded literacy and could make as much use of women's labor as men's. The "office girl" emerged as a social type who was still recognizable in the 1930s and beyond.[37] The clerical and sales forces, however, leveled off near the end of the century. Finally, the bottom-right graph of figure 5.6 also shows the later and more sustained growth of the professions and the replacement of proprietors by managers.

Three kinds of occupations—professional, managerial, and clerical—were the core of employment at the end of the century. Few of the people in these jobs worked for manufacturers, and fewer still actually touched the products their companies produced. Most companies, in fact, produced services instead of goods. Increasingly, what Americans did was provide services. Some commentators criticized the service economy, focusing on the plight of those caught in low-end service jobs.[38] But high-paid specialists like doctors, lawyers, financial analysts, and even many engineers worked in the service sector too. Service jobs are not all "McJobs."[39]

Good Jobs and Bad Jobs

The growth in complexity and the shifts among occupational types are important, but by themselves those shifts say little about the quality of jobs and how that may have changed. Social scientists have long used a measure of how the *public* values jobs, the Duncan socioeconomic index (SEI). In extensive surveys, nationally representative samples of respondents rated the "general standing" of various occupations from "excellent" to "poor." From these data, Otis Dudley Duncan calculated that popular evaluations of an occupation's standing were closely associated with the educational attainments

Figure 5.7   Socioeconomic Status of Persons Age Twenty-Five to
Sixty-Four, by Year and Gender

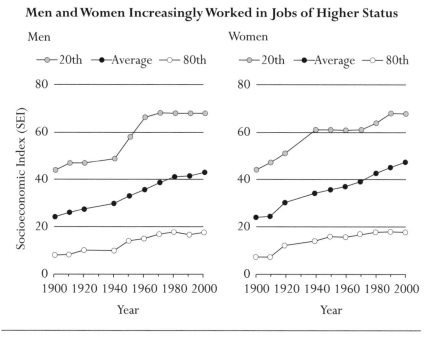

Men and Women Increasingly Worked in Jobs of Higher Status

Source: IPUMS.

and earnings of the people who actually held those jobs. A simple average of
the proportion of workers in an occupation who had above-median schooling and who garnered above-median earnings is a good indicator of Duncan's SEI and a suitable proxy for the job's "general standing."[40]

Figure 5.7 shows the *mean* Duncan SEI score for all American workers
age twenty-five to fifty-four in each census, along with the score for those at
the twentieth and eightieth percentiles of occupational scores. By this measure, more Americans held high-prestige jobs and fewer Americans settled
for low-prestige jobs over the century. The prestige gap between the workers at the top and those at the bottom of the labor market changed little in
the first half of the century, increased from 1950 to 1970, and then stayed at
the wider gap afterwards. The difference between men's SEI score at the
eightieth percentile and that of men at the twentieth percentile varied little
from its average of 38 points between 1900 and 1940, widened to 51 by
1970, and finished at 53 in 2000. Women's trends were similar.

The occupational distribution of the U.S. labor force improved in quality as it became more specialized, more service-based, and less involved with goods. A number of other desirable features accompanied these "good" and "excellent" jobs. They were cleaner, more predictable, and more interesting. Research also shows that the desirable jobs have not only intrinsic merits but also side benefits. Occupations that scored high on the SEI also offered more comprehensive pension and health benefits, more vacation time, and standard hours. But as with every aspect of American life we consider, jobs were not uniform. The engineer's desirable job was counterbalanced to an extent by the janitor's unsavory one.[41]

If we define "substandard" jobs as ones that pay low wages and do not offer pension and health coverage, then about one-seventh of U.S. jobs were substandard in 1995. Workers who were older, foreign-born, and, especially, poorly educated were likeliest to have substandard jobs. Such jobs also tended to have additional undesirable features, such as unusual work schedules or no regular schedules at all. Many of them were provided by subcontractors or employment services and required work on a project-by-project basis, with spells of unemployment between projects. It is clear that the proportion of both substandard jobs and nonstandard employment conditions increased from the mid-1980s to the end of the century.[42] These trends raised concerns that the growing inequality in wages was being accompanied by a growing inequality in working conditions as well.

Unionization

Unions represent their members in collective bargaining with management, pressing to improve members' pay, benefits, hours, working conditions, and procedures for handling conflicts. Most jobs in 2000 America were outside this system, and management set employment terms with little or no input from workers or their representatives. (A fortunate minority of individual workers, usually those with rare skills or knowledge, bargained directly with their bosses about their own jobs.) U.S. labor history is fraught with struggle, conflict, and occasional violence around unionization. Unions in the American Federation of Labor (AFL), founded in 1886, represented skilled workers, such as meat cutters, teamsters, and carpenters, across a broad range of industries and employers. Unions in the Congress of Industrial Organizations (CIO), founded in 1935, represented workers in many kinds of jobs but within specific industries, like automobile manufacturing. At its peak, the combined AFL-CIO represented 25 percent of American workers and exercised considerable economic and political clout. But by 2000, just 12 percent of American workers belonged to any union. Labor scholars attribute the decline to a combination of industrial restructuring—essentially, the decline of manufacturing, where most union jobs were

Figure 5.8   Union Membership Rates, by Year and Occupation, 1952 to 2000

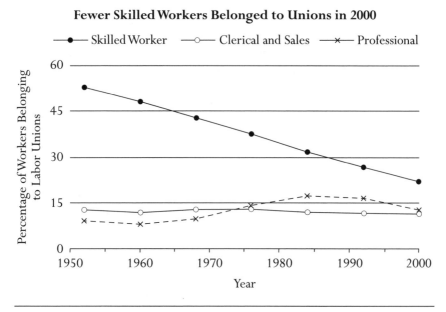

Fewer Skilled Workers Belonged to Unions in 2000

found—and the loss of union representation within previously organized industries. Most think that restructuring mattered more.[43] Most of the jobs lost in the late 1970s and throughout the 1980s were in highly unionized factories and offices. The new jobs created elsewhere were rarely covered by union contracts. Figure 5.8 displays the (smoothed) trends in union representation for all employed workers in three important, broad occupational groups from 1952 through 2000.[44]

Unions represented over half of skilled blue-collar workers in 1952; those workers formed an ever-shrinking component of the labor force through the latter half of the century, a trend that, by itself, would have reduced the role of unions in American work life. But as figure 5.8 shows, the restructuring of work was not the only source of the unions' decline: unions represented a far smaller fraction of skilled blue-collar workers in the 1990s than they had in the 1950s. The strong growth of the professions, coupled with a slight but significant increase in union representation among profes-

---

Source: National Election Studies.
Note: Data smoothed using locally estimated (loess) regressions, owing to small samples per year.

sionals, countered the slide a bit. Had it not been for the increasing presence in the labor force of professional women, who tended to be unionized more than most workers, total unionization would have dropped even more than the thirteen points it did that half-century.[45] At the peak of their strength, labor unions accomplished impressive gains for their members. Most labor economists credit them with holding down inequality, and in our previous work, we showed how they kept wages apace with productivity gains.[46] They mostly achieved that through the process of wage bargaining. But their influence clearly waned, not only in membership but also in activity. For example, work stoppages of various kinds, most typically strikes, disrupted the economy much less often toward the end of the century than they did in the 1950s and 1960s. Then, work stoppages involving 1,000 workers or more exceeded one a day (there were 412 such stoppages in 1969, for example); in 2000 there was less than one such stoppage *a week* (and just 39 for the year).[47]

Union membership was yet another fissure in the American workforce. Those in union jobs tended to earn more and to work under better conditions. They also tended to be in certain kinds of industries and in an increasingly select set, such as the last of heavy manufacturing, teaching, and, in some places, the civil service.[48] Union members typically voted differently than others of their class. As union members shrank in numbers and influence, the cleavage between them and the growing majority of nonmembers appears, according to several indicators, to have increased. For example, 9 percent more union members than nonmembers voted for Jimmy Carter in the 1976 presidential election.[49] Over the next three elections, the gap between union members and other voters grew by fifteen percentage points and stayed that high through the 2000 election. But the decline of unions meant that the social significance of this divide waned.

HOW MUCH MONEY AMERICANS EARNED AT WORK

Among the differences in social life that Americans faced in 2000, none was more stark than the difference in what they earned on the job. Among full-time workers—those who put in forty or more hours per week year-round—half earned $32,000 or more, and half earned less than that. (Mean earnings were $41,500.) However, in 1999 (as reported in 2000) the 20 percent of workers who made the highest pay earned more than $55,000, and the 20 percent who earned the least made less than $18,800. The ratio of the eightieth to the twentieth percentile in individuals' earnings was three-to-one, an unusually high ratio for a Western nation (though less than the four-to-one ratio we found for *family incomes* and report in the next chapter). Women earned less, even among full-time workers: their median was about $27,000, versus $37,000 among men. When women and men held the same jobs in the same company, they made about the same income, but typically women worked at quite different jobs, and the eighty-to-twenty ratio for them was slightly lower.[50]

These numbers on full-time workers just skim the surface of America's pay differences. Part-time workers, half of whom told interviewers that they would take a full-time job if they could find one, made less. Some worked fewer than forty hours a week every week; others worked forty hours some weeks but fewer during the rest of the year; and still others worked some combination that added up to less than two thousand hours in the year. All these workers earned hourly pay, as well as annual pay, that was significantly less than that of full-time, year-round workers. Pay differences also appeared among fully employed workers with different levels of education and among workers engaged in different occupations. Years of schooling and the type of job made a big difference in earnings. For example, men in skilled manual occupations made about $13,000 a year more if they had a college diploma rather than just a high school diploma. At the same time, men with a high school diploma made about $13,000 more a year if they were managers rather than routine white-collar workers. (And gender mattered: women earned less than men in virtually all combinations of education and occupational categories, again, mostly because they worked at the kind of companies and government agencies that paid less than the ones that employed most men.)[51] Generally, getting an incomplete college education, whether from a community college or a four-year school, did not pay off much more than having just a high school diploma. College graduates who had white-collar jobs or better earned significantly more than people in the same kinds of jobs but with less education. Male managers with a college degree averaged $75,000—pay that in effect put them in the top 10 percent of all workers.

We focus next on the strengthening connection between education and earnings. Figure 5.9 displays average earnings, adjusted for cost of living, from 1975 to 2000 by level of educational attainment for all workers. The findings are essentially the same if we look only at white men. (The reader will note that we display earnings in a ratio scale: $12,500, $25,000, $50,000, and $100,000. When we compare amounts of money, the question arises: should we subtract or divide? If one group makes $25,000 and another $50,000, should we discuss a $25,000 difference or a two-to-one ratio? Common practice in economics is to express such comparisons as ratios, and so we do too; in graphs that means using a logarithmic scale such as this one. *Why* the ratio is standard practice turns out to be a complex matter; see appendix B.) Figure 5.9 confirms the widening of earning differences by schooling: high school graduates and those without a high school diploma experienced real declines, while increases came to those with a bachelor's degree or advanced degree. In 1975 college graduates earned 50

Figure 5.9   Earnings of Full-Time, Year-Round Workers, by Year and
Education

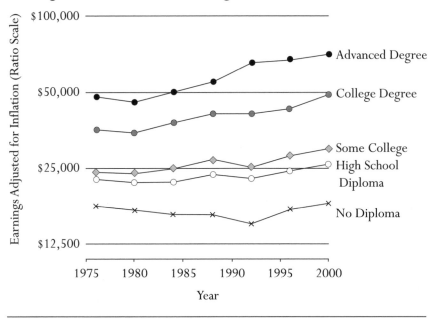

College-Educated Workers' Earnings Increased More Than Others'

Source: CPS.
Note: Annual earnings, adjusted for inflation using the CPI-U-RS series to 2000 prices.

percent more than high school graduates; by 2000, they earned 74 percent more.

Economists and sociologists debate why the differences in earnings by education had grown to be so great by 2000. A nation of farmers, factory hands, and shopkeepers had become a nation of workers in thousands of specialized niches. The skills acquired in school are certainly part of the picture. Many researchers point to the growing demand for quantitative and technical skills to explain the rising wage inequality of the 1980s and 1990s.[52] For example, a study of a redesigned food processing plant in Milwaukee concluded that the retooling required nearly every worker to process more information and make more decisions than had been necessary in the old plant.[53] Others have demurred, noting that the timing of the skills change is off and that the stock market surge might have more to do with rising inequality.[54] Either way, the differences between college graduates and the rest of the labor force rose steadily from the 1970s to the late 1990s. Differences were even greater for full-time workers than for part-timers. In 1975 college graduates who worked full-time earned 50 percent more than high school graduates who worked full-time that year; in 1999 the college graduates earned 80 percent more.[55]

Many other differences among American workers besides education, jobs, and gender affected their earnings. We consider most of them in detail when we look at family incomes in the next chapter, and so we mention them only briefly here. For example, people with different ancestries earned substantially different amounts, even when they had identical credentials and worked in the same kinds of occupations. In most comparisons, African-American workers made the least, those from the Americas (mostly Hispanic) were next, and Asian Americans earned 5 to 15 percent more than Europeans. Older workers made more—at least among those between twenty-five and fifty-four years of age. (Seniority pays, especially for men.) The highest-paying jobs were in the major metropolitan areas like New York, Atlanta, and San Francisco; among the best jobs especially, wages in the bigger "major league" cities exceeded those in the middle-sized and smaller "minor league" cities. U.S.-born workers made more than immigrants on average, but the ninety-to-ten earnings ratio *among* immigrants was nearly eight-to-one, indicating how very diverse they were.

There was more inequality in Americans' paychecks in 2000 than had been there in 1970. Figure 5.10 presents the historical trajectories in individual earnings (adjusted to 2000 dollars), distinguishing the twentieth-percentile, median, and eightieth-percentile points of the earnings distributions. The panels present the trends from 1940 to 2000 for all workers, for full-time workers, for full-time male workers, and for full-time female workers, restricting attention to people who were twenty-five to fifty-four years old.

The earnings of the lowest-paid Americans almost doubled from 1950 to 1970, sagged in the 1980s, and rebounded to $10,000 by 2000. The trends for all workers at the median and at the eightieth percentile are almost identical—a sharp increase, a sag, and a recovery. The gap between the twentieth percentile and the median in any year was much bigger for all workers (top-left graph) than for full-time workers (top-right graph). This reflects the importance of hours worked. It pretty much took a full-time schedule to earn the median amount. Full-time men earned more than full-time women, but that gap was closing. Men, especially low-wage men, did not do well after 1970. Women at each level showed continuing progress throughout the half-century. In the end, the earnings gaps for men widened. In 1950 high earners of both genders made four times as much as low earners; the multiple declined to three in 1970, but then rose to 4.75 in 2000.

Figure 5.10   Earnings at the 20th Percentile, the Median, and the 80th Percentile, by Year and Gender

Earnings Grew from 1940 to 1970; Inequality Grew from 1970 to 2000

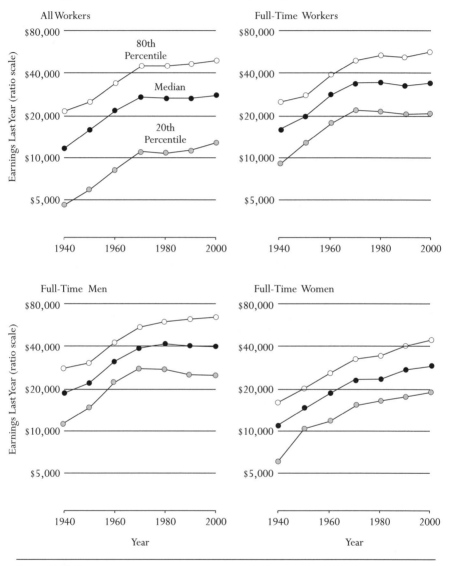

Source: IPUMS.

The national census data on earnings for the whole labor force reach back only as far as 1940. Economic historians have pushed the time horizon back further using data from particular states or particular occupations. Their consensus is that the relative equality in wages in the 1950s was the culmination of a half-century's wage "compression."[56] The wages of skilled manufacturing workers dropped during the hard economic times of the 1890s, but the wages of all blue-collar workers moved up in tandem as the economy recovered. The expansion of secondary education at the turn of the century and beyond raised skill levels at the bottom, reducing the pay advantage of the more highly educated.[57] Government policies also helped to compress wages. During World War II, the wage and price commission held down high wages to fight inflation but granted compensatory wage hikes to unskilled workers who were not making ends meet.[58] After the war, the GI Bill and the expansion of public universities allowed the supply of college-educated workers to keep pace with burgeoning demand through the 1950s and 1960s.

The government also shaped inequality starting in the mid-1930s through the minimum wage. The first minimum, in 1937, was 25 cents ($3.10 in 2000 dollars) per hour; Congress raised it to 30 cents ($3.80) the next year. Congress periodically raised the minimum wage, and it rose faster than prices and reached its peak purchasing power in 1968 at $1.60 ($8.00 in 2000 dollars). After 1968, the minimum wage lost ground to inflation. By 2000, at $5.35 an hour, the minimum wage was worth less than it had been at any time since the late 1950s. The nominal and real values of the minimum wage are displayed in figure 5.11. Classic economic theory argues that such a wage floor leads to inflation, unemployment, or both, but experience suggests otherwise.[59] It does contribute to wage compression by keeping market forces from pushing the bottom too low. In the absence of congressional action to raise the minimum wage, the erosion of the minimum wage through inflation helped inequality to widen again. The division of Americans by income is rooted in deliberate policy as well as in market forces.[60]

Another critical dimension of the earnings story is racial. African Americans made more progress in wages than others did between 1950 and 1970. Afterwards, African-American men, especially those who worked full-time, lost ground to European Americans. Moreover, fewer black men worked full-time as the industrial restructuring undermined their job opportunities more than those of any other segment of the labor force.[61] Gender differences were notably sharp and distinctive among African Americans: black women came close to attaining parity in employment and earnings with white women, but black men lagged far behind white men.[62]

Figure 5.11   Real Purchasing Power of the Minimum Wage, by Year

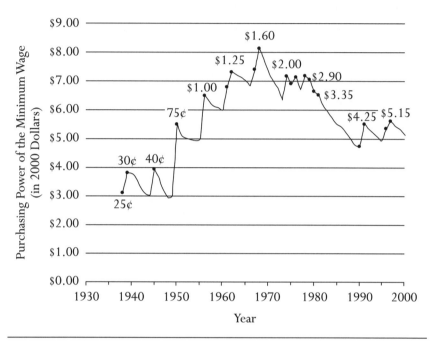

The Minimum Wage Grew Faster Than Inflation Until 1968, Then Decreased in Value

Source: IPUMS.

Note: Dots show when the minimum wage was changed; labels show the nominal minimum wage in the year it first took effect.

HOW MUCH AMERICANS WORKED

In principle, the number of hours people work can either compensate for pay differences or amplify them; it all depends on whether it is the highly paid or the lowly paid who put in more hours. If well-paid workers put in a forty-hour workweek, the poorly paid can catch up some by working longer hours or multiple jobs. The Internet journalist Matt Drudge reported on a single mother, Mary Mornin, who typified the compensating pattern: she worked three jobs to maintain a modest middle-class lifestyle.[63] Still other anecdotes describing the grueling hours of lawyers and Wall Street brokers suggest that it is the well-paid who multiply their earnings. In this section, we replace hearsay with evidence and consider quantitative data on working hours with an eye toward sorting out the inequality effects of the so-called

24/7 economy (the tendency of economic activity to go on twenty-four hours a day, seven days a week). But first, some historical perspective seems in order.

Working Hours

The prototypical job in late-twentieth-century America came with a forty-hour-a-week fixed schedule. Yet there was plenty of variation. Some people worked only a few hours a week, others sixty hours or more. Some people worked Mondays to Fridays during the day; many worked evenings and weekends. Some people started and ended at the same time every workday; millions more had varying or uncertain schedules.[64] The hard numbers for 2000 are these: American *adults* averaged thirty-one hours of paid work per week in 2000, although that average conceals that many worked much longer and many worked no hours at all. American *employees*—that is, those with a job in a business or service that someone else (or the public) owned—averaged thirty-nine hours a week. The self-employed also averaged thirty-nine hours per week in 2000. Changing the focus from all adults to all employed adults eliminates almost all of those who worked no hours at all and raises the average, but it still leaves a lot of variation around that thirty-nine hours.[65] About one-sixth worked less than thirty hours a week, and about the same proportion worked more than forty-eight hours.

The key question for income differences is whether highly paid or poorly paid employees worked longer hours. To keep things simple, we focus on working twenty-five- to fifty-four-year-olds, setting aside the eighteen- to twenty-four-year-olds, many of whom were still in school, and those fifty-five and older, many of whom were retired or preparing to retire. Even among working twenty-five- to fifty-four-year-olds, women worked fewer hours than men did in 2000—a mean of thirty-eight hours compared to a mean of forty-five hours for men. Women also more often worked part-time and less often took overtime.[66] Since women's wages lag behind men's, this tendency for women to work shorter hours led to bigger gender differences in annual earnings than in hourly wages. But education mattered even more than gender. Employed college graduates worked an average of about three hours a week longer than employed high school dropouts, but the former were especially likely to put in really long hours. Almost 40 percent of male college graduates worked a week of more than forty-eight hours; just 21 percent of male high school dropouts did.[67] The impact of education on work hours is less a matter of taste than of circumstance. While college graduates typically accept their long workweeks—most are in rewarding professions—high school dropouts typically wish they could work more in order to make ends meet. Given their low hourly wages, working increased hours is about their only viable option for higher family income.[68] At the end of the year, the longer hours of the college graduates amplified their advantage of a higher wage each hour.

Family responsibilities also distinguished those with short workweeks, at least among women. Working women with children and with husbands (or partners) averaged thirty-two hours a week; single mothers worked two hours more, women with husbands (or partners) but no children at home five hours more, and women who lived independently seven hours more a week than married mothers. A decade after the sociologist Arlie Hochschild found that couples who want to share family responsibilities nonetheless typically do little actual sharing, the "second shift" continued to constrain American women.[69] Moreover, shorter work hours limited women's career growth and lifetime earnings, especially in a nation such as the United States, which provides little public support to child-rearing.[70]

Changing Work Schedules

Distinctions between those we might call the over- and the underemployed seemed to widen in the last decades of the century—at least in the hours they worked. In 1900 most employed people worked six days a week, and farmers often seven; manufacturing workers put in ten-hour days for an average workweek of sixty hours, and men in the building trades and mining worked fewer but often grueling hours.[71] These grinding schedules wore men out, exposed them to high rates of injury, and imperiled their health through fatigue. Over the years, the combination of increasing productivity, decreasing immigration, union pressure, and government regulation reduced the norm from a ten-hour shift to an eight-hour shift. The reduction was probably clinched by the Depression. As labor shortage turned to labor surplus, job sharing became the national policy, legislated in the National Industrial Recovery Act of 1933.[72]

The Census Bureau began to collect detailed data on the workweek in 1940. By that time, significant changes in hours had already occurred, but the data nonetheless reveal the diversity in Americans' work experiences from the last days of the Great Depression until the dawn of the new century. More than 20 percent of American adults were not working at all in each year from 1940 through 2000. Among those who were employed, the median reached forty hours a week in 1950 and did not change after that. (The major reduction in working hours had occurred in the early decades of the century.) The *spread* in hours worked by Americans changed even though the average did not, first shrinking and then widening. In 1940 the workers with the longest workweeks put in fifteen hours more than the average, while workers with the shortest workweeks put in two hours less than the average. By 1960 those differences became negligible as truly long workweeks became rare; one could almost say that in those years nearly "everyone" worked forty hours a week. In the last twenty years of the century, however, a large gap opened up again. In 1990 and 2000, the one-fifth of workers with the longest workweeks put in over fifty hours on the job.

Moreover, *who* worked long hours reversed. A century ago, it was mostly factory workers who worked long hours; few office workers exceeded forty hours per week. While factory overtime became less common, office workers, especially managers and professionals, started staying late (or bringing work home).[73] We track the changes in who worked long hours by classifying workers according to their levels of education. As late as 1940, high school dropouts typically worked longer weeks than college graduates did. By 1980, that pattern had reversed, and by 2000 college graduates worked substantially longer hours than high school dropouts. We can see the crossover in long hours in figure 5.12, which shows the proportion of employees, twenty-five- to fifty-four-years-old, by education and gender, who worked more than forty-eight hours per week from 1940 through 2000. (Just two educational categories appear to keep it simple. The intermediate categories fit in between.) Among women in 1940 and in 1950, high school dropouts more often worked a long schedule than college graduates did; by

Figure 5.12   Long Hours Worked by Economically Active Persons Age Twenty-Five to Fifty-Four, by Year, Education, and Gender

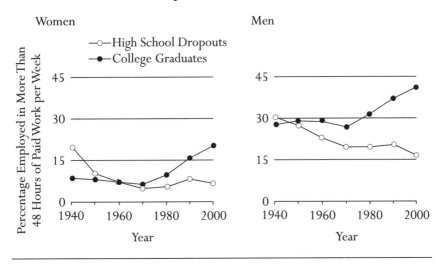

Source: IPUMS.

2000, that had reversed. Among men, there was little difference between high school dropouts and college graduates in 1940, but by 2000 just 15 percent of male high school dropouts were working more than forty-eight hours a week, while 40 percent of college graduates were. This reversal is one part of the explanation for growing earnings inequality over the last quarter of the century. Less-educated workers lost the opportunity to work longer hours to compensate for low wages.[74]

Another contributor to growing income inequality was the "marriage" of work hours. Early in the century, college graduates were relatively rare, and they most often married someone who had less education. As late as the 1960s and 1970s, most of the college-graduate husbands with long work-weeks had stay-at-home wives. By the 1980s, the expansion of higher education had given college graduates more opportunity to find matches within their own ranks (see chapter 2). And most college-educated men in the 1990s married women who were and stayed full-time workers. The result of this "educational homogamy" (like marrying like) on top of widespread college education and more women working longer hours was that the combined hours of husbands and wives rose by twelve hours a week between 1970 and 2000 (see figure 5.13). One in seven married couples put in a combined total of over eighty-eight hours.[75]

In conjunction with other trends, the changes in working hours we have reviewed illustrate how Americans' experiences of work changed over the twentieth century. In 1900 work was a lifelong, if often interrupted, activity for men; in 2000 it was a limited, if often intense, stage of life. Before, blue-collar workers and farmers toiled fifty or sixty hours per week on a six-day schedule; later, blue-collar workers were frequently frustrated because they could not get enough hours to offset their low wages. Meanwhile, some modern professionals and managers lived the 24/7 life of always being "on call." They started their careers later in life than blue-collar workers did, having spent four years in college and sometimes additional years getting a professional degree, but they followed that up with years of forty-eight-hour workweeks. We are tempted to describe them as overworked, over-paid, and overjoyed, but that would be too glib. The professionals and managers of 2000 put in longer hours, earned higher salaries, and liked their jobs better than blue-collar workers did, and they could retire closer to when they wanted to than most blue-collar workers did.[76] In a few ways, differences among workers narrowed in midcentury, but they widened again in the last quarter of the century, creating more disparate work lives.

UNEMPLOYMENT

Unemployment is the most important gauge of the health of the labor force. Business failures obviously take employees down with the company, but most employers stay open during times of low demand by reducing their

Figure 5.13   Hours at Paid Work (Husband and Wife Combined) for
Married Persons, Age Twenty-Five to Fifty-Four, Living in a
Married-Couple Household, by Year and Presence of
Children in the Household

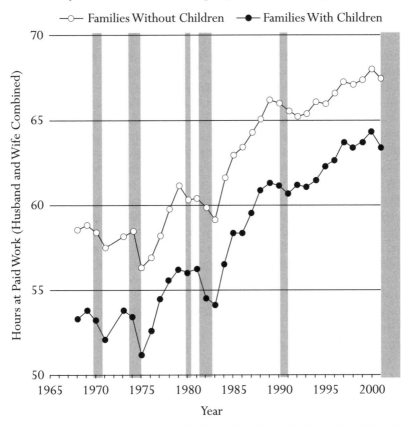

Family Work Hours Rose Rapidly—Even Among Parents

Source: CPS.
Note: Gray stripes indicate recessions.

payrolls. Unemployment thus makes for a particularly stark kind of inequality: the few lose their jobs as a means of preserving the jobs of others and, of course, preserving the investments of the owners. The alternative of sharing reduced hours among employees has happened, but rarely.[77] Economic recovery sparks hiring and employs the unemployed. And periods of sustained economic growth, as the United States experienced in the second half of the 1990s, even draws in people who had been uninterested in or hopeless about working.[78]

Data on unemployment in the first third of the century are rough, in part because of unsystematic data collection and in part because a high proportion of workers were farmers and self-employed in those days.[79] The unemployment crisis of the 1930s (see figure 5.14) spawned the data collection efforts on which we now rely. And national unemployment has stayed below the levels of the Great Depression since the government began collecting reliable data about it because economic planners use the data to keep unemployment down. By manipulating the money supply and interest rates, the Federal Reserve Bank has been able to balance inflation and unemployment within a pretty narrow range. Nevertheless, shocks have still occurred. For example, the high inflation in the late 1970s came under some control when economic planners in the Reagan administration allowed unemployment to reach its highest levels since the 1930s to deflate the money supply. With inflation under control, the unemployment rate stayed under 10 percent for twenty years, dropping as low as 4 percent in the late 1990s.

Figure 5.14 shows annual unemployment rates for the nation as a whole from 1900 to 1952 and for men and women separately from 1948 to 2002. We follow the Bureau of Labor Statistics practice of shading recession years with gray vertical bars.[80] The "CPS" data are the official annual unemployment statistics published by the BLS; the "BLS" data are from Labor Department surveys that predated the CPS. The economic historian Christina Romer compiled the estimates of unemployment before 1930.[81] The figure vividly displays the regular ups and downs of economic fortune, as well as the great shock of the 1930s. (Another peak occurred just seven years before our graph begins, with the depression of 1893.) New Deal jobs programs like WPA and CCC provided "relief"—as it was called—to about one-sixth of the unemployed starting in 1933 and to one-third of the unemployed by 1940.[82] Business cycles continued afterwards, but government intervention made recessions less frequent and painful after the first third of the century.[83] Two long runs of positive economic growth—from 1960 to 1969 and from 1992 to 2001—graced the second half of the century.

It is striking that unemployment eventually fell after 1970 even while the labor force continued to grow. Surging immigration, more women going to work, and the maturing of the baby boomers combined to increase the size of the American labor force by 80 percent (see figure 5.2). The population pressure—and serious economic troubles linked to rapidly rising oil prices—added to unemployment through 1982, but after the postwar peak that year, the labor force absorbed millions of new workers. It had done the same in the first quarter of the twentieth century, with the immigrant influx from Europe, albeit through choppier economic waters.

Figure 5.14 Civilian Unemployment Rate, by Gender, 1900 to 2002

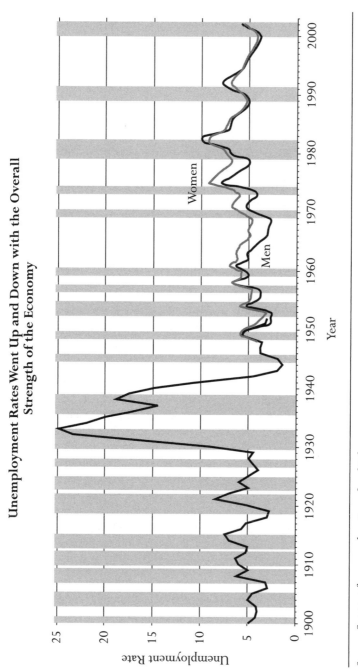

Unemployment Rates Went Up and Down with the Overall Strength of the Economy

Sources: See text for an explanation of multiple sources.
Note: Vertical bars indicate recession years.

Beyond tabulating levels of unemployment, it is important to understand the character of unemployment and who was unemployed in each era. Early in the century, unemployment was spread around; many nonfarm workers experienced a few weeks or months of unemployment in a given year. A 7 percent unemployment rate at a given time could mask short spells of unemployment for as many as half of blue-collar workers, who typically circulated in and out of jobs. The migratory employment of many farmhands, the frequent failures of family farms, and the seasonal nature of much employment (say, on the docks) added even more men to a floating pool of sometime workers. Indeed, many workers did not really have "jobs," as we understand the term today. They were hired by the day or the week; they were out of work whenever that time was up. They might be rehired by the same employer, or they might not. The notion that a laborer could keep a job indefinitely did not enter people's minds. And it did not enter employers' practices until Henry Ford's employment revolution began in 1926. Then employment patterns changed, and the labor force divided: in the later decades of the century, more workers held their jobs continuously for years at a time, while many of the laid-off were unemployed semipermanently. Unemployment during recessions before the 1930s was shared broadly by many workers, each doing without, each for short times; the burden of postwar recessions fell on the 6 to 10 percent of workers who were actually laid off. The historian Alex Keyssar summarizes the point sharply:

> Some workers acquired a virtual immunity against layoffs. Many others found that their rhythms of employment had, at the least, become more predictable. . . . Still, this new political economy had profound and important limits. The policies and reforms implemented in the 1930s did not solve the problem of unemployment. . . . The state, tacitly recognizing the permanence of a reserve army [of workers], offered financial support to its members, taxing citizens who were employed in order to underwrite the expense of maintaining pools of surplus labor. Indeed, it was precisely the thrust and function of this political economy to perpetuate the existence of a labor reserve while minimizing the suffering, the anger, the anxiety, and the threats to political order that the presence of a reserve army inescapably engendered.[84]

A gap widened, then, between workers with a steady career of employment and those with a career of frequent unemployment.

This emerging chronic unemployment gap—between those who were in the reserve army and those who were not—divided Americans along other lines. Before the Great Depression, agricultural workers and miners were more often out of work than office workers, and the recession that slowed the economy after World War I hit the steel industry harder than other sectors.[85] After World War II, two big differences marked Americans' unemployment experiences: race and education. African Americans had higher unemployment rates than others with the same education, by about three points (except right around 1970). Education's influence on unemployment increased after 1970. High school dropouts had higher unemployment rates than college graduates in every year for which data are available, but the educational gap grew in the 1970s and was even bigger than the black–nonblack gap after the recession of 1989 to 1990.

Figure 5.15 shows how education affected the chances of being unemployed after the Great Depression. (We show the data only for nonblacks because of African Americans' unusually low participation in the labor force, which we discuss later in the chapter.) The figure shows unemployment trends for three education groups. Between 1950 and 1970, after unemployment had subsided from the Depression years, less-educated workers had a moderately higher risk of unemployment than better-educated workers. After 1970, however, their risk greatly increased, while college graduates experienced continuing employment security. This is yet another in-

Figure 5.15   Unemployment, by Year and Education

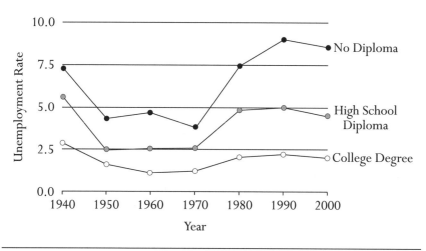

After 1970, the Risk of Unemployment Rose Most for the Least-Educated Workers

Source: IPUMS.
Note: We exclude African Americans because incarceration trends distort the data on their unemployment.

stance of how education had become more important by the end of the century. The advantage of education grew for African Americans in much the same way (not shown), but the experience of less-educated blacks was distinctive. While unemployment rates among college-graduate African Americans were comparable to those of college-graduate nonblacks (averaging 2.7 versus 1.9 percent between 1970 and 2000), unemployment rates for black high school graduates and dropouts were about double those of comparable nonblacks. Also, such official data increasingly understated joblessness among less-educated African Americans because the statistics did not count prisoners among the unemployed. Bruce Western and Becky Pettit estimate that reported unemployment among African-American high school dropouts would be as much as 50 percent higher if prisoners were counted as unemployed. As they put it, "Once prison and jail inmates are counted among the jobless, the *employment* rate of white [high school] dropouts is about 2.5 times larger than for blacks."[86]

As Keyssar suggests, workers who kept their jobs still did not escape the shadow of unemployment altogether. As we show later in the chapter, they got nervous when unemployment rose, and many began to regard their own futures as uncertain. For every out-of-work American, there were one or two others who thought they were likely to be next—that is, the percentage of people with jobs who thought that they were likely to lose them in the next six months was consistently two to three percentage points above the unemployment rate. And the happiness of the American public was significantly lower during times of rising unemployment than when unemployment was falling or holding steady.[87]

HOW AMERICANS FELT ABOUT WORK

Work is a means to an end, a way to pay for survival and for luxuries, but it can be more than that. Americans have long touted a moral stance: they emphasize work's intrinsic value. A part of the "disciplinary revolution" that catapulted northern Europe into affluence and modernity, the so-called Protestant Ethic was one of the principal disciplines in early modern times.[88] Arguably, its power persisted. When American adults in the late twentieth century were asked, "Which one thing on this list would you most prefer in a job?" half chose the answer "work that is important and gives a sense of accomplishment"; they did so consistently from 1973 to 1994. When asked, "If you were to get enough money to live as comfortably as you would like for the rest of your life, would you continue to work or would you stop working?" a consistent two-thirds of employed Americans answered that they would keep working.[89] The Protestant Ethic is deeply rooted.

Nonetheless, times and work change. We have seen the upgrading of skills, the narrowing and then widening of pay inequalities, and other developments. We close this chapter by looking at Americans' feelings about their jobs over the last three decades of the century. We can suppose that these feelings also changed in just thirty years. For example, several deep recessions after 1973 presumably made people with jobs feel lucky to be working and perhaps more content with the jobs they held. We apply the trend analyses we introduced earlier. We track changes over time in job satisfaction in the most positive answers to the question, "On the whole, how satisfied are you with the work you do?"

Levels of job satisfaction ran high in the United States throughout the 1970s, 1980s, and 1990s. Over 80 percent of American workers reported to the GSS that they were "very satisfied" with their work. But important differences emerged: more workers were very satisfied in 1975 and in the boom year of 2000 than in any other year; older and richer workers were more often satisfied than younger and poorer ones, whites more than blacks, and men more than women. The biggest differences were between educational groups. College-educated respondents more often reported high satisfaction from their work than did nongraduates, and this difference in job satisfaction increased substantially from 1975 onward, primarily because high school dropouts in particular became less and less satisfied (see figure 5.16). Differences in satisfaction between high- and low-income respondents echo these differences by education, but the education effect is both clearer and more compelling. Thus, the same group of Americans who found it hardest to get a job and hardest to keep their earnings up with inflation also found their jobs increasingly less satisfying. To be sure, three-fourths of them in 2000 reported being "very satisfied," but the least-educated never recovered the full sense of job satisfaction they reported in 1975.

Security complements satisfaction. When times get tough, even an unsatisfying job is important to hold on to. The GSS included a question about job security: "Thinking about the next twelve months, how likely do you think it is that you will lose your job or be laid off?" We track the percentage who answered, "Very likely," or, "Fairly likely." We use a method similar to what we have used in other analyses where we smooth survey data (see appendix A). But here we calibrate the answers of different groups of respondents, not with national trends but with real data on unemployment.[90] We want to see how anxiety tracked the unemployment rate. Figure 5.17 shows the trend in job insecurity for different earnings groups—those in the highest and lowest 20 percent of personal earnings and those in the middle 60 percent. The actual unemployment rate shows up as a thick gray line.

The correspondence between fluctuations in official unemployment rates and fluctuations in expressed insecurity is striking. The percentage of all workers saying they were worried (not shown on the figure) ran two to three percentage points above the actual unemployment rate. Since the question was asked only of currently employed persons, these Americans

Figure 5.16   Job Satisfaction, by Year and Education

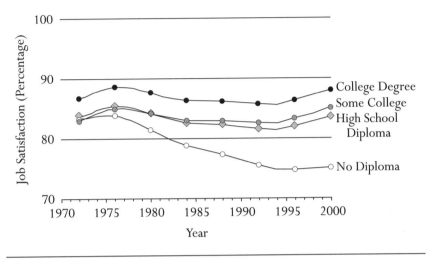

The Least-Educated Americans Became Less Satisfied with Their Jobs

Source: GSS.
Note: Data smoothed using locally estimated (loess) regression.

were responding to other people's misfortune. If unemployment was 5 percent and insecurity was 8 percent, then 13 percent of the labor force was either laid off or anticipating layoff. Furthermore, insecurity seemed to be a little "sticky"; that is, during the 1990s, when unemployment reached all-time lows, insecurity did not fall as fast as unemployment did. We see that pay levels were clearly connected to insecurity. Workers with the lowest incomes can least afford to lose their jobs. Yet they correctly sensed that their spots were more precarious than those of the average or affluent workers.

CHANCES OF MOVING UP

Among this nation's self-proclaimed titles is "land of opportunity." Americans are supposedly less bound by the circumstances of their birth than are people elsewhere. One hundred years of social mobility research have shown that Americans are neither free of nor bound by the class position into which they were born. The statistical correlation between the rank of parents' occupations and that of their children describes how tight that bond is. On a scale from 0, denoting that workers' backgrounds have no influence on the status of their current jobs, to 1, indicating that workers' backgrounds completely determine their current jobs, late-twentieth-century America scored between .3 and .4.[91] Americans in 2000 thus faced a modest

Figure 5.17   Job Insecurity, by Year and Income

Workers' Sense of Job Security Followed Actual Unemployment Trends

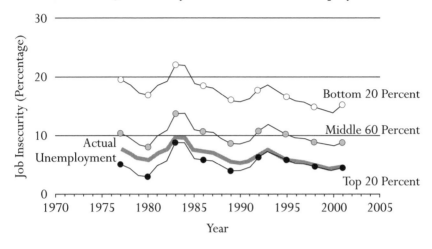

Sources: Unemployment: U.S. Bureau of the Census, *Statistical Abstract of the United States, 2002.* Attitude toward security: GSS.
Note: Gray line shows actual unemployment; data smoothed using actual unemployment plus trend.

but real restraint on their adult success from the social class circumstances of their births.[92] It was probably a weaker restraint than had been the case early in the century.

For much of the century, economic growth and the upward recomposition of jobs unloosed American youth from the fetters of modest origins. That is, individuals' chances for moving up the ladder reflected not only their parents' location on the job ladder but changes in the "ladder" itself— that is, the economy. A modernizing and growing economy raises up many people irrespective of their origins. For Americans who grew up in the 1930s, for example, the affluence of the 1960s and 1970s stand in such sharp contrast to the widespread poverty of the Great Depression that the specific conditions of their own childhoods barely shaped their futures. The correlation between fathers' and sons' economic attainments was modestly strong for that generation, as it was for others, but the upward movement from want to wealth that the whole Depression generation shared is what impresses the people who lived through it. When the General Social Survey asked people around 2000, "Compared to your parents when they were your age, do you think your own standard of living now is much better, somewhat better, about the same, somewhat worse, or much worse than theirs was?" the pattern of answers reflected this history.[93] Nearly half of those who were children or youths in the Great Depression (born between 1910 and 1939) said that their standard of living was "much better" than their parents'. More recent generations (born 1940 to 1959) also saw themselves as better off than their parents, but only a minority, about one-third, saw themselves as "much better" off, even though both generations had exceeded their fathers' occupational attainments to the same degree.[94] The point is that national economic growth contributes to people's sense of personal social mobility.

Researchers routinely make a distinction between this process, which they call "structural" mobility, and mobility that is more of an attribute of a particular person, called "exchange" mobility. Structural mobility reflects changes that affect everyone in a specific cohort, regardless of their social origins, as in the case of the Depression generation. But structural mobility tells us little about whether America gives everyone an equal chance to move up. To see that we need to focus on exchange mobility, on how people did compared to others in their cohort. Research into exchange mobility in the United States has concluded that, although the cohorts that rose out of the Depression advanced far, it was Americans born in the 1940s who experienced the most relative change and were least constrained by their social origins. It was in the 1950s and 1960s that the social institutions that affect mobility—most importantly, schools and colleges—became far more open to people of all social backgrounds. The correlation between fathers' and sons' occupations on the Duncan index fell from .4 to .3. It stayed there for cohorts born after 1950, which means that, even as the inequality in wages grew from 1970 on, the chances of youths moving up that ladder from their parents' rung did *not* grow.[95]

Although Americans pride themselves on their country's economic opportunities, comparisons of American intergenerational mobility in occupational status to that of other wealthy nations find more resemblance than difference.[96] Structural mobility matters everywhere. The level of exchange mobility in France and Sweden looks very much like the level found in the United States; Great Britain might have slightly less equal opportunity than the United States, and Germany has significantly less (that is, Germany has a higher intergenerational correlation). Studies of intergenerational mobility in earnings reach the same conclusions.[97] In short, all advanced nations share a family resemblance when it comes to opportunities for mobility; none constrain their citizens appreciably more or less than others. In the nineteenth century, the United States probably offered distinctive opportunities for migrants who came from nations still struggling to free themselves from monarchy, autocracy, and the legacy—in some cases, the persistence—of serfdom. But Europe caught up in the aftermath of World Wars I and II. Democracy and opportunity were as entrenched there in 2000 as here.

CONCLUSION

American workplaces changed dramatically in the twentieth century. The kind of work to be done and who did it both changed. Jobs became more specialized, and low-skilled, low-status jobs gave way to high-skilled and high-status jobs. Women joined men in the paid labor force, while teenagers and seniors left it. Educational differences became increasingly critical as work was restructured.

Married women were stepping out of the home and into the workplace even before World War II. Then, between 1968 and 1975, second-wave feminism appeared and helped speed the closing of the gender gap. Idealistic at first, it soon found itself in synch with economic necessity. As automobile drivers in the 1970s hoping to buy gasoline sat in lines that stretched from the pump to somewhere down the block, millions of couples probably had a similar conversation. She said, "Honey, I am keeping my job." He said, "Cool. We could use the money." Men still worked longer and made more money than women; women still did more of the housework. But every major difference between men and women—including the hours gap, the pay gap, and even the housework gap—decreased substantially over the century. Motherhood, even a baby at the breast, was far less likely to keep a woman away from work at the end than at the beginning of the century—a remarkable change that spurred considerable cultural debate (as we shall see in chapter 8).

While gender determined work less, age determined it more. Late-nineteenth-century work lives started at various times—for some, as soon as they were big enough to pick cotton or thread a machine; for others, after many years of schooling—and they ended at various times, though usually at death. By the late twentieth century, working was clearly delimited and scheduled; it was a shrinking stage in the life cycle as schooling lasted into at least the late teens for everyone and retirement began in the midsixties.

In schooling, as in the change of gender roles, idealism joined with economic necessity to revolutionize the work experience. Reformers and planners in the late nineteenth century proclaimed both the spiritual and practical merits of educating America's youth. Communities invested in buildings, grounds, and many more teachers. Secondary education expanded steadily from the 1880s to the 1980s. Postsecondary education grew as well. State universities promoted scientific agriculture; state teachers colleges staffed the new high schools. Industry and commerce discovered the productivity of educated workers. As advanced schooling became more common, those who were left behind began to look more and more different. In other chapters, we have seen how the families of college graduates, high school graduates, and high school dropouts increasingly differed in form, community, and living standards. Here we documented growing differences in the world of work: educational attainment increasingly demarcated how easily Americans could find jobs, the quality of those jobs, the hours they worked, the money they made, and even the satisfaction they felt.

The decreasing importance of gender and the increasing importance of age and education are only three of the many shifting axes of difference among twentieth-century workers. In some ways, work life was simpler in 1900. Most workers were men who toiled on farms, in factories, or in other muscle jobs; they started working for pay in their teens and stopped when they died. In other ways, work life was more complex: men bounced in and out of employment, from farm to job and back, with little security. Over the century, a new structure of work emerged. More and more specialized jobs appeared, most with defined entry requirements, career trajectories, and stability. The other kinds of jobs—farm help, day labor, temp work, and the like—formed a distinctive "secondary" labor market. In parallel, American workers divided into a primary workforce of those who found secure employment and careers and a secondary one of those who struggled chronically with un- and underemployment. The work hours of Americans declined, converged, and were standardized to the classic forty-hour week over the first half of the century, but in the rest of the century the hours of professionals and managers expanded, resulting in an increasingly wide divide between the overworked but highly paid, on the one side, and the underemployed and poorly paid, on the other. Similarly, earnings, which had compressed in the first half of the century, spread apart after 1970. Farm versus factory, blue-collar versus white-collar, women's work versus men's work—the job distinctions that had dominated the early part of the century became less critical as these other divisions emerged. Most important was a widening gap between, on the one hand, jobs with clear career tracks, security, high pay, benefits, and long hours and, on the other hand, jobs that were intermittent, insecure, short on hours, lacking benefits, and poorly rewarded.

Which side of this divide Americans ended up on was determined, in turn, by which side of the racial and, increasingly, educational divides they were on. In general, people's ancestry mattered less and less in channeling them toward bad or good jobs. Immigrant groups, as always, typically began their American histories on the lower rungs of the job ladder. The case of African Americans, however, was more complex. For black women, the twentieth century rapidly brought access to better jobs; for black men, progress stalled in midcentury, and by 2000 a sizable proportion of them were either not in the labor force at all (many were in prison) or concentrated in inferior jobs. Yet even race paled in importance compared to education by the end of the century, when how far young Americans had gotten in school and, notably, how far they had gotten in college most critically shaped their entire work lives.

CHAPTER SIX

What Americans Had: Differences in Living Standards*

AMERICANS ARE loath to describe themselves in terms of social class. Compared to the British, for example, Americans are far less likely to say that their society is composed of "haves" and "have-nots."[1] In many respects, American culture is exceptionally egalitarian; foreign visitors have long remarked on the political equality among Americans—at least, among free, white, male Americans—and noted, occasionally in horror, how little deference "common" people give to their "betters."[2] But American egalitarianism has coexisted with great economic inequality. America in 2000 was the most economically unequal nation in the developed world: it had the greatest division in wealth between haves and have-nots, and that division had grown over the previous thirty years.[3] The widening of inequality was jarring; three-fifths of Americans surveyed in 2003 said that "money and wealth should be more evenly distributed"; even Alan Greenspan, chairman of the Federal Reserve Board for almost twenty years and a closely followed economic guru, noted in 2004 that America's level of inequality "is not the type of thing which a democratic society . . . can really accept without addressing." Wide economic disparities tend to go along with high rates of social problems, civic alienation, and discontent and with low rates of economic growth.[4]

In this chapter, we move beyond our analysis of wages in chapter 5 to assess inequality in Americans' standards of living over the twentieth century.[5] We look at their annual incomes, financial assets, and consumption, and also at their subjective evaluations of their economic positions. We measure the gaps between the better- and the worse-off, and we track how those gaps

---

*Coauthored by Jon Stiles.

coincided with other axes of difference, especially race, region, and education. Americans became increasingly similar in their living standards through much of the century, but the equalizing trend stalled and then reversed around 1970. Americans then became more and more divided economically, and that division increasingly followed educational differences. Moreover, surveys show that Americans sensed the widening economic divisions among them.

LIVING STANDARDS IN 2000

Rich and poor Americans have little personal contact with one another. The British travel writer Jonathan Rabin dramatized this disjuncture in his depiction of the "air people" and the "street people" of Manhattan.[6] The air people live high above the street in condominium buildings guarded by doormen and work in offices similarly elevated and guarded. The street people include not only the homeless but also the hard-pressed; they live in buildings that require them to walk in, walk up, and be wary. They also work exposed to the street, in construction, maintenance, and service jobs. Well-dressed and well-coiffed air people encounter street people in the theater district when they exit from shows they have paid perhaps hundreds of dollars to see and search out taxis and limousines to carry them back to their homes in the air. On the sidewalk, they must work their way past panhandlers pleading for "spare change" to buy a bed for the night. These face-to-face encounters of people from the two ends of the income distribution are rare and perhaps melodramatic, but they highlight the reality of differences in living standards across all of America, not only in Manhattan. Away from the big cities, even such passing encounters are rare, since many Americans live in class-segregated communities (see chapter 7).

Just how divided were Americans in their living standards in 2000? There are at least three aspects of living standards: income, wealth, and consumption.[7] Consider, first, *annual income*, which includes not only earnings from wages or self-employment but also returns such as interest, dividends, capital gains, rents, business profits, and Social Security payments. In 2000 households with joint annual incomes that put them in the highest one-fifth of American households ranked by income averaged about $140,000 each before taxes; the one-fifth right in the middle averaged $42,000; and the lowest one-fifth of households averaged about $10,000. Using our by-now familiar eighty-fifty-twenty-percentile comparisons, the household that stood at exactly the eightieth percentile of income had about twice the income of the household at the fiftieth, and that one, in turn, had about twice the income of the household at the twentieth percentile.[8] Were these large or small differences? By international standards, they were quite large: the United States had the widest income gaps of any advanced Western society.[9]

Americans varied even more in *accumulated net wealth*—assets such as savings, stocks, pensions, and homes, minus debts. In 1998 the wealthiest one-fifth of families had an average net worth of over $1.1 million; the middle one-fifth averaged $61,000 in assets; and the least wealthy *two*-fifths of American families were worth, on average, $1,000 apiece. Thus, the richest one-fifth of families owned more than four-fifths of all the family wealth in the country, while the poorest two-fifths of families owned one-fifth of 1 percent of the national wealth. And as with income, wealth inequality was greater in the United States than in Europe.[10]

People's standards of living can also be measured by their *consumption* and the *goods* they own. At the turn of the century, all but a few households had full kitchen facilities and color televisions; 91 percent had a car or truck. Other goods appeared more often in affluent than in modest homes but were still common. For example, 90 percent of households with incomes over $50,000 had clothes washers, but so did 60 percent of those with incomes under $15,000; 90 percent of the former had stereo equipment, but so did over 50 percent of the latter. The affluent and the poor differed more in their possession of other goods, such as central air conditioning—two-thirds versus one-third—and dishwashers—80 percent versus 20 percent.[11] Still, the near-universality of household goods such as refrigerators, cars, and televisions suggests that differences in consumption were not as great as differences in income or wealth.[12]

Beyond money, assets, and goods, living standards include, in the end, the quality of life, measured perhaps by longevity, health, and security. At the end of the century, Americans varied notably in these respects. For example, people in households earning under $10,000 suffered about twenty-eight days per year of disability, compared to ten days for those with $35,000 or more; moreover, 17 percent of children were reported to be living in "food insecure" homes.[13] In the late 1990s, 66 percent of urban Americans with family incomes under $15,000 reported that there were places in their neighborhood where they were afraid to walk at night, but only 42 percent of those with incomes over $60,000 felt that way.[14] And again, the variation among Americans along these dimensions—the divide between those doing well and those getting along marginally—exceeded that of citizens in other Western nations.[15] In the pages that follow, we take up separately the expansion and division in income, wealth, and consumption over the twentieth century.

INCOME DIFFERENCES OVER THE TWENTIETH CENTURY

The twentieth century was, with the notable exception of the 1930s, one of prodigious economic advancement in America. While working fewer hours,

Americans easily quadrupled their real earnings.[16] But the pace of improvement varied for different groups of Americans. There were periods when the "have-less" quickly closed the gap with the "have-more," and periods when the have-less fell further behind. The data are spotty up to about 1960—there is some evidence on wages, some on total household income, some on capital gains, some on taxes paid—and their exact interpretation is debated. Nonetheless, the general trend is clear: as average family incomes soared through the first two-thirds of the century, variation in incomes shrank. The span closed sharply around World War I and again around World War II, then closed slowly over the next decade. (The major wars contracted the range of income because they typically led to wage controls, higher taxes, and concessions to organized labor. Other political events, such as programs for income security and health services, also helped compress incomes.) Consequently, Americans differed much less in annual income in the 1960s than in the 1900s.[17] In the last third of the century, however, average family income grew little; variation in income widened as high-income Americans pulled away from the rest.

Figure 6.1 displays the shares of the nation's income of high-earning, middling, and poorer families over the twentieth century. It displays the percentage of all family income in a year that went to the one-fifth of families with the highest income, the percentage that went to the next *two*-fifths, and then what went to the lowest-income *two*-fifths.[18] (For lack of data, we cannot use our eighty-fifty-twenty scheme to cover the whole century.) Until the 1970s, the top fifth's share of family income shrank as the middle two-fifths took more and the bottom two-fifths took a little bit more. Then the trend reversed: by 2000, the distribution had returned to roughly the 1940 level of inequality. Why it had done so, and to what effect, have been fiercely argued. We examine a few of these debates after looking more closely at the trends of the last half-century, a period for which we have more data.

Annual Incomes, 1949 to 1999

We start with the total income provided by all the related members living in a household, including households of one person, from 1949 through 1999.[19] (The decennial census-takers asked about incomes in the year before the census, which explains the odd years.) We use income before taxes, so the numbers reflect neither fluctuations in tax rates nor changes in tax credits granted to the poor. We take inflation into account by correcting for changes in the cost of living, so that all the numbers are expressed in 1999 dollars. Because we are interested in people's standards of living, we also adjust the income figures for the size of the family. We want to know how much income individuals had per family member. However, since at least the publication of the popular book *Cheaper by the Dozen* (1948; not to be con-

Figure 6.1   Shares of the National Income, by Income Segment

Income Differences Narrowed from 1900 to 1970 and Then Increased

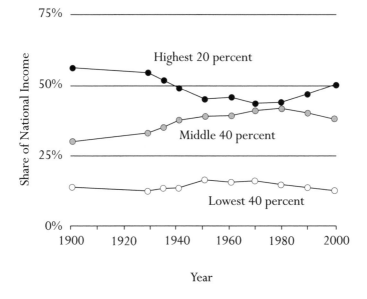

Sources: Liebergott, *The American Economy*, 498; U.S. Bureau of the Census, *Historical Income Tables—Households.*

fused with a later, different movie of the same name), it has been clear that financial demands on families do not increase in a simple, linear way: two children are not twice as expensive as one child. Research has established that an effective way to capture a family's standard of living is to divide its dollars by the *square root* of the number of family members.[20] So, for example, when a first child arrives to a couple, the family has grown by 50 percent, from two to three. But their per-person expenses have grown, by this standard formula, only 22 percent.[21] We follow this convention but express the results of our calculations as the living standard in 1999 dollars for someone in a *family of four*.[22] So when we refer to a person's "adjusted family income," we mean his or her family's total income adjusted for both inflation and size of family and expressed for ease of communication as if he or she lived in a family of four.[23] In 1949 the median American had an adjusted family-of-four income of about $19,000 (in 1999 dollars); in 1999 the median American had an adjusted family-of-four income of about $53,000.

In comparing incomes—for example, between the 1999 median of

$53,000 and the 1949 median of $19,400—we use the ratio (2.8) rather than the arithmetic difference ($33,600). As we briefly noted in chapter 5 and detail in appendix B, the standard academic practice is to use ratios for comparison. Where the choice between subtraction and division makes a substantive difference in interpretation, we point it out.

Now we can map the half-century history of income differences. The left side of figure 6.2 shows how adjusted family-of-four income, in a ratio scale, grew for the median American (the one at the fiftieth percentile—the open-circles line), for the relatively affluent American (the eightieth percentile—the top line), and for the relatively moneyless American (the twentieth percentile—the bottom line).[24] The median American's income grew rapidly from 1949 to 1969, but grew much more slowly afterwards. (Median *family income* grew some after 1969 even though median *earnings* for individual workers grew not at all [see figure 5.9] because more wives worked and they worked longer hours.) The gaps between the three levels of income seem, by visual inspection, to widen after 1969, too. The right side of figure 6.2 confirms that impression by displaying the eighty-to-twenty ratio for each year. In 1949 the eightieth-percentile American had $4.00 in adjusted family-of-four income for each $1 the twentieth-percentile American had; in 1969 the ratio had dropped to $3.13; and in 1999 it was back up to almost $3.75 to $1. (Comparing by subtraction, however, shows a steadily widening gap, from a $25,000 to a $70,000 eighty-to-twenty difference.) The great equalizing trend of the century made what has been called the "U-turn" toward inequality around 1970.

Why family incomes diverged in the last thirty years of the century is a matter of heated debate in the academic journals and even in the general media. We cannot resolve those debates here, but there is consensus that most of the answer lies in the patterns of men's earnings described in the previous chapter. Beyond earnings, changes in family structure and living arrangements contributed to the U-turn. More women went further in school, married men who also were well educated, and increasingly took well-paying jobs. Two-career couples thus moved further ahead of couples with wives who were homemakers or part-time workers and ahead of singles and single parents. Also, wealthy families rode the stock market upward in the 1990s, earning considerable investment income.[25]

Whatever the explanations for the U-turn depicted in figure 6.2, it is clear that Americans at the end of the twentieth century were more divided in terms of income than they had been for a generation, and also that this increasing divergence reversed at least two prior generations' worth of the convergence we see in figure 6.1. The inequality trend, by the way, continued into the 2000s.[26] But not all groups of Americans were equally affected by growing inequality; the most dramatic exception were the elderly.

Thanks largely to Social Security and Medicare, income differences among the elderly kept dropping. In 1949 the elderly American at the eight-

Figure 6.2   Adjusted Family Income, by Year

The Income Gap Narrowed as Incomes Rose Between 1949 and 1969, Then Widened Again

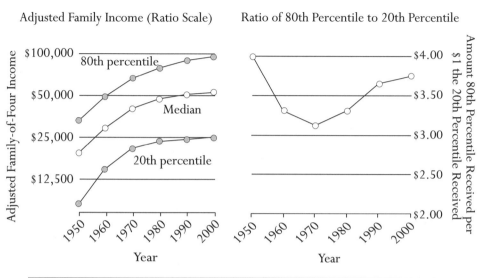

Source: IPUMS.
Notes: Families include primary individuals; incomes are adjusted for inflation using the consumer price index (research series for urban consumers), with 1999 as the base year, and for family size by dividing income by the square root of family size and then multiplying by two for the equivalent of a family of four.

ieth percentile of income among the elderly brought in $9 to each $1 of the twentieth-percentile elderly American. That ratio dropped to under $5 in 1969 and continued to drop slightly afterwards. Younger Americans, in contrast, notably parents of young children and the children themselves, experienced the sharpest U-turn. Income differences narrowed before 1970 but widened sharply after 1970. The eighty-to-twenty ratio for children rose from three-to-one in 1969 to four-to-one in 1999, a substantial widening of income inequality.[27] Thus, the late-century trends depicted in figure 6.1 and 6.2 would be even more acute if we left out senior citizens.

Differences Between Groups

We have described the narrowing and widening of income differences between those of high income and those of low income. We turn now to how differences in income lined up with other lines of division among Americans. Was

Figure 6.3   Adjusted Family-of-Four Income Medians, by Ancestry

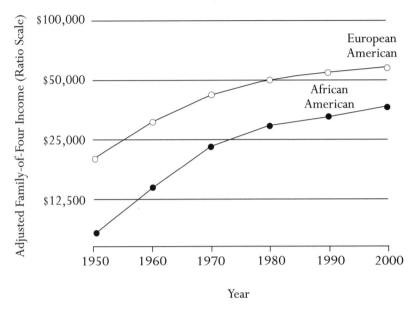

Black-White Differences in Family Income Narrowed, 1969 to 1999

Source: IPUMS.

income increasingly or decreasingly connected to those other splits? Did, for example, the income gap between blacks and whites widen or narrow?

Figure 6.3 answers that question. In 1949 the median European American had an adjusted family-of-four income of $20,500 compared to just $8,600 for the median African American; the ratio is 2.4-to-1. By 1999 median incomes had grown for both, and the European-African ratio had declined steadily to 1.6-to-1.[28] (Arithmetically, the difference *grew* from around $12,000 to about $21,000.) Over the half-century, low-income blacks, in particular, made the most rapid advance, shortening their lag behind low-income whites.[29] (Hispanics, however, fell further behind whites, and the foreign-born fell increasingly behind the native-born, both surely reflecting the influx of low-wage immigrants.)[30]

Southerners rapidly caught up with Americans from other regions between 1949 and 1979. In 1949 nonsoutherners had about $1.70 of adjusted income for each dollar of southerners' income; by 1979 the gap had shrunk to $1.15. (Even as an arithmetic difference, the gap had narrowed.)[31] Then, after 1979, there was little net change in the relative position of southern-ers.[32] Looking at the variation in incomes *within* regions reveals how much low- and moderate-income southerners gained on high-income southerners between 1949 and 1969; that gain accounts for most of the convergence be-tween Americans of lower and higher incomes nationally.[33]

Similarly, rural Americans' incomes rose relative to those of city-dwellers. Suburban residents, however, outstripped both of them. In 1949 median city and suburban people each had incomes 60 percent greater than those of people in nonmetropolitan areas. In 1999 suburbanites had incomes 50 percent greater than those of city residents, who, in turn, had incomes only 10 percent greater than those of nonmetropolitan residents. At mid-century, then, Americans living in metropolitan areas, whether in the center or in the suburbs, had about the same income and considerably more than rural Americans; by 2000 nonmetropolitan residents had caught up with center-city residents, but both were considerably behind suburbanites.[34]

The regional and urban-rural convergences can probably be explained by the migration of both business and people after 1950. Much of American in-dustry in the northern cities closed down or left town; investment moved to the South and to rural areas. At the same time, Americans with relatively few marketable skills for a modernizing economy left the rural South for the center cities of the North.[35] And well-off Americans found homes in the sub-urbs. (This geography is discussed in more detail in the next chapter.)

During this same half-century, income differences by education grew. Figure 6.4 displays the median adjusted family-of-four income by level of education (or, for children, by the household head's education). The figure shows dramatic changes, especially since 1980, as college graduates did in-creasingly well and those with less than a BA degree stagnated or fell behind. From 1949 to 1969, college graduates' incomes remained about a constant ratio of others' incomes. College graduates in 1969 reported $1.30 of ad-justed family-of-four income for each dollar reported by those with some college, about $1.50 per dollar of high school graduates, and about $2.05 per dollar of high school dropouts. Then everyone fell further behind the college graduates. By the end of the century, the ratios had become $1.50, $1.80, and $3.20, growing 15, 25, and 55 percent, respectively, for those with some college, a high school diploma, and no diploma. The college grads had moved the furthest ahead, but the gaps between all the educational groups widened.

Educational attainment became substantially more critical as a ticket to family income over only twenty years. Part of the story is the growing de-mand in the labor market for workers with advanced schooling (see chapter 5). But there was probably more involved. During these years, growing pro-portions of poorly educated men went to jail, an experience that devastated their chances of eventually finding well-paid employment.[36] Also, as we

Figure 6.4   Adjusted Family-of-Four Income Medians, by Education

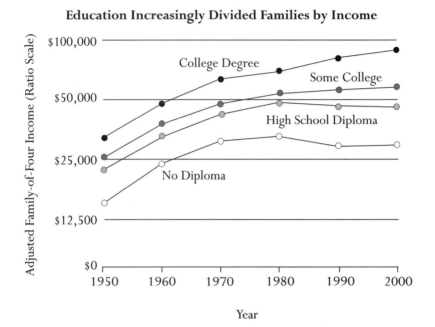

Education Increasingly Divided Families by Income

Source: IPUMS.
Note: Head of household's education is substituted for children's education.

noted in chapter 2, education increasingly determined who married whom and thus the chances of having an income-generating spouse. Better-educated Americans' incomes more often rested on two earners. Then the increasing pattern of high earners marrying high earners further contributed to the education "premium." It also probably contributed to growing income disparities—higher eighty-to-twenty ratios—*within* specific educational groups, for instance, within the set of college graduates.[37]

Summary

Through most of the twentieth century, the spread in family and individual annual incomes narrowed, as did the income differences between blacks and whites, southerners and northerners, and rural and urban Americans. After 1970, however, differences widened between very-well-off and less-well-off Americans. (We should note that the gap between the *extremely* rich and the merely rich also widened greatly.)[38] Scholars point to various forces behind this growing income inequality, including the growing importance of schooling, but also at work were the rise in single-parent families, two-career couples, and immigration and a lagging minimum wage.[39] The axes of difference that strongly lined up with income differences shifted: by 2000, black versus white, South versus North, rural versus urban, and older versus younger all mattered less in determining income than they had earlier in the century, while suburban versus city and, especially, level of education mattered considerably more.[40]

WEALTH

Although wealth is tied closely to annual income, it is a different, broader component of people's standards of living. Many Americans with a low annual income have considerable wealth—for example, some retirees own valuable homes and stock portfolios—and many Americans with high annual incomes have little wealth—for example, some self-employed entrepreneurs can have a good year but carry large debts. Wealth differences among Americans do not simply mirror differences in income.[41] Furthermore, variations in wealth have their own consequences.

A person's wealth, or "net worth," is composed of his or her assets—a home, savings accounts, stock portfolios, bonds, insurance, and similar possessions that can be cashed out—minus debts, such as mortgages and consumer loans. Researchers differ about whether to include *potential* assets, such as future Social Security and pension payouts, and personal possessions, such as appliances and furniture. Edward Wolff, a leading expert on wealth, focuses only on those assets that can be easily converted into money at close to their real value.[42] We follow his lead. Also, some items that compose wealth—goods such as houses and cars—play a double role: people both "consume" them and hold them for possible cash or collateral value. In the next section, we look at goods; here our focus is on the liquid or potentially liquid assets people hold.

Such liquid assets are important above and beyond annual incomes. Most of the critical moments in people's lives depend on their assets (or their parents' assets) more than on their annual incomes: assets more substantially determine how well people make it through critical life transitions, such as college, weddings, funerals, homeownership, career launch, unemployment, medical emergencies, children's career launches, and retirement. Also, people's sense of financial security probably rests at least as much on their assets as on their paychecks. Looking at wealth yields a different story about the diversity of living standards than does looking at income. For example, blacks made notable progress in catching up to whites in annual income but remained far behind in wealth. In the mid-1990s, the median white received $1.60 in adjusted family-of-four income for every dollar the median black received, but the median white family had *$8.30* of net worth for each dollar the median black family had. (Excluding homes yields a $33-to-$1 ratio.) If data on Americans' wealth were not so much harder to obtain than data on their incomes—the latter are included in almost every government and private poll, the former only in occasional and complex surveys—social scientists would probably have studied wealth much more. Another limitation is that researchers are largely constrained to relatively recent data.[43]

Differences between rich and poor are much greater in wealth than in annual income. As we saw, in 2000 the American at the eightieth percentile of income had an adjusted family-of-four income of $3.75 to each dollar of the American at the twentieth percentile. But the American household at the eightieth percentile of wealth had effectively an *infinite* net worth relative to that of the American at the twentieth percentile, because the least wealthy one-fifth of American households were in the red. Even compared to the *median*, the eightieth percentile's wealth advantage stands out: $6.70 to every dollar of net worth for the fiftieth percentile.[44]

The major reason differences in wealth are several times wider than annual income differences is that income differences accumulate year after year as high-income families put savings into assets that both earn money and appreciate over time, while low-income families make so little that their debts compound over time. High interest rates typically amplify financial assets while inflation wears away the buying power of wages. Gifts and bequests from parents to children allow this process of compound growth to stretch over generations, not just over one lifetime. By one informed estimate, 40 percent of wealth accumulation is the result of inheritance or inter vivos gifts.[45] Wealthy parents help their children up the ladder in other ways as well, such as buying them a good education and providing a security net for risky business or career ventures. In addition, families' decisions about how to save and invest, their financial skills, the number of earners they have, how long those earners have worked, and other personal traits contribute to variations in wealth—as does, certainly, good or bad luck.[46] Basically, wealth tends to foster more wealth, and poverty tends to foster more poverty, widening the economic differences.

Wealth at the End of the Century

In 1998 the median American household was worth $61,000.[47] Equity in the home was the major component; without it, the median household was worth $18,000. But the median hides tremendous variation. At the top, American households ranking between the eightieth and ninetieth percentiles were worth an average of over $340,000, and those in the top *1* percent over $10 million. At the lower end, about one-fifth of American households had zero net worth or were in the red. Setting aside home equity, about one-quarter of American households had no or negative net worth.[48]

We turn now to closer examination of specific assets and their distributions, standardizing again for inflation and family size and starting with the central asset, the house. In 2000 the average American homeowner lived in a house with a family-of-four value of about $134,000. But there was quite a range. The eightieth-percentile homeowner's house was worth (adjusted to a family-of-four) about $246,000, which was 3.4 times the house value of the twentieth-percentile homeowner, at $72,000.[49] Not included in this comparison are the roughly one-third of Americans who were not homeowners and therefore had zero home value. Differences in liquid wealth were yet greater. Take savings accounts: in the period 1996 to 1998, the twentieth-percentile saver had nothing in a savings account; the median saver had an adjusted account of about $15; and the eightieth-percentile saver had one of over $4,000. In checking accounts, the twentieth-percentile American once again had zero, the median had $300, and the eightieth-percentile over $2,000. The contrast in stocks and bonds was even wider because most Americans, including the median one, had none. Wealth inequality far overshadowed income inequality.

Family Wealth from 1900 to 2000

Economic historians have been creative in searching out evidence on wealth in earlier periods, drawing on estate tax returns, wills, and similar documents. Most such records include only assets of considerable value, such as houses, works of art, and farmland, and thus it is difficult to track the assets and debts of less affluent Americans. Nonetheless, scholars largely agree that variation in wealth declined during the middle of the twentieth century, dropping most sharply during the world wars and the New Deal era, and that it continued to decline into the 1960s and perhaps 1970s.[50] Then, as with annual income, wealth differences widened in the last two to three decades of the century, primarily because stock values and capital gains from selling stocks soared and because, at the other end, more Americans ran up larger debts as government deregulated the home loan and credit card industries. Differences in wealth widened so much that, by one estimate, they were as gaping in 1990 as they had been on the eve of the American Revolution.[51]

Scholars and policymakers have focused on tracking wealth differences between black and white Americans. Although wide in 2000, the black-white wealth gap had narrowed during the century, particularly between 1960 and 1980. Racial differences in rates of homeownership shrank as rates for black male heads of household rose toward those of whites. Blacks were twenty-seven points behind (39 to 66 percent) in homeownership in 1960, but only twenty points behind (52 to 72 percent) in 1980. Also, the value of blacks' homes rose faster than the value of whites' homes.[52] (We discuss what happened after 1980 later.)

While trends in homeownership can be traced over several decades, the details of other kinds of wealth are harder to track for the general population. For the fifteen years from 1984 through 1998, we look briefly at a few mini-trends that at least give us a view of what happened during the era after the U-turn. We draw on the government's Consumer Expenditure Surveys and again adjust the figures for inflation and family size.[53] Americans' *saving accounts* dropped sharply in this period, from a family-of-four median of about $120 to one of about $20. One reason seems to have been that well-off people shifted their savings strategies from banks to housing and stocks.[54] Inequality in savings grew. In the period 1984 to 1986, Americans at the eightieth percentile of savings banked an adjusted $70 for every dollar that the *median* household banked; by the 1996 to 1998 period, the ratio was $220 to $1. (Twentieth-percentile savers were at zero throughout.) Median *checking accounts* stayed roughly constant between 1984 and 1998, at about $300, but wealthier Americans' checking accounts grew. In 1984 to 1986, the eightieth-to-*median* ratio was about $6 to $1; in 1996 to 1998, it was about $7.50 to $1. (Again, the twentieth percentile had no checking accounts.)

As we noted, the most extreme inequality was in securities. Between 1984 and 1998, both the twentieth-percentile American and the median American directly owned no stock or bond assets. The American at the eightieth percentile of stock and bond ownership, however, saw the family-of-four value of his or her portfolio more than triple, from $380 in 1984 to 1986 to $1,350 in 1996 to 1998. Some of this paper wealth disappeared in the bear market of 2002, but even that did not negate the gains of the previous fifteen years. Securities explain much of the widening division in wealth, but the divergence in fortunes included other assets as well, even housing values. In 1980 the eighty-to-twenty ratio of house values was 2.9; in 2000 it was 3.4.[55] (And as with income, the super-rich moved far ahead of the merely rich.)[56] The asset-friendly tax cuts of the 1980s, the increase in consumer debt we mentioned earlier, and perhaps the growing number of single-parent households, in addition to growing income inequality, help explain the widening wealth gap between rich Americans and the rest.[57]

Wealth differences between demographic groups also widened in the last couple of decades of the century. The closing of the black-white gap in homeownership stalled. Between 1980 and 2000, the percentage of whites who owned homes rose from 70 to 74 percent, but the percentage of blacks who owned slipped a point, from 49 to 48 percent.[58] In both decades, the median black American had no savings, checking account, or stock assets. Wealth differences by education widened. Between the mid-1980s and late 1990s, the median college graduate's house values and financial accounts moved further ahead than those of the median high school graduate.[59] It is paradoxical, then, that the wealth of older Americans grew relative to that of younger ones. Both the housing equities and the savings of the median

American over the age of forty-four pulled away from those of younger adults.[60] Americans who came of age in the 1980s and 1990s fell behind the financial positions that their parents and even older siblings had attained at the same stage of life.[61] This misfortune is all the more striking given that the younger generation had more schooling than their elders and for that reason alone should have gotten richer faster than their elders. Yet hard times after the 1970s made it difficult for the new generation to accumulate wealth as fast as the previous ones continued to do.

In sum, wealth differences among Americans narrowed through most of the twentieth century; that trend stalled and then reversed in the last decades. Then the wealthier became yet wealthier compared to those of modest means. Moreover, in the last twenty-five years gaps widened between black and white, between old and young, and especially between different educational groups. Some of this divergence can be attributed to the 1990s stock market boom, but the breadth of the growing inequality—from house values to checking accounts—points to other sources too, such as the widening inequality in incomes, the rise in consumer debt, changes in marriage patterns, and tax policies.

CONSUMPTION

Some analysts argue that the best way to assess people's standards of living is not by their pay stubs or portfolios, but by what they buy. It is also argued that many people underreport (accidentally or not) their incomes and wealth to census- and survey-takers. In a 1988 national survey, for example, respondents who reported incomes under $5,000 also reported spending, on average, over four times as much money as they said they earned. Some welfare and disability recipients hide income; some middle-class families report themselves as less well-off than they are; and some wealthy people overlook a few sources of income.[62]

An entirely different reason for the income-outgo discrepancy is that many people spend their savings or borrow to sustain their standard of living. Indeed, people typically base their spending on long-term calculations rather than their immediate income. A young professional couple may, for example, spend more than they earn early in their careers because they can reasonably anticipate rapid increases in earnings (and perhaps the receipt of an inheritance); a middle-aged couple may restrain their spending to ensure their long-term health care (and perhaps to leave an inheritance).[63] Some of the reckoning works out. If a student's borrowing for college education or newlyweds' borrowing for a house pays off, if the economy does well, and if perhaps parents pitch in, borrowers get out of debt. For others, borrowing is a repeated act of desperation. If the investment or the economy sours, if kin are also strapped and make their own requests, if the indebted's ship never comes in, then they never get out of the red.[64] Typically, the poor borrow for immediate consumption and the rich save for investment, and typically, young families go into debt and retirees spend down their assets. Consequently, Americans differ less in what they consume than in their incomes and wealth.

Yet another argument for looking at spending rather than income or wealth is that Americans received increasing value for their dollars over the century. For example, in 1909 the average manufacturing worker had to labor a half-hour to afford a pound of bread and almost an hour to afford a half-gallon of milk delivered to the door; in 1970 his grandson needed to work five minutes for the bread and twelve minutes for the milk.[65] Moreover, the quality of the bread and milk—their freshness, cleanliness, and variety—improved considerably. If we want to know how standards of living changed, goes the argument, we should look at how much people spend and what they buy.

If we do, we see narrower differences than we have seen earlier. In 1998 the eighty-to-twenty ratio for adjusted family-of-four spending was only $2.50 to $1 (versus $3.75 for income and much more for assets). Table 6.1 shows that the twentieth-percentile spender reported buying about $4,000 worth of food a year for the standard family of four and the eightieth-percentile spender bought about $8,600 worth, for an eighty-to-twenty food ratio of just $2.13 to $1.[66] There is only so much one can spend on food, and there is only so little one can get by on, so the consumption differences there are not great, and they consist more in quality than quantity (filet mignon versus hamburger). As we move to housing, then clothing, and finally recreation, however, we see that the differences in spending widen. For recreation, the eightieth-percentile spender paid out $5.39 for each $1 spent by the twentieth-percentile consumer.

Consumption differences were smaller than the income or wealth differences. Nonetheless, 20 percent of American families in the 1990s reported failing to pay for some essential expense, such as a utility bill, rent, or a doctor's fee. Ten percent of American households reported some "insecurity" in having enough food, and 4 percent reported some hunger. And these counts do *not* include the homeless. At the same time, many Americans at the other end spent enough on mansions, yachts, and jewelry to inspire 1990s books such as *Luxury Fever* and *The Overspent American*.[67]

Ownership of basic consumer goods was also more evenly spread than income or wealth. At the last turn of the century, virtually every American household had, for example, a refrigerator and a color television set, and 90 percent had a car or truck. They varied more on other items. Nearly 80 percent owned washing machines, and a bit more than half owned a dishwasher, a computer, or cell phones.[68]

One way to understand ownership patterns for such goods is in terms of

Table 6.1   Adjusted Family-of-Four Spending on Categories of Goods, by Percentile Rank, 1998

	20th Percentile	50th Percentile	80th Percentile	80:20 Ratio
Food	$4,046	$6,094	$8,614	2.13
Housing	5,772	9,186	16,120	2.79
Clothing	610	1,356	2,498	4.10
Recreation	816	2,062	4,402	5.39

Source: CES.
Note: Numbers represent family spending, adjusted for inflation, divided by the square root of the size of the famiy, and multiplied by two.

diffusion. When a new consumer good, such as televisions or computers, first appears, only some people—usually those who are well-off or avant-garde, or both—get it. Then, because prices drop and familiarity increases, ownership "diffuses" across the population until virtually everyone has it. In this process, differences in ownership rates first widen and then narrow. Thus, what ownership tells us about differences in standards of living depends on where that good is in its diffusion history. For the basic items—not only refrigerators and automobiles but also indoor plumbing and television—there was considerable homogeneity in 2000. The wealthy may have driven BMWs and watched thirty-two-inch rear-projection television, and the working class may have driven old cars and watched TV on seventeen-inch screens, but both groups had the commodities. Skeptics in the debate over poverty in America point out that most of those who are defined as poor by their annual incomes nonetheless own such goods. More alarmed debaters respond that, socially and psychologically, poverty is a relative matter. The poor may have indoor plumbing, but if their children lacked computers in 2000, they remained socially disadvantaged—in this example, on the wrong side of the "digital divide." We return to an evaluation of relative need after looking at the historical trends in consumption.

Long-Term Trends in Spending

Consumption expanded dramatically for all Americans between 1900 and 2000—indeed, probably on a historically incomparable scale. But did that mean that differences in standards of living narrowed or widened? Consider, first, *spending* patterns. One way to assess living standards is to examine how people apportion their spending. When they live on the margin, people spend almost all their money on the basics, and the most basic is food; when people live well, they spend much of their money on discretionary extras, and one of the most discretionary is recreation. Therefore, the proportion that a family spends on recreation versus food indexes its standard of living.[69] Over the twentieth century, Americans spent less of each consumer dollar on food (half as much by the end of the century) and more on recreation (twice as much as before). Figure 6.5 draws on two different but consistent sources: occasional national surveys asking respondents how they spent their money and national economic data tracking the buying and selling of goods.[70] The key force pushing food spending down was, of course, declines in the real cost of food. Much of the money Americans saved on food went to "feeding" the family car, which by the end of the century took about as much of the household budget as food did; some part of that car budget should also be counted as recreation.

The same household survey data displayed in the figure also speak to class differences in spending patterns. Although much "noisier" than the income and wealth data, the household surveys suggest that class differences in spending narrowed through the middle part of the century until about 1973, and then class differences stopped narrowing or even widened.[71]

We return to the Consumer Expenditure Surveys of 1984 through 1998 for more comprehensive data on how Americans spent money over the last fifteen years of the twentieth century.[72] The proportions spent on food and recreation, which we use as indicators of standard of living, changed little, and the gap between high and low spenders on recreation barely widened.[73] Black-white differences on food spending narrowed noticeably, and differences on recreational spending narrowed marginally. Differences by the education of the head of household stayed roughly the same. We can say that the long-term convergence of black and white consumption continued into the 1990s (the end of that decade was especially beneficial to blacks) and that the class differences that had widened after 1970 stayed about the same after the mid-1980s.[74]

Several researchers have examined late-twentieth-century spending more comprehensively than we could here. Details differ among them, and with us, but some general conclusions emerge. Inequality in consumer spending continued declining from World War II to about 1973. From then to 2000, spending inequality grew again, but at a slower pace than did income or wealth inequality (perhaps because of expanded borrowing). Then the economic boom of the late 1990s stalled the trend toward more consumption inequality.[75]

Trends in What People Owned

The single most critical "good" Americans own is also their single greatest investment, a home. The proportion of American families who owned their

Figure 6.5   Consumer Expenditures for Food and Recreation, by Year

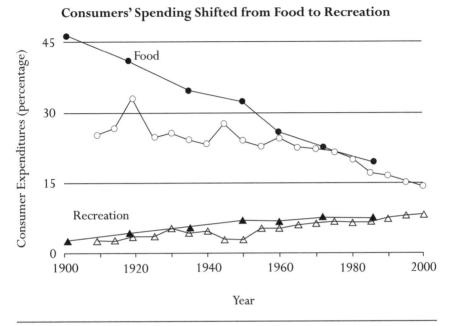

Consumers' Spending Shifted from Food to Recreation

Sources: Household surveys: Jacobs and Shipp, "How Family Spending Has Changed in the United States." National accounts: U.S. Bureau of the Census, *Historical Statistics of the United States*, 316–21; U.S. Bureau of the Census, *Statistical Abstract of the United States*, 2003, table 667, Excel spreadsheet supplement.
Note: Black data points indicate that the data come from surveys of urban consumers; white data points indicate that the data come from national accounts.

own homes jumped in the middle of the century. We see that displayed in figure 6.6 by the nearly horizontal line. A bit under half of American households owned their homes in the first part of the century; that figure jumped to over 60 percent by 1960 and stayed about there afterwards.[76] Ownership of other goods, however, increased greatly. Three that are summarized together in the gray line in figure 6.6—having an inside toilet, a telephone, and an automobile—diffused in similar ways. Each was rare in 1900 but had become nearly universal by 2000. The computer, introduced late in the century, was showing a similar, albeit more rapid, diffusion.[77]

As noted earlier, as new products diffuse, differences in ownership widen and then later shrink. We can see this process in tracking black-white differences. (Few long-term data track Americans' ownership of goods by the education, occupation, or income of the owner, but the United States has long

Figure 6.6   Households with Key Domestic Goods, by Year

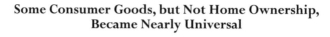

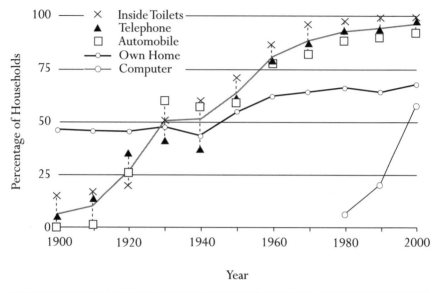

Some Consumer Goods, but Not Home Ownership,
Became Nearly Universal

Sources: U.S. Bureau of the Census, *Historical Statistics of the United States*; U.S. Bureau of the Census, *Statistical Abstracts of the United States*; Liebergott, *The American Economy*, http://factfinder.census.gov; and interpolations.
Note: The gray line shows the average of toilet, telephone, and automobile; the data points for the individual items are connected to the line.

gathered many statistics by race.) In 1890, 14 percent of whites and 5 percent of blacks had toilets—a nine-point difference; by 1940, as indoor plumbing spread, blacks lagged thirty-seven points behind whites (26 versus 63 percent), but by 2000 indoor toilets were effectively universal, so the difference was about zero. In 1900 virtually no one had a car; in 1935, 60 percent of white families had cars, but only 20 percent of black families did—a forty-point gap; in 1999, 95 percent of whites and 80 percent of blacks had a car, bringing the difference down to fifteen points.[78]

Through such diffusion, Americans of all backgrounds came to own these sorts of goods by the end of the century. In 1960 rural residents, blacks, the poorly educated, and southerners were notably less likely than other Americans to have full plumbing facilities in their homes; by 1990 the differences were gone.[79] Telephone and automobile ownership did not become universal, but the differences between groups still shrank. For example, the difference in automobile ownership between high school graduates and high school dropouts shrank from nine points in 1960 to four points in 1990.[80]

Evaluating Consumption Inequality

Thus, at the dawn of the twenty-first century Americans were all pretty similar in their ownership of nineteenth- and early-twentieth-century inventions. Certainly, wealthier Americans had more bathrooms, newer cars, and fancier phones, but almost everyone had the minimum. Even television, a mid-twentieth-century invention, was universal, meaning, for example, that almost everyone could share a common experience such as watching the Super Bowl in color. But do such commonalities mean that standards of living had generally converged? Is the growing inequality in income and wealth after 1970—and by some measures in spending—contradicted when we look at consumption of goods? Not necessarily. Consider three issues: new goods, improving goods, and public goods.

For new goods, take the example of the personal computer. Over the last quarter of the century, ownership of this new technology increasingly *divided* Americans. Figure 6.6 shows the rapid spread of computer ownership from 5 percent in 1980 to 60 percent in 2000. By 2000, ownership had become highly divided according to education: 78 percent of college-graduate households had one, 47 percent of high school graduate households, and 23 percent of high school dropout households. Similarly, ancestry and regional differences in computer ownership widened as it diffused.[81] Chances are that the future of computers will resemble that of the earlier technologies. As they passed the halfway mark, differences shrank. (Later, in chapter 9, we see a similar pattern in the diffusion of cultural values.) Nonetheless, the brief history of the personal computer reinforces one argument about goods and inequality: as old goods lose their power to mark distinctions, new products emerge that gain the power to distinguish.[82]

On improving goods, consider homeownership. As displayed in figure 6.6, ownership rates stayed relatively flat, 46 percent, between 1900 and 1940; rose rapidly between 1940 and 1960, largely owing to New Deal–era government assistance to young adults; and then flattened out again at 66 percent. Even among people in their peak years for capital accumulation, those age forty-five to sixty-four, ownership rates leveled off at 80 percent. Ownership rates did *not* converge by social class, and indeed, the class difference widened a bit in the later decades. In 1960, for example, college graduates were four percentage points likelier to own their dwellings than high school graduates (72 versus 68 percent); in 2000 they were five points likelier (73 versus 68 percent).[83] Homeownership did not follow the same diffusion pattern as did household goods. There are key differences between owning homes and owning, say, televisions. For one, as we noted earlier, homes are simultaneously investment and consumption. As an investment, their desirability varies over time. (Around the earlier turn of the century, homeownership was a conservative investment strategy that working-class rather than middle-class families often pursued.) For another, the real price of homes does not follow the price history of other commodities. Goods such as telephones and automobiles spread in great measure because their real costs decline; the same is true of manufactured goods generally. Housing, however, continues to rise in cost. Between 1918 and 1988, Americans' spending on shelter (in constant dollars) roughly tripled.[84] With larger-package goods, such as homes—and probably health care and higher education as well—costs do not decline much as a result of scale increases, and thus access does not diffuse as much. Thus, some of the basics become more available to more people—basic shelter with heat and water, simple vaccines, community college—but the ante, the middle-class standard, keeps going up, perpetuating distinctions, if not widening them.

Finally, there are *public goods*, an entirely different realm of consumption, but a critical one. When, for example, people search for a new house, they carefully weigh aspects of the neighborhood such as the local schools, traffic, health facilities, air quality, and safety. Public goods are a key part of the package. Other public goods, such as water and sewage treatment facilities, have been largely responsible for extending and equalizing life spans (see chapter 4). It is especially difficult to measure the distribution of such public goods, that is, to say anything about growing or waning public goods inequality.[85] (One effort to count "public consumption," such as the use of schools and roads, into household incomes reports an increase in inequality between 1989 and 2000.)[86] But any full accounting of living standards would need to include public consumption as well as the consumption of private goods such as televisions, cars, and shoes.

The evidence we have on overall consumption suggests that over the course of the century more and more Americans shared in what is now seen as a "middle American" lifestyle, with basic facilities, new appliances, and other goods, especially private ones, that are part of the "good life." But the evidence suggests as well that this economic convergence seemed to stall—and perhaps even reverse, as was the case with income and wealth—in the last quarter or so of the twentieth century. Equalization stalled not only in terms of several objective counts, such as spending patterns, but also in the sense that much of consumption was relative: as some goods became universal (for example, televisions), lines of division appeared around newer goods (for example, computers). It is also important to understand that *how* Americans differed in consumption changed: regional and racial differences largely narrowed, but differences by education generally widened.

SUBJECTIVE REACTIONS

Ultimately, income, wealth, and spending presumably matter because having more gives people better lives; they provide, in economists' language, "utility." Ironically, for all the attention given the careful tracking of dollars, what dollars do for people's utilities is not well established. Some scholars have studied the correlation between individuals' incomes and how "happy" or "satisfied" they report themselves being. Although the vaudevillian Sophie Tucker was no doubt right when she said, "I've been rich and I've been poor; believe me, honey, rich is better," the relationship is not linear.[87] Research suggests that, at least in well-off nations, going from having little money to having some money increases people's happiness, but going from having some to having lots adds little to happiness. Why not try, then, to assess directly Americans' utilities, through their subjective sense of well-being? Why not ask whether Americans' reports on their well-being have divided in recent decades in the same way their income and wealth have? People's reports of well-being depend, of course, on many factors besides money. For instance, married people, healthier people, and people with more friends are generally more upbeat. Here we focus on how Americans perceived their *economic* well-being—in particular, how they ranked their family incomes and how satisfied they were financially.[88]

At the end of the twentieth century, 30 percent of respondents told the General Social Survey that they were satisfied with their family's financial situation, but 25 percent said they were not. (The rest said that they were "more or less" satisfied.) Similarly, about one-fourth rated their financial situation as above average, and about one-fourth as below average.[89] The changes in these proportions over three decades are telling.

Between the early 1970s and the end of the century, the percentage of Americans who rated their family incomes as average declined from 57 to 48 percent, while the percentage who rated themselves either below or above average grew by a few points, suggesting some polarization in these perceptions. The percentage of respondents who reported being satisfied with their family's financial situation did not change much over the twenty-eight years, but as we shall see, the reports of the affluent and of the poor diverged. Thus, the polarization of income and wealth we tracked earlier is matched by a polarization in Americans' perceptions of their own incomes.[90]

We see this in more detail in the two panels of figure 6.7. The left-hand side displays GSS respondents' ratings of how their family's financial situation compared to the average, from 1 (far below) to 5 (far above average). The right-hand side uses respondents' ratings of how satisfied they were with their family's financial situation, from 1 (not at all satisfied) to 3 (satisfied). We divide the respondents into three groups according to their size-

Figure 6.7   Subjective Assessments of Family's Financial Situation and Satisfaction with It, by Income Level

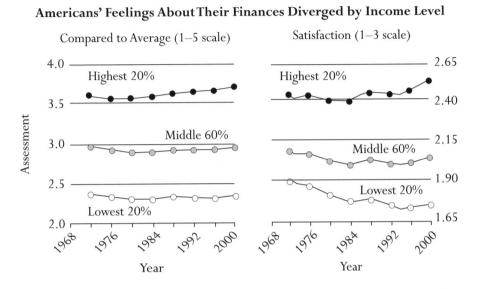

Americans' Feelings About Their Finances Diverged by Income Level

Source: GSS.

adjusted annual family incomes: the top 20 percent, the middle 60 percent, and the bottom 20 percent. The lines "smooth" the pattern using the same loess technique we described in chapter 3 (see appendix A). Differences by income grew over time, making the gaps between the poor and the affluent significantly greater by 2000 than they had been in the early and middle 1970s.[91] This polarization by income is a robust finding; it is not due, for example, to the poor in 2000 being more often Latino or single parents than in 1972. Americans' ratings of their overall "happiness" followed the same general pattern (not shown): the affluent got happier over the last three decades of the century, while the others did not.[92]

Other survey results also suggest that Americans sensed growing inequality after the 1970s. When the Harris poll asked respondents whether they felt that "the rich get richer and the poor get poorer," the proportion saying "yes" rose between 1972 and the early 1990s, then declined.[93] Similarly, the Gallup poll we noted at the beginning of this chapter, which asked Americans whether they thought of the nation as "divided into 'haves' and 'have-nots,'" reveals a trend between 1988 and 2000: the proportion who said "yes" increased from 26 percent to 38 percent.[94] In the last decades of the century, Americans perceived widening inequalities both in their own lives and in their country.

CONCLUSION

Although Americans at the end of the century were aware of widening economic differences among them, Americans have generally worried less about economic inequality than have citizens of other affluent nations, and they have been less willing to endorse government action to balance inequalities. What Americans care about more than economic equality of outcome is equal opportunity to get wealthy.[95] This stance fits their optimism: even in the job-tight year of 2003, one-third of Americans (and half of young Americans) thought it likely that they would become rich.[96] In this vein, some analysts argue that the growing inequality after 1970 matters little so long as opportunities to move up the ladder have also expanded. However, upward mobility did *not* increase and may even have decreased in the last few decades of the twentieth century.[97]

The economy at the end of the twentieth century was a major source of social division in the United States. Americans differed from one another economically more than they did socially or culturally. The cornucopia of America's productivity distributed consumer goods widely, so that differences in consumption were not nearly as wide as differences in annual income and accumulated wealth. Over most of the twentieth century, the least well-off in America—notably, the rural, southern, and black poor—made the greatest economic gains, narrowing historic differences. The two world wars, the Great Depression, and the New Deal welfare state combined to level economic distinctions substantially by midcentury. But the new economy, the new family patterns, and the new politics that emerged in the 1970s rewidened economic divisions among Americans, particularly, as we also saw in chapter 5, along lines of education. The wealthy and the college-educated drew further away from the rest. And even Americans' subjective sense of economic well-being expressed the late-century polarization.

CHAPTER SEVEN

Where Americans Lived: The Redrawing of America's Social Geography*

MANY POSTMORTEMS of both the 2000 and 2004 presidential elections explained the results by contrasting "red states" and "blue states," or even more simply, the coasts to the heartland of America.[1] One northern journalist wrote in late 2004, "There's no need to hide from this fact: The battle for the American soul that was this election is over, and the red states won." The Massachusetts legislature called for a regional convention to consider secession.[2] The elections seemed to be evidence of important and emerging social and cultural divisions by region. This conceit, however, misconstrued America's social geography and how it had changed over the twentieth century.

Americans were bitterly divided by region—in 1900. That year, perhaps one-third of Americans could vividly remember the Civil War; it was as recent to them as the Vietnam War was in 2000 to later generations, but far more vivid and painful. Politicians regularly refreshed those memories by "waving the bloody shirt." Moreover, deep sectionalism had long predated the war. Aside from political struggles over topics such as slavery and taxes, Americans had harped on cultural differences between North and South, and also between East and West. In the eighteenth century, Thomas Jefferson was already describing northerners as cool and industrious and southerners as fiery and indolent. In the nineteenth century, many Americans would use the verb construction "to Yankee," meaning to cheat.[3] Long after the war, the South still seemed a civilization apart; its racial composition was distinct, and its economic backwardness deep. So socially distant were the regions that as late as the 1910s northern employers were more likely to draw workers from Europe than from the South.[4]

*Coauthored by Jon Stiles.

In 1900 urban and rural were also far apart. The isolation of rural Americans drew national concern. A federal commission investigated the "Country Problem," which it described as comprising poverty, detachment, cultural backwardness, and an individualism that undercut cooperation. The New Deal tried—with mixed success—to bring rural Americans into the national mainstream by, for example, subsidizing electrification and sending out home economists to educate farm wives. Rural Americans held positions on cultural issues, such as alcohol and religion, that were distinctly more conservative than those of city people, a contrast dramatized in the 1920s by the Scopes "Monkey Trial."[5] City mouse and country mouse had real-world human counterparts.

In 1900 a third geographical divide was only just opening up: city versus suburb. Suburbanization was not new; affluent families had been leaving the downtowns of the largest cities for greener, outlying fields since before the Civil War. But in the early twentieth century, middle- and working-class families began moving out along streetcar lines to the close suburbs. It was not until after World War II that suburbanization became a mass movement. In 1940 about one-fifth of all Americans lived in suburbs; by 1970 almost two-fifths did, more than the proportion who lived in either center cities or nonmetropolitan areas. Suburbs became, as we will see, demographically distinct—somewhat wealthier and certainly much whiter than the cities. Moreover, as many observers in the 1950s and 1960s claimed, suburban life was culturally distinct: domestic, parochial, and caught up in rounds of sociability.[6]

How Americans sort themselves out across the regions, rural and urban places, and city and suburb matters significantly. Physical distances typically correspond to economic and social distances, to the availability of jobs and public services, to contact with different sorts of people, and to different political constituencies and agendas. It is one of America's peculiarities that its cities and even small suburbs typically have considerable authority in determining taxes, regulation, and public services.[7] Moreover, Americans are segregated by ancestry, class, and other traits: blacks here, whites there; singles in one area, families in another. Sometimes residential concentration enriches society. When students or artists congregate, for example, cultural innovation increases; when immigrants cluster, they help one another adapt to America. But often segregation, even when voluntary, is a problem. When disadvantaged families are concentrated, their problems seem to get worse, and they are isolated from people and institutions that might help them. When advantaged families are concentrated, they protect themselves, but also more easily hoard their time, money, and attention, raising the drawbridge and accentuating class differences. And yet integration may have its own drawbacks: recent studies suggest that residents of diverse communities have greater difficulty acting together for the common good than do residents of homogenous communities.[8]

In this chapter, we describe twentieth-century developments in these two aspects of social geography: how twentieth-century Americans were distributed into different kinds of communities—how they differed by region, by urban versus rural, by city versus suburb—and how segregated Americans were from one another in and between their communities. But first we consider whether geography itself remains important. Many twentieth-century commentators described their century as one in which new, space-transcending technologies, from hand-crank telephones and Model T cars to jumbo jets and the Internet, rendered distance and place moot.

PLACE MATTERS

In 1900 most Americans got from one neighborhood to another—and often from one town to another—the old-fashioned way: on foot. And most Americans' messages also traveled on foot.[9] One hundred years later, most American adults covered many miles a day by automobile, at least half had flown on airplanes, half used the Internet, and all but a handful used telephones to talk to people many miles, sometimes thousands of miles, away.[10] Space seems to have been, as some observers put it, "erased"; one could be almost anywhere physically in a short time—or arrive there "virtually" in no time at all. Except for the most disadvantaged, space and place did not seem to matter anymore.

But where people lived still mattered in 2000. Take residential mobility. Despite the popular image of an ever more rootless society, people became *more* rooted. Census data show that twentieth-century Americans moved less often than their ancestors had in the nineteenth century, and that trend continued until (and past) 2000.[11] Or take homeownership, which roots people in a community. At the beginning of the century, about half of Americans lived in homes they owned; at the end, over two-thirds did.[12] Place mattered in many other, practical ways too. Zoning, for example, began in New York City in 1916 and became widespread by midcentury. By 2000, living on one side or the other of a zoning boundary mattered, just as it mattered which side of the lines demarcating school districts, police precincts, and tax zones one lived on. These administrative differences were one more reason home buyers in 2000 faced huge disparities in prices by neighborhood, town, and metropolitan area. Median house prices in one suburban county of San Francisco were 78 percent higher than in a neighboring suburban county. Boston-area home prices were 85 percent higher than those in and around Providence, only forty miles south, and 140 percent higher than those in and around Worcester, only forty miles west. The realtors' slogan of "location, location, location" still rang true.[13]

Americans also cared about their places and the people in them. Surveys show that in 2000 a sizable majority of American adults felt good about their communities, and notably better than they felt about the nation as a whole; they reported a sense of belonging with their neighbors roughly on par with the fellowship they felt with coworkers and fellow parishioners, and almost half said that they had at least a few friends in the neighborhood.[14] The spread of "NIMBY" actions ("Not In My Back Yard" resistance to the intrusion of change from outside) around the country demonstrated how riled up Americans could get about protecting the places in which they lived. Even national politics reflected local constituencies, confirming the wisdom of legendary Speaker of the House Tip O'Neill when he said, "All politics is local."

Did twentieth-century revolutions in transportation and communications do nothing, then, to weaken Americans' connection to place? The best guess is that over the century the increasingly available means to transcend space encouraged Americans to involve themselves more in far-flung activities, interests, and social relations. Shopping, recreation, and social contacts in the immediate community shrank proportionally, but, in the end, not by much.[15] Thus, over the century geography remained important; it partly structured the nature of American differences. But which geographical differences mattered more and how they mattered shifted. Before we turn to those shifts, we describe American social geography in 2000.

AMERICANS IN PLACE, 2000

Over one-third of Americans lived in the South, and about one-fifth of Americans lived in each of three regions: the Northeast, the Midwest, and the West. Over the century, the South and especially the West had taken an extra 20 percent share of the population from the Northeast and the Midwest.[16] In 2000 the kinds of people who lived in the four regions were pretty similar. The greatest differences were by ancestral origin, as we defined it in chapter 3: midwesterners hailed overwhelmingly from Europe (81 percent), while the South had the highest proportion from Africa (19 percent) and the West a high proportion with roots in the Americas (26 percent) or Asia (8 percent).[17] Southerners made a bit less money than the rest. But no region was particularly different in terms of average age or family arrangements. For example, although Florida attracted many of the elderly, the South as a whole was not notably more aged than the rest of the country.[18]

In contrast to modest regional differences, notably different sorts of people lived in different types of communities—rural areas versus urban ones, cities versus suburbs. To organize our analysis of community differences we designed the two-by-three grid shown in figure 7.1. Metropolitan Statistical Areas (MSAs) are usually defined by the census as composed of contiguous counties with a central city or multiple central cities—such as Minneapolis and St. Paul—totaling at least 50,000 people.[19] We separate metropolitan areas into two categories: those with populations of less than 1.5 million in

Figure 7.1   Community Typology and Percentage of the Population, 2000

American Communities Varied Along Two Dimensions

	Nonmetropolitan Area	Small Metropolitan Area (less than 1.5 Million)	Large Metropolitan Area (greater than 1.5 Million)
Periphery	Countryside and village (for example, Iowa farm county)–10%	Suburb in small MSA (for example, Urbandale, Iowa)–22%	Suburb in large MSA (for example, Highland Park, Illinois)–27%
Center	Town over 2,500 (for example, Denison, Iowa)–10%	Center city, small MSA (for example, Des Moines, Iowa)–14%	Center city, large MSA (for example, Chicago, Illinois)–16%

Source: Authors' compilation.

any particular census year, and those with more than 1.5 million. In 2000, 1.5 million was just above the size of the MSA of Charlotte–Gastonia–Rock Hill, North and South Carolina (which ranked 34th among about 280 MSAs ranging from New York's 22 million to Enid, Oklahoma's 58,000).[20] The third category covers all places outside of metropolitan areas. For ease of discussion, we often refer to the horizontal axis as the "rural-urban" dimension, although that is a simplification. "Suburbs" are all the municipalities and unincorporated parts of a metropolitan area outside its center city or cities. Because the Census Bureau builds up these categories from counties, the typology is somewhat crude. (For instance, distant parts of Los Angeles County that are in the Angeles National Forest are technically counted as suburbs of a large metropolitan area.)[21] Despite its crudeness, the matrix reveals considerable American diversity.

Figure 7.2 shows how much the ancestral backgrounds, incomes, and ages of Americans varied by community type in 2000. People of European origin ("whites") predominated in the less urban and more peripheral places (top panel). Over eight in ten residents of rural or small-town America were of European origin, but only about four in ten residents of large center cities were of European origin. City people were more typically of African, American (especially Latin American), or Asian origin.[22] Similarly, the foreign-born made up barely one in fifty residents of the countryside but nearly one in four residents in the center cities of large metropolises.

Figure 7.2   Percentages of Americans Who Were of European Origin,
             Higher Income, and Unmarried, by Type of Place, 2000

Different Places Were Home to Different Kinds of People in 2000

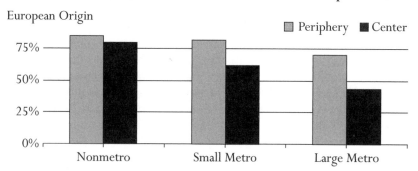

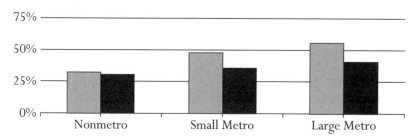

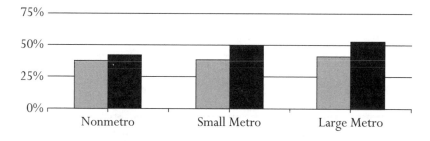

Source: IPUMS.

The more urban the area, the higher the income of residents' households (middle panel). Metropolitan Americans, especially those living in the suburbs of large areas, were the most likely by far to have household incomes over $50,000. Similarly, the more urban the area, the higher the proportion of adults with advanced education and workers with white-collar or professional jobs. Within metropolitan areas, suburban residents had a bit more education and higher-status jobs than the center-city residents. City-suburb differences in education and occupation were not as great as those of income, because the center cities, especially the larger ones, had concentrations of both young college graduates and high school dropouts—the "dual city" with a "missing middle" that many urban scholars have described.[23] The downtown cores of the center cities showed the concentration of well-educated young people even more; residents of those few census tracts typically had more education than even the suburbanites.[24]

In 2000 Americans of different ages and stages in the life cycle did not favor any particular type of community, with one noteworthy exception (see figure 7.2, bottom panel): unmarried adults concentrated in metropolitan places, particularly cities; this pattern overwhelmingly reflects the distribution of those who had never married.[25] Correspondingly, eighteen- to twenty-nine-year-olds also concentrated in city centers (not shown), especially in the downtowns.[26]

Figure 7.2 and related data reveal that in 2000 Americans differed socially by the kinds of communities in which they lived. As one traveled from rural and small-town America to the large metro areas, one would see populations that were increasingly nonwhite, affluent, and not married. And within metropolitan areas, especially large ones, as one traveled from city to suburb, one would see residents who were more often white and affluent. The city residents were more often nonwhite, unmarried, and lower-income (or more accurately, residents of large cities were divided into well-off and poorly off) compared to those outside the centers. These demographic and economic differences help account for cultural and behavioral differences, including voting patterns in 2000 that varied by type of community.

RESIDENTIAL SEGREGATION, 2000

In these ways, Americans sorted themselves—or were sorted—into different *types* of communities by ancestry, affluence, and, to a smaller extent, life-cycle stage.[27] A related but distinct question is whether and how Americans in their *specific* communities and neighborhoods were segregated by race, class, or age. African Americans were the most segregated Americans. In the twentieth century, millions of them moved from heavily black, rural counties in the South to predominantly white cities in the North and became, like most European

Americans, urban people. But in those urban areas, African Americans ended up separated from whites in different, heavily black neighborhoods.[28]

Scholars have intensively studied this history, and we address it later. Here we simply describe segregation in 2000. We measure how segregated Americans were from one another, although we do it only for *metropolitan* (city and suburban) Americans.[29] We use as our measure Theil's H, which expresses the degree to which people of a certain category—say, African Americans or children—are spread out *unevenly* across a geographical area. The lower the number, the more dispersed and integrated the particular group; the higher the number, the more group members live next to one another and apart from other types of people.[30] In our study, the smallest geographical area is the census tract, typically a contiguous "neighborhood" of several thousand residents. The following list displays the degree of segregation—as measured by Theil's H—for different kinds of Americans in 2000.[31]

Theil's Index for Segregation, 2000,

… by race, ethnicity, and origin:[32]

African Americans	.43
Hispanic Americans	.36
Non-Hispanic Whites	.36
Foreign-born	.21

… by income level:

Highest 20 percent of household income	.16
Lowest 20 percent of household income	.13

… by life cycle:

Married	.07
Children under fifteen	.02
Adults eighteen to twenty-nine years old	.05
Adults sixty-five and older	.05

Ancestral groups were heavily segregated. African Americans lived most separated from others, with the highest Theil's H, .43. Hispanics and non-Hispanic whites also clustered to a great extent, at .36 each. Researchers have noted that levels of racial segregation vary substantially by region. In large midwestern and northeastern cities like Chicago, Detroit, Milwaukee, and New York, blacks were very segregated, but less so in smaller, newer metropolitan areas such as Portland, Oregon, and Tallahassee, Florida.[33] Next, we see that high- and low-income Americans were somewhat segregated from those worse or better off than themselves in income. American neighborhoods are highly differentiated by the cost of buying or renting in them, but neighbors can be more variable in annual incomes. Some neighbors may be retired, others may be well-to-do newcomers, some may have bought homes when prices were far lower, some may be subsidized by relatives, and so on. If we knew people's long-term incomes or, better yet, knew their wealth, we would surely see considerably higher segregation scores than the roughly .15 displayed in the list.[34] Finally, we see that Americans in 2000 were least segregated by age or marital status.

Theil's H also permits us to assess *where*—at what level of geography— people were segregated. Hispanics tended to live among other Hispanics in large measure because Hispanics clustered in particular regions of the country and in particular metropolitan areas within those regions; they lived in places like greater San Antonio and Miami rather than areas like Pittsburgh or Cincinnati. On the other hand, to the extent that families with children clustered together—and it was a limited extent, with Theil's H = .02—it was not because they concentrated in particular regions, metropolitan areas, or towns, but because they clustered in particular neighborhoods within towns. The affluent tended to be separated from other Americans both because they lived in specific, tony suburbs outside the center city and because they lived in specific, tony neighborhoods within cities and towns. And the unmarried were modestly segregated because, as we saw earlier, they tended to congregate in the center cities of metropolitan areas rather than in the suburbs.[35]

Residents of metropolitan America who stepped outside their homes in 2000 were likely to see neighbors racially and ethnically very much like themselves. They would see a greater mix of neighbors in terms of income—perhaps a widow on Social Security still living in her fully paid-off home next door to a couple of young professionals who had just moved in— but typically people who lived at roughly the same economic level as themselves. And they would see neighbors of varying ages (excepting the young singles clustering in center cities). By these measures, geographic divisions among Americans in 2000 corresponded mainly to ancestry, somewhat to class, and least of all to age and life stage. Later we consider how segregation by ancestry, class, and life stage changed over the last several decades of the twentieth century. But first we tell the story of what happened to the regional cleavages that so divided Americans in 1900.

CHANGE ACROSS THE CENTURY: HOW THE REGIONS MOVED CLOSER

In 1942, when Americans first sang, "I'm dreaming of a white Christmas, just like the ones I used to know," three of every five had grown up where they would have indeed known a white Christmas. By 2000, that had reversed: only about two of every five children lived in a white Christmas region. The American population shifted from the North and Midwest, from the "Frost Belt," to the South and West, the "Sun Belt." The West, in particular, grew dramatically: in 1900 it was home to about one of eighteen Americans, but in 2000 it was home to more than one of every four Americans. As the numbers evened up, so did many long-lasting social differences between regions.[36]

In 1900 the South was racially distinct: about one-third of its residents were nonwhite, while in no other region did nonwhites exceed one-tenth. In 2000 the regions were, as we saw, much more alike racially. The major contributor to this leveling was the exodus of African Americans from the South that began around World War I. By 1980, 4 million southern-born blacks lived outside the South. The balance of immigrants and the native-born also evened out across the regions. (Starting in the 1980s, however, immigrants increasingly clustered in the West.)[37]

The regional distribution of farmers also evened out as farming declined.[38] In 1900 most southern workers were farmers, while only one in eight northeastern workers were. As fewer Americans farmed and the numbers approached only a few percent everywhere, regional differences based on the economic and social features of farming—both as an occupation and as a way of life—narrowed. In a similar way, the regions converged in income. The South, which had fallen economically even further behind the industrializing North after the Civil War, approached levels of affluence typical elsewhere by 2000.[39] And the regions became more similar in urbanization. In 1910 over half of northeasterners were in metropolitan areas, but only one-tenth of southerners were; by 2000 the difference had narrowed to 85 and 70 percent, respectively.[40] Over the century, then, the South became more like the rest of the nation racially, ethnically, and economically (see also chapter 6).

The West was distinctive in 1900 for its family arrangements—or lack thereof—in large part because it had almost thirteen male residents for every ten female ones (compared to ratios under eleven-to-ten elsewhere). Many western adults in 1900 had never married and lived as singles. By 1960 western family life was pretty much like that elsewhere in the nation.[41]

The wide social differences between the regions that had emerged in the nineteenth century contributed to noted cultural differences between them at the beginning of the twentieth. In the same vein as Jefferson, academics, essayists, and novelists described distinctive ways of life: the chivalrous, violent South; the individualistic, untamed West; the civic culture and Babbittry of the small-town Midwest; the mercantile, cosmopolitan Northeast. However accurate these stereotypes may have been in 1900, by 2000 the cultural contrasts had been muted, although not erased. Political differences by region, in particular, narrowed and were then rearranged. The South's Democratic allegiance, rooted in slavery and Jim Crow, persisted for the first half of the twentieth century. Beginning with the 1948 presidential election, Democrats from outside the South began courting the votes of blacks and liberal whites with pledges to support desegregation. Republicans reacted slowly but eventually appealed to southern whites who felt betrayed by the Democrats, winning first the presidency in 1968 (through Nixon's "southern strategy"), then Senate seats, governorships, and, ultimately, the House of Representatives in 1994.[42] This political history stimulated the post-2000 "red state, blue state" discussion we mentioned earlier. Closer examination of the voting patterns revealed that "red county, blue county" better describes that political division. More importantly, from 1970 to 2000 the regions that voters lived in became less associated with how they voted in presidential elections, while the type of community they lived in became more associated with their presidential choices.[43]

Explaining why social, economic, and cultural differences by region narrowed is another project, and a large one. Migration across regions certainly contributed, particularly to the increasing similarity by ancestry. The expansion of national markets and national media probably contributed. But economic development, occupational changes, and urbanization, particularly in the South, seem central to any full account.

CHANGE ACROSS THE CENTURY: HOW THE SUBURBS MOVED AWAY

More dramatic even than the movement of Americans from the Frost Belt to the Sun Belt was their movement from rural areas to suburban places. We again use a two-by-three layout, which captures the rural-to-urban dimension (nonmetropolitan, small metropolitan, and large metropolitan) and the center-periphery distinction.[44] Figure 7.3 shows the distribution of Americans across these types of places from 1900 to 2000. It reveals how Americans shifted from the open countryside to metropolitan areas, especially the peripheries of those areas. The percentage of Americans who lived in nonmetropolitan peripheral communities (the countryside) shrank from a majority of 55 percent (the huge white expanse at the left of the graph) to only 10 percent (the small portion on the right side); those who lived in small or large metropolitan areas but outside their center cities grew from 11 percent to 50 percent. (The percentage living in both kinds of center cities grew from 22 percent in 1900 to 32 percent in 1930 and stayed around that figure for the rest of the century.) The late nineteenth century and the twentieth century were both eras of rural depopulation, but in the nineteenth century Americans became city people and in the twentieth century they became suburban people.

Figure 7.3   Distribution of Population Across Types of Places

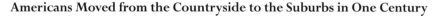

Americans Moved from the Countryside to the Suburbs in One Century

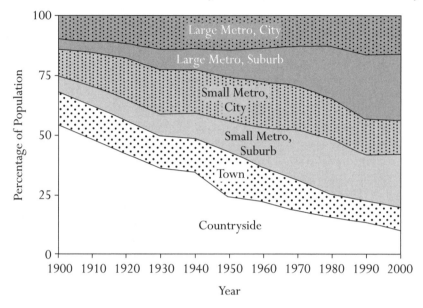

Sources: IPUMS and Bogue, "Population Growth in Standard Metropolitan Areas."

Urban scholars attribute the shift from rural to suburban to a few factors. For one, the immigrant waves both prior to 1920 and after 1970 over-whelmingly swept into metropolitan areas; relatively few newcomers became farmers. For another, individual Americans moved: country boys and girls went to the cities, and years later their children and grandchildren decamped to the suburbs. In addition, communities themselves changed. Small towns grew into cities, and their suburbs engulfed surrounding villages and open country.[45] Across the nation, farmhouses that in 1900 had nestled in fields and orchards by 2000 huddled beside tract homes and shopping malls. From a society split between rural and urban—in 1900 two-thirds of all Americans lived outside metropolitan areas, and two-thirds of the rest lived in the center cities—America became one divided between city and suburb: in 2000 only one-fifth of Americans lived outside metropolitan areas, and most of the remaining great majority lived in suburbs. This redeployment alone was a massive social change, but it coincided with a geographical re-arrangement of social differences too.

Ancestry

The shift mattered racially. Figure 7.4 uses a three-box chart to show what happened to the geographical distribution of European-origin Americans. The first box displays what happened outside metropolitan areas, the second what happened inside small metropolitan areas, and the third what happened in large metropolitan areas. Within each box, the filled-in dots represent central places—small towns or center cities—and the open dots represent the peripheries—countryside or suburbs.[46]

In the early twentieth century, figure 7.4 shows, European Americans did not concentrate in any particular kind of place; they made up between 83 and 97 percent of the residents in all kinds of places. In contrast, African Americans concentrated in the rural areas (not shown); they were 16 percent of country residents and only 2 percent of residents in the centers of large metropolitan areas. As we noted in chapter 3, the category "European-American" meant something different in 1900 than in 2000. In the urban centers, European Americans included many demeaned immigrants, such as Italians and Jews, who would not assimilate until later. They were quite different from the descendants of earlier European immigrants, such as the English, Scots, and Nordic, who made up the European Americans of rural America. In that sense, even though figure 7.4 shows an apparent similarity from rural to urban and between city and suburb in ancestry in 1900, the big cities were in fact more ethnically diverse even then than other places. And they were so recognized, often quite hostilely, in the culture of the times. Nonetheless, the diversity of European nationalities in early-twentieth-century cities was less culturally significant than would be the case with the later concentrations of peoples from various continents.

The large-scale migration of blacks from the rural South after 1940 and the immigration of Hispanic and Asian immigrants after 1970 created the great racial diversity that Americans now take for granted as typical of large metropolitan areas and center cities. From 1930 to 1970, African Americans replaced European Americans in large center cities, and Latin Americans increasingly did so after 1970. It is true that blacks, Asians, and Hispanics in the last years of the century moved to suburbs, typically those just across center-city lines. But such moves did not keep pace with the growth of the minority population, nor with the departure of whites from the center cities.[47] In these ways, Americans increasingly divided themselves racially and ethnically between city and suburb. (In the last years of the century, the white population of downtowns grew a bit, along with the gentrification of those districts.)[48] Indeed, in the late twentieth century, while more urban places continued to have the greatest concentrations of immigrants,[49] the terms "urban" and "city" became code words for "African American," as in

Figure 7.4 European Ancestry, by Year and Type of Place

Over the Century, Metropolitan Areas and Center Cities Became Much Less European-American

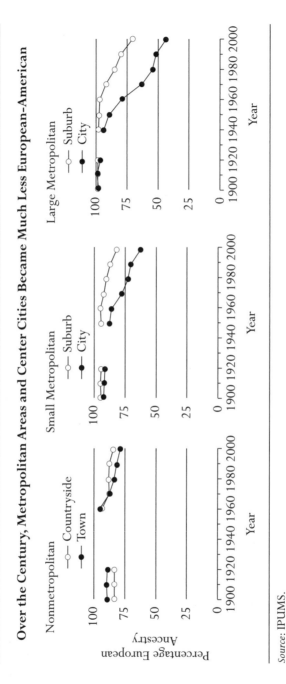

Source: IPUMS.

Note: To protect the anonymity of individuals, the Census Bureau withholds some geographical details. That precluded us from distinguishing the geography in smaller places in 1940 and 1950.

marketing slogans like "urban fashion" and "urban music"—an association that would have puzzled Americans of 1900.

Class

In contrast to ancestry, the economic situations of urban and rural Americans became more *similar* over the century. However, city and suburban residents became more *dissimilar* economically, and dissimilar in a new way. City-suburb differences reversed and widened, to a great extent displacing rural-urban as the main geographic dimension of class.

With the data we have, we can chart family incomes precisely only from the 1950 census on, but we draw on other data and other studies to get a sense of the centurylong trend.[50] At the beginning of the century, urban Americans were considerably better off than rural Americans, and city residents were better off than suburban residents.[51] At midcentury, the median American family living in a nonmetropolitan area had an income about one-third below that of the median metropolitan American.[52] Had we comparable data for earlier decades, they would show an even larger rural disadvantage in those years. Before modern farming and the New Deal, rural life was especially poor, despite occasional periods of prosperity such as World War I. Close examination of figure 7.5 shows that, over the last fifty years of the century, differences between nonmetropolitan and metropolitan areas narrowed, so that by the 2000 census the (now many fewer) families of rural America earned only about one-fifth less than urban families did.

Before 1950, city families earned more than suburban ones. Aside from a relative handful of high-status suburbs, most places right around the major cities were industrial, market-gardening or -dairying towns and villages whose residents had modest incomes.[53] The suburban disadvantage narrowed to virtually nil by 1950 and then turned into a substantial advantage afterwards. By 2000 suburban households' median income was one-fourth greater than that of center-city households.[54]

Looking yet more closely, we find that both the narrowing of the rural-urban gap in income and the widening of the city-suburban gap in income after midcentury largely reflected changes among the lowest-income Americans. Americans at the twentieth percentile of income among the rural (the sort who formed *The Other America* in Michael Harrington's famous 1962 book decrying poverty) quickly became substantially better off in the subsequent years, mostly because well-paying industrial jobs moved to the countryside and partly because many of the poorest and least-skilled residents left the countryside. But this improvement at the bottom of the income scale did *not* happen in the large center cities. The income of the twentieth percentile there hardly changed in forty years. Indeed, inner cities saw the departure of some of those same blue-collar jobs that showed up in rural places. Thus, in

Figure 7.5 Median Family Income, by Year and Type of Place

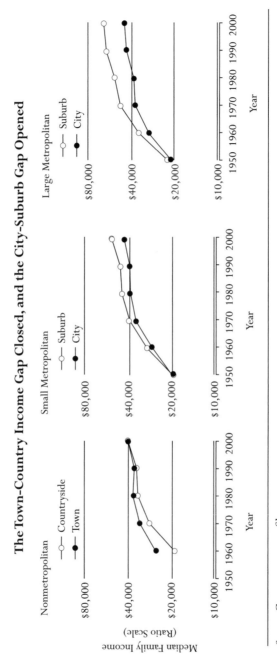

The Town-Country Income Gap Closed, and the City-Suburb Gap Opened

Source: Census summary files.
Note: Incomes adjusted for inflation (base = 2000), but not for family size.

1900 the geography of the haves and the have-nots corresponded roughly to the split between city folk and country folk; in 2000 it corresponded more to the split between suburbanites and center-city people.[55]

When we assess social class by education or occupation rather than annual income, the picture is more complex but still consistent with this description of the shifting geography of haves and have-nots.[56] One way to understand what happened is this: Americans nationwide gained far more education, and they moved up from farming to blue-collar, white-collar, and then professional work. Metropolitan residents led and rural Americans trailed in the educational and occupational transitions. The class lines distinguishing urban from rural Americans therefore marked different statuses in different eras: dividing people at high school graduation earlier in the century and at college graduation later in the century; dividing farm work from nonfarm work earlier and then dividing blue-collar from white-collar work later. In general, low-status, rural Americans substantially closed the gaps between themselves and comparable urban Americans, but low-status, inner-city Americans did not close the gaps between themselves and comparable suburban residents. Again, the rural-urban division waned in importance relative to the urban-suburban division.

Center-city residents became relatively poorer about the same time that center cities became especially nonwhite. Which was the driver in this correlation, poverty or race? Did minorities concentrate in the urban centers because they were poor? Or did cities become poor because minorities concentrated there? The likely answer is both.[57] Ancestry partly accounts for the widening city-suburb gap in median income, but even among whites suburban median income came to exceed that of city residents (although not by nearly as wide a margin). Among *non-Hispanic* whites, suburbanites slightly widened their advantage over city-dwellers over the last half of the century. The division by social class between city and suburban Americans was to a great degree tied up with race, but more than that was going on. One complicating development was the emergence in the large metropolitan center cities of a polarized, dual economy that combined clusters of poor, uneducated laborers with clusters of young, educated, and well-paid professionals, especially in places like lower Manhattan and downtown Portland, Oregon.[58]

In sum, rural-urban distinctions became decreasingly connected to social class over the century. But living in the suburbs became increasingly connected to affluence over the last half of the century, especially in the large metropolitan areas.

Life Cycle

While Americans substantially rearranged themselves geographically according to ancestry and class, they did not do so according to stage in the life cycle. Early in the century, children lived disproportionately in nonmetro-politan areas, but that difference narrowed as rural birth rates dropped to levels common in cities. Early in the century, children were also especially likely to live in suburbs rather than the center cities, but that pattern disap-peared as black and postwar immigrant families clustered in the center cities. The most substantial rearrangement of life-cycle geography was that never-married people increasingly clustered in metropolitan city centers. For most of the century, never-married adults lived in pretty much the same kinds of places that other adults did. In 1950, for instance, about one in five Americans age fifteen or older in all types of places had yet to marry. But by 2000 the kind of disparities shown in the bottom panel of figure 7.2—with more than half of center-city residents being unmarried (never-married, widowed, or divorced)—had appeared, largely the product of the presence of never-marrieds in city centers. Young adults who after the 1960s delayed marriage (see chapter 4) clustered in America's center cities and the down-towns of those cities.[59] The young singles life brings with it a distinct culture often identified with urban centers: active public spaces, entertainment businesses, and a slightly anti-establishment lifestyle. The concentration of this lifestyle in the big cities accelerated in the last decades of the century.

Summary

How Americans sorted out across types of communities changed sharply over the twentieth century. In 1900 America was a rural nation; in 2000 it was essentially a suburban nation. Within urban areas, deconcentration—growth on the outskirts eclipsing growth in the centers—accelerated. Along with shifts of population came shifts in social composition. Rural versus urban became a euphemism for native white versus "peoples of color," mainly because of the Great Migration northward of blacks and the immi-gration of Hispanics. The association of urban life with ethnic diversity, well understood early in the century when diversity meant European ethnics, grew much stronger. Not only did the more urban places continue to have concentrations of the foreign-born, but they also had concentrations of non-white residents.

More striking yet was the reorientation of city and suburb. At the begin-ning of the century, the residents of the centers and the suburbs differed much less in race and class than they would later on. Indeed, city people, im-migrant masses notwithstanding, were economically better off than people in the immediate hinterland. Then, the social distance between city and suburb widened as suburbs became more economically advantaged and remained white while the cities drew nonwhites. The new city-suburb contrast ap-peared on the ground, not just in the census: shopping malls and light indus-tries expanded in the suburbs, and abandoned plants and vacant stores multiplied in the centers; politicians increasingly catered to suburban rather than city voters; and the popular media found itself marketing "urban" styles, like hip-hop music, to white, suburban youth. The old polarities of North and South and of city and country resonated less and less, while the division of the inner and outer metropolis became more meaningful.[60]

COMING TOGETHER, DRIFTING APART: CHANGE IN SEGREGATION

Paradoxically, even as whites and nonwhites increasingly lived in distinct types of places, they became more integrated in particular neighborhoods.[61] This paradox is revealed by taking our analysis of metropolitan segregation in 2000 and extending it back forty years to 1960. Black-white segregation declined at the neighborhood level, but whites increasingly moved behind the walls of separate suburban communities. Separation by income widened, in part also because of suburban boundaries.

Segregation by Ancestry

Douglas Massey and Nancy Denton, in their award-winning book *American Apartheid*, described how African Americans in eleven of the nation's largest northern cities became much more segregated over most of the twentieth century up to 1980 and how many of them eventually lived in what the authors term "hyper-segregated" ghettos. Figure 7.6 is a schematic presentation, again using Theil's H index, of what happened after 1960 across all of metropolitan America. Had we comparable data for the earlier decades, they would show that the segregation of African Americans increased substantially from 1900 to 1960.[62] As figure 7.6 shows, however, overall segregation declined substantially after 1970. The top line of the figure traces the *total* residential segregation between blacks and nonblacks in metropolitan America from 1960 to 2000; blacks were less and less likely to live in ghettos. (Segregation patterns for Hispanics changed little over this period.[63] Also, the growing integration of African Americans applies as well to integration specifically with non-Hispanic whites; it was not simply integration with the rising numbers of Hispanics.)

The layers of this figure distinguish the *geographic level* of segregation. The bottom layer shows how much segregation between blacks and others can be accounted for by their living in different regions of the nation, the next layer up by their living in different metropolitan areas, the next up by their living in center cities versus suburbs, and the next up by their living in different places (essentially municipalities) within the suburban rings; the top layer shows how much segregation was neighborhood by neighborhood, where neighborhoods are defined as census tracts. Had we comparable data

Figure 7.6   Segregation of African Americans, by Year and Location of
the Segregation

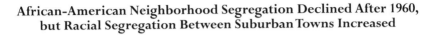

**African-American Neighborhood Segregation Declined After 1960,
but Racial Segregation Between Suburban Towns Increased**

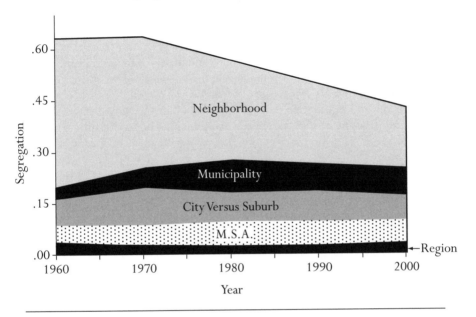

Source: Summary files from the census.
Note: Segregation measured using Theil's H measure.

for the early decades of the century, they would no doubt show that much of
the black-nonblack segregation then was a result of regional differences
(blacks were concentrated in the South) and that the locus of segregation
shifted toward the neighborhood in the middle decades of the century.[64] The
message of figure 7.6 is that the neighborhood-level segregation of blacks
declined substantially after 1970, but that segregation by municipality modestly *increased.* We interpret this to mean that black Americans increasingly
lived in more mixed neighborhoods, but that some nonblacks avoided integration by living in white suburban municipalities.[65]

Yet there is a seeming contradiction: how do we reconcile the long-term
trend for whites and blacks increasingly to live in separate *kinds* of places,
cities versus suburbs—as suggested in figure 7.4 and our discussion of it—
with the recent trend for them to live closer to one another in *specific* neigh-

borhoods, as shown in figure 7.6?[66] One part of the answer is the timing: African Americans clustered most in the center cities between 1950 and the 1970s, and European Americans left the center cities most rapidly during the same period; the major neighborhood desegregation happened afterwards.[67] Another part of the answer is that the calculations displayed in figure 7.4 combine diverse suburbs and cities into the same categories. For example, the suburbs of Houston and Seattle appear as "suburbs of large metropolitan areas," and the cities of Chicago and Los Angeles appear as "center cities of large metropolitan areas." The segregation analysis of figure 7.6, on the other hand, in effect matches and analyzes racial differences by city and suburb within specific metropolitan areas. Part of what explains the widening differences between city and suburb displayed in figure 7.4 is the shift of the white population from the eastern cities to the western suburbs. For example, 6 percent *fewer* whites lived in the Middle Atlantic states in 2000 than in 1960, while 60 percent *more* whites lived in the Pacific states in 2000 than in 1960.[68]

For these reasons, we believe both the story of greater racial differences by type of place and the story of greater neighborhood integration. Nationally, European Americans increasingly clustered in suburban communities (notably in Sun Belt suburbs), while "people of color" moved much more slowly from city to suburb. The city-suburb line, which obsessed urban sociologists in the 1960s and 1970s, became less of a barrier to racial integration as minorities moved into the inner suburbs around the big cities.[69] But municipal borders within the suburban regions became somewhat more significant barriers.[70]

For all these nuances, the trend toward neighborhood-level integration was substantial and probably the result of black economic advances, declines in racism, and enactment of fair housing legislation.[71] Urban scholars are quick to point out that segregation often persists at smaller units of geography; a block may appear integrated, for example, only because one side is all white and the other side is all black. Still, there is no gainsaying the clear decline in black segregation.

Segregation by Income

Widening economic inequality since 1970 (discussed in chapter 6) was reflected on the ground, especially in the increasing concentration of poor people. The ghettoization of poverty—that is, the tendency of poor people to live in neighborhoods with high concentrations of the poor—increased in the 1970s and 1980s and then dissipated somewhat during the booming 1990s. Paul Jargowsky estimates that in 1990, 15 percent of poor, urban Americans (30 percent of poor, urban, black Americans) lived in neighborhoods in which at least two of five residents were poor; in 2000 only 10 per-

Figure 7.7   Segregation of Richest Quintile in Family Income
by Year from Others and Location of the
Segregation

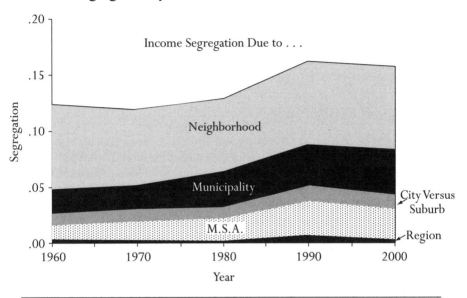

Segregation by Income Increased from 1970 to 1990

Income Segregation Due to . . .

Neighborhood

Municipality

City Versus
Suburb

M.S.A.

Region

Source: Summary files from the census.
Note: Segregation measured using Theil's H measure.

cent (19 percent of blacks) lived in neighborhoods with so much poverty.[72] Our calculations show similar but more modest trends toward more segregation by income and then, later, less segregation by income. Between 1970 and 1990, low-income urban Americans—those in the lowest quintile of household income—became moderately more segregated from other urban Americans, but their concentration abated slightly in the 1990s, consistent with Jargowsky's findings. At the other end of the spectrum, affluent Americans—those in the highest quintile—also became more segregated from other Americans between 1970 and 1990. Note that in figure 7.7 the scale of segregation is much less than in figure 7.6, because income segregation— at least for quintiles (not, say, the top 1 percent)—is much less than racial segregation. Overall, the index of segregation for the highest-income 20 percent grew from an H of .12 up through 1980 to an H of .16 afterwards.

The segregation of the affluent rose largely because they concentrated in certain metropolitan areas and in certain suburban municipalities.[73]

The trends for both black segregation and income segregation point to the growing importance of suburban municipalities. Affluent and white people separated themselves from others, not by keeping them out of their neighborhoods—that became relatively less important or perhaps less possible—but by retreating to suburban towns where housing costs and zoning laws impeded the less affluent and black from moving in.[74] In a significant parallel development over the same years, American students become more integrated *within* school districts—that is, specific schools became more diverse—but they became more segregated *between* school districts.[75]

Segregation by Stage in the Life Cycle

There has been talk of the increasing segregation of the elderly and children, the first by their migration to the Sun Belt and retirement communities and the second by the efforts of towns and developers to exclude them.[76] But we found little change between 1960 and 2000 in the clustering or dispersion of either the elderly or children. On the other hand, the segregation of the unmarried from the married and of eighteen- to twenty-nine-year-olds from others, although modest in comparison to racial or class segregation, did grow after 1960. This corresponds to our earlier finding that these groups increasingly clustered in metropolitan center cities.[77]

The evidence we have used in this discussion of segregation does not speak to centurylong trends, only to what happened in roughly the last half of the century. Americans were segregated far more by race than by income, and by income much more than by life cycle. Racial separation declined substantially, however, while income segregation rose moderately and life-cycle segregation a little. These are further signs—like those noted in other chapters—that even if Americans in 2000 remained heavily divided by race and ethnicity, those divisions were closing, and that divisions by class and, perhaps, stage in the life cycle were widening.

CONCLUSION

Key American divisions by ancestry, class, and marital status once corresponded strongly to region—the South was native-born, black, and poor, and the West unmarried—and strongly to rural-urban distinctions—people in the country tended to be farmers, to be more commonly poor and black, and to have large families. Most of these regional and rural-urban contrasts faded during the twentieth century, with the very notable exception of ancestry, and there the rural-urban contrast reversed. African Americans once concentrated in rural and small-town America and European Americans in urban places, but by the end of the century African Americans and other nonwhites were very much city people, and European Americans were rural and suburban. Given the powerful role of race in America, this new and strong connection between ancestry and type of community has profound consequences for everything from pop culture to political strategies. Yet over the century, most social divides among Americans increasingly coincided with neither region nor rural-versus-urban, but with city versus suburb. City people were more often non-European, of lower income, and unmarried. The geographic axes of American differences shifted.

Our examination of metropolitan residential segregation from 1960 through 2000 casts further light on this reorientation. Segregation—and by far the greatest segregation in America is by race and ethnicity—became relatively less important at the neighborhood level, while it became more important at the level of specific towns: segregation between center cities and suburban rings in midcentury and segregation between towns within the suburban ring later. The newer developments suggest that, with the aging of inner suburbs and the movement of minorities and poor people beyond the center city, the emerging form of residential differentiation is by specific municipality. In some cases, the suburban enclaves are not even municipalities at all, but private governments in literally or figuratively "gated" communities.[78] The old and simple polarities of America's social geography are dissolving into more finely graded, politically based mosaics. This too is of major consequence, because so much of America's civic life and the fortunes of its citizens are still tied to the places where they live.

CHAPTER EIGHT

How Americans Prayed: Religious Diversity and Change

FROM THE beginning of the nation, foreign observers noted how much more devout Americans were than the European peoples from whom they had sprung. That devotion increased over the nineteenth century as higher proportions of Americans became "churched." A century ago, British ambassador to America Lord Bryce wrote that "Christianity influences conduct [in America] . . . probably more than it does in any other modern country, and far more than it did in the so-called ages of faith." Surveys in the latter part of the twentieth century repeatedly found that among Western people Americans most commonly believed in God, practiced religion, and reported religion to be important in their lives.[1] George Bush's 2004 reelection on the wings of church-based mobilization converted the last skeptics on the importance of religion in the United States.

Americans exercise religious faith in hundreds of different ways. Immigrants brought with them faiths from around the world, and Americans launched many religious movements of their own, which then spread elsewhere—including the Unitarians, Mormons, Seventh-Day Adventists, Jehovah's Witnesses, and Christian Scientists. Even in the colonial era, this religious diversity attracted notice. The commingling of groups such as Quakers, Calvinists, Jews, Anglicans, Catholics, Mennonites, and Presbyterians, as well as people of smaller sects, "Free Thinkers," and the very many who were "unchurched," seemed bizarre to visitors from an Old World where, for the most part, every person in a region was a member of a single state-supported church. Although established churches were part of colo-

nial and early America too (until 1833—notably Congregationalism in New
England and the Church of England in the South), religious pluralism distinguished the new nation, and that pluralism only increased over the decades.[2]
    Religious diversity has repeatedly and seriously divided the nation,
most persistently Catholic immigrants' efforts to resist "Protestantization"
in matters from temperance to Bible reading in schools. Even at the end of
the twentieth century, when about half of Americans who professed a religion saw themselves as "strong" adherents, an equal fraction saw religious
people as intolerant of others' views.[3] Throughout American history, religion served to unite the nation, particularly in times of trouble. Lincoln
invoked God in his inaugural addresses, Franklin Roosevelt led the nation
in prayer during World War II, Lyndon Johnson asked for prayers following the assassination of President Kennedy, and congressional leaders burst
into a spontaneous singing of "God Bless America" following the attacks of
September 11, 2001. At the end of the last century, great majorities of
Americans felt that religion promotes a better society and better families,
and seven of ten adults wanted the influence of religion to grow. And yet,
to the bafflement of any strict theologian, Americans were also tolerant of
religious diversity, stipulating that it did not matter *which* religion gained
influence.[4]
    In this chapter, we describe American religious diversity, document its
development, and weigh its implications. Already diverse by European
standards in 1900, religion in America grew even more diverse throughout
the twentieth century. Demography was far more important than religious
conversions in creating religious difference: immigration and birth rates favored some denominations over others. A wave of immigration in the first
quarter of the century and another wave in the last quarter brought in
many millions of people from Catholic, Jewish, Buddhist, and nonreligious
backgrounds and relatively few from Protestant countries. Differences in
childbearing—mainline Protestants and Jews tended to have fewer children, conservative Protestants and Catholics to have more—amplified
these differences. For example, Protestants declined from almost 80 percent of the population in 1900 to 60 percent in 2000. This dramatic shift
led to some serious tension, fueling, for example, restrictions on immigration in the 1920s, but two factors seemed to mitigate the challenges of diversity. One was the increasing internal diversity within American Protestantism, and the other was an increasing tolerance—perhaps even
preference—for religious variety. Over the century, Americans embraced
a live-and-let-live ethos—or perhaps a pray-and-let-pray (or not) ethos. It
was President Dwight Eisenhower who famously said, "Our Government
has no sense unless it is founded in a deeply felt religious faith—and I don't
care what it is."[5]

RELIGIOUS DIVERSITY IN 2000

In the middle of the twentieth century, a best-selling book by the journalist Will Herberg, *Protestant, Catholic, Jew*, captured the common notion that the United States was a "Judeo-Christian" nation.[6] By the end of the century, Americans were acutely more aware that some people were outside that category: Muslims, Hindus, Buddhists, members of new sects, and religious skeptics. To describe the religious status of Americans in 2000, we must consider two realms of religion. One is the organized infrastructure of denominations, churches, and codified theologies that makes up *public* religion. People attend services, and they pay dues or contribute as they participate in organized religion. The second realm is that of the *private* beliefs that people hold and the rituals they practice. The public and private realms overlap only partly: in the 1990s, for example, one-third of Americans who answered "yes" when asked if they "had a religious preference" nevertheless said that they attended religious services only once a year or less. And at the same time, about half of the people who said they had *no* religious preference nevertheless said that they believed in God.

Religious Identification

We begin with the first feature of religion, its organization, looking specifically at the variety of religious identities Americans had. Figure 8.1 shows the distribution of adults among the major religious categories around 2000.[7] It is based on their answers to the question, "What is your religious preference? Is it Protestant, Catholic, Jewish, some other religion, or no religion?"[8] About 56 percent of American adults identified themselves as Protestants—counting unhyphenated "Christians" as Protestants—and about one-fourth as Catholic. Jews, also part of the Western religious tradition, were but 2 percent. Other religious traditions—Eastern or Orthodox Catholic, Muslim, Buddhist, and other Eastern religions—claimed about one-half of 1 percent each.[9] Almost 2 percent of American adults provided other sorts of replies, including "interdenominational," "pagan," and traditional faiths associated with Native Americans. Fourteen percent of American adults answered "no religion." Later in the chapter, we look more closely at these Americans who claimed no religion. We simply note here that only a minority of these Americans were explicitly atheist or agnostic in their beliefs; what generally typified these people was a rejection of *organized* religion.

Protestants come in hundreds of specific denominations. Some are large and well known, such as the Southern Baptist Convention and the Episcopal Church. Others are collections of small denominations that have merged to form larger organizations, like the Presbyterian Church (USA), the United Methodist Church, and the Church of Jesus Christ of Latter-Day Saints.

Figure 8.1   Current Religious Preferences of American Adults Age
                    Twenty-Five to Seventy-Four

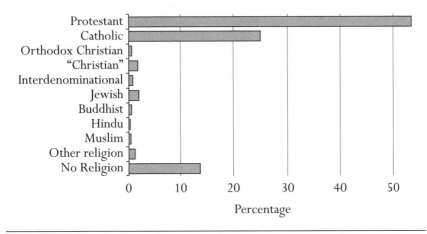

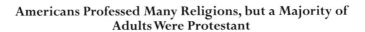

Source: GSS, 1998 to 2002.

Most are smaller or less centralized organizations of individual congregations. For example, the Christian Holiness Partnership (founded in 1867)
was "officially made up of 21 different denominations, three interdenominational missionary agencies, 48 colleges and seminaries, six Holiness publish-
ing houses, nearly 2,000 camp meetings, and hundreds of independent congregations and local churches that belong to denominations that are not
officially identified as members."[10] Figure 8.2 shows how Protestants distributed themselves across denominations and aggregations of specific denominations. We have grouped the Protestant denominations into four types
based on how conservative their doctrines were: conservative, moderate,
liberal, or not able to be categorized.[11] We do not imply that all people in a
denomination were similar in their personal beliefs; the categories are based
on the doctrinal stances of the denominations, not on individuals, who often
deviate considerably from their own denomination's theology.

   In 2000 the Southern Baptist Convention was the single largest specific
denomination, with 15 percent of Protestant adults. Other, smaller conservative Baptist organizations combined to make the largest aggregation. Together, conservative Baptists accounted for one-third of all Protestants.
Methodists of all types were next with 14 percent of Protestant adults.
Lutherans were 10 percent, but they split, with one-third of Lutherans in

Figure 8.2   Denominations of Protestant Adults

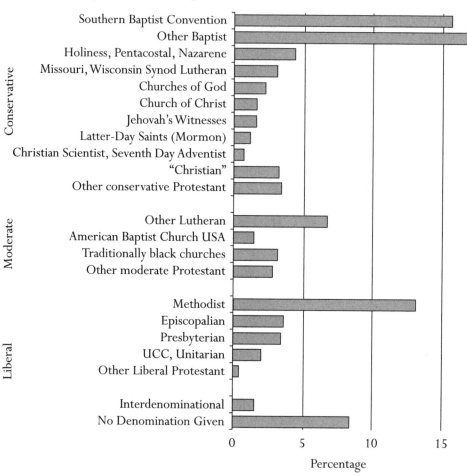

Baptist Was the Largest Protestant Denomination

Source: GSS, 1998 to 2002.
Notes: UCC = United Church of Christ. The "no denomination" category includes people who named a denomination that NORC could find no information on. Percentages sum to 100 percent.

the conservative Missouri or Wisconsin synods while the rest (mostly in the Evangelical Lutheran Church of America) were doctrinal moderates. Some highly visible denominations had fewer adherents than less prominent ones. For example, the Church of Jesus Christ of Latter-Day Saints (the Mormons) were just 1 percent of the GSS respondents.[12] The Jehovah's Witnesses were a slightly bigger share, and the Christian Scientists slightly smaller. Meanwhile, adherents of the largely invisible Holiness and Pentecostal churches were three to four times more numerous as those in the Church of God, the Church of Christ, and similar denominations. Finally, those branches of Protestantism that can trace themselves back to the Pilgrims and Puritans—so important in colonial times and in our national memory—made up but 2 percent of American adults in 2000. These groups had organized themselves into the Reformed and Congregational churches by the end of the eighteenth century and in 1957 joined to form the United Church of Christ. (In the figure, we also add to their number the Unitarians, who were originally an offshoot of the Congregationalists.) The shrinkage of these once-dominant branches of Protestantism testifies to the dynamic changes in organized religion across American history.[13]

Religious Participation

The most common connection that Americans had to their churches, synagogues, and temples was through their membership in the organization and their attendance at religious services. At the end of the twentieth century, about two-thirds of Americans claimed membership in a church or synagogue, and about one-third of Americans claimed to attend religious services weekly or nearly weekly. Scholars argue about how accurate these reports of attendance are. Most acknowledge that respondents tend to err in the direction of overreporting attendance and also that people who are religiously active are more likely to answer surveys. The survey-based estimate of church attendance is probably 10 to 30 percent too high as a measure of a typical Sunday's congregations. If we take people's statements not so literally but as an indication of their relative attachment to organized religion, we can ask both how Americans compare to other people and how some Americans compare with others.

Americans reported higher rates of attendance than did people in Great Britain, France, Germany, and the Scandinavian countries.[14] Among Americans, there was notable variation by religion and by Protestant denomination in reported rates of near-weekly attendance. For example, in the late 1990s, 60 percent of people belonging to small conservative congregations and groups reported near-weekly attendance, compared to 41 percent of those in the Southern Baptist Convention, one-third of Episcopalians and Catholics, and 9 percent of Jews.[15]

Religious Belief

Membership and attendance numbers describe Americans' connections to organized religion in 2000. What about Americans' private beliefs and practices? Surveys generally find that upwards of 90 percent of Americans said they believe in God.[16] In the GSS, 86 percent of Americans said that they believed in God, and another 8 percent believed in a "universal spirit or higher power," while only 5 percent disbelieved both. Answers to other questions reveal that huge majorities of Americans endorsed specific religious stances: 54 percent described themselves as religious, and another 30 percent said they were "spiritual"; 79 percent agreed that "there will be a day when God judges whether you go to heaven or hell"; 61 percent said that religion was "very important" in their lives; and 46 percent labeled themselves as "born again" or "evangelical." Ninety percent of Americans said that they prayed, three of four said that they prayed every day, and nearly all who prayed thought that their prayers were heard.[17]

Yet, given such intense religious feelings, it is noteworthy that 75 percent of American adults said "yes" when they were asked, "Do you think there is any religion other than your own that offers a true path to God?" and over 80 percent of those said such paths were just as good as their own. Similarly, three-fourths of Americans said that many religions—not just their own— "can lead to eternal life." This Eisenhowerian ecumenism was an important feature of Americans' religious thinking in 2000; most balanced their deep faith with a commitment to free choice and openness to other paths.[18]

RELIGIOUS DIVERSITY INCREASED IN THE TWENTIETH CENTURY

To understand how Americans reached this level of faith and diversity over the course of the twentieth century, we draw mostly on two sorts of survey data. One set tabulates the religious affiliations and convictions of representative samples of American adults, as reported to survey researchers from about 1950 through 2000. Before 1950, the data are sparse and sometimes suspect. The second set includes the answers given by respondents to the General Social Surveys of 1972 through 2000 when asked about religion in their childhoods. This allows us to extend our view back to about 1900, the adolescent years of the oldest respondents. The retrospective technique has the side benefit of removing differences by age, since it gives us a religious picture of youths in each decade of the century. The drawback of retrospection is that, to some extent, people do misremember their youths. The direction of this bias, it is reasonable to suspect, is to inflate the religiosity of childhood.

Identification

We tell the story in three parts. First, we distinguish Americans who affiliated with the dominant, Western, Judeo-Christian faiths from those who identified with other traditions and from those who professed no religious affiliation. We look closely at who claimed "no religion." Second, we examine trends in the divisions among Protestant, Catholic, and Jew. Third, we look within the largest and most diverse group, the Protestants. The left-hand side of figure 8.3 summarizes the results of Gallup polls, Roper surveys, and the GSS from 1947 through 2000 (the early ones are exclusively Gallup) to questions about respondents' religious affiliations. On the right-hand side of the figure, we use GSS respondents' answers to the question "In what religion were you raised?" to describe the religious distribution of American teenagers from about 1904 through 1995.[19] Both figures tell the same story: Americans were almost all Protestants, Catholics, or Jews into the 1960s. In 1966 *Time* magazine's cover story "Is God Dead?" sparked national discussions about faith, and indeed, around 1970 the total hegemony of mainline Western faiths started to weaken, dropping under 95 percent in 1972. Increasing proportions of Americans began reporting "other" religions[20] or no religion.[21] (Because we have "smoothed" the lines, the figures understate how suddenly the "no religion" responses increased in the 1990s.)[22] In any case, religious diversity across the global boundaries of religion increased in the last third of the century.

In understanding the increase in the tendency to prefer no religion, it would be a mistake to equate claiming no religion preference with having a secular worldview, because American adults who reported being raised with no religion (right-hand side of figure 8.3) or currently having no religion (left-hand side) were largely distinguishable not by their lack of belief but by their rejection of organized religion.[23] Most held a conventional cluster of religious beliefs. For example, about one-fifth of those who, across all the years of the GSS, reported no religious preference also said that they had no doubts that God existed; another one-fifth said that they believed in God although they occasionally had doubts; and another one-fourth said that they believed in a "higher power." In 1998 almost 60 percent of "nones" said that they believed "that God watches over me," and nearly 40 percent reported praying at least weekly. What stood out about these respondents was their aversion to religious services and their disdain for organized religion. The rejection of formal religion, much more than loss of faith, also explains (along with demographic changes such as delayed marriage) most of the 1990s upswing in the proportion claiming no religion. An additional factor contributed to that development: the increasing identification of churches with conservative politics led political moderates and liberals who were al-

Figure 8.3   Religious Preference, by Year and Type of Data

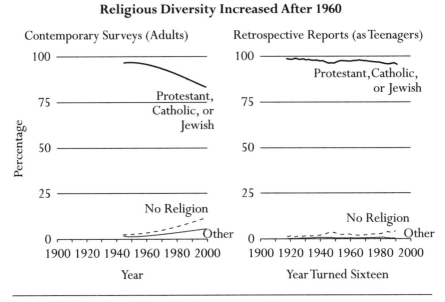

Religious Diversity Increased After 1960

Contemporary Surveys (Adults)

Retrospective Reports (as Teenagers)

Sources: Gallup and Roper polls, NORC surveys, and GSS.
Note: Data smoothed by seven-year moving average.

ready weakly committed to religion to make the political statement of rejecting a religious identification. (In other words, if being religious seemed to mean being right-wing, then they spurned a religious identity.) Whether this politicization will grow into the anticlericalism familiar to Europeans remains to be seen.[24]

The recent increases in the proportion of American adults professing no religion, together with the slight increase in people holding to religions outside the Judeo-Christian tradition, have weakened the monopoly of Western faith traditions in America. Protestantism, Catholicism, and Judaism claimed over 95 percent of Americans from 1900 to 1968, but only 83 percent of them in 2000. Culturally, the diversification may be less than these numbers suggest. Researchers have noted, for example, that non-Western immigrants at the end of the century adapted their religious practices and even their theologies toward mainstream American ones, just as Catholics and Jews had assimilated elements of Protestantism a century earlier (a point we return to near the end of this chapter).[25]

Figure 8.4   Religious Preference of Christians and Jews, by Year and Type of Data

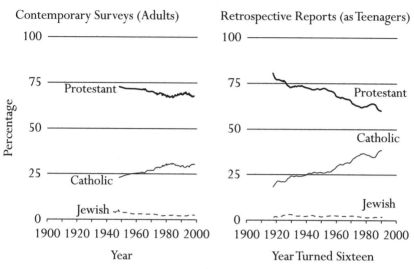

Religious Diversity Among Western Faiths Increased Throughout the Century

Sources: Gallup and Roper polls, NORC surveys, and GSS.
Note: Data smoothed by seven-year moving average.

Protestant, Catholic, and Jew

We turn next to the changes in religious affiliation among Western religions. The graphs on the left- and right-hand sides of figure 8.4 are drawn from the same data we used to make figure 8.3, but now we focus on the three major religious groups. There are a few minor discrepancies between the two sides of the figure, as one might expect given that the left-hand side describes the affiliations of adults and the right-hand side those of youth. (So, for example, Jews were 3 percent of adults but only 1 percent of teens in the late 1990s.) Nonetheless, the overall stories are parallel.[26] Protestants made up a sharply declining percentage of the Western religion category, and Catholics a sharply increasing proportion. Immigration and differences in birth rates help explain this weakening of the Protestant majority. American adults who immigrated from elsewhere early in the century were about equally as likely to be Catholic as Protestant, but among those who immigrated near the end of the century, the Catholic-reared outnumbered the Protestant-reared by better than five to one.[27] Immigration increasingly contributed Catholics (as well as "others," as we saw earlier) to America's religious diversity. The graph on the right-hand side of figure 8.4—the religious affiliations of *native* youth from 1904 on—shows a dramatic shift in proportions, from almost eighty-twenty Protestant-Catholic for those who were teens around 1910 to about sixty-forty Protestant-Catholic for those who were teens in the 1990s. (The adult lines on the left-hand side show a weaker trend toward Catholicism than do the youth figures on the right-hand side because a growing proportion of Catholics converted to Protestantism in the later years of the century—largely in reaction to the Vatican's rejection of divorce.)[28] By any measure, the numerical dominance of Protestants had declined by the end of the century. Combining the data of figures 8.3 and 8.4, we see that the proportion of all native-born Americans who professed Protestantism dropped from nearly 80 percent in the first decade of the century to 50 percent in the last decade—a tremendous diversification of American religion.[29]

The Restructuring of American Protestantism

The "mainline" denominations, which once made up two-thirds of American Protestants, declined in size—most relatively but some absolutely too. Figure 8.5 displays the retrospective youth data from the GSS. The Methodists, Presbyterians, Episcopalians, and Lutherans claimed smaller shares of American youth, while Baptists and "others" increased their shares.[30] Although American Protestants generally shifted toward the more conservative churches, they also became more organizationally diverse, with, for example, schisms producing more denominations within the larger categories (for example, more variants of Lutheranism).[31] Also, the growing "other" group was composed of dozens of small denominations and sects.

Demographic changes were largely responsible for the conservative drift among Protestants, just as they were for the declining proportion of Protestants in the general population. The shift from a sixty-forty split in favor of mainline denominations to a forty-sixty split was mostly due to the conservatives' higher fertility and earlier childbearing. A detailed analysis attributes 70 percent of the growth of the conservative denominations to their advantage in producing children; the remainder—and more of the later change—stemmed from conservative youth moving to a mainline denomination in adulthood. Historically, upwardly mobile conservative Protestants often joined an affluent and moderate denomination; by the end of the century, they more often stayed in a conservative denomination.[32]

There is also some evidence that individual churches within Protestant denominations became more doctrinally diverse. For example, both conservative and mainline denominations debated issues regarding the ordination of women and the acceptance of gays.[33] Mark Chaves's detailed analyses of women's ordination issues are exemplary on this point. He shows how dis-

Figure 8.5   Protestants' Specific Denominations, by Cohort (Year Turned Sixteen)

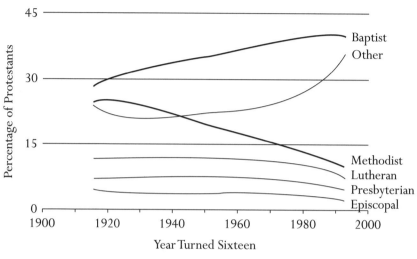

Baptists and Others Increased, While Methodists Declined

Source: GSS.

Note: Data smoothed using locally estimated (loess) regression.

putes resolved at the denominational level persisted at the local level because, even though a denomination may have taken a decision to allow a practice, traditions of local autonomy gave rise to disagreements within congregations about whether to conform. In the end, this local adaptation to a national (or international) decision led to differentiation below the denominational level.[34]

Religious Persistence and Switching

Underneath the organizational recombinations from religious mergers and schisms, and in addition to the consequences of immigration and differential birth rates, religious change is produced by individuals' personal decisions to continue in or to leave the faith in which they were raised. In 2000 almost 75 percent of adults identified with the religion of their youth.[35] Many Americans (half of people raised Protestant and 30 percent of people raised Catholic or Jewish) "shop around" for a church, but few "buy" the new brand.[36] Indeed, a follow-up question indicated that most "shopping" occurs in connection with a move from one city or town to another.[37]

Figure 8.6 shows the percentage of adults whose religion at the time they were interviewed was the same as the one they said they were raised in, arranged by the year they turned sixteen, as before. The figure permits us to see historical change in switching religions. The top row shows that Protestants' tendency to prefer the denominations of their youth differs by the type of denomination.[38] People raised in conservative denominations were less likely than other Protestants to change: overall 77 percent stayed in the same tradition. Those raised in moderate or liberal denominations were likelier to go elsewhere, averaging 68 and 63 percent "stayers," respectively. None of the three Protestant groups showed any trend toward more or less denominational persistence over the century.[39] The second row of figure 8.6 shows the religious stability of people raised Catholic, Jewish, or with no religion. Catholics born in the first decade of the twentieth century were the most stable—over 90 percent of them persisted as Catholics—but that rate dropped substantially, to merely 72 percent, for cohorts that turned sixteen in the 1970s or later. (The small number of Jews in each cohort makes the apparent decline in their persistence since the 1960s uncertain.) Finally, early in the century people raised without religion were very likely to acquire a religious preference in adulthood—typically upon marriage. That changed after World War II, and in the later years of the century people who were raised without a religion were as likely to stay in their "tradition" as were those raised in a religion.

Most people who switch move to a similar denomination.[40] Two-thirds of people who switched out of the Protestant denomination of their youth in the 1960s through the 1990s chose another Protestant destination, one-tenth became Catholic, and one-fifth said they had no religious preference. Among switchers out of Catholicism who reached adulthood after 1960, about half became Protestant and a bit more than one-third claimed no religious preference. One-third of switchers out of Judaism in that time period became Christians, and the other two-thirds adopted no religious preference. Of those people who were raised with no religion but took up religion as adults, 75 percent became Protestant, 14 percent became Catholic, and 3 percent became Jewish. Overall, religious switching for people who reached adulthood after 1960 increased religious diversity as it helped to swell the numbers with "no religion."

Yet the great majority of Americans stayed with the religion and denomination of their youth. Religious diversity increased largely as Catholic and Jewish immigrants brought their faiths with them from abroad in the early part of the twentieth century, as new immigrants brought other faiths with them after the 1970s, and as the practice of no religion at all became a sta-

Figure 8.6 Religious Immobility, by Year Turned Sixteen and Denomination

Three of Four Americans Stayed with the Denomination They Were Raised In

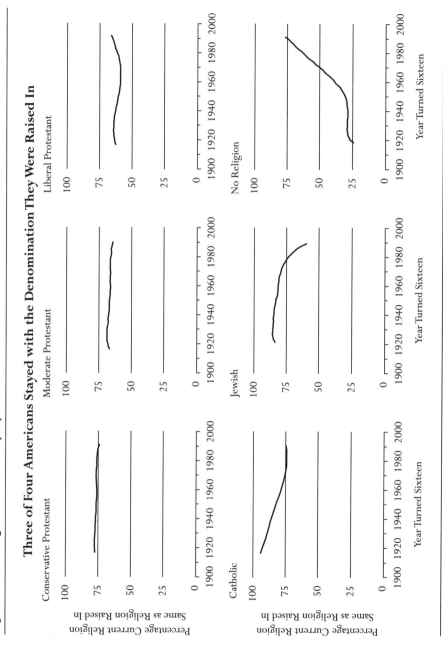

Source: GSS.

ble part of the religious marketplace. Individual change or conversion was a minor contributor to the kaleidoscope of religion in America.

AMERICAN ATTITUDES TOWARD RELIGIOUS DIVERSITY

Americans in the latter part of the century encountered increasing religious diversity, including greater numbers of fellow Americans who were outside the Judeo-Christian tradition or who stood apart from organized religion altogether. Historically, Americans have been noted as relatively accepting—relative to people of the Old World—of religious differences, and they seemed to become more so over the twentieth century. In the 1920s, the sociologists Robert and Helen Lynd studied Muncie, Indiana—which they labeled "Middletown"—as an archetypal American town. In the 1970s, other sociologists returned to Middletown to assess changes there. Much had changed, of course, but one dramatic change was a massive decline in the proportion of Middletown youth who agreed that "Christianity is the one true religion and everyone should be converted to it."[41] Another indicator of emerging tolerance is a question that the Gallup organization has asked over the years: "If your party nominated a generally well-qualified person for president who happened to be [fill in], would you vote for that person?" The options for filling in the blank are a Jew, a Catholic, an atheist, a woman, or a black. As we discuss in chapter 9, acceptance of Jewish or Catholic presidential candidates increased from 50 percent to almost all Americans between 1937 and 2000. And by 2000 about half of Americans said they were also willing to vote for an atheist, up substantially from decades earlier.[42]

Of course, telling an interviewer that one would vote for a Jew, Catholic, or atheist is different from actually doing so, but nonetheless, the change in the climate of opinion is impressive. The 1928, 1960, and 1976 presidential races can be thought of as practical tests of the avowed religious tolerance of Americans. The Democrats nominated Catholic candidates for president in 1928 (Al Smith) and 1960 (John F. Kennedy), and in 1976 they nominated a born-again Christian, Jimmy Carter. Smith lost, but Kennedy and Carter won, as did avowed "born-again" George W. Bush, Republican, in 2000. In none of these elections could the candidates have won without the support of the majorities outside their religious affiliations. Of course, people weigh many issues when making their choice for president, but public discussions leading up to each of these elections indicate that religion was on people's minds. Scholars have investigated each of these elections, especially the 1960 and 1976 ones.[43] Surveys of American voters in 1960 indicate that many took Kennedy's religion into account when they voted. However, Catholics were more likely than Protestants or Jews to say they considered

Kennedy's religion when deciding how to cast their vote, and they saw his Catholic religion as a reason to vote for him. Very few Protestants said that they voted for Nixon instead just because Kennedy was Catholic. Most tellingly, the voting tendencies of Protestants and Catholics reverted to their 1950s patterns when Johnson beat Goldwater in 1964. Similarly in 1976, the attraction of a coreligionist got Baptists who might have otherwise backed Ford to vote for Jimmy Carter in 1976; as in 1960, there is no evidence that others were dissuaded from voting Democratic by the candidate's religion.

Americans' religious tolerance also extended to the areligious or irreligious. In the last half of the century, a few polls asked respondents whether someone could be a Christian without attending church; 70 percent or more said "yes."[44] Broader evidence is to be found in the surveys taken since the 1950s that have asked people whether "somebody who is against all churches and religion" should be banned from making speeches "in your community" or whether such a person should be "allowed to teach in a college or university." The percentage of American adults who favored banning the speech of skeptics fell from 35 percent in the early 1970s to 25 percent in the period 1996 to 2000; the percentage who thought skeptics should not be allowed to teach fell from 58 to 41 percent; and the percentage who would remove a book critical of God and religion from the library fell from 38 to 29 percent.[45]

Americans also became more tolerant of intimate relations across religious lines. Polls have occasionally asked whether respondents approve or disapprove of religious intermarriage. A generational difference opened up in the 1960s, with younger Americans being more tolerant of religious intermarriage than earlier birth cohorts.[46] Behavior followed attitudes as actual intermarriage increased between Jews and Gentiles, between Catholics and Protestants, and between Protestant denominations—with the possible exception of the most conservative denominations.[47] Figure 8.7 shows the trend, by birth cohort, for the percentage of GSS respondents who said that they were Protestant, Catholic, or Jewish and that their spouse *currently espoused* a different religion (solid line). It also shows the rates of intermarriage by Protestants across major denominations (dashed line).[48] Note also that the largest change occurred between the 1920 to 1939 and the 1940 to 1959 cohorts, cohorts divided by whether they matured before or after the 1960s.

Over the twentieth century, then, and especially during the "long 1960s," Americans became much more accepting of diversity in general and of religious diversity in particular, even within their own marriages. A dramatic illustration of this widening acceptance is that in 2000 half of American Jews, who historically have severely shunned intermarriage, agreed that "it is racist to oppose Jewish-gentile marriages."[49]

Figure 8.7   Married Couples with Different Religions (Protestant, Catholic, Jewish) or Different Denominations (Among Protestants), by Birth Cohort

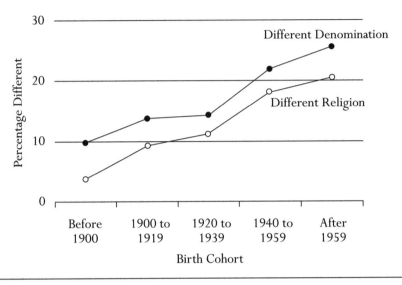

Americans Were Increasingly Likely to Be Married to Someone of a Different Religion

Source: GSS, 1974 to 1994.

PERSONAL PRACTICE AND BELIEF

The institutional diversity of American religion grew in the twentieth century, as did tolerance of that diversity. But what happened to personal piety—to belief and practice? The conventional wisdom is that modern Americans were, setting aside a handful of fundamentalists, less religious than their ancestors. But this is not what historians of religion have concluded. Although the beliefs and practices of people long ago are difficult to measure, the best assessment is that during the nineteenth century Americans became *more* religious, not less. Adults were more likely to join churches, to understand Christian theology, and to practice their faiths systematically in 1876 than in 1776. This trend of *increasing* religiosity continued through at least most of the twentieth century.[50] Here we focus on the latter part of the twentieth century and explore two general questions: In the midst of increasing diversity, how did average Americans' religiosity

change? And did Americans become more or less divided in religious practice and belief?

Public Practice: Belonging and Attending

Figure 8.8 shows long-term trends in church membership and attendance as
reported to the Gallup and Roper polls. The top line shows the proportion
of respondents who answered "yes" when asked if they "happen[ed] to be a
member of a church or synagogue"; the bottom line shows the proportion
of respondents who answered "yes" when asked if they "happen[ed] to attend
church or synagogue in the last seven days, or not?"[51] The findings should be
taken with some reservation because, as we noted earlier, respondents
sometimes exaggerate membership and attendance and religiously active
people more often answer surveys. Also, the results for the earliest years
should be taken with special reservation because polling methods were not
as accurate then.[52] But the long-term trends, rather than the absolute numbers, are what interest us here.

Two general impressions emerge from the data. First, there was not
much change in the last half of the twentieth century in either membership
or attendance, at least relative to seasonal fluctuations. Americans reported
membership rates in the low 70 percent range around 1950 and in the high
60 percent range in the late 1990s; they reported weekly attendance in the
high 40 percent range in the mid-1950s and in the low 40 percent range in
the late 1990s. Second, the marginal changes we can observe suggest that
membership and attendance rose to a peak in the 1950s, declined in the
1960s and 1970s, and then leveled off in the 1990s.

If we try to peer back before the 1940s, we have only fragmentary data—
the occasional survey here or there done with uncertain methods. But these
fragments suggest that Americans in the first four decades were *less* often
church members than was true later and that they attended services at rates
no higher than those of Americans in the latter half of the century. One example is, again, the classic study of "Middletown" conducted in 1924. The
researchers counted Sunday service attendees at "the forty-two religious
bodies" in the fall of that year and calculated that, "although the tradition is
that 'every one goes to church,'" only 16 percent of Middletown's white
men and 25 percent of its white women attended either morning or evening
services on an average Sunday. (Decades later a follow-up study concluded
that attendance rates had increased by 1977.) Such evidence reinforces the
impression that church activity peaked around 1960.[53]

The stability in attendance, at least since the rates returned in the late
1960s to pre-1950s levels, masks two countervailing trends. First, the later
in the century Americans were born, the lower their attendance rates were.
About half of those born before 1900 were likely to have attended services

Figure 8.8   Membership in Churches and Participation in Religious Services by Year

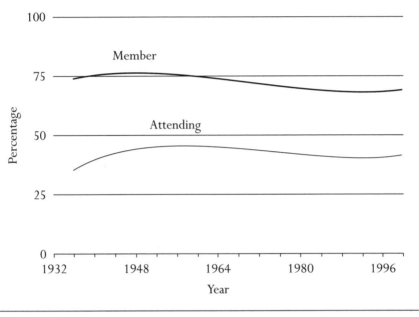

Membership in Churches and Attendance at Services Changed Little, 1937 to 2000

Source: Membership (Gallup Polls); Attendance (Gallup and Roper Polls).
Note: Data smoothed using cubic equations.

in the previous week, but only about one-quarter of those born since 1960 had. Second, people attend more often as they age, marry, and raise children, and this tendency roughly counterbalances the generational change. Since the average age of Americans rose (from twenty-three in 1900 to thirty in 1980, to thirty-five in 2000), the two tendencies produced a flat trend line after the 1960s.[54]

The trend in attendance, however, was not flat for everyone. We pooled Gallup polls from 1957—just about the peak of reported attendance—and 1968 with the later General Social Surveys and used the statistical technique described in appendix A to smooth the trend lines. Figure 8.9 shows that history of attendance varied greatly by religious affiliation. The real change was among Catholics: around midcentury, 80 percent reported weekly attendance, but by the end of the century only 30 percent did. Changes in at-

Figure 8.9   Attendance at Religious Services, by Year and Denomination

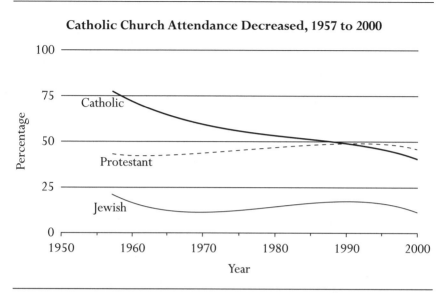

Catholic Church Attendance Decreased, 1957 to 2000

Source: Gallup polls and GSS.
Note: Data smoothed using locally estimated (loess) regression.

tendance among Protestants and Jews (also among "others" and "nones"; not shown) were not statistically significant. (Catholics similarly experienced a substantial decline in attendance across *generations*.)[55]

GSS surveys conducted in 1991 and 1998 give us a wider, albeit rose-tinted, window on the century. Respondents were asked, "And what about when you were around eleven or twelve, how often did you attend religious services then?" Assuming that these reports are accurate, the results show that between 1930 and 1960, 80 percent of children attended regularly; attendance then dropped steadily to 60 percent in the 1980s. If we assume instead some nostalgia—as would be suggested by the contemporaneous reports of attendance from earlier years that we noted before—then the drop since the 1960s was not so great. In either case, comparisons between Protestants and Catholics should not be distorted by differential tendencies to nostalgia. And these retrospective reports roughly reinforce the pattern shown in figure 8.9: relatively little change in attendance among those reared as Protestants, and a major decline since the 1950s for Catholics.[56]

The decline in Catholic attendance we observe is consistent with studies showing that about one-third of the Catholics who had been attending weekly through the years of the Second Vatican Council (1962 to 1965) became less frequent attenders immediately after the birth control encyclical, *Humanae Vitae*, in 1968. Another 10 percent or so of Catholic adults cut back on their church attendance between 1968 and 1975.[57] Since then, cohorts socialized into the less rigorous regime of occasional attendance have replaced the cohorts that maintained high standards of attendance, leading to a slow but steady decrease in weekly attendance rates for Catholics. Largely because of the Catholic trend, the data also show a *convergence* among the larger religious groups over the years (and over generations) in rates of attendance.

Although Protestants who identified with conservative denominations were more likely than liberal ones to attend services in any given week, there is no evidence of greater or lesser change in attendance for one or the other type of denomination. Methodist churches might not be as full as they used to be, and the Pentecostal and Baptist churches are presumably fuller, but that is because there are fewer Methodists and more Pentecostals and Baptists. The only noteworthy exception to the overall flat attendance trend lines for Protestants was a regional convergence: attendance among southern Protestants dropped toward the level of Protestants in other regions. Looking at change across birth cohorts reveals a *convergence* in Protestants' attendance patterns across a variety of traits, with the possible exception of parents versus nonparents.[58]

The sociologist Mark Chaves aptly called the church, even in the late twentieth century, "America's principal site of culture creation," and the changes in attendance we have reviewed here over the last half of that century are variations on a comparatively—by international and historical standards—high level of involvement. The main source of religious change during the last third was the sudden drop-off and subsequent further erosion in Catholic church attendance. Summarizing trends in church attendance from 1940 to 1985, Michael Hout and Andrew Greeley write: "Contrary to received wisdom in social science and the mass media, we could find no evidence of religious secularization as measured by the attendance at religious services in the United States over the past half-century. The downward trend in church attendance in the late 1960s and early 1970s was strictly a Catholic phenomenon."[59] We concur. The last fifteen years of the last century showed that Hout and Greeley were too optimistic about Catholic attendance by a few percentage points (they said it had stopped dropping by 1975), but their sense that other groups were unchanged and unchanging is borne out here. Some researchers, most notably the political scientist Robert Putnam, have looked at data very similar to ours and reached a more extreme conclusion. In Putnam's words, churches are "hollowed out," and "decay has consumed the load-bearing beams of our civic infrastructure."[60] His conclusion grossly exaggerates the condition of American religious participation. He uses tenuous and problematic evidence of greater religiosity in the 1950s to declare a "religious boom" and the subsequent return to pre-1950s levels as "erosion." Those are very heavy terms to lay on just two 1950s surveys done in the early history of polling.[61] And social scientists know well that the 1950s, exceptional years in several respects, were hardly a benchmark for "normal" America. We conclude that the key trend in attendance over the last half-century or more has been the decline in Catholic attendance to the level of that of mainline Protestants.[62]

Belief

The most basic religious belief, of course, is belief in God. In the last half of the twentieth century, over 90 percent of Americans answered "yes" to the question, "Do you, personally, believe in God (or a universal spirit)?" or a question like it. Affirmative answers were especially high in the 1950s and declined slightly afterwards, from 99 percent in a 1954 survey to 91 percent in 1993 and 93 percent in 2000.[63] Part of the reason for the modest decline was the replacement of earlier-born believers by later-born nonbelievers, but there was also a modest drop within generations between the 1950s and 1990s. Catholics and especially Jews were slightly less likely to say "yes" over time. But all these changes in belief in God were within a very narrow range, at 90-plus percent for Protestants and Catholics.

We can further explore belief in God by using a question that the GSS included from 1988 to 2000: respondents were asked to choose one of six options, from "I don't believe in God" and "I don't know whether there is a God, and I don't believe there is any way to find out," to "While I have doubts, I feel that I do believe in God," and "I know God really exists, and I have no doubts about it." In the short twelve-year window, 65 percent of Americans, give or take two points, gave the "I have no doubts" reply. Certainty about God increased slightly among college graduates.[64] (Across birth cohorts, belief in God declined—notably among Catholics—until the baby boomer generation born between 1945 and 1959 and then stabilized.)

This item is much better than the simple "yes" or "no" approach to belief in God from the Gallup polls, but its greater sophistication did not turn up any notable change between 1988 and 2000. We also found published results from two earlier time points: 1964 and 1981.[65] In 1964, 77 percent of Americans believed in God without doubt—compared with the average of 65 percent for the 1988 to 2000 GSS.[66] Most of the shift between the 1964 and 1988 responses is into the "While I have doubts, I feel that I do believe" option. As the percentage of Americans saying that they believe without doubt went down by twelve points, the percentage who said that, with doubts, they believed went up by ten points. (The percentage saying that they did not believe in God went up from 1 to 5 percent.) Here we have evidence that a segment of American society changed their outlook on God as well as on religion in the 1960s. Unfortunately, we have no points from the late 1960s or the 1970s that would enable us to see more precisely when the change occurred and how sudden or gradual it was.

A higher threshold of doctrinal belief concerns the *literalness of the Bible*: is it the "actual word of God," inspired by God, or just fables? Surveys using one version of this question revealed that in the mid-1960s 53 percent of adult Americans, on average, picked the "actual word" answer and that in the mid-1980s 49 percent did.[67] Surveys using a different question found that in the decade around 1980, 38 percent of respondents picked literalism, and about fifteen years later, around 1995, 33 percent did.[68] (The "fables" reply increased four points, from 12 percent to 16 percent.) Together, these polls suggest a roughly nine-point drop from the 1960s to the 1990s in the proportion of Americans who believed in Bible literalism. The most striking change in group differences from 1984 to 2000, when the GSS asked this question, is the closing of the educational gap. The proportion of high school dropouts who were literalists dropped from 60 percent to 50 percent, but the proportion of college graduates increased from 12 percent to 18 percent. Cohort patterns capture the longer-term changes. Using the GSS samples drawn from 1984 to 2000, we found that 50 percent of Americans born around the turn of the last century were literalists; that proportion declined steadily to the end of World War II, down to 30 percent, and the proportion remained there through the baby boomers and the children of the early baby boomers, those born from 1946 through 1980. Closer inspection shows that the generational differences were largely due to two factors: Americans were increasingly educated, which reduced their literalism, and over the century more high school dropouts turned away from literalism (see figure 8.10). We thus see a convergence of opinion, most strikingly because literalism increased slightly among college graduates born after 1930.[69]

Finally, we consider whether Americans believed in *life after death*. From 1944 through the early 1990s, 72 percent of Americans answered "yes" when asked if they believed in life after death; in the last years of the twentieth century, the average *rose* to 77 percent.[70] Generational differences also point to no change in this belief, or to slightly increasing belief, over the century.[71]

Different types of Americans largely *converged* toward belief in the afterlife. Mainline Protestants, Catholics, Jews, and Americans who professed no religion increasingly accepted the idea, moving them closer to the level of conviction held by fundamentalist Protestants. For example, before the 1970s, fewer than 20 percent of Jews and fewer than 40 percent of respondents who claimed no religion expressed belief in an afterlife; at the end of the century, 50 and 60 percent, respectively, did. (This upswell of belief appears as well if we group people by the religion they were raised in rather than the one they currently claimed.) Nonsoutherners increased their level

Figure 8.10   Belief in the Literal Truth of the Bible, by Year Turned Sixteen and Education

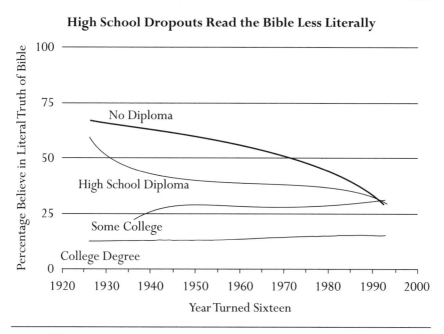

High School Dropouts Read the Bible Less Literally

Source: GSS.
Note: Data smoothed using locally estimated (loess) regression.

of belief to a level about that of southerners. And residents of metropolitan areas became more like rural residents in having faith. The key exceptions to this embrace of the afterlife were poorly educated Americans, as show in figure 8.11. Fewer high school dropouts believed in life after death in the 1990s than around 1960; Americans of higher educational attainments, however, especially college graduates, were notably more likely to believe at the end than at the middle of the century. It is almost as if the least educated had missed out on a new social wave—belief in the afterlife.[72]

CONCLUSION

We have examined closely four indicators of religious involvement, in addition to quickly looking at church membership: attendance at services and belief in God, the literalness of the Bible, and life after death. The first question we raised was: what happened to religious belief and practice in the last

Figure 8.11   Belief in Life After Death, by Year and Education

Americans' Belief in Life After Death Increased Modestly over Time, Except That of High School Dropouts

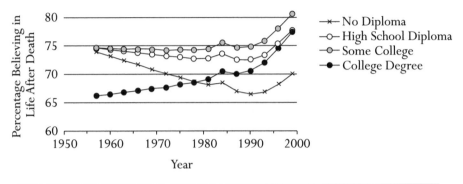

Source: Gallup polls, NORC, and GSS.
Note: Data smoothed using locally estimated (loess) regression.

few decades of the twentieth century? For the most part, the historical changes were modest; generally, faith and practice increased a bit in the 1950s and then declined a bit afterwards. Overall, indicators of religiosity did not decline much (if at all) over the last several decades of the century. This surface consistency, however, covers some internal variations.

There were generational differences: Americans born around the beginning of the twentieth century were much more religiously active and religiously certain as adults than those born in the 1960s and 1970s (excepting belief in life after death). Much of that pattern, however, reflects the connection between aging and religiosity. Comparing people of a similar age across the years reveals remarkable stability in religious belief and practice.

Clearer differences appear between Catholics and Protestants: Catholics sharply retreated from religious attendance, and this accounts for most of the national trend in attendance. Although this was almost certainly connected to internal changes in Catholicism, not their adoption of ideas or practices typical of Protestants, its consequence was to homogenize attendance rates over time. Even more consistently across the measures, college graduates' religious practice and beliefs *increased* over time relative to those of others. Given that frequently the religiosity of those with less than a high school degree declined, a *convergence* in religiosity among different educational groups thus occurred.[73] We offer no explanation for this development, which is largely unnoted in research on American religiosity, but we do observe that it is consistent with the growing implications of educational differences in America: the more-educated became increasingly integrated into central American institutions, and the less-educated less so.[74]

Stepping back from the survey data, we note that the homogenization of religious beliefs and practices is a common experience for American immigrant groups. Historians of Catholicism and Judaism in America have described the "Americanization" of both faiths by leaders and laity alike, a process that has often reflected the tension between the already assimilated members of the group and newer arrivals.[75] For Jews, Americanization entailed adopting Protestant organizational structures (for example, congregational democracy) and service practices (for example, forms of congregational singing). The founders of Reform Judaism in the late nineteenth century explicitly wanted to assimilate and renounced separatist practices such as kosher food and head coverings for men; they also adopted "American" customs such as Sunday services and choirs and embraced the Social Gospel. Catholics initially chose to construct a parallel but separate social world of schools, universities, hospitals, and communities. As the century of mass media unfolded there were Catholic newspapers and magazines, radio and television programs, and book publishers.[76] Separatist policies were dramatically reversed by the Second Vatican Council. Although Catholic institutions continued to function (and most thrived) following Vatican II, the express policy of pursuing Catholic separatism in the United States was ended.[77] These days, the model of regularly scheduled religious services presided over by a member of a professional clergy who gives an address on matters of religious interest and leads collective prayer is spreading ever more widely as leaders of Asian immigrant communities similarly adapt Buddhism and Confucianism to America.[78]

In the end, Americans in the twentieth century for the most part retained their characteristic religiosity. And even as the nation's religious structure became more differentiated, its religious culture may have become more homogeneous in both practice and belief. Ironically, Americans in the twentieth century became increasingly diverse in religious affiliation, but more similar in religious faith.

CHAPTER NINE

When Americans Disagreed: Cultural Fragmentation and Conflict

As THE twentieth century drew to a close, learned observers worried that Americans were splintering apart on cultural issues. Books with titles such as *Culture Wars, The Disuniting of America, Postethnic America*, and *We're All Multiculturalists Now* described a people divided by ancestry, lifestyles, and moral values. Many election postmortems of 2000 and 2004 claimed that voters cast their ballots more in accord with moral stances than with their economic interests. Although these claims were overblown—in 2004 the issue of terrorism certainly mattered most—they reflected a long-term concern about cultural disintegration. Other learned observers responded to these warnings by reassuring readers that Americans still formed *One Nation, After All* or "One Nation, Slightly Divisible." But division was the dominant motif among the pundits—and among average Americans too. Survey respondents expressed worry about ethnic diversity, and most rejected the suggestion that government should subsidize expressions of such diversity. In the mid-1990s over 60 percent of respondents agreed that "Americans are greatly divided when it comes to the most important values."[1]

This turn-of-the-twenty-first-century worry about fragmentation recalled similar anxieties a century earlier. Wise men then warned that immigrants were adulterating American culture (recall the sneering at Italians reported in chapter 1); labor and management fought no-holds-barred around the country; white vigilantes used lynching to maintain control in the rural South; guardians of morality and cosmopolitan literati decried one another over what was permissible in literature; "drys" and "wets" campaigned vigorously on alcohol regulation and enforcement; and religion seemed to many to be in a death struggle with science.[2]

Yet, about halfway between these two periods of what seemed to be out-of-control pluralism, pundits worried about the opposite—too little diversity. In midcentury, books such as *The Organization Man, The Lonely Crowd, Escape from Freedom*, and *The End of Ideology* described a uniform, gray-toned, mass society. Comedians joked about men returning from work and entering the wrong home because the new suburban tract houses were all alike. *Time* concluded that "either through fear, passivity, or conviction, [youth] are ready to conform"; a *New York Times* columnist described young adults of the 1950s as a cohort with "few interests, not much spirit and, in general, seemingly content to cut its coat according to the cloth"; and the president of Yale admonished graduating seniors to "once and for all live down your reputation as the silent generation." Only about a dozen years later, of course, university presidents were routed from their wood-paneled offices by an anything-but-silent, anything-but-gray-toned generation.[3]

So the question we pose is this: Did average Americans over the twentieth century become more or less "divided . . . [on] the most important values?" Or did divisions widen and narrow in different eras? Because the best evidence on this question comes from poll data and reliable polling largely began after World War II, we must focus our question on the second half of the century. We can, however, occasionally peer back into the decades before 1950.

There were good reasons in the 1950s, the years of the conformity scare, to suppose that cultural distinctions were fading—and good reasons to fear uniformity, given the recent specters of Nazi Germany and Stalinist Russia. Large corporate and governmental bureaucracies, universal schooling, brand marketing, and network media seemed to be molding Americans into similar, culturally homogeneous atoms of a mass society—an analysis that developed into the "organizational thesis" among historians.[4] Virtually all Americans heard the same explicit and implicit messages about what was normal—even if "normal" changed over the years. (On 1950s television, married couples like the Ricardos and Nelsons had separate beds; on 1990s television, shows such as *Friends* and *Sex in the City* featured unmarried women casually discussing their sexual escapades. In both eras, the entire nation looked on.) Another apparent impetus to homogeneity was the convergence in important domains such as the life span and the life cycle, family size, standards of living (at least until the 1970s), and secondary education, all of which we have covered in this book. Shared hardships, such as the Great Depression and the deprivations of wartime, and shared enemies (during World War II and the cold war) also bred commonality. Gallup polls from the Korean War era suggest that most Americans saw national unity as a key to winning.[5]

By the mid-1960s, however, observers' concerns reversed. Social movements of minorities, youth, and women repudiated mainstream culture. Soon after, renewed immigration introduced great diversity in ways of life. Increasing economic inequality after 1970 and the increasingly divergent fates of well-educated versus poorly educated Americans suggested rising incoherence in the public culture. Growing affluence, new communications, and—ironically—the mass market encouraged division: they permitted any small group to find its own distinct niche. The columnist David Brooks made the point this way:

> There is no longer a clear pecking order. . . . Everybody gets to be an aristocrat now. . . . You can be an outlaw-biker aristocrat, a corporate-real-estate aristocrat, an X Games aristocrat, a Pentecostal-minister aristocrat. You will have your own code of honor and your own field of accomplishment. . . . You can construct your own multimedia community, in which every magazine you read, every cable show you watch, every radio station you listen to, reaffirms your values and reinforces the sense of your own rightness.[6]

Perhaps both concerns, about too little diversity and about too much of it, were correct—but for different eras. Perhaps homogenization increased from 1900 to about 1950 as immigration waned and national institutions and media grew, and then homogenization may have diminished as markets diversified and immigration returned. So did the twentieth century bring more or less cultural division—or both?

A critical distinction must be made before we try to answer this question. There are at least two different ways to visualize how America might have "fallen apart," be it from the start or the middle of the century. The first imagines Americans to have once clustered together on a shared terrain of values, but the cultural landscape was then riven in two, leaving hostile camps berating one another across a growing chasm. This is the *culture wars* image. The second pictures that same, originally shared terrain as fracturing along many crisscrossing fissures; as the fissures deepened Americans gathered in small groups, each atop its own cultural mesa. This is the *fragmentation* image. Consensus is lost, not because one axis of division appears, but because Americans gather into many distinctive subcultures. We address the "falling apart" question in both of these senses, beginning with "culture wars."

CULTURE WARS

During the 1992 Republican National Convention, the political commentator and occasional presidential candidate Patrick J. Buchanan sparked heated

debate when he declared to millions of television viewers that "there is a religious war going on in our country for the soul of America." Seven years
later, Buchanan continued: "Our culture war is about one question: Is God
dead, or is God king?. . . whether God or man shall be exalted, whose moral
beliefs shall be enshrined in law, and what children shall be taught to value
and abhor. With those stakes, to walk away is to abandon your post in time
of war."[7] The academic version of this thesis posits that twentieth-century
Americans divided into two camps even before the 1960s. The secular or
theologically liberal camp welcomed religious ecumenicism, women's
equality, and the relaxation of sexual constraints. The fundamentalist camp
resisted public sexuality, abortion rights, and the upsetting of traditional
gender roles. Buchanan's ire seems understandable: Americans became
more liberal on most such cultural issues, most rapidly between 1965 and
1975. Survey respondents increasingly expressed tolerance for women
going out to work, premarital sex (but *not* extramarital sex), divorce, childlessness, and homosexuality. For example, in 1969 two-thirds of Americans
said that premarital sex was "wrong"; thirty years later, fewer than half did
(see chapter 4).[8]

The survey data suggest, however, that this liberalization was *not* the result of a widening schism in which Americans divided into oppositional
camps and the liberal camp grew faster than the conservative one. Rather,
the American center drifted toward more liberal positions.[9] Scholars recon-
ciled the findings of little polarization among Americans with the popular
impression of a culture war this way: although the great majority of Americans did *not* divide into increasingly hostile camps, the political parties and
politically active voters *did*. Starting in the 1970s, Democratic and Republican leaders took increasingly opposed positions on the hot-button cultural
issues. Before then, officeholders' and voters' stances on matters like abortion, women's rights, and race often cut across parties; there was not much
difference, for example, in Republicans' and Democrats' positions on abortion.[10] By 2000 (and beyond), party positions on such issues had become distinct and much more ideological, even though average Americans were no
more divided on these issues than they had been decades earlier. One ana-
lyst, Christian Smith, concluded that the "culture wars that we . . . see on
television . . . are being waged by a fairly small group of noisy, entrepreneur-
ial activists of the extreme." Rank-and-file Americans had not enlisted in this
war and had not become more polarized.[11]

Or so the story goes. If we push the historical horizon back—to before
the 1970s—the plot thickens. For example, Congress was just as polarized
in the early years of the twentieth century as it was in the late years; the midcentury was (once again) atypical, in this case for greater consensus between
the two parties.[12] In this section, we track trends in public opinion back before the 1970s, in some cases starting with the 1930s. The General Social

Survey, which provides the standard data drawn on by scholars studying culture wars, provides a nearly three-decade window, 1972 to 2000, on American values. That window is wide, but not wide enough, because it leaves out the 1960s and early 1970s, when many social transformations happened. (Recall, for example, how rapidly Americans changed their preferred family size between 1967 and 1973; see figure 4.11.)[13] So we combine the GSS with Gallup polls going back many years. We ask whether cleavages expanded, and we ask whether the way Americans sorted out on either side of the cleavages changed.

We canvassed a long list of poll items, tapping a wide range of cultural issues in search of topics on which surveys had asked consistent questions at least a half-dozen times and at least twice before 1970. This requirement considerably reduced the pool of items, but the exercise itself revealed an important connection between cultural controversies and survey research: pollsters, both commercial and academic, typically did not ask about even profound issues until they became divisive.[14] In the end, we examined in detail survey questions on the following topics (the list includes a few that we analyzed in earlier chapters):

- *Women's roles*: Two questions for respondents: Should married women work? Would you vote for a woman for president?

- *Ethnic prejudice*: Five questions: Would you vote for a Catholic, Jewish, or black person for president? What do you think of interracial marriage? Are blacks "pushing" too much?

- *Capital punishment*: Do you support the death penalty?

- *Ideal size of families*

- *Religion*: Two questions: Do you believe in God? Do you believe in life after death?

- *Abortion*: Three questions on the conditions under which respondents would allow abortion

- *Drinking*: Would you "have occasion to use alcoholic beverages?"

We also briefly treat two questions with a limited time span, having been asked only since 1970:

- *Homosexuality*

- *Premarital sex*

The Diffusion of Public Opinion

Items of culture, including opinions, generally spread or "diffuse" in a population. The pace at which people adopt new items, whether a personal computer or the idea that women should get equal pay, is slow at first as only a handful of visionaries take them up; then the pace speeds up rapidly as the bulk of the population joins in, and finally it slows down again as only the hard-core resisters are left. This account describes the S-shaped diffusion pattern familiar to students of technological innovation. (See, for example, figure 6.6, showing the spread of consumer goods, or figures 2.2 and 2.3, showing the diffusion of educational degrees.) Figure 9.1 presents a stylized version of this process, showing the diffusion of an item from 10 percent to 90 percent of the population. During this process, some groups are "early adopters" ahead of the curve; their adoption history is shown by the darkened circle line. The history for the "late adopters" is shown by the open circle line. The key observation for us is that, as diffusion proceeds, the gap between the early and late adopters, marked by the gray bars, widens and then narrows.[15]

We cannot, in the survey data, identify people who were disposed to be early or late adopters. Instead, we know that people in certain groups—the young, the urban, the northern, and the better-educated, for example—tend to be early adopters and that their counterparts tend to be late adopters. These social attributes serve as rough proxies for early versus late adopters in our analyses. Conversely, the dynamics of early versus late adoption generate division by those same groups. As a new idea starts to spread, the young and the old, for example, increasingly find themselves at odds on it. A cultural skirmish between generations has developed. This is how we use the connection between people's group memberships and their willingness to innovate to index the waxing and waning of "culture wars."

Over the twentieth century, Americans adopted new cultural views on some matters nearly as rapidly as the idealized curves in figure 9.1 imply. On others, change was more glacial. And on yet other topics, Americans moved first one way and then another. Clearly, this abstract process is conditioned by the substance of the issue under consideration. Not all opinion change has been in the liberal direction, as we see in the cases of, for example, abortion and capital punishment. By using this diffusion framework, we can see when and along what cleavages a twentieth-century culture war might have broken out. And by drawing on polls going as far back as the 1930s, we can put the late-century debate on culture wars into historical perspective.

We divided the attitude items into three broad categories: those issues on which American opinion clearly shifted in one direction, those for which there was a reversal of trends, and those that showed little change over the

Figure 9.1   Hypothetical S–Shaped Diffusion Curves

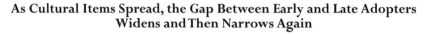

**As Cultural Items Spread, the Gap Between Early and Late Adopters
Widens and Then Narrows Again**

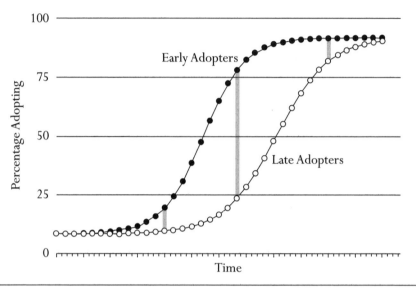

Source: Authors' compilation.

period for which we have evidence. In our analysis, we again used the
adapted loess technique, first described in chapter 3 (and appendix A). We
used all available published survey results to estimate the national trend for
a specific question from as far back as the 1930s up to 2000, and then we
used the raw survey data available in specific years from Gallup or the GSS
to estimate the trends for specific subpopulations.

Long-Term Changes

One cultural issue that roughly mimicked the pattern in figure 9.1 was
women's roles. Beginning in 1938, Gallup asked the question, "Do you approve or disapprove of a married woman earning money in business or industry if she has a husband capable of supporting her?" Either Gallup or the
GSS asked this question through 1998.[16] Over those sixty years, the balance
of American opinion shifted dramatically, from 20 percent approving to 80
percent approving. Figure 9.2 (top graph), labeled "all," shows that pattern.
The circles are the actual percentages saying "approve" in each year ("ob-

Figure 9.2   Approval of Married Women Working for Pay, by Year, Age, and Type of Place

As Americans Accepted Working Women, Gaps in Approval Among Groups First Widened, Then Narrowed

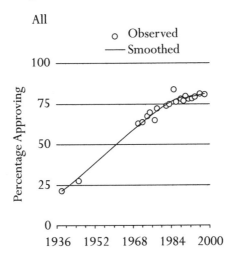

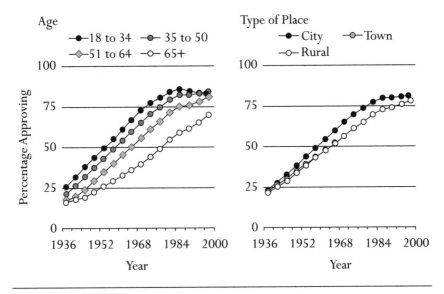

Sources: Gallup polls and GSS.
Note: Data smoothed using locally estimated (loess) regression.

served"). The solid line "smooths" the trend, using our adapted loess method (see appendix A). It shows much of the classic, stretched-out S-curve of innovation diffusion, although the left tail is missing. We can imagine what the numbers would have been had this question been asked in polls around 1910 or 1920 and speculate that we would be displaying a long, flat line leading up to the 22 percent in 1938.

The top graph thus shows that Americans' approval of wives working for pay generally followed an S-curve diffusion pattern in the twentieth century. But we are mainly interested in how cleavages around this issue changed over time. As before, we estimated the trends for subgroups of Americans by seeing how they deviated from the smoothed trend for the total population. In the bottom-left graph, for example, we display the trends in approval of working wives for four different age groups: eighteen- to thirty-four-year-olds, thirty-five- to fifty-year-olds, fifty-one- to sixty-four-year-olds, and those sixty-five and older. (For clarity, we have dropped the national trend line and the specific points, showing only the smoothed lines for the subgroups.) We can see that, initially, there was little difference by age in opinions; then the differences widened, reaching their greatest width around the 1960s and 1970s; finally the differences narrowed by the end of the century. The bottom-right graph shows the same pattern of divergence, and then convergence between city residents, on the one hand, and town and rural residents, on the other.[17]

Put another way, a generation gap and a community gap developed on this issue, climaxed around 1970, and then dissipated by the end of the century. A similar story can be told about regional differences: a gap developed between easterners, on the one hand, who were more accepting, and southerners and midwesterners, on the other, who were less approving; the gaps then closed by 2000 (not shown). We also examined differences by education, although we could track only those from 1945. The difference between high school dropouts and high school graduates widened from ten points in 1945 to nineteen in 1972, and then narrowed to nine points in 1998. In sum, around 1940 the great majority of Americans agreed that wives should stay at home, and there were no wide divisions on that question. During the 1960s and 1970s, however, younger, urban, coastal, and better-educated Americans shifted toward the feminist position, opening up major divisions on the issue by social background. By the 1990s, as social conservatives adopted egalitarian positions, Americans overwhelmingly approved of wives working.[18]

Another question on women's roles often asked by pollsters is (as originally phrased by Gallup), "Would you vote for a woman for president if she qualified in every other respect?" In the mid-1930s, 29 percent of men and 42 percent of women said "yes"; by the end of the century, about 90 percent of both men and women said "yes." The patterns of change by subgroup were similar to those we described for the working wives question. That is, differences by age, region, education, and place widened to their greatest extent around the 1970s and then closed by the end of the century.[19] Group divisions on women's roles tell us about the pace of the culture wars and suggest that the feminist front erupted in the 1960s and 1970s and quieted down afterwards.

Another major cultural front concerned religious and racial diversity. Americans' tolerance—or at least what they were willing to say aloud—advanced substantially.[20] The questions used by poll-takers over the longest period asked whether respondents would vote for a Jewish, Catholic, or black candidate for president. We see a diffusion pattern similar to that with the items on women, although not as clearly because the pollsters started asking the presidential questions only after about half of the public was already saying "yes." That is, survey researchers started tracking these opinions when, according to the S-curve model, group divisions were already the widest. The top-left graph of figure 9.3 shows the overall percentages of Americans who said they would vote for a Jewish, Catholic, or black person, excluding Jewish, Catholic, and black respondents from each result, respectively. The trends are jagged because the questions were asked only a handful of times. Still, we see approximations of the elongated S-curve, though the initial leg of that curve is missing. (Post-2000 polling shows that "yes" answers leveled off at 90 percent.)[21]

The top-right graph of figure 9.3 shows the pattern of opinion among non-Jews on the Jewish question by region of the country. Regional differences, especially between the South and other regions, widened from the late 1930s to the late 1950s and then narrowed afterwards, so that by the 1990s they were negligible. Differences by place and age followed similar trends.[22] Answers to the question about a Catholic candidate, which was asked only a few times, are shown by place of residence in the bottom-left graph of figure 9.3. Differences by place narrowed between 1958 and 1983.[23] History does not always move so smoothly, of course, and the black-for-president question is illustrative. The bottom-right graph of figure 3 displays the percentage of nonblacks, by education, who said "yes" to voting for a black candidate (or "Negro" before 1978, and "black man" through 1987). Generally, the more educated the respondent, the more likely he or she was to answer affirmatively. Between 1958 and 1980, those with less than a BA degree started to catch up with the college graduates in their support, but in the 1980s support for a hypothetical black candidate sagged. (It is tempting to offer a post-hoc explanation for this trend by pointing to the candidacy of Jesse Jackson in the 1980s, but as we discuss later, the retreat on African-American issues was not limited to presidential politics.) Support resumed rising in the 1990s, with all the educational groups converging to near-universal affirmation. There was similar convergence of white Ameri-

Figure 9.3   Citizens Who Would Vote for a Catholic, a Jew, or a Black for President

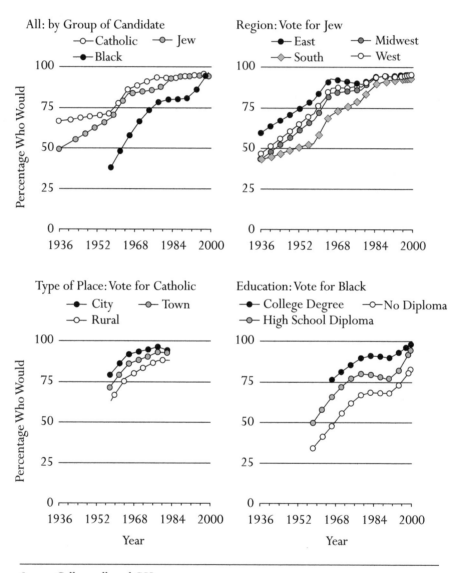

Differences on Minority Presidential Candidates Widened When National Views Were Evenly Split and Then Narrowed as Tolerance Grew

Sources: Gallup polls and GSS.
Note: Data smoothed using locally estimated (loess) regression. Question not asked of members of the group in question.

cans across age, place, religious, and regional divides in their willingness to say they would vote for a black. For example, in 1958 only 11 percent of white southerners said "yes," compared to 54 percent of white easterners; by the late 1990s, the percentages were over 90 percent everywhere.[24]

Then there is the question, discussed in chapter 3, about racial intermarriage. Between 1963, when it was first asked, and 2000, the percentage of nonblacks who said "no" to laws against it—that is, the percentage who accepted interracial marriage—rose from 37 to 87 percent. The retreat on race observed in the 1980s in the black-for-president question (see figure 9.3) shows up in the intermarriage question too. The now-familiar waxing and waning of group differences appears again: widening differences in accepting intermarriage by age, education, region, and religion in the 1960s and 1970s and then shrinking differences in the 1980s and especially the 1990s as most older, less-educated, southern, and Protestant respondents came to tolerate racial intermarriage.[25] Figure 3.9 shows the trend by birth cohort. The difference between the Depression generation (born 1930 to 1944) and their parents' generation (born 1900 to 1914) grew from fifteen points around 1963 to thirty points around 1985, then declined to twenty points in 2000 as most of the remaining survivors of the parental generation came to accept racial intermarriage.[26] The survey question discussed in chapter 3 (figure 3. 10) on whether blacks "push too much," also asked from 1963 through 2000, shows patterns that are less definitive, probably because the national position on this question leveled off at 50 percent and stopped moving. Differences by age, cohort, and education on the topic widened from 1963 to 2000; differences by urbanism and region widened and then narrowed.

These survey items on women's role and minorities tell similar stories—that as opinion first liberalized a gap opened up, and then, as the liberal stance became predominant, gaps closed. Attitudes toward premarital sex, which we discussed in chapter 3, also followed this pattern. We do not analyze that topic in detail here, because we lack the requisite comparable data before 1970. But attitudes on the subject seemed to shift sharply around 1970, and for the most part, Americans converged toward accepting premarital sex *for adults*. From 1982 to 2000, 62 to 64 percent of Americans said it was only sometimes wrong or not wrong at all. Americans shifted their positions to and fro a bit, depending on their religious affiliations, but after 1982 the social landscape was relatively stable.[27]

We see that, in general, younger, northern, more-educated, and more-urban Americans typically adopted new cultural positions first and that older, southern, less-educated, and less-urban Americans did so later. The waxing and waning of these social divisions shows that the peak of battle was roughly from the late 1950s to the early 1970s, or what some historians label the "extended 1960s." Much of the culture war controversy after the

1970s was its fading echo, as in the comment by conservative Supreme Court Justice Samuel Alito: "The late 1960s and early 1970s . . . was a time of turmoil at colleges and universities. And I saw some very smart people and very privileged people behaving irresponsibly. And I couldn't help making a contrast between some of the worst of what I saw on the campus and the good sense and the decency of the people back in my own community." Or as the documentary filmmaker Ralph Arlyck put it, more bluntly, "The '60s pissed off a lot of people."[28] But cultural controversy hardly ended in the 1960s, of course, or with the reactions to that decade. New ideas and new divisions on ideas always emerge. For an illustration, consider the question of homosexuality.

Starting in 1973, the GSS asked, "What about sexual relations between two adults of the same sex—do you think it is always wrong, almost always wrong, wrong only sometimes, or not wrong at all?" In 1973, 11 percent of Americans said homosexuality was "not wrong at all"; in 2000, 27 percent did; that proportion had increased to 31 percent by 2004. Moral acceptance of homosexuality grew (although acceptance of gay marriage stalled).[29] As this attitude spread, divisions by age, region, education, and religion widened.[30] At the end of the twentieth century and beyond, the widening political divides around homosexuality increasingly coincided with social divisions in the general public.[31] The point we would stress is that, even as divisions on some hoary issues like race and gender roles seemed to narrow in the 1980s and 1990s, divisions on other, newer cultural items widened.

Not all topics of cultural controversy, however, involve a steady progression from novelty to universal acceptance. In some cases, the direction of opinion change reverses. Resistance develops; circumstances change. (When and why reversals occur is a complex topic beyond our scope here.) Take abortion, a topic that roiled American politics for the last third of the century, showed the greatest polarization, and was well tracked in the polls.

Cycles of Opinion

From 1962, when pollsters first asked about abortion, public opinion moved quickly in the direction of easing constraints; then, after about 1977, opinion moved slowly in the other direction. For example, the percentage of Americans who approved of abortions performed because the woman could not afford to raise a child was under 20 percent in 1962, over 50 percent in 1977, and down to 40 percent by 2000. We combined respondents' answers to three specific abortion questions—approving of abortion because of a defective fetus, because of the mother's health, or because of low income— into a scale ranging from 0 (no to abortion for any of the three reasons) to 3 (yes for all three reasons).[32]

From 1962 to 1977, Americans moved from an average score of 1.6

Figure 9.4   Scores on Abortion Scale, by Year and Education or Region

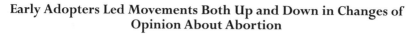

Early Adopters Led Movements Both Up and Down in Changes of Opinion About Abortion

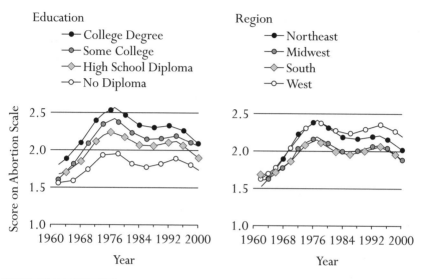

Education
    —•— College Degree
    —•— Some College
    —◆— High School Diploma
    —○— No Diploma

Region
    —•— Northeast
    —•— Midwest
    —◆— South
    —○— West

Sources: NORC surveys and GSS.
Note: Data smoothed using locally estimated (loess) regression.

(agreeing to about half of the abortion questions) to an average of 2.2. Then the tide shifted. By 2000 agreement was down to an average of 2.0 on the scale (agreeing with two of the questions). Figure 9.4 shows the trajectory by education and by region. In the first part of the cycle, 1962 to 1977, the more-educated respondents shifted toward the pro-choice position at a faster rate than the less-educated ones did, and the respondents in the East and West shifted faster than did southerners and midwesterners. In the second part of the cycle, 1977 to 2000, the more-educated shifted *away* from the pro-choice position faster than and toward the less-educated; easterners shifted *away* faster than and toward the southerners and midwesterners.[33] Trends by age groups and by urbanism are similar. The early-adopting sectors of the population moved fastest toward a pro-choice position and also faster away from it. Other Americans were more conservative and less volatile. The period of greatest division was around 1975 to 1980, when the gaps by education, region, age, and place were widest.[34]

    Americans' opinions on the death penalty also cycled. From the mid-1930s to about 1960, support for it dropped, then rose sharply until about

Figure 9.5   Support for Death Penalty, by Year and Region

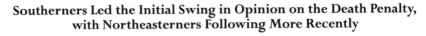

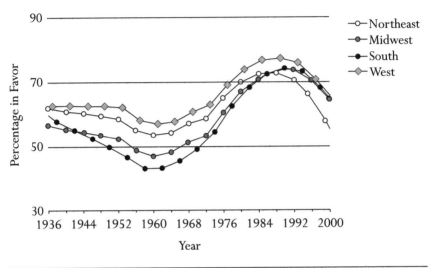

Southerners Led the Initial Swing in Opinion on the Death Penalty, with Northeasterners Following More Recently

Sources: Gallup polls and GSS.
Note: Data smoothed using locally estimated (loess) regression.

1990, and then dropped again. The timing of this cycle and the small differences in opinion between groups suggest that Americans' attitudes on the death penalty largely followed the national homicide rate, which cycled similarly over those years.[35] Figure 9.5 shows differences of opinion by region as great as fifteen points around 1960, and then again of ten points around 2000. The figure also reveals an exception, from 1936 to 1990, to the general diffusion pattern. *Southerners* were the most volatile; they led the first swings of opinion against the death penalty from 1936 to about 1960 and then moved fastest toward favoring it after 1960. (Throughout, westerners most often supported the penalty.)[36] In the 1950s, southerners more typically opposed capital punishment than easterners did. Also in this era, better-educated and urban Americans supported the death penalty more than less-educated and rural Americans. Then southerners moved rapidly in favor of the death penalty, matching the position of easterners around 1990. The last swing of opinion, after 1990 and away from capital punishment, was led instead by the familiar, early-adopting easterners—and also by better-educated and younger Americans. By 2000, in contrast to 1955, these avant-garde groups gave capital punishment the least support.[37] The reason for the 1936 to 1990 exception, with southerners leading the move, may have something to do with the special nature of crime as a topic of concern and the proportion of southerners who were black.

In chapter 4, we noted another cycle in opinion: from the 1930s to the late 1950s, Americans gave increasingly larger figures as their ideal number of children; then, from the 1960s into the 1990s, they gave progressively smaller numbers. Although the desired size of a family is not a topic typically connected to the culture war issues, the rapid fluctuations in preferences (figure 4.11) were part of the postwar and then the 1960s cultural changes. The first part of the cycle corresponded to the baby boom itself: an increase from an average "ideal" of 2.8 children in 1936 to a high of 3.6 in 1962, a surge in pro-natalism that departed sharply from the long-term historical decline in actual family sizes. The next phase, after 1962, was a rapid drop in the ideal to about 2.5 children by the mid-1990s. Because we lacked the necessary survey data, it was hard to parse group differences in the earlier, upward part of the cycle. But around 1955, there were wide differences in preferred family size—by region, gender, age, religion, and place.

Figure 9.6 presents one of the longer series we found on the ideal size question. In the 1950s, clear differences in opinion separated rural, town, and city residents. Those differences evaporated as the late-adopting groups caught up with the opinion leaders by the 1980s in favoring smaller families. All kinds of Americans reduced their ideal family size, but those in sectors that had preferred larger families in the 1950s reduced their ideal even more. Those in favor of larger families around 1955 generally reached the small family size preferences of the early adopters—an average of 2.5 seemed stable—by the late 1980s. We see, again, the extended 1960s as a period of substantial change, but in this case (as in capital punishment), the action was the closing rather than the widening of gaps. These examples illustrate that trends in cultural stances can reverse. In most cases, it seems that the early-adopting sectors pushed the newer trends pro and con, although that was not so for capital punishment.

Long-Term Stability

Finally, there are social issues on which American opinion changed little, in net, over most of the century. Drinking is a key example. For many generations, struggles over alcohol drove local, state, and eventually national politics, but the issue seems to have reached some sort of settling point by the 1950s, roughly two decades after the repeal of Prohibition. Continuously between 1945 and 2000, about two-thirds of American adults reported that they had occasion to use alcohol; the percentage changed no more than three points up or down over those fifty-five years.[38] Underneath this consis-

Figure 9.6   Ideal Number of Children, by Year and Type of Place

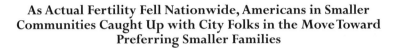

**As Actual Fertility Fell Nationwide, Americans in Smaller
Communities Caught Up with City Folks in the Move Toward
Preferring Smaller Families**

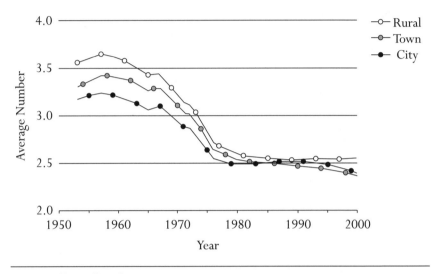

Sources: Gallup polls and GSS.
Note: Data smoothed using locally estimated (loess) regression.

tency, however, notable group differences are apparent. For example, in the 1990s young Americans were thirty percentage points likelier to drink than the elderly, men ten points more likely than women, and Catholics twenty points more likely than conservative Protestants. Along with these roughly stable contrasts were historical changes in differences consistent with those we have described before: regional differences narrowed during the 1960s and 1970s as more southerners said they drank, and they narrowed again in the 1980s and 1990s as more easterners said they did not; rural-city differences narrowed in a similar fashion. We have seen such convergences on many other issues. But educational differences widened after the 1960s as those without any college exposure increasingly forswore alcohol. This educational divergence is confounded with generations. Most cohorts began adulthood with drinking rates around 70 percent or more and then gave it up as they aged. But the later in the century Americans were born, the slower they were to give up their youthful drinking, so that cohort differences tended to widen. In the end, drinking, which over fifty-five years showed no general trend or even a cycle, tells us little about S-curve diffusion. And yet it is not the case that nothing happened. On this seemingly settled issue, we saw the narrowing of regional and place differences and the widening of educational (and generational) ones.

A glance back at chapter 8's discussion of religion gives us a couple of other examples of relative stability. Between the 1940s and 1990, 72 percent of Americans said they believed in life after death; there was little trend. After 1990, the percentage rose to 78 (and to over 80 percent by 2004). This was a modest change, and as such, it was led by baby boomers and the better-educated (see figure 8.11). Similarly, from the mid-1940s to the late 1990s, the percentage of Americans who said that they believed in God dropped by only two points, from 95 to 93 percent. If one zooms in on that tiny change, it is possible to see a slightly greater decline among men, whites, Jews, baby boomers, and college graduates. If this were the start of a twenty-first-century shift to agnosticism—a big "if"—these groups would be the early adopters.

The topics on which public opinion has been static tell us little about current or recent culture wars; the battles were in the past or perhaps are in the future. They do hint, however, at some of the general trends in Americans' axes of difference—for example, the declining significance of region and the rising significance of education.

Summary

We largely confirm here what other researchers have found for the years from 1972 to 2000 (and we should, since most of our data for those years came from the GSS, as did theirs). On hot-button topics like women's roles, race, abortion, and sex, Americans generally became no more divided by region, place, age, education, or religion. (Indeed, despite the prevalent view that the culture wars are fought along the religious-secular line, differences in responses between frequent and infrequent church attenders widened for only three topics over those three decades and more often narrowed.)[39] But it is too simple to dismiss entirely the culture wars thesis. One reason is that the 1972 to 2000 period was largely one of completion, quieting, and reconciliation after the tumultuous "extended 1960s." So, for example, by the 1990s the great controversies over whether wives should work had been resolved in the affirmative; so had the principle (if not the practice) of racial equality. There is another reason not to dismiss culture wars too facilely: we must acknowledge that new issues did emerge that divided Americans—as in the case of homosexuality—and they will do so again, although perhaps without the multiple battle fronts of the 1960s.

We have, then, two broad findings, the first on the general process of cultural division and the second on the specifics of twentieth-century history.

First, as new cultural possibilities emerge and spread—and this is happening all the time—controversies arise and divisions open up between social groups, such as young and old, or urban and rural. These divisions typically then narrow as the new ideas become widely accepted or widely rejected (although they may cycle, as with abortion, or reach some steady equilibrium, as with drinking). If we attend to those topics when they are at their most controversial—say, by asking questions on premarital sex only starting in 1970—we find that a culture war is under way. We may even see it dissipate over the subsequent years but miss the "natural history" of the controversy, the process we describe as the S-curve. Second, the extended 1960s were years of particularly great division on several issues at once—race, gender, and sexuality, in particular. One might say that the culture war is a reality, but a reality of much longer ago.[40] For the century and the public as a whole, we suggest that there was no unilinear trend toward more division or less division, toward more or less culture war. But we can see some signs that an emerging key axis of division on cultural issues, when there is division, is education.

A FRAGMENTING AMERICA?*

As we noted in the early pages of this chapter, there is another way to think about cultural division than the two-camps-at-war image so forcefully expressed by Pat Buchanan: we can ask whether the American people fragmented into more and smaller cultural islands. The strongest claim would be that the great majority of Americans once shared a common set of worldviews and ways of life. Then, over the twentieth century, this unity splintered, so that by 2000 Americans divided along many, crisscrossing lines—by their personal traits, such as race, religion, and class, by combinations of those traits, and by varied combinations of cultural stances. As a result, there were churchgoers who were sexually conservative and those who were sexually liberal, college graduates who supported a stronger government and those who opposed it, African-American feminists and African-American traditionalists, and so forth. America became a nation not of one society but of many mini-societies—so goes the argument.

The idea that Americans have fragmented—if not really from a single community, at least from several large groups to many smaller ones—underlies many discussions of whether America is "falling apart."[41] Two kinds of research touch the fragmentation thesis at least indirectly.

One kind is "business geography." Several companies have developed place-based typologies as marketing tools. They combine vast amounts of

---

*Jane Zavisca conducted the statistical work for this section.

demographic information about geographic units such as zip codes or census block clusters with proprietary commercial data on those areas. Think of the warranties you fill out that ask for your zip code, the magazines delivered to your address, and the sales revenues of the nearest Starbucks. The firms' researchers churn these massive amounts of data through statistical machines to yield grand typologies of American households. One company, Claritas, divided Americans in 2005 into sixty-seven types, such as the Blue Blood Estates, New Empty Nests, and Mayberry-ville. (The 2.2 percent of American households who populated Mayberry-ville were, Claritas said, white, small-town high school graduates—"middle-class couples and families [who] like to fish and hunt during the day, and stay home and watch TV at night.") Claritas and others like it sell retailers information about which neighborhoods are home to the customers they are seeking. Ford, for example, should probably locate its dealers near neighborhoods with many Mayberry-villes, since that group tends to include many Ford owners. The researchers make one assumption that is critical to the whole endeavor—that people are so sharply segregated by tastes that "you are like your neighbors." With respect to our question, business geographers assert that fragmentation has grown in America: "Forget the melting pot. America today would be better characterized as a salad bar. . . . America has fractured into distinctive lifestyles, each with its own borders." Whether because of real social change, because it gathered more kinds of data, or because of shrewder marketing, the sixty-seven types of Americans counted by Claritas in 2005 had grown from sixty-two in 2000 and a mere forty in the 1970s and 1980s.[42]

The other kind of research is academic (and much less profitable). Scholars who attempt to identify cultural "lifestyles" argue that, in affluent societies, people define themselves less by their residential communities, ethnicities, or occupations and more by their leisure and consumer tastes, such as their music, clothes, and food. Some analysts describe "clusters" or even "cultural tribes," such as "down-shifters, environmentalists, nonsmokers, residents in gated communities, clubbers, and hackers." Researchers identify such clusters from surveys in which respondents are asked questions ranging from their opera attendance to their potato chip consumption to matters of faith. Computer programs applied to the surveys identify sets or clusters of respondents who tend to answer questions the same way; each combination of answers can be read as a distinct lifestyle or cultural type. For example, heavy chips-eaters may also typically love country music, NASCAR, and attending church; the opera lovers may tend to be people who also like camping and reading *The New Yorker*. Researchers subsequently ask whether sharing certain lifestyles emerges from certain backgrounds, such as particular occupations or communities. Some political analysts adopt such methods to identify and target distinct voter groups, such as the "Republican Heartland Cultural Warriors."[43]

Transferring these approaches to our concern about cultural fragmentation, we ask whether Americans divided over the last three decades of the twentieth century into more and more separate clusters defined by distinct combinations of social values and social backgrounds.

Measuring Fragmentation

We undertook what can only be considered an initial exploration, not a resolution, of this question. (We hope to extend this work.) Ideally, we would examine large samples of Americans, drawn over many decades, who were all asked a long and unchanging list of questions about key cultural issues, such as faith, family life, morality, and the like. We would then test the notion that Americans went from consensus to dissensus, or more realistically, from fewer distinct clusters into more distinct clusters—say, not just religious conservatives and secular liberals but also secular conservatives and religious liberals. If this kind of fragmentation occurred, we would find that later in the century American survey respondents gave more diverse combinations of answers than respondents did earlier in the century, and this would reveal the splintering of the public landscape into many cultural "mesas."

Such data do not exist. Instead, we make do with more limited information over a much shorter time frame, the last third of the century. We use again the General Social Survey, because it asked many identical questions repeatedly over three decades. To track the connections between various positions—do people who, for example, abhor capital punishment typically favor women's equality and also tend to be well educated?—we need to have the same set of questions—in this example, capital punishment, gender roles, and education—posed to the entire sample. And to address the historical issue, that combination needed to exist over thirty years. These requirements drastically reduce the number of questions, respondents, and years that we could explore, even in the GSS (and they made use of other surveys impossible). In brief, we proceeded as follows. (Appendix C lays out the data and other methodological issues in detail.)

We scanned the GSS for questions on relevant cultural issues that were asked over the last three decades of the century and selected for analysis those respondents in each year who were asked all of these questions, totaling over twelve thousand individuals. We found thirteen behavioral and opinion items that could be used:

Respondents' self-ratings on a politically conservative-to-liberal scale

Reported frequency of church attendance

Attitudes toward:

Abortion

Premarital sex

Homosexuality

Easing divorce laws

Whether women are suited for politics

Prayer in schools

The ideal number of children

Capital punishment

Government spending for the environment

Government spending for minorities

Whether racial intermarriage should be legal

We also categorized respondents on seven social background traits, their answers to questions about age, ancestry, region (South/non-South), place (nonmetropolitan, suburb, city), education, household income, and religion (conservative Protestant, other Protestant, Catholic, other, or none).[44] Given the limited number of cases available and the complexity of the analysis, we pooled the GSS surveys into three time periods: the 1970s (the 1974 and 1977 surveys), the 1980s (1982, 1985, 1988, 1989, and 1990), and the 1990s (1991, 1993, 1996, 1998, and 2000).

We wanted to assess, for each decade, how respondents sorted themselves out according to these twenty different views and traits. How many distinct groupings were there in each decade? How large were they? How could they be described? We tailored latent class analysis (LCA) to our own purposes, as explained in appendix C. Simply described, the LCA program examines the associations among the twenty items, how answering each question went with answering every other one, in combinations that number several hundred million possibilities. It seeks the most parsimonious summary of the associations by assigning people to the fewest clusters of respondents consistent with the complexity of the data.

Clusters of Americans, 1970s to 1990s

Our LCA estimates suggest that nine clusters most efficiently summarize how respondents answered the twenty questions in the 1970s, whereas ten clusters most efficiently summarize the combinations of answers in the 1980s and in the 1990s. (Appendix table C.2 displays the tests that yielded this conclusion.)[45] Put another way, the largest three clusters together accounted for 49 percent, 51 percent, and 44 percent of the respondents in each of the three decades, respectively. What are we to make of these results? The shift from nine to ten clusters from the 1970s to the 1980s is not a substantial increase, because a difference of only one cluster is statistically subtle, more a matter of nuance than a clear-cut difference. Also, we had notably fewer cases in the 1970s than in the 1980s or 1990s, and that may have worked to suppress the number of clusters in the 1970s.[46] The decline between the 1980s and 1990s in the percentage covered by the three largest clusters, 51 to 44 percent, suggests that, while fragmentation did not increase, Americans were more evenly distributed across the different clusters in the 1990s.[47]

The answer to our key question, then, is that there was not much fragmenting between the 1970s and the 1990s, if any at all. (Perhaps the fragmenting that did occur took place, like the "culture wars," in the extended 1960s, before the 1970s.) Americans seemed, however, to divide into somewhat more balanced clusters in the 1990s. We can go further and describe what these clusters look like. They were fairly consistent over the three decades, although we can find some subtle changes. (Appendix table C.3 presents the full statistical descriptions of each cluster.) In table 9.1, we simplify those results by comparing just the 1990s and the 1970s. The table includes a row describing each of the ten clusters. We align the 1970s and 1990s clusters that seemed clearly to include the same sorts of people in the two periods, list the traits that show their consistency, and note in some cases particular differences between the 1970s and 1990s versions of those clusters. For example, cluster I was the largest in both periods, with 21 percent of the respondents in the 1970s and 16 percent in the 1990s. In both eras, cluster I largely consisted of white, well-to-do, well-educated suburbanites who were liberal on race and gender issues but supportive of capital punishment. In the 1970s, they were also disproportionately mainline Protestants, but in the 1990s cluster I also included many Catholics. (The distinctive feature of clustering in the 1980s—which we do not review here for reasons of space and simplicity—seems to have been the emergence of a mainly Latino cluster. In the 1970s and 1990s, Latinos instead largely appeared among the heavily Catholic clusters, notably cluster VII.) What does table 9.1 suggest about fragments of Americans?

Note first how, in each period, the clusters do indeed represent distinctive combinations of traits and attitudes. Take an example from the 1970s. The respondents in clusters II and V agreed on several social issues. People in both groups strongly opposed premarital sex, homosexuality, and easier divorce, and people in both clusters tended to call themselves conservatives.

Table 9.1 Capsule Descriptions of the Cultural Clusters, 1970s and 1990s

Cluster Number	Traits That Distinguished the Cluster in Both Decades	1970s			1990s		
		Number	Percentage	Special Features of the 1970s	Number	Percentage	Special Features of the 1990s
I	Affluent; educated; suburban. *Support capital punishment; somewhat liberal on race and gender.*	1	21	Mainline Protestant.	1	16	Mainline Protestant and Catholic.
II	Middle-aged. *Politically conservative churchgoers; very conservative on family issues (abortion, sex, and so on).*	2	14	High school graduates; middle-income.	5	11	
III	Nonsouthern, older, mainline . Protestant; low-income. *Lean conservative on social issues, moderate on abortion.*	3	14		7	8	Moderate on capital punishment.
IV	Young, urban, nonsouthern, well-educated, middle-income. *Secular; self-labeled liberals; liberal on social and racial issues.*	4	11		4	11	

(Table continues on p. 236.)

Table 9.1 (*Continued*)

Cluster Number	Traits That Distinguished the Cluster in Both Decades	1970s			1990s		
		Number	Percentage	Special Features of the 1970s	Number	Percentage	Special Features of the 1990s
V	Poorly educated, elderly, southern, rural; conservative Protestant. *Socially conservative, especially on interracial marriage, premarital sex, and homosexuality.*	5	10		10	4	Low-income. *Socially conservative on issues such as interracial marriage, women in politics, and homosexuality.*
VI	Southern, rural. *Racially conservative, but relatively moderate on most other social issues except homosexuality; favor small families.*	6	10	Not elderly, conservative Protestant, but rarely attend church.	3	14	Middle-aged. *Favor capital punishment.*
VII	Catholic, young, disproportionately Latino.	7	8	One-fifth Latino. *Slightly liberal, except anti-abortion.*	8	8	Two-fifths Latino, nonsouthern. *Politically and socially moderate, except anti-abortion.*
VIII	Almost all black, urban. *Racially liberal; liberal on capital punishment, divorce law, premarital sex.*	8	7		6	9	

Cluster	Description						Demographic
IX	Black, southern, conservative Protestants; church attenders. *Racially liberal and opposed to capital punishment; conservative on social and gender issues.*	9	5	Almost all black, poor, poorly educated.	9	9	Mostly black high school graduates.
X	Appears only in 1990s; seems to emerge from the sorts of people who formed clusters I and IV in the 1970s				2	15	Suburban, young high school graduates; two-fifths with no or "other" religion. *Secular, very liberal on social and gender issues, but favor capital punishment; favor small families.*

Source: Authors' analysis of the GSS.

Note: All clusters were at least 93 percent white, unless otherwise indicated. Non-italic entries refer to demographic and social attributes, italicized entries to attitudes.

But 95 percent of cluster II respondents *approved* of interracial marriage, and 93 percent in cluster V *opposed* it; also, almost all respondents in cluster II reported being frequent church attenders, yet only about half in cluster V did. (In addition, cluster V was much more southern, rural, aged, and poorly educated, while cluster II was about average in these respects.) Or compare the 1990s' two predominantly black clusters, VIII and IX. Although similar demographically and politically and on racial issues, the respondents in the two clusters differed greatly on issues of sexuality (83 percent of cluster IX said premarital sex was always wrong versus 8 percent of cluster VIII) and in their church attendance (66 percent of cluster IX said they attended frequently versus 28 percent of cluster VIII). Complexity—rather than simple polarization—characterizes the groupings.

Note, second, the continuity across decades. Excepting the emergence of cluster X in the 1990s, the profiles of each pairing in table 9.1 changed only modestly.[48] The major puzzle is explaining the new cluster X, which, although composed of people who were similar in some ways to people in 1970s clusters I and IV, seems to have emerged from 1970s clusters I and III. That is, the respondents in 1990s cluster X appear to be the more liberal and less religious "descendants" of those 1970s conservative and religious clusters.[49]

Note, third, that despite the complexity of cross-cutting groupings, we can find a few segments of the population that appear polarized. In both the 1970s and 1990s, Americans in cluster IV were stereotypically liberal: half claimed to be non-Christian or of no religion, the great majority rarely went to church, they formed the most solidly liberal cluster on issues such as premarital sex and homosexuality, and 75 percent labeled themselves "liberal" or "slightly liberal." On the other side of the spectrum were at least two clearly conservative clusters. Cluster II was most opposed to the liberals of cluster IV: virtually all were Christians, frequent church attenders, self-described political conservatives, and highly critical of abortion, premarital sex, homosexuality, and divorce—and they became more so in the 1990s. In both decades, the ideological liberals of cluster IV formed 11 percent of the sample; the strongly conservative cluster II included 14 percent of the 1970s respondents and 11 percent of the 1990s ones. People in cluster V were also relatively consistent cultural conservatives. Add the three clusters together—IV's liberals with the conservatives of II and V— and we can estimate that about 35 percent of the 1970s sample, but fewer (26 percent) of the 1990s sample (roughly 40 percent and 30 percent of the white respondents in each decade), seemed consistently liberal or conservative. The gap between the ideologically consistent liberals and conservatives may have widened a bit, but fewer Americans were in those fragments. Most Americans by far held more jumbled and not easily simplified views.

Summary

This preliminary exploration, using cluster analysis, generally discounts the claim that America fragmented between the 1970s and 1990s. We found that ten clusters in the 1980s and 1990s and nine clusters in the 1970s best capture the GSS respondents' patterns of answers. We also found that a slightly smaller percentage of the respondents fell into the three biggest clusters in the 1990s than in 1970s. But these are small and, as we noted, perhaps only technical fluctuations. The broader picture shows much more continuity than change in the thirty years. Of course, the fragmentation of America may well have occurred before the available data, during those turbulent 1960s we focused on in our "culture wars" exploration.

E PLURIBUS UNUM

Both sets of results, those on the culture wars, 1935 to 2000, and those on fragmentation, 1970 to 2000, suggest that, at least after the 1970s, Americans in general did *not* become notably more polarized or divided on matters of cultural or moral values. The politically active did divide after 1970, because the political parties increasingly lined up along the social cleavages, not because the general public increasingly took sides. Other findings in this book, of course, do document increasing polarization in other arenas, such as work and income, especially by amount of education. But there was as much consensus on social and cultural views around 2000 as there had been around 1970—and perhaps greater consensus than before on topics like premarital sex, women's roles, and interracial marriage. The contemporary intensity of the political debate comes not from the distance between the partisans, we suggest, but from the fact that they are so evenly matched, as witnessed in the close elections of 2000 and 2004. New issues always arise that divide the public, so no one can project consensus into the twenty-first century. But our best estimate is that the twentieth-century era of truly substantial divisions was—as popular impression would have it—the "extended 1960s." (Another era of exceptional cultural divisions may have been, as some historians suggest, the 1920s, but those years are over our data horizon.) Perhaps most remarkable is how much consensus on ideas, values, and attitudes has persisted—recall our findings on religion in chapter 8—in the face of considerable division along demographic, economic, geographical, and educational lines.

CHAPTER TEN

Conclusion: The Direction of Americans' Differences

ON SEPTEMBER 1, 2005, deep in the American South, only about five hundred miles from where Italians were lynched in 1900, the Tampa Bay Devil Rays baseball team featured "Italian Heritage Night"—to be followed by Polish and Irish Heritage Nights. (That same summer the San Francisco Giants presented "Asian-American Heritage Night" in their ballpark at China Basin, only a brief walk from the place where Chinese immigrants were murdered in the nineteenth century.) The Italians who over a century before had marched out of Washington Square in Manhattan to honor Columbus (see chapter 1) could hardly have imagined how conventional celebrations of their ancestry would have become only a few generations later. (October is Italian-American Heritage Month.) They could also hardly have imagined that being Italian American would become so inconsequential to the fate of their grandchildren. By 2000, Italian ancestry might have become a source of pride, good humor, and good food, but it had little effect on where Americans lived, how they lived, how well they lived, or even who they married.[1] Other things—especially how much schooling they got—determined their grandchildren's fates far more. The marchers' descendants lived in a society more diverse and divided in different ways than the one the marchers of 1900 sought to join.

Americans of the late twentieth century were a varied lot; that was evident everywhere we looked in our survey of who Americans were, how they lived, and what they thought. They varied in age and gender, of course, but also in how they organized themselves in (or out of) families; in their educations, occupations, and incomes; in their racial and ethnic ancestries; in their religions; and in their values. Some of these differences became more salient over the century, others less so. In both cases, looking at these differences often tells us more about Americans than we learn from tracking an "average American" across the century. For example, we understand more about American living standards if we keep in mind that wealth, poverty, and the contrast between the two expanded between 1975 and 1995 than if we are content simply to know that average family income rose a little. Similarly, the implications of the longevity revolution between 1900 and 1940 are more profound than the simple twelve-year increase in the average life span suggests, because that revolution mainly extended the lives of the short-lived. One-fifth of Americans born in 1900 died in childhood, but most Americans born in 1940 who, because of poor nutrition, sanitation, and the like, would have been in that ill-fated group instead lived well into middle age, long enough to grow up, marry, and parent their own children. Another illustration is the decline in average birth rates from the start to the end of the century; this decline was large and consequential, but we better understand what happened when we see that the century's fertility revolution was a decline in the extremes. Fewer American women had many children, and fewer had no children, and eventually most had two or three. Variation matters, and the nature of those variations changed over the century.

We use this chapter to summarize the insights that emerged from our attention to a century of differences, and we then go on to focus on a few major themes that cut across the specific topics of the previous chapters.

A RECAP

Americans became dramatically more educated over the course of the century. One in five had a high school diploma in 1900; 85 percent did by century's end. College education, once a perk of the elite, spread throughout the middle class; by 2000, 70 percent of young people attended college or another postsecondary institution, and 30 percent earned a college degree. During this vast expansion, the least-educated gained more schooling at about the same pace as the most-educated did; in this sense, educational inequality did not increase. And yet educational attainment increasingly divided Americans economically, socially, geographically, and politically. In practically every topic we raised, the most- and the least-educated Americans were further apart in 2000 than they had been earlier.

Americans at the turn of the twenty-first century could see growing diversity most obviously in the complexions of their newest fellow Americans and hear it most clearly in their languages. Ethnic diversity had actually declined through much of the twentieth century, because 1920s legislation virtually shut off the flow of immigrants from outside the hemisphere. New laws and new economic realities after 1965 attracted immigrants from parts of the world that had previously sent relatively few people to America. The new immigrants appeared to be better prepared for American society and faster learners than those of the early century. Their English-language knowledge on arrival was greater, their acquisition of it after arrival was quicker, and they brought more educational credentials. Immigrants in general found greater acceptance from native-born Americans over the century. Where once people who came from anyplace other than northwestern Europe had been commonly denounced, by 2000 celebrations of multiculturalism like heritage nights and heritage months abounded. Americans still argued about the best course for eliminating discrimination and injustice, but only a small minority held on to the sorts of nativist views once common among both elites and the general public. By most measures of "social distance," Americans were more tolerant of Americans unlike themselves at the end of the century than they had been in the 1930s when such measurements began. Most significantly, intermarriage across ethnic and racial lines was on the rise, although mixed marriages for African Americans remained notably rare.

However visible and critical racial and ethnic diversity was, Americans differed in many other, deeper ways as well—in longevity, fertility, and family life. Changes in birth, marriage, and death drove other social changes. Most profound was the dramatic decline in infant and child mortality in the first forty years of the century. In 1900 parents frequently lost babies and toddlers to infections, waterborne parasites, and diseases like measles, smallpox, and pneumonia. And children lost their parents to accidents, heart disease, and epidemics of tuberculosis and influenza. Few Americans born in 1900 reached adulthood without having lost either a sibling or a parent. Because death in 1900 was so often the product of forces beyond Americans' understanding (like germs) or control (like mosquitoes), it did not spare any class, race, or gender (although it stalked the cities more than the countryside). When families lost adult members, the survivors moved in with relatives and formed extended families. In 1900, 20 percent of children lived with a grandparent, aunt, or uncle; 45 percent of seniors lived with an adult child. But by 1970 only 10 percent of children and 12 percent of seniors lived in extended families like that. Controlling death thus dramatically altered family patterns.

Extending a process that had started in the nineteenth century, parents increasingly planned and limited their families. They had fewer children and spaced them further apart. Even during the baby boom of 1947 to 1962, Americans started limiting their broods to four or fewer; in the last quarter of the century, Americans had too few children to replace themselves.[2] Often unnoticed, however, is how uniform these family patterns became: the great majority of Americans had just two or three children.

Yet differences in family life did emerge, notably between those with stable marriages and those without—a difference that corresponded strongly to levels of education. As the less-educated regularly encountered unwedded parenthood and divorce, college graduates married, remained married, or quickly remarried after divorce.

Late-century media coverage often highlighted and fretted about the decline in the proportion of nuclear families. But the news coverage typically missed the fastest-growing household type, the "empty nest" of a married couple whose children had grown up and moved out. Thanks mainly to the control of death and improved financial security, fifty- and sixty-year-olds in 2000 lived out an age-old wish: to see all their children grown to maturity with families of their own. Single-adult households also became far more common, but they too were diverse. Some included a parent and children; many had only one, affluent twentysomething; and most contained a long-lived widow or widower who preferred to live independently.[3]

The variety of what Americans did for a living expanded greatly over the twentieth century. A few ancient occupations, like farmer, miner, and shopkeeper, topped the list of common job titles, but our index of occupational diversity doubled in one hundred years as new kinds of jobs, like pilot, television repairman, paralegal, and web designer, emerged. The nature of work changed substantively too. In 1900 Americans worked mainly with things—growing things, making things, selling things. In the latter half of the century, Americans largely worked with other people and, increasingly, with information—reading, writing, and talking. The information demands of the new economy degraded the value of a high school diploma and enhanced that of higher degrees. Many employers started looking for college graduates to do the work they once entrusted to high school graduates. Some observers call this "credential inflation," but most social scientists consider employers to be rational: they were willing to pay a premium because jobs increasingly demanded more people and data skills than many employees had.

Variations in Americans' wages accounted, in large part, for variations in their living standards—that is, for the nation's economic inequality. Early in the century, inequality was substantial. The financial collapse of 1929 and the Great Depression of the 1930s destroyed much paper wealth and put millions of people (25 percent of the labor force in 1932; see figure 5.14) out of work. The hard times reversed the rise of inequality and compressed the distribution of incomes. World War II accelerated that equalizing trend as it brought high taxes to the wealthy and high wages to industrial workers. Then the economic boom of the 1950s and 1960s not only lifted all boats, in President Kennedy's famous metaphor, but most especially lifted the rowboats of the poor out of the muck. Between 1967 and 1973—the golden age of postwar prosperity—the richest million Americans saw their incomes rise by 19 percent while the poorest million's incomes rose even faster, by 24 percent, pushing income inequality down to its lowest point on record.[4] But after 1973 the rich continued to get richer—the top 5 percent had in-flation-adjusted incomes that were 83 percent higher in 1995 than in 1975—while the poor not only failed to keep pace but lost ground. By 1995 the poorest 10 percent of American families had lower incomes, after ad-justing for inflation, than the poorest 10 percent had in 1975. Variations in wealth were always far greater than variations in income, and they too ex-panded in the latter third of the century. Americans' levels of consumption, however, did not differ nearly as much as their incomes, because the rich save and the poor borrow, and because increased productivity gave even low-income Americans access to new and better products. Yet differences in consumption also seemed to widen near the end of the century. And cer-tainly, differences in economic security became more pronounced in the last decades. The economic leveling of midcentury America had turned into eco-nomic pyramiding in late-century America.

Migration patterns, like patterns of birth and death, also reshaped Amer-ican diversity. In 1900 Americans were a rural people: they largely lived in towns, villages, and open countryside, and New York, Chicago, and Philadel-phia were the only cities with over 1 million inhabitants. By 2000, however, three of four Americans lived in a metropolitan area, mainly in the suburban rings of large center cities. In 1900 region really mattered. People over forty-five years old could remember the Civil War, and younger Americans were schooled in the importance of regional history. Laws in the South di-vided blacks and whites into two castes, a system foreign to the rest of the nation. The West was still wild; Oklahoma, New Mexico, Arizona, Alaska, and Hawaii were not even states yet. The movement of people—out of the South and Southwest in the 1930s and then toward the Sun Belt after World War II—helped level regional differences. Economic growth brought the South into the national economy. Technology and the popular culture it spawned in the form of national radio and television networks and nation-wide distribution of movies bridged regional cultures. By the end of the cen-tury, the geographic divide that mattered most was no longer regional but the distinction between the center cities of metropolitan areas and their sub-urban rings. Furthermore, hints emerged in the last four decades, mostly in the form of growing economic segregation, that suburbs themselves were becoming more socially distinct and segregated from each other, that the fracture lines within metropolitan regions were emerging as important axes of difference.

Religious diversity, like ethnic and occupational diversity, also expanded greatly, at least in terms of professed religions; Americans came to identify with literally hundreds of different denominations, most of them varieties of

Christianity. In 1900 most Americans were members of mainline Protestant denominations. By 2000, mainline Protestants were outnumbered by the members of conservative Protestant denominations and Roman Catholics; indeed, the proportion of Americans who were Protestants of any stripe had declined from four in five to one in two. Also, late in the century, the fraction of American adults who eschewed any religious affiliation increased from 7 to 14 percent. That development was tied to both generational succession (the cohorts born between 1900 and 1919 were the greatest church joiners) and the politicization of conservative denominations (which alienated some liberals).[5] Yet, as Americans dispersed into ever more "niche" denominations or even looser "spiritual" practices, they converged in how they practiced their faiths and in what they believed: devotions took on an increasingly standard format of weekly services presided over by professional clergy, and more and more Americans shared a belief in life after death. In the spirit of ecumenicism, tolerance of other people's religious faiths grew as well.

Americans' interest in cultural differences has always been rooted partly in the possibility that difference means social fragmentation, conflict, and possible collapse. In the later years of the century, the ethnic, class, and lifestyle diversity of America worried many a commentator. Such worries are somewhat ironic: pundits and best-selling authors of the midcentury warned readers of too much homogeneity. Nonetheless, while American politics repolarized after a relatively harmonious period at midcentury, popular attitudes and beliefs for the most part neither led nor followed this sharpening division. Issues arose, and Americans disagreed for a while about them, but most controversies had a natural life cycle. If there was a period of "culture war," it was not near the end of century but during the exceptional, extended 1960s, when cultural struggles over family, gender, and race peaked. Abortion was the only truly polarizing topic in the last quarter of the century. Nor is there much evidence for the claim that Americans at the end of the century were fragmenting into increasingly many distinctive cultural camps. Even though marketers had some success with targeting their audiences with directed appeals based on zip codes, Americans' social attitudes and demographic characteristics clustered pretty much the same way in the 1990s as they had in the 1970s. Underneath the variety of addresses, ethnic loyalties, occupations, churches, organizations, brand loyalties, pastimes, and pop-culture tastes that made for the kaleidoscopic quality of the American people in 2000 was a common core of shared outlooks and values.

As we covered the range of twentieth-century American variations, from diversity in life spans to diverse opinions on homosexuality, some themes recurred. One, of course, is the increasing weight of education, but there are a few others worthy of attention as well.

EMERGING THEMES OF TWENTIETH-CENTURY AMERICA

In trying to summarize a century's worth of social change, we have by necessity been unable to dwell on many critical developments, each of which—from the extension of life spans to the role of culture in political struggles—demands more intensive study. Similarly, in summing up, we can only draw the reader's attention to three general themes that recurred throughout the previous chapters.

The Force of "Vital Events"

In many public debates on topics such as family, work, and values, discussion typically focuses on the question of what shall we—individually or as a nation—do. Should one marry someone of a different faith? What effect would legal recognition of same-sex couples have on Americans' families? But looking at matters over a century's duration provides a more humbling perspective on what shapes social life. Much, it turns out, is the product of deep transformations in what demographers call "vital events," notably death rates, but also patterns of births, marriages, and moves. Earlier in this chapter, we discussed the effect of the increasing postponement and equalizing of death in rearranging the American life cycle and family structure. The spurt in births in the 1950s and 1960s helped create a shared culture of "familism"—as well as a subsequent traffic jam in schools and colleges—and it will create an elderly-heavy society and perhaps intergenerational conflict in the mid-twenty-first century. Migration patterns added new ingredients to the ancestral mix and introduced novel religious strands; decades later these patterns had produced unfamiliar ethnic and racial combinations that challenged the ability of some Americans to even identify their race in the decennial census.

To underline the role of demography is not to suggest that demographic shifts appear from nowhere and alter society willy-nilly. They may sometimes seem to do so, especially in the short run, as in the case of pandemics or bursts of immigration. More typically, however, demographic shifts are subject to collective decisions (although not always made with collective foresight). Once set in motion, demographic shifts often shape social life below the radar of public debate. As we pointed out, for example, some commentators on the "disappearing" nuclear family seemed unaware that the driving force behind those numbers was the increasing longevity of married couples. Our public discourse would be richer if it better appreciated these deep currents of vital events.

The Special Case of African Americans

Often in describing the course of American social history, we have had to as-terisk our declarative statements with a qualifier, "except for African Amer-icans." For example, diverse ancestral groups intermarried at higher and higher rates over the century, children in 2000 were about as likely to be in two-parent nuclear families as in 1900, and American communities had few and transient ethnic ghettos—but these and similar claims did not hold for blacks. Americans have long known, or should have known, that the greatest division among them is between the descendants of slavery and everyone else. Alexis de Tocqueville predicted thirty years before Emancipation that this would be so, and the early sociologist W. E. B. Du Bois famously pro-claimed that "the problem of the twentieth century is the problem of the color-line." The chasm between the slaves' offspring and other Americans did, in many ways, narrow over the twentieth century. African Americans gained more legal rights, more education, better jobs, higher incomes, more political say, and more acceptance. Even residential segregation declined in the final three decades. But in a few ways the chasm actually widened, and so did divisions among blacks themselves. For example, black children in-creasingly lived apart from their fathers, and young black men increasingly spent years in prison—both of these trends occurring at exceptionally high rates. And even where historical change moved African Americans closer to the European-American majority, the distance remaining was great. Black residential segregation, while dropping, remained an order of magnitude greater than that of other minorities; black intermarriage rates, while rising, remained an order of magnitude lower than that of other minorities. In more subtle ways too, the estrangement of African Americans was of a spe-cial quality. In survey after survey, for example, African Americans at the end of the century typically answered questions in more critical, alienated, skeptical, and dissatisfied ways than did other respondents, reflecting a cyn-icism that was an understandable heritage of three centuries under a caste system.[6]

Education as a Great Divider

While the gap between African Americans and whites remained profound, it narrowed some. In contrast, the division between the less- and the more-ed-ucated grew and emerged as a powerful determiner of life chances and lifestyles. In 1900 what set Americans apart were differences that were easy to see, even at birth. Men and women led different lives, as did blacks and whites, southerners and northerners, natives and immigrants, Protestants, Catholics, and Jews, and those born into big families or small ones, into rich ones or poor ones. Through the century most of these differences abated. By midcentury, significant differences by region, nativity, and family size in how people lived had largely disappeared. Also, prosperity was more widespread than ever before, and poverty decreased rapidly. Americans were beginning to leave behind discrimination against women, blacks, Catholics, Jews, and other groups. And in the second half of the century, the consequences of gender, racial, and religious differences moderated further. Economic differences and their consequences, however, widened after 1970. Also, new and consequential differences defined by marital status and, especially, by education appeared. Broadly speaking, the differences that came to have greater consequences shifted from differences at birth to the differences at the beginning of adult life.[7]

This pattern reminds us of William Julius Wilson's characterization of *The Declining Significance of Race*. In that controversial 1978 book, Wilson argues that "now the life chances of individual blacks have more to do with their economic class position than with their day-to-day encounters with whites."[8] Being black, though once paramount in their struggle for economic success, had been partially supplanted by economic circumstances in the mid-1970s. Most circumstances of birth were, we suggest, overshadowed by economic realities in twentieth-century America. In fact, evidence for the declining significance of gender, region, ancestry, and nativity is stronger than for the declining significance of race.

"Class," understood in its broadest sense, had been a diminished concern in midcentury America, but it reemerged by the end of the century as a key axis of difference—albeit with important changes. Social scientists of the early decades of the twentieth century paid much attention to class (when not obsessing about the adjustment of immigrants). They documented poverty in the inner cities and unveiled the class scaffolding behind the facades of American small towns.[9] The Depression accentuated these concerns and widened the audience for class-based fiction, cinema, and politics. But class seemed to matter less after the war, during the economic boom and the baby boom, and in the turbulent 1960s. (There were certainly struggles then, but they were not class struggles.) It was unclear what class even meant in the American context. It clearly seemed to mean money, but did not seem to mean the kind of inherited, frozen, cultural rank it meant in Europe. After 1970, however, growing economic inequality pushed class more and more into public debate, even demanding attention from those who warned against "class warfare." At the same time, class itself seemed to have been transformed. In 1900 a family's class—and its consequent life ways—rested on real property and the father's job; in 2000 class seemed to rest most on the educational attainments of husband and wife.

Credentials earned and cognitive skills learned in school increasingly sorted workers into better versus worse jobs and into highly paid versus lowly paid occupations. Education influenced family life more too. By 2000, college graduates were an especially distinctive set of Americans. They earned higher incomes than other Americans, of course, but they also were likelier to marry, to remarry faster after divorce, to have higher-income spouses, to live in higher-income neighborhoods, to benefit from more job security, to have better health, and to express a cheerier outlook on life. Political alienation, to take another example, increased in the last decades of the century, but it was highest and rose most rapidly among the poorly educated, while it was lowest and rose only slowly among the well-educated.[10] Some of the advantages that college graduates garnered came from the sorts of skills and social values provided by higher education itself, and some came indirectly from the better jobs and higher incomes yielded by the degrees. Together all these advantages increasingly set the highly educated apart.

There was debate in the 1990s about whether this emerging and nearly ubiquitous pattern meant that the United States was developing a "meritocracy" in which an educated (and presumably worthy) elite sat high atop American society. For some, the combination of ability and effort leading to success while irrelevant factors like region, race, and gender no longer held deserving individuals back would be a positive development. Some critics of this trend worried, however, that the advantages the elite garnered could be handed on to the next generation, stalling social mobility; other critics faulted the criteria and unfair procedures that opened the educational door into the elite.[11]

We have noted that the connection between education and an open opportunity society is complex. Education, aside from its intrinsic value, became in the twentieth century *the* ticket to a better and different life. But it is a ticket that can be distributed in a couple of different ways—inherited or not. If the amount and quality of young persons' schooling depend heavily on the resources they bring from home—their parents' educations, wealth, connections, and so on—then opportunity for moving up the social ladder is less open. The handing on of advantage from generation to generation through education is acceptable in American culture—more praiseworthy than, say, getting a job through nepotism or inheriting the family business— because young people earn their educational credentials in a competition that appears, albeit misleadingly, to have nothing to do with family background. On the other hand, if progress in school depends less on students' family backgrounds, then the education ticket is a way for the less advantaged to move up in an open society.

How much family background determined schooling shifted historically. From as far back as good data can be found and up to the early 1980s, it appeared that family background, including parental class and ancestry, was mattering less and less to attaining a college degree and that a wider range of American youth were getting that ticket to the good life. After the early 1980s, the connection between family origins and educational attainment tightened, mostly because the cost of college went up.[12] Thus, access to a better life—which meant not only more money but also better work, a better neighborhood, and a more stable marriage—shrank, even as college and postgraduate credentials became all the more critical. Education began to matter more as access to it in the 1950s and 1960s expanded; it mattered even more as access to it narrowed in the 1980s and 1990s.

Education mattered more at the end of the century in terms of the material fortunes that amount to class, broadly conceived. It also mattered more in terms of personal life, tastes, culture, lifestyles, and politics. By 2000, the divisions between high school dropouts, high school graduates, college graduates, and, more and more, postgraduates were deep and growing.

COLLECTIVE SELF-DETERMINATION

Although many of the forces that drove twentieth-century social change were out of the control of individuals—and often of institutions too—we also have been struck by the extent to which Americans, collectively, shaped the unfolding patterns of differences. The vehicle of that collective effort was, of course, government.

The politics of the last quarter of the twentieth century blended a resurgent emphasis, at least rhetorically, on individualism—self-reliance, entrepreneurship, freedom from taxes, and so on—with a corrosive distrust of public institutions. Yet the beneficent changes of the century were often due to public institutions. Municipal efforts in the first quarter of the century to filter and chlorinate water, remove waste, regulate food and milk, and eliminate pests largely explain why infants and children lived so much longer.[13] Later, publicly financed and mandatory inoculation curtailed the spread of measles and eradicated smallpox and polio. In more recent decades, research grants from the National Institutes of Health led to medical breakthroughs that saved older Americans who might have been stricken down by cancer and heart disease. The family revolution of the "empty nest," of couples living longer together, is one consequence of government action in health and income security.

Public primary and secondary education was a necessary ingredient in the transformation of the nation's economy from muscles applied to things to brains applied to people. The early proponents of public schools were more convinced that mass education would promote democracy than be of economic value. But both goals were realized in the last century. Citizens may be criticized for not reading the newspapers as much or as closely as they should, but an educated electorate remains a necessity as Americans debate complex issues like global warming, stem cell research, and the ethics of prolonging life through medical means. (The efficacy of public education was also debated in the last quarter of the century, but test scores and graduation rates suggest that the "crisis" in public schools was overblown.)[14] Public education did what private education could not.

The expansion of higher education, by providing both trained workers and innovative research, was especially critical to the most recent growth and transformation of the American economy. At the end of World War II, there was space enough in colleges and universities for only one-fifth of Americans age eighteen to twenty-two; by the early 1990s, there was space enough for about four-fifths of them.[15] The expansion came about almost solely through the construction and subsidization of *public* higher education. Ohio State University, for example, quadrupled in size between 1955 and 1975. Our own positions at the University of California are the long-term result of California's famous 1960 "Master Plan for Higher Education" and state taxpayers' continuing support for building a world-class system of higher education. (We thank our fellow Californians.) Increasing access to higher education after World War II shrank economic gaps among Americans, but as we just noted, cutbacks in funding and in need-based scholarships after the 1970s reversed that trend.

Public investment in the southern and western states hastened their incorporation into the national economy. The rural electrification program and the Tennessee Valley Authority, the defense contracts of World War II and the cold war, hydroelectric projects, Eisenhower's national highway system, Kennedy's Appalachian programs, and even the decision to put NASA in Houston were among the many ways in which the federal government helped replace the agricultural economies of the South and West with modern, post-industrial ones.

Americans also used government to narrow differences among them more directly. In chapter 5, we documented how the minimum wage kept economic inequality in check. Add to that Social Security, Medicare, and the other "safety net" programs. Twentieth-century Americans built a floor that, despite some splintering and cracking in the later decades, helped keep up living standards. And in the arena of ethnic and cultural differences, explicit policies, from antidiscrimination laws and voting rights enforcement to symbolic expressions like Martin Luther King Jr. Day, have, with some modest success, reduced intergroup tension and the cost of being in a minority. The federal government was late to embrace the cause of civil rights, but when it finally engaged the issue—starting roughly from President Truman's order to integrate army units in 1948—progress in race relations came much more quickly than it had in the preceding seventy-five years.

We are underlining the point that many of the important convergences that Americans experienced in the twentieth century were the product of their own collective will and action in closing differences. To be sure, many were also the product of economic dynamics—such as the increased productivity fostered by technological change—and of cultural shifts—such as the spread of ecumenicism. Some were also the unintended consequences of deliberate action. (For example, the rapid expansion of higher education in the 1950s and 1960s reduced the income premium paid to college gradu-ates.) But it is critical to appreciate the extent to which both the closing of many gaps—through devices such as public health campaigns, infrastructure investment in the Sun Belt, and the federal minimum wage—and the widen-ing of other gaps—through decisions such as allowing health insurance cov-erage to lag and the minimum wage to succumb to inflation—are the result of purposeful policy rather than the unfolding of impersonal forces.

At the beginning of the new century, what strikes us most is, on the one hand, the impressive absorptive and uniting quality of American culture and, on the other, the widening class divisions since 1970. The narrowing of regional differences may have taken generations, but it was mainly accom-plished by about the 1950s. European national ancestry is not the weighty matter it was a century ago; it figures more now in baseball "heritage nights" than in life chances. Even race has become somewhat less consequential, and many of the remaining racial differences reflect economic disadvantage more than overt racism. As economic inequality grew over the last genera-tion, however, class—more and more centered on education as its key com-ponent—increasingly shaped Americans' lives. Still, neither these widening class divisions nor the culture wars chatter of the 1990s have diminished Americans' overwhelming sense of being one nation. *E Pluribus Unum*.

APPENDIX A

Combining Parametric and Nonparametric Regressions to Study How Trends Differ Among Subpopulations*

WE ANALYZED for this book dozens, maybe hundreds, of social trends over the period 1900 to 2000 in the United States. We were interested in two aspects of the trends: their general direction (increase or decrease), and whether subpopulations were becoming more similar or more different from one another (convergence or divergence). Locally estimated ("loess") regression smoothing techniques provide a useful approach to analyzing the direction of the trend, but we found them to be unsatisfactory for figuring out whether subgroups were converging or diverging.[1] This appendix describes how we blended loess with parametric regression techniques to analyze trends and how they differed across subpopulations.

The blended approach takes three steps:

1. Obtain a loess fit for the general trend (without regard to subpopulations or covariates)

2. Generate a new variable that assigns the loess fitted values to each time point

3. Enter the trend variable (generated per step 2), interesting covariates, and terms for the interactions between natural time (not recoded) and the covariates into a multivariate parametric regression

*Special thanks to Gretchen Stockmayer, who implemented the technique in a simple, elegant, and flexible form, and to Leo A. Goodman, who provided useful comments and suggestions.

The simple, traditional approach would be to use ordinary least squares (OLS) regression and some combinations of interaction effects involving time to analyze the trends. The problem with that approach is its treatment of time. Researchers have to choose either dummy variables for each period—a very inefficient alternative—or a mathematical formula for the trend (such as the polynomial option on Microsoft's Excel program), an approach that is too constraining. The loess approach is far more efficient than dummy variables and far more flexible than specifying a mathematical formula for the trend.

The main effects for covariates derived in step 3 describe how far above or below their intercepts they are compared to the national trend and thus tell us about basic group differences—say, whether southerners were generally less supportive of racial intermarriage than northerners. The interaction terms—say, South by time and South by time-squared—describe the trajectory of each group as deviations from the overall national trend. Then we can assess the degree to which subgroups converge and diverge over time. We see the fruits of this analysis later when we pursue a concrete example.

Other researchers have addressed the analysis of trends with statistical smoothing methods since Cleveland first introduced loess in 1979. But the literature focuses on identifying the trend; the approach introduced here blends nonparametric and parametric regressions in a way that is better suited to the question of convergence versus divergence. So, for example, the procedure outlined by John DiNardo and Justin Tobias is optimal for researchers whose focus is on the shape of the trend line (or another relationship of primary interest), but it does not answer the question of variations in trend across subpopulations that occupied so much of our project.[2]

THE MODEL

Let y_{it} be some outcome of interest—for example, the probability of agreeing that states should not make laws prohibiting marriages between people of different races—for person i in year t.[3] Suppose that: (1) y varies among important subpopulations and over time; (2) the variation among subpopulations is well expressed in terms of a general linear model (perhaps made flexible by the use of dummy variables); and (3) variation over time is not easily captured by a simple function. A mathematical formulation of our suppositions to this point would look like this:

$$y_{it} = \beta_0 + \sum_{k=1}^{K} \beta_k X_{ik} + \lambda_g G(t) + \varepsilon_{it} \qquad (A.1)$$

In this formulation, the differences among the groups encoded by the X variables do not change over time. The expected value of y_{it} goes up and down over time according to g(t), but differences among groups are constants represented by the β_k terms.

Many of the dependent variables of interest to us were dichotomies—agree or disagree that states should not make laws prohibiting marriages between people of different races, attending or not attending religious services, being satisfied or dissatisfied with a job, and so forth. The two most common methods for analyzing binary outcomes—logit and probit regression—are, unfortunately, ill suited to our questions of convergence and divergence. The problem is that logit and probit methods start with nonlinear transformations of the probability of a positive response. Thus, the probabilities for different combinations of X variables calculated from estimates of the coefficients in equation A.1 might show convergence or divergence, even though the model contains no convergence or divergence terms. That is because the logit and probit transformations fit curves, not simple straight lines, to the probability of a positive outcome.[4]

To make the differences among social categories dynamic, we need to allow them to change over time. A first thought might be to interact them with g(t), since that is the time element in equation A.1. But that would be a peculiar form of social change—indicating that social differences are large when y_{it} trends upward and small when y_{it} trends lower. More interesting for our purposes is the prospect that the differences are increasing or decreasing as natural time moves ahead from 1900 to 2000. Those ideas imply a model that scales the interaction terms to natural time instead of to the smoothed series g(t). Simple linear change seems improbable, however, so we include polynomials with respect to time in the interaction effects:

$$y_{it} = \beta_0 + \sum_{k=1}^{K} \beta_k X_{ik} + \sum_{k=K+1}^{2K} \beta_k X_{ik} T_t + \sum_{k=2K+1}^{3K} \beta_k X_{ik} T_t^2 + \lambda g(t) + \varepsilon_{it} \quad (A.2)$$

where $T_t = t - t_0$ and t_0 is the first year in the series. Note that as we have no "main effect" of time other than the time variation captured by g(t), we estimate interaction effects involving T_t and T_t^2 for each covariate (instead of the usual practice of deleting one of the interaction effects to identify the effects).

In principle, it might have been possible to write a statistical algorithm that would estimate g(t), then the βs, then reestimate g(t), then the βs, and so forth, until some convergence criterion was met. That was more elaborate than our needs dictated. So we, in effect, stopped after one iteration.

Survey research organizations such as the Gallup poll began using some questions of considerable interest in national surveys in the 1950s (and occasionally even earlier). In most cases, we could get published data for the overall marginals from the earliest surveys and polls, but individual data could only be obtained from the last quarter of the century. We decided to incorporate published marginals in estimating our loess regression even when we did not have access to individual data for those surveys, because doing so improved our estimates of g(t), especially for the first few years of our individual-data series.

EXAMPLE: LAWS AGAINST RACIAL INTERMARRIAGE

In chapter 3, we took up the topic of laws against interracial marriage. The question is: "Do you think there should be laws against marriages between blacks and whites? [yes or no?]" It was first asked in a national survey in 1963, again in 1967 and 1970, and then incorporated into the GSS from 1972 onward. Figure A.1 shows the percentages recorded for all adults in each survey by year (circles) and the locally estimated (loess) regression estimates (gray line). Opposition to restricting marriages between blacks and whites climbed sharply through the first fifteen years—from around one-third to about two-thirds of nonblacks opposing. The upward trend stalled somewhat between 1978 and 1986 or 1987 before rising more sharply thereafter.

Figure A.1   Opposition to Laws Banning Marriages Between Blacks and Whites for Persons of All Ages, by Year

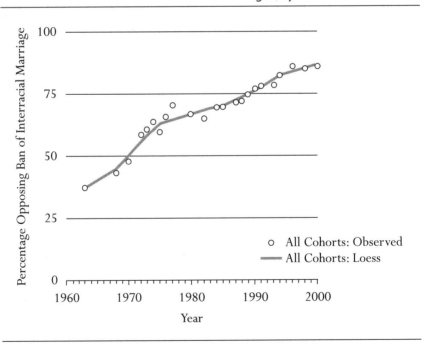

Sources: NORC Tolerance Surveys (1963 to 1970) and GSS (1972 to 2000).
Note: Excludes African-American respondents.

Most observers would immediately ascribe the trend to events, the succession from the civil rights movement to the busing backlash in the late 1970s. How or why the thrust upward resumed in the late 1980s is less clear from that perspective. Glenn Firebaugh and Kenneth Davis provide an alternative explanation. They hypothesize that the passing of the deeply prejudiced cohorts and the emergence of cohorts of young people raised in less prejudiced times were responsible for most of the trend.[5] To apply Firebaugh and Davis's findings to our own analysis, we separate the respondents into six cohorts: people born before 1900; between 1900 and 1914; between 1915 and 1929; between 1930 and 1944; between 1945 and 1959; and 1960 onwards. We fit the model in equation A.2 on individual-level data from the earlier NORC survey and the GSS. To each individual record we attach our estimate of g(t) from figure A.1 as an additional independent variable in the equation. (It varies over time but not among individuals in a time period.) In effect, we are controlling for the overall national trend in order to test whether specific subgroups have their own trends that differ significantly from that national average. The estimates are in table A.1.

Both cohort and period contribute significantly to differences in attitudes. Opposition to laws banning interracial marriage rose sharply from the mid-1960s to the mid-1970s in all cohorts old enough to have been adults in those years. Controlling for the replacement of the most prejudiced cohorts by new cohorts that harbored significantly less prejudice reveals backsliding from the mid-1970s to the late 1980s (especially in the oldest cohorts) that was hidden in the national trend. The baby boom cohorts (1945 to 1959) opposed these laws far more strongly than their elders had—in 1970, 68 percent of baby boomers opposed restrictions on interracial marriage, compared to 28 percent among people born before 1900. The cohorts born since 1960 appear close to the baby boomers in figure A.2, a consequence of the way their positive and negative coefficients balance out. (Note that the reference year is 1960—the year the oldest among them were born—they were not interviewed until 1978.)

Cohorts diverged in the 1970s and converged during the 1990s. The model captures this reversal in the bigger negative terms for the cohort-by-time interactions for the older cohorts than for the younger cohorts coupled with the significant positive squared-term for the 1900 to 1914 cohort. (The pre-1900 cohort had effectively disappeared by the late 1980s.) In using the loess technique, we formally tested whether each pair of coefficients differed significantly. For example, the difference between the cohort-by-time interaction for the 1915 to 1929 cohort and that for the 1930 to 1944 cohort is $(-.021 - -.013)$, which equals .008; the t-test for that difference turns out to be 2.61, which is statistically significant at the conventional .05 level (and beyond). Thus, the trend lines for the two cohorts differ significantly. Throughout the book, our claims of convergence or divergence between groups largely rest on t-tests of this sort.

Table A.1   Coefficients for Model of Trends in Attitudes Toward
Interracial Marriage: Percentage Opposing Laws That
Prohibit Marriages Between Blacks and Whites, by Cohort

Variable	Coefficient	Robust Standard Error	p
g(t)	1.533	.158	<.001
Cohort			
Before 1900	—	—	—
1900 to 1914	.069	.036	.051
1915 to 1929	.163	.034	<.001
1930 to 1944	.210	.033	<.001
1945 to 1959	.316	.044	<.001
1960 and up	.118	.142	.408
Cohort by time[a]			
Before 1900	−.024	.007	.001
1900 to 1914	−.028	.005	<.001
1915 to 1929	−.021	.004	<.001
1930 to 1944	−.013	.004	.001
1945 to 1959	−.012	.003	<.001
1960 and up	.001	.010	.950
Cohort by time-squared/1,000			
Before 1900	.166	.321	.604
1900 to 1914	.404	.105	<.001
1915 to 1929	.181	.071	.011
1930 to 1944	.035	.062	.570
1945 to 1959	.003	.060	.955
1960 and up	−.174	.168	.300
Intercept	−.315	.063	<.001

Source: Authors' analysis of pooled Gallup/GSS data set.
[a] Time = year − 1960 (that is, time = 0 in 1960, 10 in 1970, and so on).

The graphic display in figure A.2 makes all of the several parts of the complex change clearer. The cohort effects are evident in the clear separation of
each cohort's line from its predecessor's (except for the way the 1960-and-
up cohort overlaps the 1945 to 1959 cohort), and the period effect is evident in the overall upward slant of the trend lines. The divergence by generation is subtle, masked by the sharp upward trend at the time cohorts were
diverging. The convergence of the 1900 to 1914 cohort with later ones after
1988 is clear.

Figure A.2   Opposition to Laws Banning Marriages Between Blacks
and Whites, by Year and Cohort: Loess Regression Results

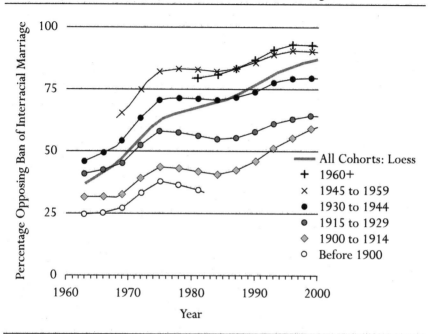

Sources: NORC Tolerance Surveys (1963 to 1970) and General Social Surveys (1972 to 2000).
Note: Excludes African-American respondents.

APPENDIX B

Income Differences or Income Ratios?

SCHOLARS HAVE developed many statistical measures of inequality.[1] The standard procedure is to use some version of a ratio measure that essentially treats the comparison proportionally—the difference in logged dollars, for example, or the proportion of total dollars garnered by each quintile, or some yet more complex measure, such as Gini or Theil coefficients. All of these show a trend toward a more equal distribution of income before 1970 and a steady trend toward a less equal one between 1970 and at least the middle 1990s.[2] Why ratio measurement is the standard is not obvious. There is some intuitive appeal to using an arithmetic difference instead. Take, for example, the numbers in figure 5.9: in 1999 full-time workers with a BA degree made $49,250, while high school graduates made $26,100, for a difference of $23,150. At the typical hourly wage of a high school graduate in 2000 ($12.30), he or she would have to find an additional thirty-six hours of work a week to close the gap.[3] The result is intuitive and is sometimes different from that generated by ratios. Similar calculations based on arithmetic differences suggest that income inequality started growing in the United States starting in 1960 rather than 1970, as suggested by ratio measures.[4]

Our efforts to pin down the logic behind the consensus on using ratio measures, as we have done in this book, were not fully successful. Different sources and different authorities provide different rationales. Some authorities prefer the ratio measure because of the empirical observation that income and wealth data are right-skewed, or because research suggests that there are declining marginal returns to additional dollars, or because statistical models assuming proportionality better fit the data. Others prefer it because of the formal requirement that the inequality measures be "scale-invariant" (not changing if all the measures are multiplied by a constant) or because of some other technical consideration.[5]

Yoram Amiel and Frank Cowell introduce popular opinion to the issue. In questionnaires administered to four thousand college students from several countries, they found that only about half clearly endorsed the notion of "scale independence," that is, proportionality, a key principle behind using ratios.[6] Fewer still endorsed "translation independence," that is, arithmetic differences. But many believed that evaluations of differences rest on the initial level of affluence. When incomes are low, absolute increases—everyone gets a $100 raise—promote equality; when incomes are high, proportional increases—everyone gets a 3 percent raise—do. (The students' judgments also failed to conform to other basic principles in economic models of inequality, a noteworthy problem considering that most of them were economics students.)

In the end, the essential rationale for assessing income differences in ratio terms is psychological: the more dollars someone has, the less each new dollar "means." A $1,000 raise to someone earning $100,000 means less—psychologically and practically—than it does to someone with a $10,000 income; it may yield perhaps only one-tenth as much utility to the wealthier as to the poorer person. The rationale also draws on the consensus that humans judge fairness as a ratio; we see people's deserts as "just deserts" when they are rewarded proportionally to their efforts.[7] In the end, we adopted the conventional approach, measuring differences in dollar earnings, income, and wealth, all as proportions.[8]

One modest test of these two standards of comparison—arithmetic difference versus ratio—can be constructed by looking at trends in black and white family incomes. A difference measure—white family-of-four median income minus black family-of-four median income (figure 6.3)—shows that the income gap between blacks and whites widened between 1970 and 2000 (by about 8 percent), while a ratio measure—white income divided by black income—shows that the gap narrowed (by about 14 percent). How did African Americans' subjective evaluations of their financial position change in that same period? From 1972 through 2000, the General Social Survey asked respondents to rate their family's financial position compared to the "average." Over those years, African-American respondents became somewhat *more* positive about their financial situations. (The proportion saying that their family's situations was below average dropped from 50 percent in the mid-1970s to 40 percent at the end of the century, and the proportion saying above average grew from 5 percent to over 10 percent.) The perceptions of American blacks were more consistent with the ratio measure.

APPENDIX C

Procedures and Data for the
Fragmentation Analysis in Chapter 9*

OUR OBJECTIVE is to identify cultural clusters in the American population. We cannot observe such groups directly. Instead, we observe a variety of attributes and then look for patterns of association between these attributes to identify groups. There is no one correct answer to the question: "How many groups are there in American society?" The number depends on the attributes selected to characterize groups, the criteria used to sort people into groups, and the threshold for deciding when a model adequately represents the data. The precise number of groups might vary using different characteristics and criteria than are used here. However, informal sensitivity tests (changing the list of variables, recoding variables, varying the weight on parsimony in model selection) suggest that our findings on trends over time are robust to minor changes in variable selection, coding, and model selection criteria.[1]

DATA SOURCE AND CODING

To examine trends in cultural clustering we need a dataset with consistent questions about cultural values over time. To our knowledge, the General Social Survey is the only nationally representative survey that meets these criteria. We can thus analyze change only over the three decades that the GSS has been fielded. Potentially, we would have available over forty thousand cases and dozens of cultural and social variables. However, the GSS did not ask all its questions in every year, and more critically, the split-sample design to which the GSS moved in the 1980s further limits the set of vari-

---

*Written by Jane Zavisca.

ables we can use for a cluster analysis. With the advent of the split sample, most questions on cultural values were asked of only two-thirds of the sample. Thus, relatively few respondents were asked an entire set of relevant questions. Three different ballots were used: ballots A, B, and C. Split questions were asked either on ballots A and B, B and C, or A and C. For example (X indicates that the question was asked):

Question	Ballot A	Ballot B	Ballot C
Capital punishment	X	X	
Legalize drugs		X	X
Woman for president	X		X

The split-ballot design ensures that at least one-third of the sample will be asked any given pair of questions such that all bivariate relationships can be examined. However, no individuals were asked all the questions, and we need to model the joint associations between many variables. We therefore restricted analysis to questions that were asked on ballot A.[2] (That collection of questions turned out to be more interesting than those that were on ballot B or ballot C.) Since not all questions were asked in all years, we had to drop some years of data from the analysis. We selected variables so as to balance the need for multiple items against the need for adequate sample size. A small number of cases (thirty-two) that were missing data on more than two variables were dropped. In the final dataset, we pooled data across years into three periods as follows:

1970s (1974, 1977) − N = 2,886

1980s (1982, 1985, 1988, 1989, 1990) − N = 4,674

1990s (1991, 1993, 1996, 1998, 2000) − N = 4,705

We included variables measuring both demographic attributes and cultural and political attitudes. All variables were coded as nominal or ordinal categorical variables. Most variables were coded as such in the original questionnaire; we recoded the only continuous variables, age and years of education, into ordinal scales for ease of interpretation and because their effects were expected to be nonlinear. We combined categories to eliminate those with less than 5 percent of responses. On ordered responses, we combined "don't know" responses with a middle or neutral category. We dropped a few variables from our initial list because they poorly distinguished clusters or were highly correlated with other variables. Given the computational demands and complexities of our statistical procedures, it behooved us to simplify where we could.[3]

The coding for variables included in the analysis is listed here. Note that, for ease of interpretation, variables regarding political or cultural values were coded so that lower numbers indicate a more "conservative" or "traditional" response, while higher numbers indicate a more liberal response.

Variables and Coding for Cluster Analysis

PLACE3: Type of place of residence
1 urban
2 suburban
3 rural
SOUTH: Place of residence in the southern region
0 no
1 yes
RACE3
1 white/other
2 black
3 Latino
AGE3: Age group
1 twenty-one to thirty-five
2 thirty-five to sixty-four
3 sixty-five and older
EDUC3: Educational attainment
1 less than high school degree
2 high school degree/some college
3 college degree
INCCAP3: Per capita income percentile
1 0 to 40 percent
2 41 to 80 percent
3 81 to 100 percent
RELIG4: Religious affiliation
1 conservative Protestant
2 other Protestant
3 Catholic
4 other
ATTEND3: Frequency of church attendance
1 rare
2 sometimes
3 frequently

POLVIEW3: Political views
  1 conservative
  2 moderate/don't know
  3 liberal
CAPPUN: Attitude toward capital punishment
  0 support
  1 oppose/don't know
NATENV2: Government should spend more on environment
  0 no/don't know
  1 too little
NATRACE: Government spending on minority conditions
  1 too much
  2 about right/don't know
  3 too little
RACMAR: Interracial marriage should be legal
  0 no
  2 yes
FEPOL: Women are suited for politics
  0 no/don't know
  1 yes
ABORTION
  1 always wrong
  2 sometimes wrong
  3 always okay
PREMAR: Premarital sex is:
  1 always wrong
  2 sometimes wrong/don't know
  3 not wrong
HOMOSEX: Homosexuality is:
  1 always wrong
  2 sometimes wrong/don't know
  3 not wrong
DIVLAW: Divorce law should be:
  1 more difficult
  2 stay the same
  3 more lenient
NOPRAYER: Against prayer in school
  0 no
  1 yes
HLDIDEL: Ideal number of children
  1 one or two
  2 three

3 four or more
4 as many as want

THE LATENT CLASS MODEL

We use the method of latent class analysis to determine the number and nature of groups. The model hypothesizes the existence of a latent (underlying, unobserved) partitioning of the population into "classes" or "clusters." The latent variable "explains away" or accounts for the associations observed between the variables. Unlike traditional cluster analysis, latent class analysis is a probabilistic, model-based approach—response patterns are assigned probabilities of latent class membership.[4]

To explicate the model, consider a dataset with four observed categorical variables A, B, C, and D, and a hypothesized latent variable X. The model is written as follows, where π^X_t denotes the probability of membership in class t of the latent variable X, and $\pi_{it}^{A|X}$ is the conditional probability of being in category i of variable A, conditional on membership in latent class t.

$$\pi^{ABCDX}_{ijklt} = \pi^X_t \, \pi^{A|X}_{it} \, \pi^{B|X}_{jt} \, \pi^{C|X}_{kt} \, \pi^{D|X}_{lt}$$

or the equivalent loglinear parameterization:

$$\ln\big(f^{ABCDX}_{ijklt}\big) = \lambda + \lambda^X_t + \lambda^A_i + \lambda^B_j + \lambda^C_k + \lambda^D_l + \lambda^{AX}_{it} + \lambda^{BX}_{jt} + \lambda^{CX}_{kt} + \lambda^{DX}_{lt}$$

with standard identifying restrictions such that the conditional probabilities for each indicator variable sum to 1 across all T classes, and the probabilities of latent class membership also sum to 1.[5]

We fit variants of the basic model as implemented in Latent Gold software. Parameters for ordinal variables are constrained using fixed scores for distance between the categories.[6] We also included "direct effects" or "local dependencies" for associations between variables that were poorly accounted for by the latent class analysis and that we believe to derive from some process external to the latent variable of interest.[7] For example, the association between attitudes on homosexuality and premarital sex (HOMOSEX and PREMAR) and between attitudes toward government spending on racial minorities and government spending on the environment (NATRACE and NATENV2) remained high even under models with many latent classes. This presumably stems from similarity in question wording and context in the order of questions on the GSS. The strong association between age, education, and income (INCCAP3, EDUC3, AGE3) is in part a cohort effect that was also not of interest and that we did not want to allow to have a strong influence on the classification process. Similarly, we added a direct effect between SOUTH and PLACE (urban to rural) as a known association not of interest in our analysis.

MODEL SELECTION AND FIT

Latent Gold uses a complex mixed algorithm for model estimation. The algorithm combines Expectation-Maximization (EM) and Newton-Rhaphson (NR) maximum likelihood estimation with a Bayesian prior to avoid boundary solutions. For each model run, we set Latent Gold to generate 15 random sets of starting values, with up to 50 NR and 250 EM iterations and an EM convergence tolerance of e^{-10}. Each model run was then replicated at least five times to check for local maxima.

If L^2 follows a chi-squared distribution, as is typically assumed, the model can be said to fit well in a "conservative test" vis-à-vis the saturated model when the p-value exceeds .05. However, the likelihood ratio comparison with a saturated model is also not appropriate for these data because the data are extremely sparse (there are many empty cells in the cross-classification table), and therefore the likelihood test does not follow a chi-square distribution. Instead, we use the Bayesian information criterion (BIC) to select between competing models. (Smaller values of the BIC indicate a superior model.) A rule of thumb for the BIC is that there should be at least five and ideally at least ten observations per parameter.[8] Thus, a motivation for combining categories to reduce the size of the cross-classification table was not so much to reduce sparseness (which would be an issue in any model with more than five or six variables given the sample size) as to reduce the number of parameters that would be required to fit models with a relatively large number of classes. No formal test of model fit is available for sparse data, but as an informal assessment, we report the percentage reduction in L^2. Since the likelihood is known to be off by an unknown constant with sparse data, the percentage reduction in L^2 will be underestimated and can be interpreted as a minimum indicator of the proportion of variance explained. Table C.1 presents the tests for the best-fitting models.

INTERPRETATION OF RESULTS

Conditional Probabilities

Because they are for a nonlinear model, the parameter estimates produced in a latent class analysis can be difficult to interpret. Calculation of conditional probabilities can be more informative. Clusters are characterized by the probability of given responses, conditional on cluster membership.

Table C.1   Models Tested for Cluster Analysis

Model	BIC(LL)	Npar	L^2	Percentage Reduction in L^2	Classification Errors
1970s					
1 cluster	103614	44	60366.28	0	0
2 clusters	100727.1	69	57280.17	5.1	0.0776
3 clusters	99282.97	94	55636.9	7.9	0.073
4 clusters	98772.06	119	54926.8	9.1	0.1236
5 clusters	98315.89	144	54271.44	10.3	0.1423
6 clusters	98222.11	169	53978.47	10.6	0.1807
7 clusters	98150.64	194	53707.81	11.1	0.1838
8 clusters	98104.87	219	53462.85	11.4	0.1977
9 clusters	98092.56	244	53251.35	11.9	0.2032
10 clusters	98099.65	269	53059.25	12.1	0.2249
11 clusters	98140	294	52900.41	12.4	0.2285
1980s					
1 cluster	165331.7	44	91592.32	0	0
2 clusters	160261.9	69	86311.28	5.8	0.076
3 clusters	158602.9	94	84441.06	7.9	0.0786
4 clusters	157589.9	119	83216.82	9.2	0.1249
5 clusters	156952.4	144	82368.04	10.0	0.1466
6 clusters	156704.6	169	81908.97	10.6	0.181
7 clusters	156464.6	194	81457.75	11.0	0.1841
8 clusters	156272.3	219	81054.14	11.5	0.1851
9 clusters	156154	244	80724.6	11.9	0.1898
10 clusters	156072.1	269	80431.46	12.2	0.2241
11 clusters	156076.9	294	80245.08	12.4	0.2392
1990s					
1 cluster	166039.7	44	93519.19	0	0
2 clusters	161382.7	69	88650.78	5.1	0.083
3 clusters	159422.7	94	86479.37	7.5	0.0825
4 clusters	158320.2	119	85165.48	8.9	0.1273
5 clusters	157744.5	144	84378.41	9.7	0.1444
6 clusters	157393.7	169	83816.1	10.4	0.1732
7 clusters	157252.3	194	83463.36	10.7	0.1916
8 clusters	157147.5	219	83147.13	11.1	0.2222
9 clusters	157094.9	244	82883.14	11.3	0.2297
10 clusters	157072.1	269	82648.9	11.7	0.2325
11 clusters	157088.9	294	82454.25	11.8	0.2408
12 clusters	157115.3	319	82269.23	12.0	0.252

Table C.2 Parameters for Clusters in Best Models of 1970s, 1980s, and 1990s

	Summary Cluster									
	I	II	III	IV	V	VI	VII	VIII	IX	X
1970s cluster number	Cluster 1	Cluster 2	Cluster 3	Cluster 4	Cluster 5	Cluster 6	Cluster 7	Cluster 8	Cluster 9	None
Cluster size	0.21	0.14	0.14	0.11	0.10	0.10	0.08	0.07	0.05	
Ethnic (white-black-Latino)	W	W	W	W	W	W	W/L	B	B	
South	-0.82	-0.28	-1.37	-1.00	1.71	1.54	-1.00	0.31	1.55	
Rural-suburban-city	.98 SU	.41 SU	0.17	.83 U	1.26 R	1.07 R	-0.38	2.21 U	.68 R	
Education	1.08	0.81	-1.13	1.87	-1.95	-0.65	0.03	-0.11	-1.65	
Per capita income percentile	1.20	0.36	-0.45	0.47	-1.11	-0.51	-0.16	-0.55	-1.64	
Age	-0.45	0.43	1.50	-1.89	1.84	-0.99	-1.21	-1.10	0.81	
Religion	1.53 OP	1.02 CA	1.13 OP	2.88 OTH	1.31 CP	2.20 CP	4.21 CA	1.79 CP	2.16 CP	
Attend church	-0.49	3.83	-0.96	-1.94	0.92	-0.86	0.63	-0.13	0.95	
Political self-ranking	-0.27	-0.79	-0.18	1.94	-0.31	-0.04	0.65	0.51	0.26	
More for environment	0.16	-0.37	-0.79	1.94	-1.02	-0.18	0.63	0.74	-0.06	
Anti-capital punishment	-0.77	-0.35	-0.73	1.16	0.12	-0.43	0.02	1.17	1.18	
More for minorities	-0.38	-0.18	-0.62	0.87	-0.60	-0.79	-0.02	2.74	2.30	
Interracial marriage OK	2.47	0.44	-1.79	3.91	-3.81	-1.22	1.45	7.77	7.74	
Women in politics OK	0.67	-0.45	-0.42	1.70	-1.56	-0.15	0.22	0.36	-0.47	
Abortion OK	1.63	-1.70	0.39	2.06	-1.12	-0.11	-0.51	-0.13	-1.62	
Easier divorces	0.57	-1.70	-0.41	1.40	-1.44	0.09	-0.12	1.53	0.25	
Premarital sex OK	0.89	-1.89	-0.16	2.16	-2.77	0.10	0.64	1.50	-1.21	
Homosexuality OK	0.79	-1.64	-1.28	2.46	-2.25	-0.96	0.48	0.36	-1.42	
No prayer in schools	0.36	-0.23	-0.02	1.49	-1.27	-0.45	0.44	-0.38	-1.56	
More kids ideal	-0.99	0.59	0.09	-1.09	0.99	-0.65	0.26	0.55	1.21	

(Table continues on p. 270.)

Table C.2 (Continued)

				Summary Cluster						
	I	II	III	V	VI	IV	VII	VIII	IX	X
1980s cluster number	Cluster 2	Cluster 4	Cluster 5	Cluster 7	Cluster 1	Cluster 6	Cluster 10	Cluster 8	Cluster9	Cluster 3
Cluster size	0.17	0.11	0.10	0.07	0.18	0.07	0.04	0.06	0.05	0.16
Ethnic (white-black-Latino)	W	W	W	W	W	W	L	B	B	W
South	−0.89	−0.20	−1.68	2.99	0.78	−0.65	0.36	0.15	1.66	−1.16
Rural-suburban-city	0.72 SU	0.28 R	0.35 R	1.53 U	0.62 R	1.41 U	0.72 U	1.85 U	0.94 U	0.42 SU
Education	1.72	0.87	−1.84	−1.72	−0.48	2.18	−1.66	0.23	−2.33	0.15
Per capita income percentile	0.92	0.31	−1.86	−1.16	0.07	0.69	−1.04	−0.14	−2.60	0.57
Age	−0.43	−0.06	3.53	1.35	−0.31	−0.92	−1.08	−0.85	0.64	−0.95
Religion	1.77	1.13	1.5 OP/CA	2.17 CP	0.65 CP	2.76 OTH	2.72 CA	1.16 CP	2.27 CP	1.1 OTH
Attend church	0.27	4.36	0.70	1.12	−0.71	−1.45	0.18	−0.01	0.59	−2.04
Political self-ranking	−0.05	−1.07	−0.25	−0.48	−0.30	2.12	0.27	0.69	0.16	0.17
More for environment	0.56	−0.21	−1.06	−1.29	−0.01	2.39	−0.29	0.67	−0.54	0.23
Anti-capital punishment	0.09	−0.17	0.07	0.03	−1.05	1.37	0.44	1.06	1.49	−1.39
More for minorities	0.23	−0.15	−0.25	−1.22	−1.12	1.24	0.30	3.45	1.75	−0.48
Interracial marriage OK	3.22	0.52	−1.64	−3.39	−1.55	3.82	0.73	3.91	0.34	1.61
Women in politics OK	1.11	−0.56	−0.83	−1.66	−0.19	1.45	0.03	0.35	−0.78	0.71
Abortion OK	0.35	−2.13	−0.77	−1.30	0.16	3.15	−0.91	0.28	−1.41	1.59
Easier divorces	−0.38	−1.66	−1.03	−0.96	−0.14	0.90	0.46	1.18	0.60	0.98
Premarital sex OK	0.50	−2.44	−1.29	−3.32	0.19	1.88	0.12	0.94	−0.42	1.82
Homosexuality OK	0.93	−6.48	−1.26	−2.81	−1.93	2.67	−0.17	−0.16	−1.08	1.10
No prayer in schools	0.59	−0.63	−0.40	−1.60	−0.67	3.03	−0.14	−0.64	−1.15	0.61
More kids ideal	−0.25	0.70	0.73	0.54	−0.69	−0.54	0.85	0.17	1.08	−0.79

1990s cluster number	Cluster 1	Cluster 5	Cluster 7	Cluster 10	Cluster 3	Cluster 4	Cluster 8	Cluster 6	Cluster 9	Cluster 2
Cluster size	0.16	0.11	0.08	0.04	0.14	0.11	0.08	0.09	0.05	0.15
Ethnic (white-black-Latino)	W	W	W	W	W	W	W/L	B	B	W
South	−0.64	0.14	−0.70	2.15	1.29	−0.93	−0.86	0.48	1.00	−0.75
Rural-suburban-city	0.52 SU	0.68 SU/R	0.67 R	1.48 R	0.73 R	0.86 U	0.57 U	1.2 U	0.8 U	0.52 SU
Education	1.32	0.58	−1.05	−2.99	−0.75	2.14	−0.94	−0.68	−0.37	−0.11
Per capita income percentile	1.00	0.14	−1.11	−2.18	0.15	0.60	−0.60	−1.07	−0.49	0.24
Age	−0.34	0.26	3.53	2.89	−0.23	−0.72	−1.03	−0.50	−0.52	−0.68
Religion	1.67	1.08 CP	1.13 OP	1.65 CP	1.06 CP	2.12 OTH	2.48 CA	1.27 CP	1.49 CP	1.35 OTH
Attend church	0.70	3.69	0.09	1.14	−0.54	−1.19	−0.25	0.03	1.53	−2.43
Political self-ranking	−0.24	−1.54	−0.24	−0.49	−0.44	2.18	0.00	0.31	0.02	0.28
More for environment	0.18	−1.13	−1.08	−1.24	−0.01	1.48	−0.08	0.23	0.37	0.46
Anti-capital punishment	−0.45	−0.09	−0.16	0.48	−1.55	1.12	0.35	0.75	1.62	−1.45
More for minorities	−0.10	−0.68	−0.41	−0.72	−1.40	0.98	0.13	2.68	1.92	−0.51
Interracial marriage OK	5.04	0.21	−1.62	−3.70	−1.22	3.68	0.14	1.17	1.56	1.06
Women in politics OK	0.92	−0.52	−0.80	−1.93	−0.50	1.47	−0.33	0.05	−0.19	0.63
Abortion OK	0.06	−2.26	−0.07	−1.17	−0.05	2.53	−0.73	0.24	−1.24	1.29
Easier divorces	−0.62	−1.96	−0.74	−0.94	−0.17	0.62	0.66	1.31	0.02	0.61
Premarital sex OK	0.40	−3.15	−0.81	−2.61	−0.18	1.75	0.44	0.70	−2.83	1.96
Homosexuality OK	0.64	−4.23	−1.15	−3.15	−1.38	2.78	−0.14	−0.20	−2.31	1.05
No prayer in schools	0.40	−0.73	−1.04	−1.98	−1.17	3.12	−0.26	−0.87	−1.04	0.88
More kids ideal	−0.13	0.74	0.36	0.98	−1.12	−0.57	0.65	0.59	0.71	−0.79

Source: Authors' analysis of the GSS.
Notes: The categories for each variable are in the list in appendix C. Entries are primarily log odds ratios.

Odds Ratios

Odds ratios are useful for comparing the degree to which response probabilities for one cluster differ from other clusters. For dichotomous variables, we calculate the odds ratio for a given response for each cluster versus the rest of the sample (excluding that cluster):

$$\frac{P(X=1|C=c)*P(C=c)}{P(X=2|C=c)*P(C=c)} \bigg/ \frac{P(X=1|C\neq c)*P(C\neq c)}{P(X=2|C\neq c)*P(C\neq c)} = \frac{P(X=1|C=c)*P(X=2|C\neq c)}{P(X=2|C=c)*P(X=1|C\neq c)}$$

Note that we do not put the marginal probability in the denominator; the cluster of interest contributes to that marginal probability, and for large clusters that could wash out the relative difference from the rest of the population.

For nominal variables, we calculate odds for the most prevalent category in a cluster versus all the other categories. For ordinal variables, we use Agresti's "generalized odds ratio," which reduces to the standard odds ratio in the case of a two-by-two table. The generalized odds ratio is the probability of "concordance" divided by the probability of "discordance." For comparing two ordinal distributions Y_1 and Y_2 (in our case, the distribution of a cluster versus the distribution of the rest of the sample), the measure estimates $P(Y_2>Y_1)/P(Y_1>Y_2)$.

We report log (generalized) odds ratios for ease of interpretation, since this makes the distribution of the statistic symmetric around 0. For interpretation, $\ln(OR)=.3$ corresponds to $OR=1.33$; $\ln(OR)=.7$ corresponds to $OR=2$; and $\ln(OR)=1.1$ corresponds to $OR=3$. Standard errors can be calculated for both the simple and generalized log odds ratio, but we do not report them since the test statistic was significant in all cases where the log odds ratio was substantively interesting (equivalent to a ratio difference in odds of at least one-third).

Table C.2 displays the log odds ratios for the conditional probabilities for each cluster for the best-fitting models for each decade, lining up the clusters according to our best match.

NOTES

CHAPTER 1

1. "Italian Societies Parade," *New York Times*, October 13, 1900, 14; "No Alien Labor on the Tunnel," ibid., January 23, 1900, 1; "Favors American Labor," ibid., January 4, 1900, 1; "Irishmen Fight Italians," ibid., August 12, 1900, 12; "Little Italy Disinfected . . . Inhabitants Taken by Surprise," ibid., July 11, 1900; "Italy Asks Reparation," ibid., January 14, 1900, 4; "The Killing of Italians in Mississippi," ibid., July 21, 1900, 5.
2. "Columbus Day Parade Set," *Bronx Times*, October 10, 2002, available at: www.bxtimes.com/News/2002/1010/Front_Page/059.html (accessed May 30, 2005).
3. As reported in Roth, "I Got a Scheme," 79.
4. Bender, "New York in Theory."
5. Citro, Cork, and Norwood, *The 2000 Census: Interim Assessment*; General Accounting Office, *Census 2000: Design Choices*; Anderson and Feinberg, *Who Counts*; Edmonston and Schultze, *Modernizing the U.S. Census*.
6. Ruggles et al., *Integrated Public Use Microdata Series:Version 3.0*.

CHAPTER 2

1. *Education Is Good Business* (1947), General Pictures Production, available at Prelinger Archives: http://www.archive.org/details/Educatio1947 (accessed February 16, 2006). Note that the documentation does not establish the chamber's sponsorship, which nevertheless can be inferred from the content.
2. Jencks and Riesman, *The Academic Revolution*; Hout, "The Politics of Mobility;" Fischer et al., *Inequality by Design*, 152–54.
3. The census did not actually ask for people's education until 1940, so if we use the average educational level of people in the year of the cen-

sus, we lose the early decades. Almost everyone was done with their schooling by their early twenties, so birth dates allow us to track the entire century of education. We mark each birth cohort by the year its members turned twenty-one. Using birth cohorts to see historical changes introduces slight distortions (such as the effects of differential mortality) but is unlikely to change any substantive conclusions. Finally, we do not have an estimate for 2001 because those born in 1980 had not yet completed their schooling.

4. The census initially coded years of education and then in 1980 switched to credentials. To reconcile the different schemes IPUMS coders created broad categories (for example, having completed one, two, three, or four years of school as one category), so deriving estimates from these categories required some interpolation.

5. See, for example, Kaestle, "Public Education"; Tyack, "Preserving the Republic by Educating Republicans"; Licht, *Getting Work*, ch. 5; Lassonde, "Learning and Earning."

6. Hochschild and Scovronick, *The American Dream and the Public Schools*.

7. Lieberson, *A Piece of the Pie*, 137–50.

8. Orfield, Losen, and Weld, "Losing Our Future."

9. Church, "Collegiate Education," 2531–32. Thomas Kane ("College-Going and Inequality") describes how subsequent changes in the costs and consequences of going to college in the last quarter of the twentieth century affected who enrolled and who did not. His main conclusion is that the gap between the affluent and the poor—already large in 1975—increased. Although the changing costs and changing payoffs of college are both implicated as probable causes of the trends, correlated factors, like a growing propensity of highly educated parents to invest a larger share of whatever money they have in their children's educations, cannot be ruled out in explaining the widening gap in attendance. The unmistakable point of Kane's review, however, is that the asset that is the greatest contributor to growing economic inequality—education—became itself more unequally distributed between 1975 and the turn of the century.

10. Danziger and Gottschalk, *America Unequal*.

11. Yossi Shavit and Hans-Peter Blossfeld ("Persisting Barriers") show that the gender pattern was not unique to the United States: women attained more education than men in most rich countries after 1980 (and in some as early as the mid-1960s).

12. See Fischer et al., *Inequality by Design*, ch. 8, for one review of research on race and academic testing.

13. Hout, "Educational Progress for African Americans and Latinos"; Conley, *Being Black, Living in the Red*.

14. James, "City Limits on Racial Equality"; Reardon and Yun, "The Changing Structure of School Segregation."

15. For starters, see, for example, Zhou, "Are Asian Americans Becoming 'White'?"; Stevenson, Chen, and Lee, "Mathematics Achievement of Chinese, Japanese, and American Children"; Schneider and Lee, "A Model for Academic Success."

16. Fischer et al., *Inequality by Design*, ch. 8.

17. Wilson, *The Declining Significance of Race*. Many studies document that discrimination declined but did not disappear.

18. Norman Nie, Jane Junn, and Kenneth Stehlik-Barry (*Education and Democratic Citizenship in America*) and John Helliwell and Robert Putnam ("Education and Social Capital") debate this issue. Jon Stiles ("Education: Comparisons of Absolute Versus Relative Measures") shows that in a few cases the relative measure can yield different results. For example, a smaller proportion of thirty- to forty-four-year-old men with BA degrees held elite professional jobs in 1990 than in 1940, but a larger proportion of thirty- to forty-four-year-old men in the top quartile held elite professional jobs in 1990 than in 1940. The implication is that the educational requirements for such jobs increased over time such that a BA alone became less sufficient and that elite professional jobs remained a preserve of the very best-educated, whatever "best-educated" entailed in that generation. But these were particular instances; overall, credentials serve well as the measure of educational position (once we take age into account).

19. On income differences, see chapters 5 and 6. Claudia Goldin and Lawrence Katz ("The Returns to Skill in the United States Across the Twentieth Century") estimate that the returns to education were highest at the start and end of the century and lowest in the middle. Lisa Keister (*Wealth in America*, 145) reports that education became a greater determiner of wealth after 1960. On family differences, see chapter 4 and, for example, McLanahan, "Diverging Destinies," and Goldstein and Kenny, "Marriage Delayed or Marriage Forgone?"

20. See Becker, *Human Capital*, and Bowles and Gintis, *Schooling in Capitalist America*.

21. Schwartz and Mare, "Trends in Educational Assortative Marriage."

22. The sociological literature is brimming with late-twentieth-century studies that show, often in an "everybody knows" way, that educational attainment shapes all these outcomes. We will cover some of the literature on jobs, income, and families, but decades of studies show that more highly educated people are more socially connected, more involved in the community, more trusting of others, and even a bit happier (Witter et al., "Education and Subjective Wellbeing").

23. Hout, "More Universalism, Less Structural Mobility."

24. See Lucas, "Effectively Maintained Inequality," and Kane, "College-Going and Inequality."

25. Blau and Duncan, *American Occupational Structure*, 429–31.

26. James Davis ("Achievement Variables and Class Cultures") explicitly addresses this point, but countless other studies point to the same conclusion.
27. The statistics in this paragraph are our own calculations from the General Social Survey.
28. National Center for Educational Statistics, "Trends in International Mathematics and Science Study," table 7.
29. Orfield et al., "Losing Our Future."

CHAPTER 3

1. Edward E. Corwall, "Are the Americans an Anglo-Saxon People?" *New York Times*, January 14, 1900, 21.
2. Waters, *Ethnic Options*, 147, 165.
3. Wilson, *The Declining Significance of Race*.
4. Many academics critique not only the scientific usefulness of racial categories but also the practice of referring to population groups as "races." In some parts of our analysis, we refer to groups defined by their "continents of origin." But the census forms we rely on generally instructed census enumerators and family respondents to fill in or check a "race" for each person. So we call their answers "races" on the supposition that some enumerators or respondents would have given different answers if the questions had not used the word "race."
5. Bean et al., "Immigration and Fading Color Lines in America," 7. This Population Reference Bureau report is an excellent source on the changing ethno-racial makeup of Americans.
6. Lieberson, "Measuring Population Diversity," 851–52.
7. About the only counties in those parts of the country with diversity scores greater than .15 were those in the Boston, Chicago, Detroit, Milwaukee, and St. Louis metropolitan areas. Some Indian reservations in Montana and the Dakotas raised their counties above the lowest diversity level.
8. The percentage of American Indians who were native-born in 2000 was not 100 percent, as might be expected. In one of the many changes leading up to Census 2000, the Office of Management and Budget (OMB) decided that indigenous people from Central and South America who immigrated to the United States would be counted under the umbrella category "American Indians." See OMB, "Revisions to the Standards for the Classification of Federal Data on Race and Ethnicity."
9. Bean et al., "Immigration and Fading Color Lines in America," 1.
10. We also coded as "American" anyone whose answer was one of the

fifty states. See also Lieberson and Waters, "The Rise of a New Ethnic Group"; U.S. Bureau of the Census, "Ancestry."

11. Takaki, *Debating Diversity*.

12. For a history of race, see Sollors, "What Race Are You?" and Frederickson, *Racism*.

13. Frederickson, *Racism*.

14. Gossett, *Race: The History of an Idea in America*.

15. American Sociological Association, *The Importance of Collecting Data and Doing Social Scientific Research on Race*. See also Fischer et al., *Inequality by Design*, ch. 8.

16. Anderson, *The American Census*.

17. Nobles, *Shades of Citizenship*, appendix A.

18. Census-takers asked respondents for the race of any absent members (at least in 1950 through 1970). They also followed the rule that mixed-race persons had the race of their fathers until that rule was changed to mother's race for the 1970 census. In 1950 the Census Bureau told enumerators to "assume that the race of related persons living in the household is the same as the race of your respondent, unless you learn otherwise. For unrelated persons (employees, hired hands, lodgers, etc.) you must ask the race, because knowledge of the housewife's race (for example) tells nothing of the maid's race" (see 1950 instructions at: www.ipums.umn.edu/usa/voliii/inst1950.html#114). We have no information about the instructions the Census Bureau gave on this matter prior to 1950. Since the 1970 census introduced self-enumeration, respondents have been instructed to give their best assessment for each person in the household.

19. Self-identification began on a limited basis in 1960, but 1970 was the first census designed to be answered entirely by the respondents themselves.

20. Farley, "Racial Identities in 2000."

21. Hispanics were first counted in 1970 on the census long form, which is sent to only a fraction of the population. The Hispanic-origin question was added to the short form, which all American households receive, in 1980.

22. OMB, "Revisions to the Standards."

23. Anderson, *The American Census*; Prewitt, "Ethno-Racial Classification in Public Policy."

24. "What Is the Proper Name for the Black Man in America?" *New York Daily Tribune*, June 10, 1906, pt. IV, p. 2.

25. Quoted in *Newsweek*, June 30, 1969, 62.

26. "Report from Black America: A *Newsweek* Poll," *Newsweek*, June 30, 1969, 20.

27. See also Smith, "Changing Racial Labels."
28. Sigelman, Tuch, and Martin, "What's in a Name?"
29. For example, according to a survey conducted by the Pew Hispanic Center in 2002, 53 percent favored either "Hispanic" or "Latino," 34 percent preferred "Hispanic," and 13 percent preferred "Latino/a"; see Sigelman et al., "What's in a Name?" We use both "Hispanic" and "Latino."
30. See, for example, Fredrickson, *White Supremacy*, and *Racism*; Jacobson, *Whiteness of a Different Color*; Omi and Winant, *Racial Formation in the United States*; Williamson, *The New People*.
31. More precisely, our coding scheme is as follows:

    1. *Europe*: Those (a) coded only white on race, or (b) coded white plus Indian/Alaskan, or (c) coded white plus "other" race.

    2. *Africa*: Those (a) coded only "Black," "Negro," or "Mulatto," or (b) coded black plus any other race.

    3. *Americas*: Those (a) coded American Indian, Alaskan Native, or any other tribal response, and not coded white or black, or (b) coded Hispanic according to the rule described in this note.

    4. *Asia*: Those (a) coded any Asian or Pacific Islander response (including Filipino, Asian Indian [Hindu], or Native Hawaiian), or (b) coded one of these categories plus any other race except black, or (c) coded "other" in 1910.

    We treated cases recorded as "other race, not elsewhere classified," as missing data, except for 1910, when they were coded as Asian because birthplace data indicated that the great majority of that category were immigrants from Asian nations. Also treated as missing data were cases coded with a write-in of "Spanish" after 1970 but not coded as Hispanic.

    Regardless of the racial categorization, we coded people as Hispanic—and thus put them in the "Americas" category—if they: (a) were coded "yes" in the Hispanic questions of 1970 through 2000; or (b) were born in Puerto Rico, the Caribbean Islands, or Central or South America; or (c) were reported to have a mother tongue of Spanish (in 1910, 1920, 1960, and 1970); or (d) were designated as having a Spanish surname (in 1920 through 1980); or (e) were reported to have a mother or father born in the regions listed in item b (in 1900 through 1920).

    Clearly, there is some error in these assignments. We assign Hawaiians to Asia (prior to 2000, they petitioned the OMB to be considered American Indians but were denied); some Hispanics who reported

Spanish ancestry were classified in the Americas, not as European (but the numbers are small); and our assignment of multiple-race individuals follows hypo- and hyperdescent rules (although it is similar to OMB's formula for reducing to single-race populations). Still, we are confident that we are able to capture the major patterns with accuracy.

32. Lieberson, *A Piece of the Pie*. The inclusion of "lesser" European groups together with the dominant northwestern European groups has the effect of narrowing early-century social differences between Europeans and others. Given our argument that such differences generally declined over the century, this procedure works against our line of analysis.

33. Because of the large slave population (18 to 19 percent of the total), Europeans formed only 80 percent of the population from 1790 until 1840; see Gibson and Jung, "Historical Census Statistics on Population Totals by Race," table A-1.

34. It would be unreasonable to assert that the trend shown in figure 3.5 is purely an artifact of the changes in how race and Hispanic origin have been measured over the last one hundred years, but it would be equally unreasonable to assert that we have measured the real changes with perfect accuracy.

35. Castles and Miller, *Age of Migration*, 26.

36. Martin and Midgley, "Immigration": 20. This figure is based on net immigration. Not all immigrants who are admitted to the United States remain permanently. In 1995 the Immigration and Naturalization Service (INS) (*1997 Statistical Yearbook of the Immigration and Naturalization Service*) estimated that, from 1901 to 1990, approximately 30 percent of all immigrants admitted to the United States eventually emigrated elsewhere.

37. INS, *2000 Statistical Yearbook of the Immigration and Naturalization Service*, table 2, p. 21.

38. Passel, "Unauthorized Migrants: Numbers and Characteristics."

39. See, for example, Shanahan and Olzak, "The Effects of Immigrant Diversity." Other social scientists argue that increased diversity decreases civic participation; see Costa and Kahn, "Civic Engagement and Community Heterogeneity."

40. Between 1901 and 1910, 8.8 million immigrants arrived; between 1991 and 2000, 9.1 million arrived; and between 1921 and 1960, 8.2 million arrived. U.S. Citizenship and Immigration Services, *Fiscal Year 2003 Yearbook of Immigration Statistics*, table 1.

41. "The Melting Pot," *Fortune* 20, July 1939, 76.

42. Gossett, *Race*.

43. During this period, Roosevelt was also delivering his famous "race death" speeches—he is often misquoted as having said "race suicide"—exhorting native-born white women to increase their birth rates because they were being outbred by immigrants and minorities.

44. The raw total was surpassed late in the twentieth century by the 1,536,483 admitted in 1990 and the 1,827,167 admitted in 1991. However, these figures include legalizations of previously undocumented immigrants and specially designated agricultural workers authorized under the 1986 Immigration Reform and Control Act. Without those additions, the immigration figures for 1990 and 1991 would be 656,111 and 704,005, respectively (INS, *1997 Statistical Yearbook of the Immigration and Naturalization Service*, table 4).

45. Literacy tests that required immigrants to be able to read and write in their native languages were introduced in 1917, along with an "Asiatic Barred Zone," which barred immigrants from across South and Southeast Asia.

46. The key 1924 legislation used 1890 and a slightly higher quota. Five years later, it was amended to a total quota of 150,000, divided according to the proportion of the national-origin group in the total U.S. population as counted in 1920. For a detailed description of U.S. immigration laws, see INS, *1997 Statistical Yearbook of the Immigration and Naturalization Service*, appendix 1.

47. Gossett, *Race*, 407.

48. In fact, during the Great Depression more people emigrated from the United States than immigrated.

49. Naturalization was officially limited by the federal government in 1790 to "free white persons." The Fourteenth Amendment extended the right of citizenship to blacks in 1868.

50. Representative Philip Burton (D-Calif.) argued: "Just as we sought to eliminate discrimination in our land through the Civil Rights Act, today we seek by phasing out the national origins quota system to eliminate discrimination in immigration to this nation composed of the descendants of immigrants." Representative Emanuel Celler (D-N.Y.) explained: "With the end of discrimination due to place of birth, there will be shifts in countries other than those of northern and western Europe. Immigrants from Asia and Africa will have to compete and qualify in order to get in, quantitatively and qualitatively, which, itself will hold the numbers down. There will not be, comparatively, many Asians or Africans entering this country. . . . Since the people of Africa and Asia have very few relatives here, comparatively few could immigrate from those countries because they have no family ties in the U.S."; *Congressional Record*, August 25, 1965, 21813 and 21812.

51. For one thing, by 1965 most European-born Americans had few immediate relatives still living with whom to be reunited. Their average age was fifty-two, and one-fourth of them were sixty-five or older. (In the 1970 census, the mean age of foreign-born white adults was fifty-

seven, and the seventy-fifth percentile of their age distribution was seventy, by our calculation. We subtracted five years from each of these to get the 1965 estimates.) Older Europeans who might have considered moving had home-country pensions and no American ones. Working-age Europeans faced far better home-country opportunities than in 1900.

52. Massey, Durand, and Malone, *Beyond Smoke and Mirrors*.

53. Fix and Passel, "U.S. Immigration at the Beginning of the Twenty-first Century." The 2000 census counted 30.1 million foreign-born residents of the United States. Legal permanent residents (9.3 million) and naturalized citizens (another 9.2 million) account for 18.5 million out of that total; 2.3 million refugees (700,000 of whom became U.S. citizens) and almost 1 million legal non-immigrants (including students, workers who are in the country both legally and temporarily, and diplomats) bring the tally up to 21.6 million. The difference between the census count of 30.1 million and the administrative count of 21.6 million yields the estimate of 8.5 million undocumented. This number, though substantially higher than previous estimates, is consistent with the fact that the 2000 census count itself exceeded projections by 8 or 9 million. An amnesty in 1986 legalized 2 million formerly undocumented immigrants (and facilitated the legal immigration of their relatives).

54. Ibid.

55. The Irish and Germans had also been measured against earlier British immigrants. For example, in 1865, claiming to be "100 percent American" was implicitly an anti-Irish comment. In 1938 the same slogan graced campaign posters for New York's Irish-American congressional hopeful, John J. O'Connor, Senate hopeful John Burke, and William McDonough, a candidate for state assemblyman; *Fortune*, "The Melting Pot."

56. Borjas, *Heaven's Door*; Jacoby, *Reinventing the Melting Pot*.

57. Bean et al., "Immigration and Fading Color Lines in America," figure 4.

58. Portes, "English-Only Triumphs."

59. We identified the earlier immigrants as non-natives listed in the 1900 through 1920 censuses who had been in the United States anywhere from fewer than six to more than twenty years at the time of the census, and the later immigrants as non-natives listed in the 1980 through 2000 censuses who had been in the country during the same period. We left out those who had emigrated from English-speaking nations. (For a list of these nations, see Bleakley, "Language Skills and Earnings," appendix table 1, panels A and B.) We defined speaking English as any "yes" answer on the IPUMS "speakeng" variable. However, the

measure of English ability was not consistent over the century; see
note 60 for details.

60.   One methodological question is whether the census measures of English proficiency were comparable in the two eras. The question about
English-language proficiency for the 1980 through 2000 censuses is
superior to the one used for 1900 through 1920. As the IPUMS code-
book describes the questions: "In 1900–1920, enumerators simply
asked the respondents if they could speak English; it is not possible to
tell how well persons who answered 'yes' could actually speak English. In 1980 and 1990, respondents indicated whether or not English
was their only language. If it was not, they were to indicate how well
they could speak English: very well, well, not well, not at all. Information is not available for 2000 on whether English was their only language" (although, in fact, over 2 million cases were coded just that in
2000). For the analysis described here, but not shown, we coded English proficiency as a "yes" in 1900 through 1920 and as a "speaks very
well" or "speaks English only" in 1980 through 2000. Given these differences in questions, any biases would inflate *old* immigrants' ability
to speak English relative to that of new immigrants. Thus, our conclusion that the new immigrants knew more English is especially robust
with respect to the wording of the question.

61.   According to the economist Joel Perlmann (*Italians Then, Mexicans
Now*), the Mexican second generation has been slower to close the
wage gap with native-born Americans than earlier second-generation
Europeans were, but the differences partly can be explained by the
economic climate in America during the two periods. Early in the century, economic inequality was decreasing. Over the last three decades
of the twentieth century, earnings inequality increased sharply (see
chapter 5), just as the new wave of immigrants arrived.

62.   We use the GSS data on first marriages to measure intermarriage
rates, based on native-born respondents' reports of their and their
spouse's race, religion, ethnicity, or national origin (as appropriate).
We define marriage cohorts using the respondents' age at first marriage. If mixed-ancestry marriages have a higher propensity for divorce than homogamous marriages, then we may understate the rate
of intermarriage in the past. Also, to the extent that spouses simplify
their ancestral backgrounds when answering the interview and do so
in ways that match one another, the GSS data understate intermarriage throughout the period; Lieberson and Waters, "The Ethnic Responses of Whites." The GSS last asked age at marriage in 1994, so we
have no marriage cohorts after that. Fuller studies of intermarriage,
drawing on census data, lead to roughly similar conclusions; see, for
example, Kalmijn, "Intermarriage and Homogamy"; Lieberson and

Waters, *From Many Strands*, ch. 6; Pagnini and Morgan, "Intermarriage and Social Distance"; and Bean et al., "Immigration and Fading Color Lines in America." One advantage of using the GSS is that we can distinguish Jewish respondents, which is not possible using the IPUMS.

63. Past intermarriage over several generations made it harder for the twentieth-century Germans, Irish, and British to increase their out-marriage rates by our definition of out-marriage. We label each person according to the ancestry he or she "feels closest to" (that is the question wording). We consider them out-married, however, only if *none* of their ancestries match any of their partner's ancestries (each can mention up to three). If we consider only the ancestries the respondents and their spouses feel closest to when we define intermarriage, then the rates for the Germans, Irish, and British increase between 19 and 26 percent in each marriage cohort. A similar increase occurs for people who report American Indian ancestry using this definition of out-marriage.

64. Hout and Goldstein, "How 4.5 Million Irish Immigrants Became 40 Million Irish Americans."

65. Waters, *Black Identities*.

66. See, for example, Bean et al., "Immigration and Fading Color Lines in America"; Lee and Bean, "Beyond Black and White"; and Gans, "The Possibility of a New Racial Hierarchy."

67. U.S. Supreme Court, Loving v. Virginia, 388 U.S.1(1967), 2.

68. "Do you personally hate the Japanese people?"; Roper Center, accession 0264372, Lexis-Nexis Academic Universe (accessed May 28, 2006).

69. "It has been almost half a century since the war with Japan ended. What would you say your feelings are toward the Japanese people at present: Friendly, unfriendly, or neutral?"; Roper Center, accession 0228116, Lexis-Nexis Academic Universe (accessed May 28, 2006).

70. Schuman, Steeh, and Bobo, *Racial Attitudes in America*.

71. The respondents were students attending U.S. universities who were all enrolled in social science classes. The racial breakdown of the sample was similar to that of the entire country in each year. Regional diversity was also a factor in the sample design; see Owen, Eisner, and McFaul, "A Half-Century of Social Distance Research."

72. The average score (an average of all the responses for all thirty groups) dropped from 2.14 in 1926 and 1946 to 1.93 in 1977. The spread of scores—the difference between the highest- and lowest-rated group—declined even more, from 2.85 in 1926 (the difference between the 1.06 given to the English and the 3.91 given to Asian Indians) to 1.37 in 1977 (the difference between the 1.25 given to Americans and the 2.63 given to Koreans).

73. The trends refer to the ratings of white, Protestant, native-born respondents between 1964 and 1992. See also Schuman et al., *Racial Attitudes*, and Rosenfield, "The Polls: Attitudes Toward American Jews."

74. Gallup Poll, "Poll Topics and Trends: Immigration," available at: http://www.gallup.com (accessed July 17, 2005). See also Barkan, "Return of the Nativists?" on the attitudes of Californians during the era of rapid immigration.

75. Schuman et al., *Racial Attitudes in America*, is the definitive source on questions asked about African Americans over the decades.

76. Hout, "How Trends Differ Among Subpopulations."

77. The smoother used here is a loess regression (invented by William S. Cleveland; see *Elements of Graphing Data*), using the STATA software package, with a bandwidth of .50 in our analyses of opinion data. We experimented with the polynomial functions more commonly found in spreadsheet software, but discovered that they often yield clearly ill-fitting curves, particularly when summarizing data with long periods between points.

78. Ludwig, "Acceptance of Interracial Marriage at Record High," Gallup Poll "Tuesday Briefing," available to subscribers at: http://www.gallup.com (accessed June 1, 2004). Note that, in 2003, almost the same percentage of non-Hispanic whites, 66 percent, said that they would approve of such a marriage for their own children or grandchildren. In 1958 the key phrase was "white and colored people" and, until 1983, "whites and nonwhites."

79. Calculation based on using the Firebaugh-Davis ("Trends in Antiblack Prejudice") method. They reached a slightly different but commensurate conclusion because they did not consider data from the 1963, 1967, and 1970 surveys.

80. For a fuller discussion of these kinds of changes, see Alwin, "Generations X, Y, and Z."

81. As first shown by Firebaugh and Davis, "Trends in Antiblack Prejudice."

82. Among blacks, the responses were 27 percent to 66 percent. On the question of whether affirmative action programs should be increased, 22 percent of whites said "yes" (33 percent said "decrease," and 36 percent said "keep the same"), compared to 57 percent of blacks (versus 4 percent and 28 percent); Gallup Poll, "Social Audit: Black-White Relations in the United States—2001 Update" (July 10), available to subscribers at: http//:www.gallup.com (accessed January 22, 2002), 20–21. We should not, however, exaggerate whites' opposition. That same year, 2001, 44 percent of non-Hispanic whites told Gallup that they favored "affirmative action programs for racial minorities"; Gallup Poll, "Poll Topics and Trends: Race Relations," available to subscribers at: http://www.gallup.com (accessed July 18, 2005).

83. Research on other items does not reveal a backlash; see Taylor, Sheatsley, and Greeley, "Attitudes Toward Racial Integration."
84. Even about one-third of African Americans agreed.
85. Greeley and Sheatsley, "Attitudes Toward Racial Integration."
86. Schuman and his colleagues (*Racial Attitudes*) reach a similar conclusion using items that more explicitly address neighborhood integration.
87. A 1999 Princeton Survey Research Associates poll asked: "Racial and ethnic diversity strengthens my community because people's different experiences and points of view help when trying to solve problems. Racial and ethnic diversity is a burden on my community because people's differences make it harder to get things done. Which one comes closer to your view?" The replies were 69 percent "strengthens" and 19 percent "weakens"; Lexis-Nexis Research, accession 0412573 (accessed July 28, 2005). In another 1999 Princeton Survey Research Associates survey, respondents were asked: "Tell me whether you think each thing is a major reason, a minor reason or not a reason that America has been so successful in this century. . . . The cultural diversity of our people . . . ?" The replies were 71 percent "major," 20 percent "minor," and 6 percent "not"; Lexis-Nexis Research, accession 0331720 (accessed July 28, 2005).
88. Ross, "The Causes of Race Superiority," 88–89.
89. Lieberson, *A Piece of the Pie*, 383.
90. On life expectancy, see chapter 4 and Arias, "United States Life Tables, 2002"; on incarceration, see Western, *Prisons and Inequality*; on happiness, see Hout, "Money and Morale."

CHAPTER 4

1. The categorization by Ruggles and Brower ("Measurement of Household and Family Composition") is comparable to ours. Note that homeless people are almost certainly undercounted in the census, but those who are included are typed by the same criteria as people who live in a permanent residence.
2. For historical consistency, we follow the 1970 definition of group quarters as a household situation that contains five or more unrelated individuals. We combine the two small categories of group quarters and nonrelatives for ease of presentation and to deal with definitional problems between 1900 and 1910.
3. Our approach is consistent with the observation by Ruggles and Brower ("Measurement of Household and Family Composition," 93) that, given various methodological issues, studies should use individuals rather than families as the units of analysis.
4. This is the "POSSLQ" estimate (see Casper, Cohen, and Simmons,

"How Does POSSLQ Measure Up?"). In the 2000 CPS, the POSSLQ estimate was 24 percent larger than the unmarried partners count; see http://www.census.gov/population/socdemo/hh-fam/tabUC-1.pdf (accessed May 26, 2004). See Fitch, Goeken, and Ruggles, "The Rise of Cohabitation," for an extensive effort to provide more accurate historical estimates.

5. See, for example, Smock, "Cohabitation in the United States." Census table UC-1 cited in the previous note yields an estimate of 4 percent; using POSSLQ rules on the 2000 census yields 4.6 percent. A Gallup poll in 2002 found that 37 percent of married Americans reported having lived together before marriage (51 percent of those under age fifty); Jones, "Public Divided on Benefits of Living Together."

6. The Census Bureau's counts of children living with parents are somewhat higher because they do not separate out extended households as we do here. (Later we examine trends for children the same way the census does.) In 2002 the bureau estimated that 69 percent lived with two parents, and 73 percent did if cohabitation is counted; Fields, "Children's Living Arrangements, 2002," table 1. This estimate is based on the Census 2000 finding that 5.7 percent of children were living in "unmarried partner households" (5.1 percent with opposite-sex partners, 0.6 percent with same-sex partners); U.S. Bureau of the Census, "Household and Family Characteristics of Children," Census 2000 PHC-T-30, "Characteristics of Children," table 2, available at: www.census.gov/population/cen2000/phc-t30/tab02.pdf (accessed May 26, 2004). We return to the extended household issue later.

7. The children estimate adds those in married-with-children to those in extended household; the institutions estimate refers to the group quarters segment of the "shared quarters" category.

8. The table in this note shows the results treating cohabitation as "marriage." Counting cohabiting couples is complex, given the variety of arrangements that might qualify. Our goal was to use a common classification system across the century rather than rely on the "unmarried partner" question of the 1990 and 2000 censuses. We count households as cohabiting-couple households if there was a person present who was the opposite sex to the household head, who was age fifteen or older, and who was identified as a "partner," "friend," or "visitor." We excluded as cohabiters foster children, people paying to live in the household, and employees. (Possible cohabiting couples in the household that do not include the head were not counted.) This method overestimates cohabitation to the extent that some partners, friends, or visitors are simply roommates, and it underestimates cohabitation to the extent that some who pay or work to live in the household may actually be in a quasi-spouse relationship with the head. These alternative counts make

a negligible difference before about 1970. Others whom we cite use different procedures for cohabiting counts in 1990 and 2000, but the numbers are similar. Our counting procedure resembles that of Fitch et al., "The Rise of Cohabitation," although they prefer a seventeen-year-old cutoff.

Household Type, by Age, Counting Cohabitors as Married, 2000

	Zero to Seventeen	Eighteen to Twenty-Nine	Thirty to Forty-Four	Forty-Five to Sixty-Four	Sixty-Five and older
Married with children	66.1%	35.4	52.5%	28.3%	5.0%
Married without children	0.0	13.7	12.5	36.1	43.3
Single parent	15.6	9.0	8.2	5.6	3.7
Extended household	16.5	17.2	11.4	12.7	12.6
Primary individual	0.0	9.5	10.2	14.2	28.8
Shared quarters[a]	1.9	15.1	5.2	3.0	6.7

Source: Authors' compilation.
[a] Non-relatives and group quarters.

9. Treating cohabiting adults as if they were married changes the percentages only a few points. One major racial contrast is that cohabiting white women married far more often than did cohabiting African-American women; Raley, "Recent Trends and Differentials in Marriage and Cohabitation." The rates we report are all snapshots. If we focus on the proportion of children who *ever* lived in a given arrangement, cohabitation makes a modest difference but does not alter our conclusions. African-American and Hispanic children in the 1990s were 30 percent likelier than non-Hispanic whites to have ever lived with a cohabiting parent; Graefe and Lichter, "Life Course Transitions of American Children." Similarly, African-American and Hispanic children spent, on average, more of their childhoods in a cohabiting arrangement than white children did—11 percent and 7 percent of those years, respectively. In the end, however, the basic differences in the 1990s between blacks and others remain dramatic: the percentage of children's childhoods spent with a couple, married or cohabiting, was 87 percent for whites, 79 percent for Hispanics, and 27 percent for African Americans; Bumpass and Lu, "Trends in Cohabitation."
10. Bachu and O'Connell, "Fertility of American Women: June 2000." See also Cherlin, *Marriage, Divorce, Remarriage*, ch. 4.
11. This figure of 14 percent of black men compares to 7 percent of His-

panic men and 5 percent of non-Hispanic white men. A methodological note about racial differences with a substantive implication: African-American men between thirty and forty-four years old were notably more likely to be recorded as living in a married-couple household than were African-American women, by about nine percentage points. Given the very small percentage of African Americans who marry nonblacks, this is an odd discrepancy. The discrepancy lies not in the numbers of African-American men and women who were married—that was about right—but in the base number of African-American men and women. Census Bureau researchers counted notably fewer African-American men age thirty to forty-four than African-American women in that age category. Some of the missing were men who lived with a "spouse surrogate" but were not reported. A much larger group were African-American men living in unconventional, uncounted, and typically unpleasant housing arrangements. Because these marginal African-American men were missing in the denominator, the census data made it seem that a higher percentage of African-American men were married than was actually true. Jon Stiles analyzed these data. On the African-American undercount, see Hogan and Robinson, "What the Census Bureau's Coverage Evaluation Programs Tell Us"; Darden, Jones, and Price, "Ethnographic Evaluation of the Behavioral Causes of Undercount"; West and Robinson, "What Do We Know About the Undercount of Children?"

12. There is some evidence, however, that Mexican-origin Americans are moving toward a higher single-parent pattern; Wildsmith, "Race-Ethnic Differences in Female Headship."

13. Cohabitation has little effect on the pattern, and looking only at non-Hispanic whites makes little change in the pattern. The thirty-nine-point difference between most- and least-educated shrinks only four points if we include cohabiting parents, since less-educated couples cohabit more often than more-educated couples. And the thirty-nine-point gap narrows only nine points when we restrict our focus to non-Hispanic white children. This means that the education differences are not simply mirroring racial or ethnic differences, and vice versa. On cohabitation differences, see Graefe and Lichter, "Life Course Transitions of American Children."

14. And 41 percent of young, unmarried women with some college were mothers. These numbers refer to women age twenty-five to forty-four. The ideal statistic would look only at never-married women. Nonetheless, the differences are clear. In another view of these differences, 54 percent of births to high school dropout women in 2000 were out of wedlock versus 4 percent of births to women with a BA degree; Bachu and O'Connell, "Fertility of American Women: June 2000."

15. Among adults age thirty to sixty-four, 68 percent of college graduates lived in a married-couple household, versus 58 percent of high school graduates and 44 percent of high school dropouts.

16. No doubt there is some causality running the other way: youngsters who become unwed parents often drop out of school. But overall, we can assume that educational diversity drives the variety of household patterns we see here. Later in the chapter, we look more closely at the "normal" life cycle.

17. Mosher and Bachrach, "Understanding U.S. Fertility."

18. Preston, "Mortality Trends."

19. White and Preston, "How Many Americans Are Alive Because of Twentieth-Century Improvements in Mortality?"

20. Cutler, "The Economics of Health." In another calculation, Peter Uhlenberg ("Death and the Family") estimates that families in 1900 had a better than three-to-two chance of losing a child before he or she reached age sixteen; those odds had dropped to one in twenty by the 1970s. Conversely, in 1900 a child had a one-in-two chance of losing a parent or sibling before reaching sixteen; that had dropped to one in ten by the 1970s.

21. Cutler and Miller, "The Role of Public Health Improvements in Health Advances"; Preston, "Mortality Trends," and *Mortality Patterns in National Populations*, esp. 183–86. See also specific studies, such as Wells, "The Mortality Transition in Schenectady."

22. The data behind figure 4.2 come from historical vital statistics available from the National Center for Health Statistics. We used actual cohort experiences up through 1998 and projected the rest assuming that age-specific death rates will change half as much between 2000 and 2050 as between 1950 and 2000. Our spreadsheets are available at: http://www.russellsage.org/publications/books/060711.219626.

23. See, for example, Williams and Collins, "U.S. Socioeconomic and Racial Differences in Health."

24. Of women in their early thirties in 1900, about one-fifth had never given birth and one-fifth had done so seven or more times. Fewer than one in eight had had a specific number of births between one and six.

25. These figures are based on the vital statistics reports in Heuser, "Cohort Fertility Tables," and subsequent data posted on www.cdc.gov/nchs.

26. The calculations in the previous paragraph refer to so-called "period" estimates—the number of births a woman would have if she experienced at each age what the women that age in year t experienced. The calculations behind figure 4.3 eliminate the synthetic nature of the period estimate by tracking a real cohort of women as they progressed through each age one year at a time. Even though this approach provides a better description of how life works out, demographers often

look at the period fertility rate to keep tabs on younger women who are just beginning their childbearing years.

27. McFalls, "Risks of Reproductive Impairment in the Later Years of Childbearing"; Mencken, "Age and Fertility"; Morgan, "Late-Nineteenth and Early-Twentieth-Century Childlessness."

28. For discussions on causes of the baby boom, see, for example, Klein, *A Population History of the United States*, ch. 6; Nugent, *Structures of American Social History*, 126ff; Westoff and Westoff, *From Now to Zero*. A recent paper argues that rising real wages between 1800 and 2000 drove down birth rates, because the opportunity cost of children rose, but that new household and child-rearing technologies introduced in mid-century reduced those opportunity costs for a while, thus temporarily spurring fertility; Greenwood, Seshadri, and Vandenbroucke, "The Baby Boom and Baby Bust." On consequences, see, for example, Macunovich, *Birth Quake*.

29. Fitch and Ruggles, "Historical Trends in Marriage Formation," esp. figure 4.7. See also Westoff, "Marriage and Fertility in Developed Countries"; Goldstein and Kenny, "Marriage Delayed or Marriage Forgone?"; and authors' own calculations from the March CPS data files. The fraction of nineteenth-century women who never married was probably significantly higher yet, although precise national figures are not available. Data for Massachusetts indicate that the proportion single at age fifty rose from 15 percent in the cohort born in 1830 to 22 percent for the cohort born in 1890 (see Uhlenberg, "A Study of Cohort Life Cycles"), but women outside the Northeast were likelier to marry.

30. Age-at-marriage data are from IPUMS for the 1940 to 1980 censuses and from the June 1985 and June 1995 CPS.

31. With 20 percent still unmarried, we might suspect that many women born in the 1970s will never marry. But recent projections indicate that all but 6 or 7 percent of the women in these cohorts will be married by 2010; Goldstein and Kenny, "Marriage Delayed or Marriage Forgone?"

32. This estimate of 35 percent is calculated from Bramlett and Mosher (*Cohabitation, Marriage, Divorce*, table B) and covers women age twenty to twenty-nine at the time of a 1995 survey. Cohabitation was defined in the survey "as being unmarried, but 'having a sexual relationship while sharing the same usual address'" (89).

33. See Fitch and Ruggles, "Historical Trends in Marriage Formation"; Oppenheimer, "A Theory of Marriage Timing," "Men's Career Development," and "The Continuing Importance of Men's Economic Position"; Furstenberg et al., "Growing Up Is Harder to Do." A recent study of unmarried parents found that many were waiting for financial

stability before marrying; Gibson et al., "High Hopes but Even Higher Expectations." See also Edin and Kefalas, *Promises I Can Keep*.

34.   The pre-1970 increase in divorce is exaggerated by the tendency early in the century for census respondents to hide their divorces or abandonment. So, for example, the percentage of ever-married Americans between the ages of eighteen and sixty-four who were recorded as divorced grew from 0.6 percent in 1900 to 4.6 percent in 1970 (more than a fivefold increase), but when we also count those who reported that their spouses were "absent" on census day, then the "spouseless" grew from 4.3 percent to 9.8 percent, a twofold increase (calculated from IPUMS data). These estimates by year of marriage are based on GSS data because the census does not inquire about married peoples' previous marriages, information vital to figuring out whether a person has ever been divorced. We made these estimates by sorting respondents by age within birth cohorts and smoothing the percentage who had ever been divorced.

35.   See Bramlett and Mosher, "Cohabitation, Marriage, Divorce, and Remarriage in the United States." The decline continued into at least 2003 (http://www.cdc.gov/nchs/data/nvsr/nvsr52/nvsr52_22.pdf).

36.   On explaining the rise in divorce rates, see, for example, Ruggles, "The Rise of Divorce and Separation in the United States" (and subsequent comments); South, "Time-Dependent Effects of Wives' Employment on Marital Dissolution"; Friedberg, "Did Unilateral Divorce Raise Divorce Rates?"; and Thornton and Rodgers, "The Influence of Individual and Historical Time on Marriage Dissolution." Andrew Cherlin (*Marriage, Divorce, Remarriage*, 45ff) contends that the no-fault laws were only coincidental. On reasons for the later decline, see Heaton, "Factors Contributing to Increasing Marital Stability in the United States."

37.   Calculated from the 2000 1 percent Public Use Microdata Series (PUMS).

38.   To be more precise, the probability of an early 1960s marriage lasting ten years was 80 percent for all educational groups. For 1980s marriages, only college-graduate women had an 80 percent chance of reaching their tenth anniversary; only 65 percent of high school graduate wives and 50 percent of high school dropout wives reached their tenth anniversary; Martin and Parashar, "An Education Crossover in Divorce Attitudes," figure 1 (drawn from the CPS). See also McLanahan, "Diverging Destinies"; Martin, "Growing Evidence for a 'Divorce Divide'?"

39.   Donehower, "The Demographic Foundations of Change in U.S. Households." How much declining fertility explains the move from elderly coresidence is unclear. See Ruggles, "The Transformation of American Family Structure"; Kramarow, "The Elderly Who Live Alone in the

United States"; and Schoeni, "Reassessing the Decline in Parent-Child Old-Age Coresidence."

40. See Watkins, Mencken, and Bongaarts, "Demographic Foundations of Family Change," for estimates of how the demographic changes altered family life. Family historians have increasingly stressed the "strategic" use of coresidence to deal with life shocks such as migration and death. See, for example, Anderson, "Family, Household, and the Industrial Revolution"; Modell, "Changing Risks, Changing Adaptations"; and Hareven, "The History of the Family and the Complexity of Social Change."

41. In 1910 nearly 25 percent of white mothers and over 30 percent of black mothers under the age of thirty-five and without husbands reported having some children who lived apart from them; Moehling, "Broken Homes."

42. Some of the 16 percent living in an extended household lived there with a single parent or, less commonly, with both parents. We return to this complication later in the chapter.

43. This table shows the proportion of each age group living in a married-couple or cohabiting-couple nuclear household in three key years. (Our coding rule for cohabitation is discussed in note 8.)

Age	1900	1960	2000
0 to 17	70%	78%	66%
18 to 29	52	67	49
30 to 44	62	76	65

Source: Authors' compilation.

44. See, for example, Popenoe, *Disturbing the Nest*; Skolnick, *Embattled Paradise*; and Coontz, *The Way We Never Were.*

45. Goldscheider and colleagues estimate that in 1900, 40 percent of mothers with children under five had a mother or adolescent daughter at home, but that in 1990, 25 percent did; Goldscheider et al., "The Growing Isolation of Parenthood in the Life Course"; Short, Goldscheider, and Torr, "Less Help for Mother."

46. Carole Shammas (*A History of Household Governance in America*) makes the erosion of patriarchal authority a key theme of American social history. On wives' increasing autonomy, see also, for example, Cott, *Public Vows*; Hartog, *Man and Wife in America.* On youth independence, see, for example, Mintz, *Huck's Raft*; Bahr et al., "Trends in Family Space/Time, Conflict, and Solidarity."

47. See, for example, May, *Great Expectations*; Ruggles, "The Rise of Divorce and Separation"; and Ono, "Historical Time and U.S. Marital Dissolution."

48. Modernization theory in the Parsonian mode stressed the isolation of the conjugal family (see, for example, Parsons, "The Kinship System of the Contemporary United States"; Riesman, *The Lonely Crowd*). A stream of subsequent research (for example, Sussman, "The Isolated Nuclear Family"; Litwak, "Geographic Mobility and Extended Family Cohesion") challenged the notion that nuclear households were really isolated—kin lived nearby—although not necessarily the notion that such households were a problem.

49. A related question was whether single-parent or stepparent families formed by divorce were more damaging to children than ones formed by the death of a parent. That may well be so. On these issues, see, for example, Cherlin, *Marriage, Divorce, Remarriage*, ch. 3; Cherlin and Furstenberg, "Stepfamilies in the United States"; McLanahan, "Life Without Father"; Biblarz and Raftery, "Family Structure, Educational Attainment, and Socioeconomic Success"; Hawkins and Booth, "Unhappily Ever After."

50. A small percentage of middle-aged Americans living in a childless couple never had children, of course. But that group is sufficiently small that the label "empty-nester" is reasonably accurate.

51. Among younger Americans, the era of greatest commonality was the 1950s and 1960s, when over 70 percent of those under forty-five were in nuclear households. (Even most of the eighteen- to twenty-nine-year-olds were.) Conformity was notably greater than earlier in the century, when many young adults lived in extended households and in shared quarters. After 1970, family diversity increased substantially for these groups, with more young Americans living alone or in single-parent households, although the two-parent-plus-child(ren) household remained the dominant choice. The degree of diversity in the households of older Americans changed little, but those over age forty-five went through the major shift we just described from more complex to simpler households. These comments are based on a diversity index calculated across the six types of households. In abbreviated form, the index shows the following pattern by age:

Age Group	1900	1960	2000
0 to 17	.46	.37	.56
18 to 29	.72	.64	.80
30 to 44	.65	.52	.70
45 to 64	.71	.74	.76
65 and older	.73	.75	.71

Source: Authors' compilation.

52. These numbers exclude group quarters; including them would steepen the decline in size variability.
53. See note 8 for our rules on coding cohabiting-couple households.
54. The single-adult category in figure 4.8 includes a few percent of children who were nonrelatives in a household or who lived in an institution.
55. For similar results, see Tolnay, "The Living Arrangements of African-American and Immigrant Children." This conclusion must be partly qualified by evidence that the marriage rate for African Americans was somewhat exaggerated early in the century; thus, the divergence is not quite as sharp as shown here, but it is nonetheless substantial. On the exaggeration issue, see Morgan et al., "Racial Differences in Households and Family Structure at the Turn of the Century"; Pagnini and Morgan, "Racial Differences in Marriage and Childbearing"; and S. Philip Morgan, personal communication, June 7, 2004.
56. For technical reasons, we have the count only since 1910. (The 1900 sample was updated in the midst of our analyses, and manpower constraints prevented us from redoing the work; it is unlikely to have made a serious difference.) We counted each child living in a nuclear household "embedded" within an extended household as having two parents. (This figure also includes up to 1 percent of residents seventeen or younger who were the *spouses* in an embedded nuclear household, but that complication has negligible consequences for our results.)
57. As noted earlier, black marriage rates were exaggerated early in the century. This distortion does not affect our household analysis, because we count widows and married women whose husbands were absent as unmarried.
58. The debate goes back to the classic works of scholars such as Melville Herskovitz, W. E. B. Du Bois, E. Franklin Frazier, Herbert Gutman, and Daniel Patrick Moynihan. For the latest analyses, see, for example, Cherlin, *Marriage, Divorce, Remarriage*, ch. 4; Wilson, *The Truly Disadvantaged*; Ruggles, "The Origins of African-American Family Structure"; Pagnini and Morgan "Racial Differences in Marriage and Childbearing"; Morgan et al., "Racial Differences in Households and Family Structure at the Turn of the Century"; Bennett, Bloom, and Craig, "The Divergence of African-American and White Marriage Patterns"; Fitch and Ruggles, "Historical Trends in Marriage Formation"; Goldscheider and Bures, "The Racial Crossover in Family Complexity in the United States"; Taylor, "Postbellum African-American Culture"; and Katz, Stern, and Fader, "The New African-American Inequality." On the issue of imprisonment, see, for example, Pettit and Western, "Mass Imprisonment and the Life Course." On the college-educated, see, for example, Qian and Preston, "Changes in American Marriage"; Lichter and Qian, *Marriage and Family in a Multiracial Society*.

59. A technical note: we could think of educational differences not in terms of diplomas but as relative standing. As we report in chapter 2, as long as we compare more- and less-educated people of the same age, the results are the same as we reported: relative educational differences in household arrangements widened.

60. See, for example, Kalmijn, "Shifting Boundaries"; Schwartz and Mare, "Trends in Educational Assortative Marriage."

61. The distribution of thirty- to forty-four-year-old non–African Americans by their nativity and household types is given in this table. The percentage in extended households goes down for the native-born but, after 1970, up sharply for the foreign-born. Cohabiting households do not change this story.

	1900	1910	1920	1940	1950	1960	1970	1980	1990	2000
Foreign-born										
Couples	.62	.58	.64	.68	.66	.72	.74	.67	.56	.58
Extended	.15	.15	.15	.15	.16	.14	.12	.16	.22	.26
Single	.24	.27	.22	.17	.18	.13	.13	.18	.22	.16
Native-born										
Couples	.62	.63	.65	.67	.73	.79	.81	.76	.69	.70
Extended	.22	.21	.21	.20	.17	.12	.08	.06	.06	.08
Single	.16	.16	.14	.13	.10	.09	.11	.18	.24	.22

Source: Authors' compilation.

62. For more extensive discussion of this topic, see Glick, Bean, and Van Hook, "Immigration and Changing Patterns of Extended Family Household Structure."

63. For example, in the early years an unusual proportion of white thirty- to forty-four-year-olds in the western region lived as "singles"—31 percent compared to 13 to 20 percent elsewhere. By 2000 the rates in all the regions were between 29 and 31 percent. Similarly, early in the century the elderly in the West were especially unlikely to be in extended households, while the opposite was true of the elderly in the South; by 2000 this difference had also disappeared.

64. This analysis is made difficult and approximate by certain data issues (discussed in chapter 7). Here we use a simple three-part division: nonmetropolitan areas, the center cities of metropolitan areas, and the remaining—largely suburban—parts of metropolitan areas. This table illustrates the general trends, showing the distribution of household types for white thirty- to forty-four-year-olds. The trends are roughly similar for zero- to seventeen-year-olds and for those age sixty-five and older.

Place	Household Type	1900	1950	2000
Nonmetropolitan	Couple households	66%	75%	68%
	Singles	15	9	26
	Extended households	20	15	6
Metro: outside	Couple households	57	75	66
center city	Singles	22	9	25
	Extended households	21	17	9
Metro: center city	Couple households	58	67	47
	Singles	22	15	41
	Extended households	20	18	11

Source: Authors' compilation.

65. On the social psychology of living alone, see, for example, Fischer and Phillips, "Who Is Alone?"; U.S. Bureau of the Census, "Families and Living Arrangements," table HH-4. Available at: http://www.census.gov/population/socdemo/hh-fam/hh4.pdf.

66. U.S. Bureau of the Census, *Historical Statistics*, 41–42; U.S. Bureau of the Census, table HH-4.

67. The one-point decline after 1980 might be the result of the sag in earnings for young workers, some of whom consequently stayed in or returned to their parents' households. According to a 1980s Bureau of Labor Statistics (BLS) estimate, it cost at least 25 percent more for all parties combined if a young adult set up a separate household from his parents (Levy, *Dollars and Dreams*, 153–56). See also Michael, Fuchs, and Scott, "Changes in the Propensity to Live Alone."

68. From 1900 to 1950, divorced and separated women were about equally likely to live in either extended households or single-parent households (30 percent in each situation); toward the end of the century, they were over three times more likely to live as single mothers than in an extended household.

69. Steven Ruggles ("The Transformation of American Family Structure" and "Multigenerational Families in Nineteenth-Century America") estimates that only 3 percent of the change in elderly white women's coresidence with children was due to demographic shifts.

70. Quoted from Kobrin, "The Fall in Household Size and the Rise of the Primary Individual," 79.

71. Similarly, Ruggles ("The Transformation of American Family Structure," 127) explains the change by saying that in "every sphere of family life, there has been a loosening of bonds of obligation among kin." However, it may be that some elderly see their obligation to their children as avoiding being a burden to them. It makes more sense to speak of cultural change toward more autonomy. In "Multigenerational Fam-

ilies," Ruggles lays out the argument about the decline of farming. On this debate, see also Kramarow, "The Elderly Who Live Alone in the United States"; Schoeni, "Reassessing the Decline in Parent-Child Old-Age Coresidence"; McGarry and Schoeni, "Social Security, Economic Growth, and the Rise in Elderly Widows' Independence"; Elman, "Old Age, Economic Activity, and Living Arrangements," and "Intergenerational Household Structure and Economic Change"; Ruggles, "The Demography of the Unrelated Individual"; Michael et al., "Changes in the Propensity to Live Alone"; and Heaton and Hoppe, "Widowed and Married."

72. The literature on this subject includes: Modell, "Changing Risks, Changing Adaptations," and *Into One's Own*; Chudacoff, *How Old Are You?*; Hareven, "Historical Changes in the Life Course," and "Aging and Generational Relations"; Shanahan, "Pathways to Adulthood in Changing Societies"; Buchman, *The Script of Life in Modern Society*; Furstenberg, "Family Change and Family Diversity"; Rindfuss, "The Young Adult Years"; Gutmann, Pullum-Pinon, and Pullum, "Three Eras of Young Adult Home Leaving"; Stevens, "New Evidence on the Timing of Early Life Transitions"; and Stanger-Ross, Collins, and Stern, "Falling Far from the Tree."

73. See, in particular, Shanahan, "Pathways to Adulthood in Changing Societies"; Buchman, *The Script of Life in Modern Society*; Furstenberg, "Family Change and Family Diversity"; Rindfuss, "The Young Adult Years"; and Stanger-Ross et al., "Falling Far from the Tree."

74. Stevens, "New Evidence on the Timing of Early Life Transitions."

75. We measure this correspondence with a statistic we term the Goodman association; it ranges from 0 (no correspondence) upward with no numerical limit. It moved steadily upward from 0.87 in 1900 to 1.41 in 2000. By way of a standard for comparison, the Goodman measure is .41 for the association between voters' social class position and their candidate choice in presidential elections. Many measures of the association between categorical variables analogous to the correlation coefficient for interval and ratio variables were developed over the course of the twentieth century, but consensus on which is best has eluded us. This measure was proposed by Leo Goodman and popularized in the analysis of voting differences; it is the standard deviation of elementary coefficients from a multiplicative (or log-linear) model of association; Goodman, "Measures, Models, and Graphical Displays." The Goodman measure, like the correlation coefficient, is 0 when the variables being compared are statistically independent, but there is no upper bound to the Goodman measure (the correlation coefficient cannot be greater than 1.0). The comparison with class voting comes from Manza and Brooks, *Social Cleavages and Political Change*, 110.

76. Other studies, as we noted, found increasing disorder in the last few decades. Jordan Stanger-Ross and his colleagues ("Falling Far from the Tree"), for example, report that the "congruence" and "integration" of early adult life transitions rose sharply from 1900 through midcentury and then fell some after about 1960.

77. We excluded those who answered the question with something like, "As many as I want," and we coded all answers "six and higher" as "six" to avoid distortion by extreme scores.

78. The drop is *not* the result of shifting from Gallup to GSS polls; it shows up in the Gallup polls alone.

79. We also analyzed the trends using as a dependent variable whether a respondent answered "three or more." The results are similar, although somewhat noisier.

80. The specific figure is 96 percent. Gallup found that 72 percent of adults had children, 6 percent wished they had had children (but had waited too late), 16 percent wanted to have children sometime in the future, and 4 percent did not want children; Frank Newport, "Desire to Have Children Alive and Well in America," Gallup Organization, 2003, available at: http://www.gallup.org (accessed August 20, 2003).

81. Some (for example, Westoff and Ryder, *The Contraceptive Revolution*) have dismissed the shift in survey responses as just a consequence of fertility control; they argue that women, now with fewer births, no longer had to rationalize the births they had not wanted. But we see more to it than that. Adults of all ages answered this question about ideal family size, not just parents. The sudden drop from three or more births to two births as "ideal" occurred all at once and for all age groups (including those who were done with child-rearing and those who were anticipating it); the trend is very similar for respondents thirty and younger and for those over thirty. Also, the change was too widespread and happened too fast to be merely the end of rationalization. Even more tellingly, after the 1960s people over fifty seemed to stop "rationalizing" the "extra" births that they had rationalized a decade earlier. Forty percent of respondents to the 1972 through 2000 GSS who had in fact parented three or more children said that fewer than three children was ideal. These and similar findings suggest that the drop was a real and widespread shift in American preferences, not a casual rationalization.

82. Statistical tests for interaction effects were significant, except for the Protestant-Catholic differences.

83. On the general topic, see, for example, Smith, "The Dating of the American Sexual Revolution," and "American Sexual Behavior"; and Rothman, *Hands and Hearts*. The survey was of Chicago residents and was reported in Laumann, Mahay, and Youm, "Sex, Intimacy, and Fam-

ily Life in the United States," 13. Nationally, 30 percent of girls born around 1940 had premarital intercourse before turning twenty; 40 percent of girls born around 1950 had; and 60 percent of girls born around 1960 had. But then came a decline: 55 percent of girls born around 1970 and 50 percent of girls born around 1975 had premarital sex as teens. These statistics on intercourse by age nineteen are combined from Hofferth, Kahn, and Baldwin, "Premarital Sexual Activity Among American Teenage Women," table 3, and the 1995 National Survey of Family Growth, as reported in Abma et al., "Fertility, Family Planning, and Women's Health," 4. See also Seidman and Rieder, "A Review of Sexual Behavior in the United States," and Lindberg et al., *Teen Risk-Taking*. Young women during the 1960s were especially likely to engage in sex early. Edward Laumann and his colleagues (*The Social Organization of Sexuality*, 197–99, 213–14) found that there was a big change in rates of premarital sexuality between the 1933 to 1942 cohort of women and the 1943 to 1952 cohort—most of the latter were in their teens and twenties in the 1960s—but that there were only minor differences between the 1943 to 1952 cohort and subsequent cohorts. On first-time births, see Bachu, "Trends in Marital Status of U.S. Women at First Birth." The out-of-wedlock trend has two elements: fewer women were giving birth, and more of those who were giving birth were doing so out of wedlock.

84. Gallup, "Current Views on Premarital, Extramarital Sex," available to subscribers at: http://www.gallup.com (accessed June 24, 2003).

85. Readers will notice that, although the trends were similar for Gallup and the GSS, the absolute levels of "not wrong" answers were quite different: 26 percent for GSS in 1972 and 43 percent for Gallup in 1973. This testifies to the important effect on responses of how questions are worded. See also Harding and Jencks, "Changing Attitudes Toward Premarital Sex."

86. In the GSS, 71 percent of respondents during the mid-1970s said that extramarital sex was "always wrong" (85 percent that it was always or almost always wrong); 78 percent (90 percent) said that in the mid-1990s. Americans in a 1986 survey were far less tolerant specifically of teenagers having sex, suggesting that increasingly "premarital sex" came to mean sex between adults rather than teens; see Thornton, "Changing Attitudes Toward Family Issues"; Smith, "The Dating of the American Sexual Revolution"; and Axinn and Thornton, "The Transformation in the Meaning of Marriage."

87. For example, in 1978 about six in ten baby boomers—who were in their twenties then—said premarital sex was "not wrong at all," but in 2000, when these baby boomers were in their late forties or so, only about four in ten said it was "not wrong at all."

88. Harding and Jencks, "Changing Attitudes Toward Premarital Sex."
89. On this topic, the Gallup and GSS questions are too different to merge. Harding and Jencks ("Changing Attitudes Toward Premarital Sex") make a strong effort to sew the two series together.
90. Between 1985 and 1990, 51 percent of African-American respondents said premarital sex was "not wrong at all," and 24 percent said it was "always wrong"; in the years between 1994 and 2000, the percentages were 34 percent "not wrong at all" and 41 percent "always wrong." African Americans born after 1960 were less accepting of premarital sex than baby boomer African Americans. Blacks' decreasing endorsement in the 1990s of early sex roughly matches a reported drop during that decade in early sexual activity among black high school students (Lindberg et al., *Teen Risk-Taking*). Also, rates of births to unwed mothers among African Americans dropped through the 1990s and beyond, while rates for whites stayed roughly constant (National Center for Health Statistics, *Health United States*, 132, 142). Similarly, rates of teen births dropped sharply among African Americans in the 1990s (U.S. Department of Health and Human Services, *National Vital Statistics Reports*, 5).
91. For the categorization of Protestants, see chapter 8.
92. The 1960 question was "Should divorce be made more difficult to get, easier to get, or should things be left as they are now?" Both Gallup poll results were obtained through the Lexis-Nexis service: 1960, accession 0036871; 1966, 0038989 (accessed May 28, 2006).
93. On attitude trends, see Cherlin, *Marriage, Divorce, Remarriage*, 45ff; Thornton, "Changing Attitudes Toward Family Issues," and "Changing Attitudes Toward Separation and Divorce."
94. The percentage answering that divorce should be "easier" are shown in this table by education and year. The numbers for 1960 and 1966, from Gallup, are the observed percentages; those for 1975 through 2000, from the GSS, are smoothed.

	1960	1966	1975	1985	2000
Total sample	9%	18%	30%	24%	23%
College graduates	22	29	36	24	14
Some college	6	21	30	23	22
High school graduate	6	15	26	21	24
High school dropout	8	17	24	24	32

Source: Authors' compilation.

95. Martin and Parashar ("An Education Crossover in Divorce Attitudes") argue that women without a BA degree increasingly faced risky marriages and single motherhood; presumably more of them viewed easy

divorce as a potential escape from a bad choice. Another dynamic was that women with a BA became more socially conservative. It was not as clear why the education crossover happened for men, but Martin and Parashar speculate that young people generally, "particularly college graduates, [were] becoming more concerned about negative consequences of divorce."

96. The 1957 estimate is from a National Opinion Research Center survey (Michael Forstrom, NORC Archives, personal communication, June 28, 2001). The raw data provided by the GSS are affected by the question's setting in the interview schedule. The numbers we report are corrected for that, and the results reported are robust (see Smith, "Timely Artifacts").

97. The education by year interaction effect is robust in regression analyses.

98. Duane Alwin ("Coresidence Beliefs in American Society") has suggested the economic argument in his analysis of these data through 1991. See also Goldscheider and Lawton, "Family Experiences and the Erosion of Support for Intergenerational Residence."

99. Differences by race declined as white opinion shifted toward sharing blacks' greater support for extended households. Differences by religion (Protestants and Jews were more likely to say, "Bad idea") and ethnicity (Latinos were much less likely to say, "Bad idea") changed little. For more on this and the correlates of attitudes toward coresidence, see Burr and Mutchler, "Race and Ethnic Variation in Norms of Filial Responsibility"; Alwin, "Coresidence Beliefs in American Society"; Goldscheider and Lawton, "Family Experiences and the Erosion of Support for Intergenerational Residence."

CHAPTER 5

1. The estimate of 1900 wages is based on U.S. Bureau of the Census, *Historical Statistics*, 168. The 2000 estimates are more complex, and the figures depend on whether or not salaried workers are included (see http://www.census.gov/hhes/www/income/ histinc/incpertoc.html); see also Caplow, Hicks, and Wattenberg, *First Measured Century*, 160–61.

2. Employment figures are based on our calculation from the 1900 census data and on U.S. Bureau of the Census, *Statistical Abstract of the United States, 2000*, 372.

3. In 1900, 26 percent of boys age ten to fifteen worked (excluding farmwork); in 1930, 6 percent did (Goldin, "Labor Markets in the Twentieth Century," 573). In Pennsylvania at the turn of the century, children contributed 40 percent of the income of households whose heads were unskilled (Kleinberg, *The Shadow of the Mills*).

4. For 1880 and 1950, see Costa, *Evolution of Retirement*; 2000 retirement figure based on our calculations.
5. U.S. Bureau of Labor Statistics, *Occupational Outlook Quarterly*, Summer 2002.
6. The environmental engineer's job exists in large part because of new government regulations. We do not have much to say here about government's role in the economy—except as an employer—but we acknowledge here that it too underwent big changes in the last century.
7. Annual data suggest that the narrowing trend continued through 1974; see Burtless and Jencks, "American Inequality and Its Consequences." Pay data were not collected prior to the 1950 census, so we focus on the 1949 to 1999 period, but historical estimates point to the onset of the Great Depression as a turning point in American inequality (see Plotnick et al., "The Twentieth-Century Record of Inequality and Poverty"; Fischer et al., *Inequality by Design*, ch. 5).
8. These ratios of the eightieth percentile to the twentieth capture the trend in wage inequality, but they do understate its magnitude somewhat. Comparisons of the ninetieth to the tenth percentile are more conventional. Statisticians use several measures that take the full range of wages into account. We could dramatize our findings by using one of these alternative measures, but all measures lead to the same conclusion: inequality retreated in the middle of the twentieth century and expanded in the last decades.
9. The political economists who followed Adam Smith originated this idea. It matured into two very different expressions in Marx and Engels's *Communist Manifesto* in 1848 and Émile Durkheim's *Division of Labor* in 1893. Although the intellectual traditions that grew up from these seminal works are usually characterized as polar opposites, the followers of Marx and the followers of Durkheim generally compete over how best to represent this claim, all the while agreeing that it is, ultimately, true.
10. "The Americas" includes Native American Indians in some chapters, but here it refers only to Latinos. Detailed breakdowns show that American Indians have significantly lower labor force participation rates than these charts indicate. In other features of American life, Latinos and Native Americans are not very different, so we can ignore the small residual difference between them without losing valuable information. Here the differences are too large to ignore, but we do not have enough observations of Native Americans to make up a reliable separate category. To keep a clearer sociological reference in our analyses we leave the native North Americans out of the discussion at this point.
11. Gary Becker formalized the theory in *Human Capital* in 1964. When he

won the Nobel Prize in Economics in 1992, the citation called his work on human capital his most important contribution.

12. Thurow, *Generating Inequality*; Featherman and Hauser, *Opportunity and Change*; Danziger and Gottschalk, *America Unequal.*

13. Cain, *Married Women in the Labor Force*; Reskin and Padavic, *Women and Men at Work.*

14. We present some data on how Americans think about working women in our last chapter. The data on women's occupations and pay come up later in this chapter.

15. Hochschild, *The Second Shift*; Bianchi et al., "Is Anyone Doing the Housework?"; Cowan, *More Work for Mother.*

16. This is a very strong statistical relationship. Nonetheless, it impresses us that the United States has so many supermoms. American mothers with three preschool children at home participate in the labor force as much as European women who have just one preschool child at home; see Stier, Lewin-Epstein, and Braun, "Welfare Regimes, Family-Supportive Policies, and Women's Employment."

17. On the complexities of these decisions, see Gerson, *Hard Choices.*

18. U.S. Bureau of the Census, *Statistical Abstract of the United States, 2002.*

19. Data are from March of the census years, so we miss teenagers' summer jobs.

20. These statistics count the 1.5 million wives of farmers and shopkeepers as employed even though half of them listed no occupation in the census. We overruled their reports, figuring that they worked without pay on the family farm or in the family shop. Two other categories of women could also have been counted as working: those who took in boarders and lodgers for pay and those who did "home work" such as sewing, making collars, or weaving hats, but we have no way to count them in the IPUMS. Nancy Folbre ("Women's Informal Market Work") estimates that one-third of married women in Massachusetts in 1880 worked in all these senses, although the rate dropped by 1900 as farming declined. The official rates can best be interpreted not as work for pay but as work for pay outside the home. On children in the labor force, see Goldin, "Labor Markets in the Twentieth Century," 573; and Mintz, *Huck's Raft*, ch. 7.

21. See note 19.

22. Katzman, *Seven Days a Week.* For examples of garment workers, see Glenn, *Daughters of the Shtetl*, and Hareven, *Family Time and Industrial Time.* See also Matthaei, *An Economic History of Women in America*, and Gabin, "Women and Work."

23. Goldin, "Life-Cycle Labor Force Participation of American Women"; Cookingham, "Working After Childbearing."

24. Oppenheimer, "Demographic Influences on Female Employment."

25. The censuses miss this episode in American history because the war started and ended between the 1940 and 1950 censuses.
26. One study found that the increase in work by mothers of young children in the 1970s and 1980s was in part a result of demographic changes—mothers were older and more educated and had fewer children—and equally a result of the relative decline of their husbands' incomes, although most of the change remained unexplained; Leibowitz and Klerman, "Explaining Changes in Married Mothers' Employment."
27. Dora Costa, *The Evolution of Retirement*.
28. This is our own calculation from data on employment rates and death rates tabulated by age and sex. The U.S. vital statistics system does not record the employment status of the deceased on their death certificate, but if we assume that employed people have the same death rate as non-employed people of the same age and sex, then we can calculate the probability of holding a job and dying in the same year from age-and-sex-specific employment and death rates. With the assistance of Gretchen (Stockmayer) Donehower, we did that for each census year from 1900 to 2000.
29. The figures for 1900 are from Kaplan and Casey, "Occupational Trends," and the latest figure is from the Bureau of Labor Statistics website (www.bls.gov).
30. We learned about pilots' certification issues when United Airlines declared bankruptcy in 2002. United's critics faulted the airline for having too many different kinds of airplanes and thus being unable to deploy pilots as efficiently as competitors with fewer kinds of planes.
31. Abbott, *The System of the Professions*.
32. More specifically, we applied Theil's E formula, $E = \sum_i p_i \ln(1/p_i)$, to the detailed occupation data (each occupation was represented by the i index in the formula) for each decade's census. We divided the E value for each year by the value of E in 1900 to get the numbers displayed in figure 5.5.
33. Our figure and our description refer to the relative size of the manufacturing sector. In absolute terms, manufacturing jobs continued to increase from 1960 to 1985, declining only in the last fifteen years of the century; see Hout et al., "The Political Economy of Inequality in the Age of Extremes."
34. See, for example, Zunz, *Making America Corporate*.
35. Our calculation from IPUMS data that cross-classify sales occupations with manufacturing industries.
36. U.S. Bureau of the Census, *Occupational Trends, 1900–1950*.
37. See Frederick Lewis Allen's reference to office girls in *Only Yesterday*, written in 1931.

38. Bluestone and Harrison, *The Deindustrialization of America*.
39. We do not go as far on this point as Gregory Mankiw, chair of the President's Council of Economic Advisers in 2004, who proposed re-classifying fast-food restaurants as factories, a reclassification that would have made burger-flipping a manufacturing job; see report in *Pittsburgh Post-Gazette*, March 13, 2004.
40. For details on the index, including the exact formula for calculating the SEI from census data on education and occupation within an occu-pation, see Duncan, "A Socioeconomic Index for All Occupations," and Hauser and Warren, "Socioeconomic Indexes." In addition to the year-by-year occupational details, the IPUMS data file includes the code that the occupation would have received if the 1950 scheme had been used throughout the century. It is very convenient that Duncan's 1961 paper gave the SEI scores for each occupation classified accord-ing to the 1950 scheme, including some distinguished by employment status and others by industry, and we take advantage of it here. Thus, all of our SEI calculations refer to the occupations coded according to the 1950 rules, no matter when the data were collected. This practice has the advantage of removing pseudo-trends that might introduce methodological artifacts into the time series. It has the disadvantage of coding all the new occupations created after 1950 into more generic categories. Because the index is composed of occupational education levels and earnings levels, many people wonder if the SEI is just a proxy for the person's own characteristics instead of an independent measure of the goodness of his or her job. That would be so if occupa-tions were homogeneous. But the wide variation in education in most occupations, and in income in all of them, lowers the correlation be-tween individual education and income and the SEI of a person's job to 0.4. See Hauser and Warren, "Socioeconomic Indexes," for more discussion of this issue.
41. Kalleberg, Reskin, and Hudson, "Bad Jobs in America."
42. Fligstein and Shin, "Shareholder Value Society."
43. Ibid.
44. Data drawn from the National Election Studies; information and orig-inal data are available at www.umich.edu/~nes. Because we have few cases per occupational group per year, we pooled men and women. (Preliminary analyses by gender found no differences for male and fe-male white-collar workers, and over 85 percent of the blue-collar workers were male, so we dropped the gender distinction.) We smoothed the data to highlight the trends and reduce the influence of sampling fluctuations.
45. The declining membership of male blue-collar workers implies a nine-point drop in union membership; blue-collar men's declining

share of the total U.S. labor force implies another additional drop of seven points, for a total of a sixteen-point drop between 1952 and 2000. The actual decline was only thirteen percentage points because professional women increased as a share of the labor force and they were increasingly likely to be union members (although just 9 percent of them belonged to unions in 2000).

46. Hout et al., "Inequality by Design."
47. U.S. Bureau of the Census, *Statistical Abstract of the United States, 2003*, table 655.
48. Fantasia and Voss, *Hard Work*.
49. This and subsequent calculations in this chapter are our own from the General Social Survey. See Hout, Manza, and Brooks, "Classes, Unions, and the Realignment of U.S. Presidential Voting," for multivariate results that show that the gap in voting between union members and other voters increased over time, net of other trends.
50. On women's jobs, see Petersen and Morgan, "Separate and Unequal." For men, the median, the eightieth percentile, and the twentieth percentile of wage and salary income in 1999 were $40,000, $86,000, and $18,100 (among full-time, year-round workers with positive earnings); for women, they were $29,000, $45,000, and $14,800. The ratio of the ninetieth percentile to the tenth, a more common measure of inequality than the eightieth-to-twentieth ratio we use in this book, was 4.75-to-1 for all full-time, year-round workers and for men in that category, but just 4.05-to-1 for full-time, year-round women.
51. Petersen and Morgan, "Separate and Unequal."
52. Danziger and Gottschalk, *America Unequal*.
53. Fernandez, "Skill-Biased Technological Change."
54. Card and DiNardo, "Skill-Biased Technological Change"; Fligstein, *Architecture of Markets*.
55. Day and Newburger, "The Big Payoff," figure 2.
56. Goldin and Margo, "The Great Compression."
57. Goldin and Katz, "Education and Income in the Early Twentieth Century."
58. Margo, "The History of Wage Inequality in America."
59. Card and Krueger, *Myth and Measurement*.
60. John DiNardo, Nicole Fortin, and Thomas Lemieux ("Labor Market Institutions") demonstrate that the downside of the trend shown in figure 5.11 contributed to rising inequality after 1975. On the general role of government policy, see Fischer et al., *Inequality by Design*, and Hout, "Inequality at the Margins."
61. Farley, *New American Reality*, 255–59; Wilson, *When Work Disappears*.
62. Katz et al., "The New African-American Inequality."

63. "Drudge Report," February 8, 2005, available at: http://www
    .drudgereportarchives.com/data/2005/02/08/20050208_220000
    _flashss.htm.
64. Presser, *Working in a 24/7 Economy*.
65. A few people were on leave of some kind and showed up in the "with
    a job but not at work" category.
66. The overall means for all *adults* are twenty-seven for women and
    thirty-eight for men. Most *workers* worked full-time (thirty-five hours
    or more), but women worked part-time more than men did: 25 per-
    cent of women employees worked less than thirty hours a week com-
    pared with just 10 percent of men. And women took less overtime: 10
    percent of women worked more than forty-eight hours a week com-
    pared with 26 percent of men.
67. The details of these four measures of working hours by gender and ed-
    ucation are available at: http://www.russellsage.org/publications/.
68. See, for example, Jacobs and Gerson, "Overworked Individuals or
    Overworked Families?"; Fligstein and Sharone, "Work in the Post-
    industrial Economy in California"; Hochschild, *Time Bind*; Fligstein
    and Shin, "Shareholder Value Society."
69. Hochschild, *Second Shift*.
70. Stier et al., "Welfare Regimes, Family-Supportive Policies, and
    Women's Employment."
71. Costa, "The Wage and the Length of the Workday"; Whaples, "Hours of
    Work in U.S. History."
72. Roediger and Foner, *Our Own Time*; Goldin, "Labor Markets in the
    Twentieth Century": Costa, "The Wage and the Length of the Work-
    day."
73. Costa, "The Wage and the Length of the Workday."
74. For discussion of the inequality point, see Costa, "The Wage and the
    Length of the Workday"; Fogel, *The Fourth Great Awakening*, 218–22;
    Fligstein and Shin, "The Shareholder Value Society."
75. Hout and Hanley, "The Overworked American Family"; Fligstein and
    Shin, "The Shareholder Value Society."
76. Hout and Hanley, "The Overworked American Family"; Fligstein and
    Shin, "The Shareholder Value Society."
77. The widespread unemployment of the Great Depression prompted
    this kind of response more than the narrower unemployment in other
    periods. "Major employers like Sears, General Motors, and Standard
    Oil scaled down their workweeks, and Kellogg's and the Akron tire in-
    dustry pioneered the six-hour day [in the 1930s]"; Whaples, "Hours of
    Work in U.S. History," n.p.
78. Social policy affects employment too, of course. The Works Progress
    Administration (WPA), Civilian Conservation Corps (CCC), and

other programs created jobs during the Depression (1933 to 1940). The Personal Responsibility and Work Opportunity Reconciliation Act (PRWORA) of 1996 did create auxiliary new jobs, but it required far more people—mothers mainly—to seek paid employment.

79. Lebergott, "Changes in Unemployment."

80. The National Bureau of Economic Research (NBER) is the accepted (nonpartisan) arbiter of when the economy has lapsed into recession and when recovery has begun. It dates recessions from the first month of economic contraction to the first month of positive growth thereafter. We have shaded a year as a recession year if the economy was in recession for six or more months that year. The details are available at: http://www.nber.org.

81. Christina Romer, "New Estimates of Prewar Gross National Product and Unemployment."

82. Goldin, "Labor Markets in the Twentieth Century."

83. Romer ("Changes in Business Cycles," 42) summarizes her findings as follows: "In essence, we have replaced the pre[–World War I] boom-bust cycle driven by animal spirits and financial panics with a post[–World War II] boom-bust cycle driven by policy."

84. See Keyssar, Out of Work, 295, 297. See also Jensen, "The Causes and Cures of Unemployment in the Great Depression"; Jacoby and Sharma, "Employment Duration and Industrial Labor Mobility"; Carter, "The Changing Importance of Lifetime Jobs"; and Goldin, "Labor Markets in the Twentieth Century."

85. Grob, Steelworkers in America.

86. Western and Pettit, "Beyond Crime and Punishment," 41 (emphasis added).

87. Frey and Stutzer, Economics of Happiness.

88. Gorski, Disciplinary Revolution.

89. Our calculations are from the GSS.

90. That is, in our other analyses of survey responses we examine subgroup differences in trends by calculating each group's deviation from the pooled national trend (see appendix A). Here we replace the national opinion trend in the equations with the national unemployment rate.

91. Featherman and Hauser, Opportunity and Change; Hout, "More Universalism, Less Structural Mobility."

92. Of course, ethno-racial ancestry and gender are circumstances of birth that affect adult success too. The social class correlations apply within racial, ethnic, and gender categories as well as between them. Some scholars argue that continuity between parents and children is largely the result of the genes they share (see, for example, Jencks, "Does Inequality Matter?"), but there is no consensus among scholars on that yet.

93. We pooled the 1998, 2000, and 2002 GSSs to increase the sample size and diminish the risk of sampling error.

94. In both generations, 30 percent of respondents had moved up five points or more in Duncan's socioeconomic index.

95. Rytina, "Is Occupational Mobility Declining in the United States?"

96. Erikson and Goldthorpe, "Intergenerational Inequality"; Ganzeboom, Treiman, and Ultee, "Comparative Intergenerational Stratification Research"; Beller and Hout, "Intergenerational Social Mobility."

97. Solon, "Cross-Country Differences in Intergenerational Earnings Mobility."

CHAPTER 6

1. For example, in August 1988, Gallup asked national samples of Americans and Britons: "Do you yourself think that [America/Britain] is divided into haves and have-nots, or don't you?" Twenty-six percent of Americans and 73 percent of Britons said "yes, divided" (Gallup Report #275 [August], 8). In early 2003, 41 percent of Americans agreed; Ludwig, "Is America Divided into Haves and Have-nots?" Gallup Poll, available to subscribers at: http://www.gallup.com (accessed September 8, 2004).

2. We refer to not only the classic "visitors," such as de Tocqueville and Trollope, but many others as well. For overviews, see, for example, Woodward, *The Old World's New World*; Simmons, *Star-Spangled Eden*; and Handlin and Handlin, *From the Outer World*.

3. The distinctiveness of the United States is well documented. A recent report is Gottschalk and Smeeding, "Empirical Evidence on Income Inequality in Industrialized Countries."

4. On the 2003 survey, see Ludwig, "Is America Divided?" Greenspan is quoted in Peter Grier, "Rich-Poor Gap Gaining Attention," *Christian Science Monitor*, June 14, 2005. On the consequences of inequality, see, for example, Williams and Collins, "U.S. Socioeconomic and Racial Differences in Health"; Hagan and Peterson, *Crime and Inequality*; Harper and Steffensmeier, "The Differing Effects of Economic Inequality"; Muller, "Democracy, Economic Development, and Income Inequality"; You and Khagram, "A Comparative Study of Inequality and Corruption"; Kenworthy, *Egalitarian Capitalism*; Hagerty, "Social Comparisons of Income"; Rahn and Rudolph, "A Tale of Political Trust in American Cities"; and Fischer et al., *Inequality by Design*. Some of these claims—notably those about the association between inequality in a community and ill health—have stirred methodological debates (Beckfield, "Does Inequality Harm Health?"). Gary Burtless and Christopher Jencks ("American Inequality and Its Consequences")

present a more cautious appraisal of the effects of inequality. A good source on these issues is Neckerman, *Social Inequality*. The briefest summary of what we know is that inequality does no good and probably does some ill to a community and a nation.

5. An earlier and more detailed version of this chapter is available as a working paper, "Differences Among Americans in Living Standards," at: http://ucdata.berkeley.edu:7101/rsfcensus/wp.html.

6. Rabin, *Hunting Mister Heartbreak*.

7. Our income data come largely from the IPUMS. Wealth and consumption spending data are largely from the Consumer Expenditure Survey (Harris and John Sabelhaus, *Consumer Expenditure Survey Family-Level Extracts*). Consumer goods data again come largely from the IPUMS. Another category of living standards we discuss later is public goods.

8. These gaps were, of course, many times wider at the extremes. For example, the household at the ninety-fifth percentile had an income in 2000 about fourteen times that of the household at the tenth; DeNavas and Cleveland, "Money Income in the United States: 2000," table C.

9. The Luxembourg Income Study regularly tracks and compares income distributions in many nations. In its latest tabulations, the United States was substantially more unequal than other nations. For example, the ratio of the eightieth to the twentieth percentile in disposable income was, in 1997, 3.0 for the United States, 2.8 for the United Kingdom (1995), 2.4 for Canada (1997), 2.2 for France, and 2.1 for Germany (1994); Luxembourg Income Study, "Income Inequality Measures." Even taking into account differences in living costs, the American variation was greater than that elsewhere. Indeed, though affluent and middle-class American families had more buying power than families elsewhere, American families with below-average incomes had less buying power than comparable families in most other advanced nations; Gottschalk and Smeeding, "Empirical Evidence on Income Inequality in Industrialized Countries"; Smeeding and Rainwater, "Comparing Living Standards Across Nations." For a general discussion of American inequality in historical and cross-national contexts, see Fischer et al., *Inequality by Design*.

10. The last detailed data on twentieth-century wealth covered 1998; see Wolff, "Recent Trends in Wealth Ownership"; Keister and Moller, "Wealth Inequality in the United States"; and Spilerman, "Wealth and Stratification Processes."

11. Numbers drawn and calculated from U.S. Bureau of the Census, *Statistical Abstract of the United States, 2002*, tables 946 and 947.

12. Michael Cox and Richard Alm (*Myths of Rich and Poor*) are among a group of scholars who point to such consumption as evidence of *declining* inequality.

13. Numbers drawn from U.S. Bureau of the Census, *Statistical Abstract of*

the United States 2000, tables 177, 211, and 233, which notes: "Food secure means that a household had access at all times to enough food for an active healthy life, with no need for recourse to emergency food sources or other extraordinary coping behaviors to meet their basic food needs."

14.   Calculated from the General Social Survey "fear" item for 1998 and 2000. This comparison includes only respondents living in metropolitan areas. Overall, the percentages were 49 and 30.

15.   For example, the World Health Organization (*World Health Report 2000*) calculated an index of "equality of child survival" based on local-area variability. The United States ranked thirty-second in the world. See also the literature on health inequality cited in note 4.

16.   Lebergott, *The American Economy*, and Cox and Alm, "Time Well Spent," provide overviews.

17.   Key references include Williamson and Lindert, *American Inequality*; Soltow, "Wealth and Income Distribution"; Lebergott, *The American Economy*; Piketty and Saez, "Income Inequality in the United States"; Goldin and Katz, "Decreasing (and Then Increasing) Inequality in America"; Plotnick et al., "The Twentieth-Century Record of Inequality and Poverty in the United States."

18.   The pre-1970 numbers are estimates provided by Lebergott in *The American Economy*, 498; the rest are from U.S. Bureau of the Census, "Historical Income Tables—Households," table H-2. The percentage gained by the top 5 percent ranged from a high of 36 percent in 1900 to a low of 16 percent in 1980, then up to 22 percent in 2000.

19.   We exclude those living in group quarters and unrelated individuals sharing a household with a family. For a household of only nonrelatives, the head is included as a resident of a one-person household.

20.   See Atkinson, Rainwater, and Smeeding, *Income Distributions in OECD Countries*; Smeeding, "Changing Income Inequality in OECD Countries." Although our adjustments are far less complex than those made by other scholars (note especially Slesnick, *Consumption and Social Welfare*), we do take into account the basic reality that family needs increase with the number of family members, but at a negatively accelerating rate. And since family size is highly associated with stage in the life cycle (Slesnick, *Consumption and Social Welfare*, 148), this adjustment captures much of the life-cycle variation as well, allowing us to hold roughly constant changes in the demographic profile of the American population.

21.   That is, the increase from the square root of two to the square root of three.

22.   We first calculate an adjusted per-person income, or what some economists call "equivalent personal income" for each individual, by (1)

taking the total income of all related members of the individual's household, (2) dividing that figure by the square root of the number of related members of the household, and (3) calculating what it would be for a family of four. Step 3 is the simple exercise of doubling the result of step 2, because the square root of four is two.

23. This procedure also removes historical changes in family size as a factor in comparing family incomes.

24. Many analyses of inequality look at comparisons of the ninetieth versus the tenth percentile. We use eightieth-twentieth for a couple of reasons. One is that Jon Stiles found inconsistencies between census and CPS data at the tenth percentile, originating in the fact that the CPS found more people at very low income levels. Also, the eightieth-twentieth comparison is consistent with our other analyses in this book.

25. See, for example, Fligstein, *Architecture of Markets*; Lichter, "Poverty and Inequality Among Children"; Campbell and Allen, "Identifying Shifts in Policy Regimes"; Kenworthy, "Do Social-Welfare Policies Reduce Poverty?"; Chevan and Stokes, "Growth in Family Income Inequality"; Karoly and Burtless, "Demographic Change, Rising Earnings Inequality."

26. U.S. Bureau of the Census, *Income, Poverty, and Health Insurance*, 36.

27. This table contrasts the trends in income inequality for the elderly and for children:

Ratio of Eightieth- to Twentieth-Percentile Adjusted Family-of-Four Income

	1949	1959	1969	1979	1989	1999
Among the elderly	8.7	4.9	4.6	3.6	3.8	3.7
Among children age zero to seventeen	3.6	3.0	2.9	3.3	3.8	3.9

Source: Authors' compilation.

Some economists and policymakers have criticized the formula used to adjust seniors' Social Security checks for inflation, saying that the formula exaggerates inflation's effects and thus raises their incomes too rapidly. Our inflation adjuster is the research series. If the Social Security Administration had used it instead of the formula it did, Social Security benefits would not have risen as fast, and inequality among seniors might have increased during the years of greatest inflation (1974 to 1975 and 1977 to 1981).

28. "Others" gained even more ground relative to whites, but that change is hard to interpret given that who the "others" were changed after 1965, especially with the strong influx of middle-class families from Asia.

29. Between 1949 and 1999, the adjusted family income of the twentieth-percentile black increased 480 percent; the incomes of average and wealthy blacks grew 415 percent. The adjusted family incomes of all levels of whites increased about 290 percent.

30. The conclusion about Hispanics is not based on our data but on median family incomes collected by the Current Population Survey and reported by the Census Bureau (*Statistical Abstract of the United States, 2000*, table 743). Between 1972 and 1999, the median non-Hispanic white family's inflation-adjusted income rose 23 percent, while that of the Hispanic family rose 3 percent, with a rise in the ratio of non-Hispanics to Hispanics from $1.40 to $1.70. Adjusting for family size might mute this widening gap, but not enough to negate the point. As for the foreign-born, in 1949 the median native-born American's adjusted family income was 90 cents per dollar of that of the median foreign-born (who was likely be an older European-American immigrant); by 1990 the median native-born's income was $1.20 per dollar of that of the (now-increasingly Latin or Asian) foreign-born.

31. In 1949 the median southerner had a family-of-four adjusted income that was $8,800 less than that of Americans from other regions (that is, the average of the medians of the other regions); in 1979 the arithmetic difference was $7,200; in 1999 it was $6,800.

32. In 1999 the median northeasterner earned $1.20 on the southerner's dollar. The West fell notably behind the Northeast and the Midwest after 1980, most likely reflecting the inflow of low-income immigrants. The median incomes are shown in this table:

Median Adjusted Family-of-Four Income

	1949	1959	1969	1979	1989	1999
Northeast	$22,200	$33,200	$44,600	$49,600	$59,400	$56,000
Midwest	21,200	30,800	42,400	50,400	51,200	54,000
South	13,200	22,400	34,000	42,800	46,200	46,800
West	22,800	33,200	43,400	50,000	53,200	50,000

Source: Authors' compilation.

33. There is another way to view this change. Between 1949 and 1969, the twentieth, fiftieth, and eightieth percentiles in each region all roughly doubled their adjusted family income, except in the South. There the fiftieth percentile increased two and a half times, and the twentieth percentile increased three and a third times.

34. Analysis of nonmetropolitan, center-city, and suburban differences is complicated by missing data for many cases after 1980 (see chapter 7).

Nevertheless, the general trends are strong enough to be reliable. This table shows the rounded figures:

Median Adjusted Family-of-Four Income

	1949	1959	1969	1979	1989	1999
Nonmetropolitan	$15,200	$24,500	$34,250	$39,800	$40,300	$41,700
Metropolitan center city	24,100	31,900	40,400	44,200	46,000	46,300
Nonmetropolitan outside center city	24,800	35,600	48,000	54,500	63,500	69,300

Source: Authors' compilation.

35. See Kim, "Economic Integration and Convergence," plus subsequent discussion in the *Journal of Economic History* 59(3, 1999): 773–88.
36. By one estimate, in 1999, 15 percent of white men age thirty to thirty-four who had dropped out of high school had ever been imprisoned, and *60 percent* of similar black men had. These men, especially the black men, had slim hopes for finding quality jobs; see Western and Pettit, "Beyond Crime and Punishment."
37. Among college graduates, the eighty-to-twenty ratio increased from 2.47 in 1970 to 2.98 in 1999. Similar substantial increases occurred within other educational groups. On marriage patterns, see Kalmijn, "Intermarriage and Homogamy"; Schwartz and Mare, "Trends in Educational Assortative Marriage"; and DiPrete and Buchmann, "Gender-Specific Trends in the Value of Education."
38. The share of the national income garnered by the top one-tenth of 1 percent "more than doubled [after] 1980 to 7.4 percent in 2002. The share of income earned by the rest of the top 10 percent rose far less and the share earned by the bottom 90 percent fell"; David Cay Johnston, "Richest Are Leaving Even the Rich Far Behind," *New York Times*, June 5, 2005, A1.
39. For general discussion, see, for example, Karoly and Burtless, "Demographic Change, Rising Earnings Inequality"; Danziger and Gottschalk, *America Unequal* and *Uneven Tides*; Hout, Arum, and Voss, "The Political Economy of Inequality in the Age of Extremes."
40. In 1949 Americans age thirty to forty-four had $1.82 of adjusted family income for each dollar of those age sixty-five or older. In 1999 the ratio was down to $1.30.
41. Lisa Keister (*Wealth in America*) reports a correlation of .25 between wealth and income when income from investments is excluded.
42. Wolff, "Recent Trends in Wealth Ownership." See also Davies and Shorroks, "The Distribution of Wealth."

43. On the importance of wealth compared to income, see, for example, Conley, *Being Black, Living in the Red*. On our estimate of black net worth, see Wolff, "Racial Wealth Disparities," table 7. See also Keister, *Wealth in America*; and Spilerman, "Wealth and Stratification Processes."

44. Compared to an adjusted family income eighty-to-fifty ratio of $1.80. Wolff ("Recent Trends in Wealth Ownership") notes that in 1998, 18 percent of households had zero or negative net worth. The eighty-to-fifty ratio is interpolated from his table 2.

45. That informed estimate is in Davies and Shorroks, "The Distribution of Wealth." Keister's analysis of the determinants of net assets among Americans in their thirties, "Family Background and the Racial Wealth Gap," shows that, holding constant all sorts of personal and family characteristics, parents' incomes and the receipt of an inheritance significantly increased respondents' wealth. Dalton Conley ("Capital for College") shows that parental assets, net of their income and other factors, improved their children's chances of attending and graduating from college; see also Keister, *Wealth in America*. Wolff ("Inheritances and Wealth Inequality") found that bequests and gifts *reduce* inequality, because what low-income people receive is *proportionately* greater relative to their current wealth than is true of wealthier recipients. Wolff qualifies this finding methodologically in various ways, however, and points out that, given poorer persons' lower savings rates, their inheritances are less likely to promote future wealth.

46. For a review of factors that influence wealth accumulation—in the context of the black-white gap—see Scholz and Levine, "U.S. Black-White Wealth Inequality."

47. We use 1998 Consumer Expenditure Survey (CES) data because it is the last dataset in the century we could use. For analysis of the CES, we draw on the Bureau of Labor Statistics datasets prepared by the National Bureau of Economic Research. The CES is a study conducted by the BLS that asks respondents (about five thousand during each administration) to provide detailed information on their assets and their spending, using both detailed interviews and diaries (see http://www.bls.gov/cex/home.htm). The version of the data we used is drawn from extracts of the survey developed by the Congressional Budget Office (CBO) and available from the NBER (Harris and Sabelhaus, "Consumer Expenditure Survey Family-Level Extracts"). Although the CES began in 1980, we start with 1984 in part because that is when the sample became national rather than urban only and in part because other procedural changes made pre-1984 data hard to compare with later data.

48. Wolff, "Recent Trends in Wealth Ownership," tables 1 and 3.

49. These calculations were based on the "Consumer Expenditure Survey

Family Level Extracts: 1981:1 to 1998:2," created by John Sabelhaus and continued by Ed Harris of the CBO and distributed by the NBER.
50. See Shammas, "A New Look at Long-term Trends in Wealth Inequality"; Soltow, "Wealth and Income Distribution"; Piketty and Saez, "Income Inequality"; Spilerman, "Wealth and Stratification Processes"; Lindert, "Three Centuries of Inequality"; Keister, *Wealth in America*.
51. Keister, *Wealth in America*; Spilerman, "Wealth and Stratification Processes"; Smith, "Why Is Wealth Inequality Rising?"; Wolff, "Recent Trends in Wealth Ownership." On debt, see especially Sullivan, Warren, and Westbrook, *The Fragile Middle Class*. On wealth disparities on the eve of the American Revolution, see Shammas, "A New Look at Long-term Trends in Wealth Inequality."
52. According to William Collins and Robert Margo ("Race and Homeownership"), the independent effect of race on ownership dropped from fifteen to nine percentage points; see also Wolff, "Racial Disparities"; Scholz and Levine, "U.S. Black-White Wealth Inequality."
53. The CES was conducted before 1984, but those data are not comparable.
54. Between 1980 and 1998, the real value of the eightieth percentile's savings dropped by about half. James Smith ("Why Is Wealth Inequality Rising?") estimates that each additional dollar in capital gains led Americans to reduce savings by 18 cents.
55. Family-of-four house values, 1960 to 2000:

Family-of-Four House Values, 1960 to 2000

	1960	1970	1980	1990	2000
Twentieth percentile	$32,786	$39,038	$60,312	$57,778	$71,814
Median	61,336	70,980	105,522	113,488	134,350
Eightieth percentile	96,386	115,912	175,870	240,744	245,968
80:20 ratio	2.94	2.96	2.92	4.17	3.43

Source: IPUMS

56. Johnston, "Richest Are Leaving Even the Rich Far Behind."
57. See, for example, Smith, "Why Is Wealth Inequality Rising?"; Wolff, "Recent Trends in Wealth Ownership"; Keister and Moller, "Wealth Inequality in the United States." Some analysts note changes in family size, but our estimates control for that.
58. U.S. Bureau of the Census, "Supplemental Survey Data Report, 2002." These numbers are a bit different from earlier ones reported, which referred to households headed by blacks. See also Denton, "Housing as a Means of Asset Accumulation."

59. Between the mid-1980s and the late 1990s, the adjusted house value for the median college graduate grew from 1.5-to-1 of the high school graduate to 1.6-to-1, and the median adjusted house value for high school graduates grew from 1.15-to-1 of that of the median high school dropout to 1.4-to-1. (These numbers are for urban residents only. Note also that we dropped all cases coded as "no formal education," because in 1987–88 the CES had treated missing data as zero years of education and lumped those cases in with those who had not graduated from high school.) Similarly, the ratio of median college graduates' savings to median high school graduates' savings increased from about twelve-to-one around 1983 to over two hundred–to-one in the late 1990s; the ratio for money in a checking account rose from three-to-one to five-to-one. (Even stock ownership became more polarized: the ratio of the eightieth-percentile college graduate's adjusted stock value to that of the eightieth-percentile high school graduate's rose from less than ten-to-one to more than thirteen-to-one.) There is no point comparing the nonhousing financial assets of high school graduates to those of high school dropouts: the median high school dropout had no savings, checking account, or stock account.

60. For example, in the mid-1980s the house of the median American age sixty-five or older was worth about $1.10 to the dollar house value of the median American age thirty to forty-four; in the late 1990s that had risen to nearly $1.15. For savings, checking, and stocks, the holdings of the elderly were too marginal and fluctuated too much from year to year for similar calculations. But we can compare the savings of thirty- to forty-four-year-olds with those of forty-five- to sixty-four-year-olds. In the mid-1980s, the median forty-five- to sixty-four-year-old had 95 cents in savings compared to the median thirty- to forty-four-year-old, but by the late 1990s that was up to about $1.50. In checking accounts, however, the thirty- to forty-four-year-olds gained by a couple of cents relative to the forty-five- to sixty-four-year-olds. Generally, the older drew further away from the younger; Consumer Expenditure Survey, three-year moving averages.

61. For example, Levy, *Dollars and Dreams*; Duncan and Smith, "The Rising Affluence of the Elderly."

62. On the 1988 national survey, see Brown, *American Standards of Living*, 372, 461; see also Lebergott, *Consumer Expenditures*, ch. 1. On the validity issue, see, for the poor, Edin and Lein, *Making Ends Meet*, and, more generally, U.S. Bureau of the Census, "Money Income in the United States, 1998," appendix E. Recent census surveys have counted 89 percent of the comparable total income and 99 percent of wages and salaries, as has the Bureau of Economic Analysis using sources other than household interviews. The implication is that unearned in-

come, such as investment returns and side businesses, is the bulk of the understated income.

63. For general discussions of income versus consumption, see, for example, Slesnick, "Consumption, Needs, and Inequality," and *Consumption and Social Welfare*; Federman et al., "What Does It Mean to Be Poor in America?"; Jencks and Mayer, "Do Official Poverty Rates Provide Useful Information . . .?"; Jorgenson, "Did We Lose the War on Poverty?"; Cox and Alm, *Myths of Rich and Poor*; and Cutler and Katz, "Rising Inequality?"

64. On debt, see, for example, Sullivan et al., *Fragile Middle Class*. On kin ties, see Goldstein and Warren, "Socioeconomic Reach and Heterogeneity in the Extended Family."

65. Calculations of work time based on U.S. Bureau of the Census, *Historical Statistics of the United States*, 170, 210, and 213.

66. As for income and wealth, we correct for inflation and divide by the square root of the size of the family, then multiply by two to get a family-of-four equivalent. Daniel Slesnick (*Consumption and Social Welfare*) shows how sensitive trend analyses of consumption are to estimates of household "need."

67. On failure to pay essential bills, see Bauman, "Extended Measures of Well-being." On food insecurity and hunger, see U.S. Bureau of the Census, *Statistical Abstract of the United States, 2000*, table 233.

68. U.S. Bureau of the Census, *Statistical Abstract of the United States, 2003*, tables 996, 997. These numbers are for 2001; the prior data were for 1997.

69. Dora Costa ("American Living Standards") develops an economic model for using recreational spending as a mark of living standards. We use a simpler but similar procedure.

70. The household survey numbers are drawn from Jacobs and Shipp, "How Family Spending Has Changed in the United States," and refer only to urban wage-earning and clerical families. (This makes it difficult to integrate more recent CES data. The CES shows 14 percent spending on food and 5 percent spending on recreation in 2000, but these results cannot be "stitched" together with the older data.) "Recreation" refers to "entertainment and reading." The national accounts data through 1955 are drawn from the U.S. Bureau of the Census, *Historical Statistics of the United States*, 316–21, and U.S. Bureau of the Census, *Statistical Abstract of the United States, 2003*, table 667. Although various details make the sources somewhat different from each other, and comparisons of the two types of data complex, the overall trend lines are clear.

71. The numbers referred to are presented in the table in this note. Our calculations are simple but nonetheless suggestive. We use Claire Brown's *American Standards of Living*, which compiles household ex-

penditure studies from 1918 through 1988. She distinguishes spending by urban laborers, wage-earners, and salaried workers (all white). The table shows how much each group spent on average on food and recreation over the century, adjusted as follows: (1) we correct for cost of living, using the BLS "inflation calculator" (http://stats.bls .gov/), which is for urban costs; (2) we divide each spending amount by the square root of the *average size of family for that class group* in that year; and (3) we multiply by two to get a family-of-four equivalent. Part A shows the dollar amounts, and part B the ratios between groups. Note that differences in food spending changed modestly, although they did narrow between salaried workers and laborers between 1918 and 1950. Differences in recreational spending changed more, with the gaps narrowing substantially to 1973 and then widening by 1988.

A. Annual Amount Spent on Food and Recreation Adjusted to a Family of Four, by Class and Year (in 2000 Dollars)

	Food			Recreation		
	Laborers	Wage-Earners	Salaried Workers	Laborers	Wage-Earners	Salaried Workers
1918	$4,966	$5,480	$6,886	$440	$620	$1,194
1935	5,394	6,242	8,212	806	1,058	2,520
1950	8,362	9,384	10,742	1,720	2,262	2,970
1973	7,764	8,216	9,972	3,382	3,948	5,508
1988	7,108	7,902	9,190	4,260	5,244	8,550

B. Ratio of Spending Between Class Groups, by Type of Spending and Year

	Food			Recreation		
	Salaried: Wage-Earner	Wage-Earner: Laborer	Salaried Worker: Laborer	Salaried Worker: Wage-Earner	Wage-Earner: Laborer	Salaried Worker: Laborer
1918	1.26	1.10	1.39	1.92	1.41	2.71
1935	1.32	1.16	1.52	2.38	1.31	3.13
1950	1.14	1.12	1.28	1.31	1.31	1.73
1973	1.21	1.06	1.28	1.39	1.17	1.63
1988	1.16	1.11	1.29	1.63	1.23	2.01

Source: Authors' compilation.

72. See note 47 for further details.
73. Around 1986, the eightieth-percentile respondent in recreation spending spent 4.2 percent more on recreation than the twentieth-percentile respondent (five-year-moving averages); around 1996 the difference was 4.5 percent. Differences had not narrowed. In that sense, the centurylong convergence was stalled.
74. Whites' percentage of spending devoted to food stayed at 13 percent from the mid-1980s to the mid-1990s; blacks' percentage dropped from 18.5 percent to 16 percent. Both groups' spending on recreation increased very slightly, leaving the difference the same. Slesnick (*Consumption and Social Welfare*, ch. 6) finds a drop in consumption inequality by region from 1947 to 1973 and little net change afterwards. He reports little in the way of between-group trends for race or gender of household head.
75. Studies of consumption are difficult because they involve rare and "noisy" data (a typical condition with the Consumer Expenditure Survey) and require numerous judgment calls and estimates. (For example, how should one count the "spending" represented by an owned house? By a paid-off car? How should one calculate the needs of a young person versus an old one?) Slesnick (*Consumption and Social Welfare*) finds a drop in inequality from World War II to 1973 and then essentially no trend through 1995. He thus rejects claims of widening inequality based on income trends. His calculations, however, seem notably sensitive to his assumptions. For example, he calculates that the percentage of elderly who were poor dropped from 13 percent in 1947 to 0.6 percent in 1994 (page 182); few scholars would credit that 0.6 percent. Dirk Krueger and Fabrizio Perri ("Does Income Inequality Lead to Consumption Inequality?") find that consumption inequality increased in the 1980s but almost leveled off in the 1990s, in part, they suggest, because people increasingly borrowed money to offset fluctuations in their incomes. David Johnson, Timothy Smeeding, and Barbara Boyle Torrey ("United States Inequality Through the Prisms of Income and Consumption," especially table 3) also find that spending inequality grew in the 1980s and leveled off in the 1990s.
76. Ownership is heavily conditioned by the age of the head of the household and by marital status. For Americans age forty-five to sixty-four, the prime earning years, the historical trend line is the same except that it is shifted upward, with ownership rates leveling off at 80 percent in the last third of the century. The trend diverged for married-couple households and other households after 1960: rates for the married rose into the low 80 percent range in 1990s, compared to 65 percent for all households combined.
77. The numbers in this section are drawn from census data (U.S. Bureau

of the Census, *Historical Statistics of the United States*, and *Statistical Abstract of the United States, 2003*, and Lebergott, *The American Economy*, 272, 289–90); a few estimates are calculated by interpolation or modeling (for example, the early estimates for telephones are based on the number of telephones per household). For more on the diffusion of the automobile and telephone, see Fischer, *America Calling*.

78. The historical racial estimates are from Lebergott, *The American Economy*, 99, 290. Other estimates are from the IPUMS, except for 1999, which is from the Annual Housing Survey (U.S. Bureau of the Census, *Annual Housing Survey*).

79. IPUMS and U.S. Bureau of the Census, *Annual Housing Survey*. For example, in 1960 only 71 percent of southerners, compared to 93 percent of northeasterners, had full plumbing; in 1999, 99 percent of both did.

80. These numbers come from the IPUMS dataset and refer to individuals living in households with such facilities. A roughly thirty-point difference between whites and blacks and between college graduates and high school dropouts in having telephone service in 1960 became around a ten-point difference in 1990. The 1990 data on cars are adjusted to reflect the counts of cars found in 1960, 1970, and 1980 data by subtracting out estimated "truck-only" households.

81. Computer ownership data come from six supplements of the Current Population Survey.

82. See the discussion of consumption as comparative distinction in, for example, Douglas and Isherwood, *The World of Goods*; Rainwater, *What Money Buys*; Frank, *Luxury Fever*; and McCracken, *Culture and Consumption*.

83. The 1960 numbers are from the IPUMS; the 2000 numbers are from the CES website.

84. Between 1983 and 1999, for example, the cost of televisions declined by 45 percent, the cost of interstate telephone calls dropped by 28 percent, and the cost of new cars rose by 28 percent, but the cost of homeownership rose 88 percent. On the history of home owning, see, for example, Tobey, Wetherell, and Brigham, "Moving Out and Settling In"; Tobey, *Technology as Freedom*, ch. 4; Chevan, "The Growth of Homeownership"; Harris, "Working-Class Homeownership"; Luria, "Wealth, Capital, and Power"; Thernstrom, *The Other Bostonians*. The recent price changes are from U.S. Bureau of the Census, *Statistical Abstract of the United States, 2000*, table 770; the cost of homeownership is calculated as "rental equivalent" and does not include insurance. The 1918 to 1988 comparison is from Brown, *American Standards of Living*, 455. Many have noted that, over the years, the size and quality of the housing Americans could buy increased; in per-footage or per-amenity terms, housing costs may not have nearly tripled (see, for ex-

ample, Cox and Alm, "Time Well Spent"). This point does not negate the comparison we are making between types of goods. First, other commodities also improve in quality—for example, automobiles have improved dramatically in speed, safety, and comfort. Second, rising standards also raise the cost of the minimum "housing package" people can buy. Because of legal, market, and cultural "floors," they cannot realistically buy, say, two-room houses without running water, electricity, and standard ceiling heights.

85.   We tried. For example, the Annual Housing Survey (AHS) provides respondents' ratings of various aspects of their neighborhoods over a quarter-century. Conducted by the Census Bureau for HUD and renamed the American Housing Survey in 1983—it was administered annually from 1973 to 1981 and biannually afterwards—the AHS covers about five thousand households in major metropolitan areas. Over four waves, forty-six metropolitan areas are covered, with about a dozen in any given survey. Because of this sampling procedure and because of various changes in procedures, year-to-year and even decade-to-decade comparability is difficult.

The AHS asked respondents a series of questions about neighborhood conditions, one of which was whether it had crime. "Yes" answers rose strongly from 17 percent in 1974 to a peak of 24 percent in 1991, and then dropped rapidly to 14 percent in 1999—roughly in tune with nationwide crime statistics. During the rise, black-white differences and city-suburban differences widened; during the dramatic decline in crime of the 1990s, racial and place differences stabilized, but educational differences still widened. The General Social Survey asked a similar question: was there anywhere in their neighborhoods where respondents were afraid to walk? Between 1973 and 2000, the percentage who said "no" varied from a low of 52 to a high of 63, with little net change over the quarter-century. The results differed some from those of the AHS, but once again, educational groups seemed to diverge over the quarter-century in a similar way: high school dropouts were slightly less likely to feel secure, and high school graduates more likely. Other results from the AHS are mixed, however. For example, AHS respondents' ratings of the quality of their neighborhoods and homes seemed to converge. This is a limited exercise, and more comprehensive research needs to be done on the distribution—and changes in the distribution—of public goods.

86.   Wolff, Zacharias, and Caner, "Household Wealth, Public Consumption, and Economic Well-being." This heroic effort to estimate individual households' use of public goods is unable to take into account within-state differences in the value of goods such as roads or health

care, and thus cannot tell us whether, say, the closing of public clinics in particular locations is widening inequality.

87.   Tucker quoted in *The Columbia World of Quotations*.

88.   Hout ("Money and Morale") explores the following topics in greater depth. On happiness correlates, see appendix B concerning the nonlinearity between money and utility. See also Lane, *The Loss of Happiness*, for an extensive review—albeit somewhat overstated—of the evidence that money does not buy happiness.

89.   These are responses to GSS items SATFIN ("So far as you and your family are concerned, would you say that you are pretty well satisfied with your present financial situation, more or less satisfied, or not satisfied at all?") and FINRELA ("Compared with American families in general, would you say your family income is far below average, below average, average, above average, or far above average?"), combining the 1998 and 2000 samples.

90.   Similarly, the Pew Research Center ("Economic Inequality Seen as Rising") asked survey respondents in 1992 and 2001 whether they were satisfied that they could afford the housing, cars, vacations, and similar things that they wanted. The affluent respondents in 2001 were more satisfied than were the affluent in 1992, but 2001's low-income respondents were at the same level as the 1992 ones.

91.   The statistical estimates show that, with respect to income comparisons (left-side panel), the slope of the top-twentieth-percentile trend is significantly different from that of the other two groups. (The bottom-twentieth-percentile trend line is not significantly steeper than the middle line.) On financial satisfaction (right-side panel), the slopes of all the lines are significantly and substantially different from one another.

92.   See Hout, "Money and Morale."

93.   Ladd and Bowman, *Attitudes Toward Economic Inequality*, 99; Lexis-Nexis reports.

94.   Figures on have-nots through 1998 from Gallup Poll, "Social Audit: Haves and Have-Nots," available to subscribers at: http://www.gallup.com/poll/socialaudits/have_havenot.asp (accessed May 15, 2002). For the 2000 figure, see Lexis-Nexis reports; in 2004 it was 37 percent.

95.   On American ideas about economic equality, see Hochschild, *What's Fair*; Rainwater, *What Money Buys*; Gans, *Middle American Individualism*; Smith, "Social Inequality in Cross-National Perspective"; Kelley and Evans, "The Legitimation of Inequality"; and Verba and Orren, *Equality in America*. On attitudes toward redressing inequality, see these sources and Ladd and Bowman, *Attitudes Toward Economic Inequality*. From 1978 through 2000, the GSS asked adults to place themselves on

a seven-point scale ranging from support for the position that "government should reduce income differences" (coded 1) to support for the position that it should not (coded 7). Respondents' average position on EQWLTH was 3.8 in 1978–80, 3.5 in 1990–91—moving toward government action—and 3.9 during the boom years of 1998–2000, reversing that mini-trend.

96. David M. Moore, "Half of Young People Expect to Get Rich," Gallup Poll News Service, March 11, 2003, available to subscribers at: http://www.gallup.com. The median respondent defined "rich" as an income of $122,000 and assets of $1 million.

97. Bradbury and Katz, "Issues in Economics." On consumption inequality, see Johnson et al., "United States Inequality." Also, there is evidence that the college attendance of youth became more strongly tied to their parents' affluence over these years, a trend that would dampen mobility (Kane, "College-Going and Inequality"). In a 2005 special report, *The Economist* ("Ever Higher Society") summarized several studies all pointing to either no change or a decline in upward mobility; see a similar account in David Wessel, "Escalator Ride: As Rich-Poor Gap Widens in the U.S., Class Mobility Stalls," *Wall Street Journal*, May 13, 2005, A1.

CHAPTER 7

1. An earlier, more detailed draft of this chapter appears as a working paper available at: http://ucdata.berkeley.edu:7101rsfcensus/wp .html.

2. Anthony Violanti, "Blue State Christmas Blues; More Than the Holiday Spirit Is in the Air," *Buffalo News*, December 5, 2004; see also Hitt, "Neo-Secessionism."

3. On cultural differences, see, for example, Doyle, *The Social Order of a Frontier Community*. Jefferson cited in Tindall, "Regionalism," 532. On "to Yankee," see Barron, *Mixed Harvest*, 139; see also Sellers, *The Market Revolution*, ch. 12.

4. Rosenbloom, "The Extent of the Labor Market in the United States."

5. On the "Country Problem," see U.S. Senate, *Report of the Country Life Commission*; Larson and Jones, "The Unpublished Data from Roosevelt's Commission on Country Life"; Ward, "The Farm Woman's Problem." On New Deal efforts to bring rural Americans into the national fold, see Kline, *Consumers in the Country*. On social differences, see Kirschner, *City and Country*; Baker, *The Moral Frameworks of Public Life*.

6. We define "suburb" in this chapter as the residual metropolitan area, including both what the census counts as incorporated "places" and

what it counts as rural parts of metropolitan areas. Jackson, *Crabgrass Frontier*, is the classic one-volume history of American suburbanization. On early suburbanization, see Gardner, "The Slow Wave." On the suburbs' cultural image and reality, see, for example, Donaldson, *The Suburban Myth*; Marsh, "From Separation to Togetherness"; Gans, *The Levittowners*; Fischer, *The Urban Experience*, ch. 9.

7.   Monkonnen, *America Becomes Urban*, 223; Briffault, "Our Localism"; Keating, *Comparative Urban Politics*, ch. 2.

8.   On the problems of concentration, see, for example, Wilson, *The Truly Disadvantaged*; Massey and Denton, *American Apartheid*; Venkatesh, *American Project*. On the costs of diversity, see, for example, Costa and Kahn, "Civic Engagement and Community Heterogeneity."

9.   Aside from city streetcar systems, other conveyances—trains, horses and carriages—were available to only a relative few. Outside of business, telegraph systems were used only for emergencies, and only a relative handful of Americans had telephones in their homes. For some history on these subjects, see Fischer, *America Calling*.

10.   On use of airplanes, see Gallup Poll, "Airlines," available to subscribers at: http://www.poll.gallup.com/topics/. On Internet use, see Pew Internet and American Life Project, "Internet Use by Region," 2.

11.   Fischer, "Ever More Rooted Americans." Census coverage is spottier the further back in history one goes, but the net result of missing people in the nineteenth century was probably to underestimate mobility, especially by the young, the poor, and the black (see symposium in *Social Science History*, Winter 1991). Interstate migration appears to have risen over time (Rosenbloom and Sundstrom, "The Decline and Rise of Interstate Migration in the United States"), but a careful analysis by Patricia Kelly Hall and Steven Ruggles ("'Restless in the Midst of Their Prosperity'") indicates that serious long-distance migration probably declined. They show that a rebound in late-twentieth-century interstate moves largely reflected suburbanization (for example, from the city of Philadelphia to the New Jersey suburbs). The rate of residential moves from 2003 to 2004 (the latest available data) was the lowest on record, and rates of distant moves were on a slow, downward trajectory; see U.S. Bureau of the Census, "Geographical Mobility/Migration."

12.   Calculated from IPUMS data (Ruggles et al., *Integrated Public Use Microdata Series: Version 3.0*). These percentages exclude from the base those living in group quarters.

13.   In 2000 neighborhoods were even more segregated by house costs than by race. The top and bottom quintiles of households ranked on house value each had segregation indices of Theil's H of .44. (For an explication of this segregation measure, see the discussion later in the

chapter on segregation.) The median sale prices of all homes in the San Francisco area for December 2000 are from DQNews.com, "Bay Area Home Sales Down," and those for existing single-family homes in New England are from U.S. Bureau of the Census, *Statistical Abstract of the United States, 2001*, table 943. A 2005 comparison showed that comparable houses were worth twice as much in Houston as in Phoenix, double that in San Francisco, and 50 percent more again in La Jolla, a beach suburb of San Diego (see Kelly Zito, "$1 Million Houses Coast to Coast," *San Francisco Chronicle*, February 6, 2005, A1).

14. The Harris poll asked, "We'd like to know whether or not you feel good about various things in this country and in your life. Do you feel good about [name of city, town, or county in which you live] or not?" Eighty-two percent said they felt good about their community— fewer than for family (95 percent) or home (91 percent) but more than for the "state of the nation" (63 percent). Only 85 percent felt good about the "morals and values of people in your community," but that was considerably higher than the 39 percent who felt good about "morals and values of Americans in general." The Harvard Saguaro Seminar Survey asked, "What gives you a sense of community or a feeling of belonging?" and listed some answers. Over three-fourths selected living in their particular town and the people in their neighborhood—fewer than the percentage who picked friends, about the same as those who chose fellow parishioners and coworkers (for those who worked), and far more than those who selected people they met online. Peter Hart Associates in 2000 asked Americans, "How many friends do you currently have from . . . your neighborhood . . . none, one or two, a few, or a large number?" Forty-four percent of respondents said they had a few or more friends from the neighborhood, a lower percentage than said they had friends from work, about the same as those whose friends were from church, and more than those whose friends came from clubs, high school, and other places. These data were obtained from the Lexis-Nexis Reference website.

15. See the discussion and analysis in Fischer, *America Calling*, ch. 7. Some readers will recall the 2000 book by Robert Putnam, *Bowling Alone*, which reports general declines in Americans' social activities after the 1960s. Putnam argues that two major reasons for this decline have been increased television-watching and longer commutes, both of which encourage staying home. One might infer that staying home more may have also led people to care more about their localities.

16. These are the regional definitions for 2000: Northeast—Connecticut, Maine, Massachusetts, New Hampshire, Rhode Island, Vermont, New

Jersey, New York, and Pennsylvania; Midwest—Illinois, Indiana, Michigan, Ohio, Wisconsin, Iowa, Kansas, Minnesota, Missouri, Nebraska, North Dakota, and South Dakota; South—Delaware, Florida, Georgia, Maryland, North Carolina, South Carolina, Virginia, West Virginia, Alabama, Kentucky, Mississippi, Tennessee, Arkansas, Louisiana, Oklahoma, Texas, and Washington, D.C.; West—Arizona, Colorado, Idaho, Montana, Nevada, New Mexico, Utah, Wyoming, Alaska, California, Hawaii, Oregon, and Washington. In 1900 Hawaii and Alaska were excluded, as they were until 1960, but all of the mainland territories were included.

17. To recap from chapter 3, our categories for ancestry are based on geographic origin but translate roughly as (before 1970) Europe equals whites, Africa equals blacks, Americas equals American Indian or Alaskan native, Asia equals Asian or Pacific Islander and other. After 1970, all these categories refer to *non-Hispanic* groups and Hispanics are classified in the Americas-origin group.

18. The dozen "major" counties (that is, counties with at least 100,000 people) with the oldest residents were all in Florida in 2000. The oldest was Charlotte County, Florida, north of Fort Myers on the Gulf Coast, where 34 percent of the population was 65 years or older; see U.S. Bureau of the Census, "Population and Ranking Tables of the Older Population." For fuller breakdowns of regional statistics, see the appendix for this chapter, available at: http://www.russellsage.org/publications/books/060711.219626.

19. A metropolitan area is defined by the Office of Management and Budget as one or more counties containing "a large population nucleus [usually a city of 50,000 or more], together with adjacent communities having a high degree of social and economic integration with that core." See U.S. Bureau of the Census, "State and County QuickFacts: Metropolitan Statistical Area."

20. See U.S. Bureau of the Census, "Metropolitan Areas Ranked by Population," http://www.census.gov/population/cen2000/phc-t3/tab03.pdf (accessed January 12, 2006).

21. These categories are not easily constructed and filled out from census data. Jon Stiles undertook the complex task of marrying various sorts of data. A long description of the process and the results are presented in the appendix to this chapter available at: http://www.russellsage.org/publications/books/060711.219626. To summarize, the 1900 to 1920 and some of the 1940 data were derived from the individual-level IPUMS files, the 1970 to 2000 data came from aggregated census files, and the 1950 and 1960 data came from combinations of IPUMS and published census tables. For another approach, see Gardner, *The Metropolitan Fringe.*

22. The data are presented here in full:

Continent of Origin	Nonmetropolitan		Small Metropolitan		Large Metropolitan	
	Periphery	Center	Periphery	Center	Periphery	Center
Europe	84%	79%	81%	62%	69%	43%
Africa	8	9	7	18	9	23
America	6	9	8	14	14	24
Asia	0	1	2	3	5	7

Source: Our calculations from the STF3 data file of the 2000 census.
Note: The residual is "other."

23. In large metropolitan areas, 30 percent of suburban residents over twenty-five years of age had graduated from college, compared to 27 percent of center-city residents—but notably, 25 percent of all center-city adults never finished high school, the same proportion as in the countryside. (The proportion of residents with exactly a high school degree declined steadily with increasing urbanization.) The occupation data refer to employed civilians age sixteen and over.
      One marker of status—homeownership rates—worked in the reverse way. Eighty-one percent of households in the countryside (peripheral nonmetropolitan) owned their homes, but only 46 percent of large metropolitan center-city households did. Clearly the geographical pattern of homeownership says more about space, congestion, and housing prices than it does about social status.

24. Birch, "Who Lives Downtown."

25. Had we been able to remove from the tables teenagers living with their parents, the differences would no doubt be greater.

26. For center cities of metropolitan areas, 21 percent (small metros) and 20 percent (large metros) of residents were eighteen to twenty-nine years old; in all the other categories of places, the percentages were 14 to 17 percent. Eugenie Birch ("Who Lives Downtown") shows that twenty-five- to thirty-four-year-olds were heavily concentrated in the downtown cores of center cities.

27. The segregation discussions here and in a later section draw on Fischer et al., "Distinguishing the Geographic Levels."

28. This point—about African Americans' move from regional to neighborhood segregation—is explicitly made in Massey and Hajnal, "The Changing Geographic Structure of Black-White Segregation."

29. Data on small geographical units (census tracts) are not consistently available outside of metropolitan areas, especially in the earlier censuses.

30. More complete discussions of the measure appear in Fischer et al., "Distinguishing the Geographic Levels," and in James and Taeuber, "Measures of Segregation."

31. As described in Fischer et al., "Distinguishing the Geographic Levels," these calculations are based on all metropolitan census tracts in 2000. The measures are for total segregation from the tract level up.

32. These categories differ from the ancestry categories we developed in chapter 3 and use elsewhere in this chapter because we draw the data from census summary files, SF1 and SF3, rather than the IPUMS.

33. For an overview, see Charles, "The Dynamics of Racial Residential Segregation."

34. Using American Housing Survey data on micro-neighborhoods, Yannis Ioannides ("Neighborhood Income Distributions") reports that clustering by income is substantially higher among those under sixty-five (testifying to the distortion introduced by retirees in most analyses of income) and that clustering by property value is substantially higher than by income. In addition to the life-cycle variations in income, errors—honest and otherwise—in reporting incomes tend to mask greater class differences. For instance, William Dickens ("Comments") calculates segregation indices (D) for estimates of "permanent incomes" and reports them to be 20 to 30 percent higher than the standard estimates.

35. More details on these geographic distinctions are in Fischer et al., "Distinguishing the Geographic Levels," and in the appendices to this chapter available at: http://www.russellsage.org/publications/.

36. The percentage of Americans living in the Northeast shrank from 27 percent in 1900 to 19 percent in 2000, and in the Midwest from 35 percent to 23 percent, while the percentage in the South rose from 32 percent to 36 percent, and in the West it boomed from 6 percent to 22 percent.

37. Tolnay, "The African American 'Great Migration' and Beyond." In 1910 the South was virtually all native-born, while the proportion of foreign-born ranged as high as 26 percent in the Northeast. Differences shrank as immigration fell. In 1980 the West had a high of 11 percent foreign-born. With renewed immigration, differences widened but remained narrower in 2000 than in 1900, from 5 percent foreign-born in the Midwest to 19 percent in the West. The detailed numbers on regional differences are provided in the appendix to this chapter at: http://www.russellsage.org/publications/.

38. This table displays the changes in farming—the percentage of employed civilians, age sixteen and older, who were farm owners, managers, or laborers—as tabulated from the IPUMS:

	Northeast	Midwest	South	West
1900	13%	36%	54%	25%
1950	3	13	19	10
2000	1	2	1	2

Source: Authors' compilation.

39. Kim, "Economic Integration and Convergence"; Easterlin, "Regional Income Trends."
40. Hobbs and Stoops, *Demographic Trends in the Twentieth Century*, 41.
41. The sex ratio data are from Hobbs and Stoops, *Demographic Trends in the Twentieth Century*, 63. In 1900, 28 percent of westerners fifteen and older were living alone or as unattached adults, compared to 20 percent or fewer in other regions. By 1960 the rate was 13 to 15 percent across all regions.
42. Data on racial attitudes, for example, show substantial regional convergence (see chapter 3; see also Schuman et al., *Racial Attitudes in America*). There was also general convergence on the sorts of cultural issues covered in chapter 9. A study of spending patterns showed regional convergence in consumption over the century (Lebergott, *Consumer Expenditures*, ch. 4). But there is also a sizable literature that documents continuing regional differences, especially between the South and the rest of the country, on matters such as violence, religiosity, and individualism; a recent example is Hayes and Lee, "The Southern Culture of Honor and Violent Attitudes." On politics, see Manza and Brooks, *Social Cleavages and Political Change*.
43. This comment is based on our analysis, using the GSS, of voting in presidential elections in the 1970s, 1980s, and 1990s (including 2000). See also Manza and Brooks, *Social Cleavages and Political Change*.
44. The metropolitan area (MA) classification for recent decades—the one we used earlier for the 2000 data—is familiar, but it did not exist before 1950. For 1950 through 2000, we use the actual population of the MAs as they were defined in those years by the Office of Management and Budget to distinguish large from small. The 1940 PUMS, created in a collaboration between the Census Bureau and the Center for Demography and Ecology at the University of Wisconsin, identified the same set of MAs as existed in 1950, and the IPUMS staff eliminated identification of any of those MAs that did not meet the criteria applied in 1950. For 1900 through 1920, IPUMS applied the 1950 criteria to groups of counties to create MA equivalents. For all of these pre-1950 data, we divided large from small MAs according to population estimates based on the IPUMS microdata. The exception to this was for total counts, which we derived more directly, using Donald Bogue's classifications ("Population Growth in Standard Metropolitan Areas," appendix 1). For more details, see the appendix to this chapter available at:http://www.russellsage.org/publications/books/

060711.219626. See Gardner, *The Metropolitan Fringe*, for data carrying back measurements into the nineteenth century.

45. Technically, growth and expansion show up in the reclassification of nonmetropolitan places into metropolitan ones. When the Census Bureau identifies a new metropolitan area, it recognizes the emergence of an urban center; when it adds a formerly rural county to an existing metropolitan area, it is recognizing suburbanization on the ground. In these senses, the reclassification is a technical step that recognizes a substantive social change.

46. In this analysis, as for others to follow, data for certain decades are unfortunately unavailable. Full tables for the data reported here and below are available at: http://www.russellsage.org/publications/books/060711.219626.

47. See, for example, Frey, "Melting Pot Suburbs"; Berube and Foreman, "Racial Change in the Nation's Largest Cities." Some research suggests that Asian immigrants were not as likely to move through center cities on their way to assimilation and not as segregated from whites as blacks and Latinos were (Alba et al., "Strangers Next Door"; Massey and Denton, "Suburbanization and Segregation in U.S. Metropolitan Areas").

48. Note that these widening distinctions between places by ancestry are not simply the result of immigration flowing to urban centers. At the beginning of the twentieth century, the foreign-born also congregated in larger metropolitan areas and city centers. (In fact, the concentration was greater then. In 1900, 33 percent of residents in large metro-center cities were foreign-born, compared to 7 percent of residents in the countryside—a twenty-six-point difference; in 2000 it was 23 percent versus 2 percent—a twenty-one-point difference. The center-periphery difference within large metropolitan areas stayed about the same, at eight points.) But in 1900 the foreign-born were largely European, and at the end of the century they were overwhelmingly "people of color." On whites living downtown, see Birch, "Who Lives Downtown."

49. This table displays the percentage of foreign-born:

	1900	1910	1920	1940	1950	1960	1970	1980	1990	2000
Nonmetropolitan periphery	7%	7%	6%			2%	1%	2%	1%	2%
Nonmetropolitan center	14	14	10			3	2	3	3	4
Small metropolitan periphery	18	19	16		6%	5	4	4	4	7
Small metropolitan center	22	21	18		7	5	5	5	6	9
Large metropolitan periphery	25	26	22	16%	11	7	6	9	11	14
Large metropolitan center	33	37	31	24	19	14	12	15	19	23

Source: Authors' compilation.

50. Because of data limitations preventing us from consistently connecting individuals in the IPUMS to location, "family incomes" here are adjusted for inflation but *not* for family size. We drew them from summary tables.

51. Occupational data from 1900 to 1920 and from 1950 to 2000 show a wide advantage to the more urban places at the beginning of the century, mainly because of farming's dominance in rural areas. They also show that city residents had higher occupational positions than suburban residents, in part because many "suburbanites" were farmers, but the advantage for city-dwellers persists even when we exclude farmers; see the appendix to this chapter available at: http://www.russellsage.org/publications/books/060711.219626.   Todd Kelly Gardner ("The Slow Wave" and *The Metropolitan Fringe*) looks at center-fringe differences in occupations from 1850 through 1940 and reports that large differences favored city residents in the nineteenth century and then declined to 1940.

52. Although the data do not allow us to estimate median household income for nonmetropolitan towns and countryside separately in 1950, they do allow us to estimate median household income for the nonmetropolitan population as a whole: $13,900, which was over $5,000 less than that of any other category of place.

53. See, for example, Jackson, *Crabgrass Frontier*, and Binford, *The First Suburbs*, as well as Gardner, "The Slow Wave."

54. Corroborating evidence for the widening of city-suburb differences comes from Schwirian, Hankins, and Ventresca, "The Residential Decentralization of Social Status Groups." In 1950, in most metropolitan areas, center-city residents were more educated than those outside the center city; by 1980 the difference had flipped.

55. To be more specific, between 1960 and 2000 the household income of the twentieth-percentile person in the countryside grew by a factor of 2.6, substantially faster than in any other place category, but the household income of the twentieth-percentile person in large center cities grew by 15 percent, substantially slower than any other place category. The incomes of eightieth-percentile households rose about the same amount in all community categories, by factors of 1.7 to 2.1 times. One consequence was that economic inequality, the eighty-to-twenty ratio (see chapter 6), declined in rural areas but widened in metropolitan areas, and did so especially in large center cities. In the center cities of large metropolises, the eighty-to-twenty ratio rose from 2.7 in 1950 to 4.0 in 1980 and 4.6 in 2000—a marker of the emerging "dual city." Among whites (non-Hispanic whites in 2000), the trend was similar but much smaller in scale, meaning that the concentration of blacks and Latinos in the

center cities was substantially connected to the increasing inequality in center cities.

56. Between 1960 and 2000, basic education improved so rapidly in the nonmetropolitan periphery that the rural-urban gap in high school graduation rates narrowed. (In 1960 the difference in the percentage of residents, twenty-five and older, with a high school degree between the large metropolitan periphery and the nonmetropolitan periphery was twenty points—31 percent versus 51 percent. In 2000 it was nine points—75 percent versus 84 percent.) In the same years, college education, which had been rare, became somewhat more common, but mainly in metropolitan places, so that the rural-urban gap in BA degrees widened. (In 1960 the college graduate difference was seven points—4 percent versus 11 percent—and in 2000 it was sixteen points—14 percent versus 30 percent.) City-suburban differences are discussed later in the chapter; see appendix table B.6, available at: http://www.russellsage.org/publications/books/060711.219626.

Because farming virtually disappeared, the occupational distributions of different types of places became more alike. But if we bracket farming, we find that metropolitan residents found more high-status jobs than did nonmetropolitan Americans, widening differences. From 1900 to 1920, 30 percent of nonfarm workers in all sorts of places held white-collar or better jobs. At the end of the century, however, 50 percent of nonmetropolitan workers were in these careers, while over 60 percent of metropolitan workers were. (The percentages are of employed civilian adults age fourteen and older for 1900 through 1970, and sixteen and older for 1980 through 2000, excluding those employed in farmwork; see appendix table B.5 available at: http://www.russellsage.org/publications/books/060711.219626.) City-suburban differences are discussed later in the chapter. The patterns of occupational and educational change are similar even if we look at whites only.

57. That is, differences in disposable income partly explain why minorities concentrated in centers and whites in suburbs, but race-based housing markets also partly explain why low-income people concentrated in center cities.

58. Educational differences between city and suburb are complicated. The differences in the proportion who were college graduates changed little over a half-century; in large metropolitan areas, the suburban advantage on both high school and college graduation rates widened and then narrowed modestly. But the slimness of the differences may be misleading because, as we saw earlier, young adults—many of whom were recent college graduates—tended to concentrate in the center cities. Many then moved to the suburbs during their parenting years. At the same time, for other reasons, high school dropouts, particularly

those who were black and Latino, also concentrated more in the center cities. From 1980 on, large metropolitan cities had the smallest proportion of residents with only a high school degree (or some college) of the six place types, but they also had the second-largest proportion (after their suburbs) of college graduates.

City-suburban differences in nonfarm occupational positions favored the cities before World War II; afterwards, they evened up or, in large metropolitan areas, favored suburbanites. The new city-suburb gap was in the category of nonprofessional white-collar workers, not professional workers. (In 1950, 35 percent of large metropolitan city workers were white-collar versus 32 percent of large metropolitan suburban workers; in 2000 the respective percentages flipped in favor of the suburbs, 44 to 41 percent. For professionals, however, the differences were +4 for the suburbs in 1960 and no difference in 2000; see appendix tables available at: http://www.russellsage.org/publications/books/060711.219626.) Again, these are signs of the emerging "dual city," or the "hourglass" character of large cities. See also Birch, "Who Lives Downtown."

59.   This table displays the percentage of Americans age fifteen or older who were never married, by type of place:

	1900	1910	1920	1940	1950	1960	1970	1980	1990	2000
Nonmetropolitan periphery	34%	33%								
Nonmetropolitan center	37	35	30%				26%	26%	25%	25%
Small metropolitan periphery	35	35	31				24	24	23	23
Small metropolitan center	39	37	32		22%	22%	27	29	30	32
Large metropolitan periphery	38	38	33		22	20	25	26	26	26
Large metropolitan center	39	39	35	32%	24	25	29	33	35	36

Source: Authors' compilation.

These data unfortunately include dependent teenagers—the consequence of which would be to *understate* the geographical concentration of the never-marrieds in center cities. Here is another way to see the change in the distribution of the unmarried: in 1900 and 1970, unmarried adults were 1.1 times more likely than other Americans to live in the center cities of metropolitan areas; in 2000 they were 1.3 times more likely; for more detail, see appendices available at: http://www.russellsage.org/publications/books/060711.219626. Research covering 1955 to 1975 suggests that the spatial separation was more a matter of married couples being drawn to the suburbs than of the unmarried being drawn to the cities (Frey and Kobrin, "Changing Families and Changing Mobility"), but that may have changed after 1970.

Our analysis of eighteen- to twenty-nine-year-olds also shows a trend toward concentrating more in center cities, but that trend was much weaker. (We do not have usable age numbers for the midcentury, but in 1970 there was a two-point difference between large metropolitan centers and their suburbs in the proportion of residents who were eighteen to twenty-nine, 19 percent versus 17 percent; by 2000 the difference had more than doubled to five points, 20 percent versus 15 percent. A similar change occurred in small metropolitan areas: 20 percent versus 18 percent in 1970 had changed to 21 percent versus 14 percent in 2000.) This trend toward city concentration was weak, probably because the age group includes both family dependents and college students. Birch's analysis ("Who Lives Downtown") focuses on twenty-five- to thirty-four-year-olds and reveals a very strong increase between 1970 and 2000 in the proportion who lived in downtowns.

60. Scholars identified even newer, complex developments in the city-suburban contrast during the last decade or two of the twentieth century. Aging suburbs nearer to metropolitan centers took on some characteristics of center cities, and pockets of middle-class, family-oriented revitalization in center cities emerged. These events suggest that new spatial arrangements may develop in the twenty-first century.

61. This section also draws from Fischer et al., "Distinguishing the Geographic Levels"; see that article for more details.

62. Cutler, Glaeser, and Vigdor, "The Rise and Decline of the American Ghetto"; Massey and Denton, *American Apartheid*.

63. That consistency appears to be the product of two conflicting trends: continuing immigration, which pushed segregation up, and increasing residential integration by longtime and second-generation Hispanics.

64. We infer this from the analyses of Massey and Hajnal, "The Changing Geographic Structure of Black-White Segregation in the United States."

65. David Cutler and his colleagues ("The Rise and Decline of the American Ghetto") make a similar argument: that white resistance shifted from direct opposition to black newcomers to a willingness to pay housing premiums to flee blacks.

66. Others have also found declining neighborhood segregation; see, for example, Iceland, Weinberg, and Steinmetz, "Racial and Ethnic Residential Segregation in the United States"; and Charles, "The Dynamics of Racial Residential Segregation."

67. In large metropolitan areas, the greatest city-suburb difference in the

percentage of African Americans was in 1970: 27 percent of center-city residents were black versus 5 percent of suburban residents. By 2000 the difference had narrowed significantly (23 percent versus 9 percent).

68. U.S. Bureau of the Census, *Statistical Abstract of the United States, 1961*, 31; U.S. Bureau of the Census, *Statistical Abstract of the United States, 2001*, 26. (The latter refers to single-race identities, using the count of one race only.) The decomposition of the Theil index is such that city-suburban differences, such as those seen in figure 7.4, are appropriately distributed to larger units. The contrast between, say, suburban Scottsdale, Arizona, and center-city Detroit, Michigan, is attributed to regional and metropolitan effects.

69. The peak Theil H for the city-versus-suburb effect was .11, in 1970; by 2000, H for city-suburb had dropped to .07.

70. The Theil H associated with segregation between places within the suburban rings went up from 1970 to 2000 (.06 to .08) and did so in all regions except the West (up .02 in the Northeast, .05 in the Midwest, and .03 in the South and down .05 in the West).

71. Blacks' segregation from nonblacks declined in all regions. The total Theil H dropped .12, .18, .23, and .35 points in the Northeast, Midwest, South, and West, respectively, between 1970 and 2000; the tract-level H dropped .13, .22, .24, and .25 points, respectively. See also Charles, "The Dynamics of Racial Residential Segregation," table 1.

72. Jargowsky, "Stunning Progress, Hidden Problems."

73. Douglas Massey and Mary Fischer ("The Geography of Inequality in the United States") report trends consistent with our findings.

74. Suburban moat-building started before the period highlighted in our data, the 1980s. For example, the historian Lizabeth Cohen (*A Consumer's Republic*, ch. 5) describes various efforts by New Jersey suburbs in the 1950s to zone out buyers of modest income. On the coordination of planning and segregation, see, for example, Weiss, "Planning Subdivisions"; Jackson, *Crabgrass Frontier*. There is a sizable literature on "suburban persistence," that is, the ability of suburbs, especially affluent ones, to maintain their exclusivity over decades. See, for example, Logan and Schneider, "Racial Segregation and Racial Change in American Suburbs"; Stahura, "Suburban Socioeconomic Status Change."

75. James, "City Limits on Racial Equality"; Reardon and Yun, "The Changing Structure of School Segregation."

76. For example, a 2003 *New York Times* story describes efforts by suburban towns to discourage housing for families because they bring in children whose education then requires much taxing and spending; Laura

Mansnerus, "Great Haven for Families, but Don't Bring Children," *New York Times*, August 13, 2003, 1.

77. The increase in marital-status and age segregation occurred at the tract, place, and suburb level versus the city level; see Fischer et al., "Distinguishing the Geographic Levels."

78. See, for example, Blakely and Snyder, *Fortress America*.

CHAPTER 8

1. Finke and Stark, *Churching of America*; Bryce, *American Commonwealth*, 2:943. On the surveys, see, for example, Halman and de Moor, "Religion, Churches, and Moral Values"; Greeley, "American Exceptionalism"; and Caplow, "Contrasting Trends in European and American Religion."

2. See, for example, Butler, *Becoming American, Awash in a Sea of Faith*, and "Magic, Astrology, and the Early American Religious Heritage"; see also Nobles, "Breaking into the Backcountry." For general histories of religion in America, see, for example, Marty, *Pilgrims in Their Own Land*; Finke and Stark, *Churching of America*.

3. Unless otherwise stipulated, survey data come from the General Social Survey.

4. For more on Americans favoring more religion, see Public Agenda, *For Goodness' Sake*. Seventy-six percent said that the particular religion did not matter. Tending to dissent on the desire for more religion in public life were Jews, those with no religion, and journalists.

5. Quoted in "President-Elect Says Soviet Demoted Zhukov Because of Their Friendship," *New York Times*, December 23, 1952, 16. A variant of this statement, "America makes no sense . . . ," has long circulated, but this quotation is the only version we have been able to find.

6. Herberg, *Protestant, Catholic, Jew*.

7. We combine data from 1998 to 2002 to increase the sample size for the smaller denominations. We include only twenty-five- to seventy-four-year-olds because the data exclude institutional populations, making the sample unrepresentative of older and younger persons.

8. Different surveys of religious affiliation differ in some details, depending on technical issues like sampling and question wording, but the general picture shown here is reliable.

9. Although these small groups get considerable media attention and their numbers are mostly growing, they remained small as of 2000. Claims in particular about the size of the Muslim population after the events of September 11, 2001, were larger than we estimate them to be (see, for example, Gustav Niebuhr, "Studies Suggest Lower Count for Number of U.S. Muslims," *New York Times*, October 25, 2001).

However, all of the scientifically reliable tabulations of Muslim adults put their share of the U.S. population at less than 1 percent. The average of American Muslims is significantly younger than the average age of American Jews and Christians, so their share goes up when children are included in the count. Even after that adjustment, however, Muslims are at most 1 percent of the total population. See Smith, "Religious Diversity in America."

10. Christian Holiness Partnership, www.holiness.org/ourstory.htm (accessed 2002; defunct 2004; also at: http://www.faithand values .com/fg_profiles/Christian_holiness.asp [accessed May 28, 2006]).

11. Smith, "Classifying Protestant Denominations."

12. That fraction was higher in the GSS surveys of the 1980s, when more primary sampling units were, by chance, in Utah.

13. The key changes occurred late in the nineteenth century and are thus beyond our time horizon. Suffice to say that the evangelization movement known as the Second Great Awakening and twentieth-century demographic trends left the Congregational and Reformed churches with a smaller, older population than most others.

14. Greeley, *Religion in Europe*.

15. Membership figures are from Gallup Poll, "Gallup Poll Topics A-Z: Religion," available to subscribers at: http://www.gallup.com//poll/ releases/pr991224.asp. The attendance figures are from the General Social Survey, 1998 to 2002. On the controversy about attendance, some scholars maintain that there is no bias, and one study of an Ohio county suggests that these estimates are double the true rates. See Hadaway, Marler, and Chaves, "What the Polls Don't Show," and the follow-up symposium on church attendance in the February 1998 issue of the *American Sociological Review*.

16. So, for example, a May 18, 2004, Gallup poll reported that 90 percent of Americans said that they believed in God. George Bishop ("Americans' Belief in God") is a skeptic on this point.

17. The Gallup poll frequently asks questions about religion and reports similar results. For example, around 2000, 83 percent of Americans said that they believed in heaven, 71 percent in hell, 79 percent in angels, and 68 percent in the devil; Winseman, "Eternal Destinations." On praying, see Gallup Poll, "As Nation Observes National Day of Prayer," available to subscribers at: http://www.gallup.com/ content/defaultaspx?ci=3874.

18. Other items are from Gallup Poll, "Gallup Poll Topics A-Z: Religion" (see note 15). On Americans' beliefs about eternal life, see Pew Research Center, "Americans Struggle with Religion's Role," 54. On their thinking about religious diversity, see, for example, Smith, "The Myth of Culture Wars."

19.   We downloaded the Gallup data from the Gallup website (www.gallup.com). We calibrated the percentages to exclude missing data. Only after 1992 were Orthodox Christians and Mormons distinguished from "others," so they are pooled here with "others." Where Gallup reported multiple polls in one year, we averaged them to create a single estimate. The Roper data were collected and standardized by our Berkeley colleague Henry Brady (with the assistance of Laurel Elms) and made available to us through the facilities of the UC Berkeley Survey Research Center. The GSS makes distinctions among "others" only after 1996, so "others" remain pooled here. Both the left- and right-hand sides of the figure are smoothed using locally estimated regression (for a discussion of locally estimated regression, see appendix A).

   For the graph on the right-hand side of figure 8.3, we calculated the percentages for each birth cohort and added sixteen years, and then used locally estimated regression to smooth the results. To be sure that we are looking at American youngsters, we examined only respondents who reported that they were living in the United States when they were sixteen years old. Using reported childhood religion to measure past religious diversity presents a few technical problems but can still give us an overview. Since some religious groups have high birth rates, they had more representatives alive at the end of the century to report on their religions at age sixteen. This gives an impression that there were more, say, Catholic families earlier in the century than was really the case. Similarly, to the extent that some religious groups have shorter life expectancies, they are underrepresented for earlier years in the century. Nevertheless, these biases are not likely to affect the general conclusions we draw from the data.

20.   "Others," sociologists have found, include respondents who did not choose the mainstream labels but were in fact Christians of some sort. See Sherkat, "Tracking the 'Other.'" In 1998 and 2000, the GSS more carefully coded "others" and found that about half labeled themselves Christian Orthodox, "Christian," or "inter-denominational." Only 15 percent of "others" (fewer than 1 percent of all respondents) claimed an Eastern religion, and only 10 percent claimed Islam (about one-half of 1 percent of all respondents).

21.   One complication in the trends is the proportion of Americans who claimed no religion in the last decade of the century. The Gallup poll reported a decline from 11 percent in 1991 to 6 percent in 2000, while the GSS reported an increase from 7 percent to 14 percent. We are inclined to trust the latter estimate more because the GSS response rate is substantially higher and because other sources, such as the American National Election Study and the Pew surveys, also esti-

mated that between 12 and 14 percent of adults claimed no religion in 2000.

22. See Hout and Fischer, "Explaining the Rise of Americans with No Religious Preference."

23. This discussion draws on ibid.

24. Data from 2002 and 2004 show the percentage of American adults with no religious preference holding steady at 14 percent.

25. Yang and Ebaugh, "Transformations in New Immigrant Religions"; Dolan, *The American Catholic Experience*.

26. The data points in figure 8.4 are, again, from pooled Gallup and Roper polls and the GSS. However, the Roper polls were distinctive in showing a sharper increase in Catholics from the mid-1970s to 1992 (the last date for which religion was available in the Roper series).

27. These estimates are based on the GSS data on the religion in which respondents were raised. Among those raised abroad in one of the Western faiths, 45 percent of those who were sixteen in the 1920s had been raised Catholic, but 80 percent of those who reached sixteen in the 1980s were raised Catholic.

28. Rates of conversion from Catholicism to Protestantism among the very earliest-born GSS respondents were 10 to 15 percent. But only 7 percent of the cohort that turned sixteen around 1920 converted. That figure climbed steadily upwards into the 15 to 17 percent range for cohorts that turned sixteen around 1970. (These figures include only respondents who had been sixteen in the United States and had reached age thirty at the time of the interview. Rates of conversion were lower for the most recently born, but they had not yet been "exposed" long to "opportunities" for conversion.) On the other hand, rates of Protestant-to-Catholic conversion (for the same sorts of people) fluctuated little and never exceeded 5 percent. In sum, the increasing loss of many Catholic-reared adults to Protestantism accounts for the difference in the youth and adult trend lines shown in right and left panels respectively of figure 8.4. For more, see Hout, "Angry and Alienated."

29. See also Smith and Kim, "The Vanishing Protestant Majority."

30. "Others" includes members of many small, often fundamentalist or evangelical denominations and of independent churches and Protestants with no particular denominational attachment.

31. Sutton and Chaves, "Explaining Schism in American Protestant Denominations," figure 1.

32. Hout, Greeley, and Wilde, "The Demographic Imperative in Religious Change." Many authors—for example, James Hunter, *American Evangelicalism*, and *Culture Wars*, and Robert Wuthnow, *The Restructuring of American Religion*—attribute the growth of conservative Protestant

denominations and sects to conversions of mainline Protestants to conservative ones. That kind of conversion did not change significantly over the seventy-five years of available data and thus could play *no* role in the changing distribution of American Protestants.

33. On gays, see, for example, Moon, *God, Sex, and Politics.*

34. Chaves, *Denominations in America.*

35. This calculation excludes the 4 percent of adults who were raised with no religion.

36. Religious scholars have lately come to refer to a "religious marketplace"; see, for example, Finke and Stark, *Churching of America*; Roof, *Spiritual Marketplace.*

37. Roof, *Spiritual Marketplace.*

38. Some religious changes do not count as "switching" by our reckoning. For example, a shift from Free Will Baptist to Southern Baptist (or vice versa) would not be counted as a switch because it is a move from one kind of Baptist to another. It would count as a move if it involved crossing a denominational boundary—for example, a Southern Baptist becoming a Pentecostal.

39. Our earlier analysis of moves within Protestantism noted a drop in conversions from conservative to mainline Protestant. That decreased mobility was offset by an increase in the tendency of conservative Protestants to switch to no religious preference. The decrease in conservative-to-mainline religious mobility was canceled out by the increase in conservative-to-no-preference mobility.

40. Sherkat and Wilson, "Preferences, Constraints, and Choices in Religious Markets."

41. Robert Lynd and Helen Lynd, *Middletown*; Caplow et al., *All Faithful People*, ch. 4; Caplow and Bahr, "Half a Century of Change in Adolescent Attitudes." In 1924, 91 percent of high school students agreed; in 1977, 41 percent did.

42. Voting data are from the Gallup website, http://www.gallup.com/poll/releases/pr990329.asp (accessed August 4, 2000).

43. Our discussion draws from Manza and Brooks, *Social Cleavages and Political Change*, ch. 4.

44. In 1957 Gallup asked respondents, "Do you think a person can be a Christian if he doesn't go to church?" In 1996 Queens' University (Canada) researchers asked an American sample whether they agreed or disagreed with the statement, "I don't think you need to go to church in order to be a good Christian."

45. Data from the GSS.

46. In 1959 Gallup asked Protestants and Catholics, "Would you have a serious objection to a daughter or son of yours marrying a [Catholic/Protestant]?" Christians and Jews were asked the same

question about a Jewish-Gentile marriage. In 1968 Gallup asked, "Do you approve or disapprove of marriage between (a) Catholics and Protestants; (b) Jews and non-Jews?" The questions cannot be directly compared, but we can examine generational differences. In 1959 there were essentially no generational differences. In 1968 we see a notable difference between the pre-1920 and the 1920 to 1939 cohort, a change that continues into the following cohort. The gaps emerge only in the 1960s. This table presents the percentage of those who would not have objected to (in 1959) or would have approved of (in 1968) intermarriages:

Type of Marriage	Survey Year	Year of Birth			
		Before 1900	1900 to 1919	1920 to 1939	After 1939
Protestant-Catholic	1959	61%	62%	63%	—
	1968	—	58[a]	66	72%
Jewish-Gentile	1959	49	53	53	—
	1968	—	52[a]	63	68

Source: Authors' compilation.
[a]Cell includes respondents born before 1900.

47. Kalmijn, "Intermarriage and Homogamy," esp. 410–11. Evelyn Lehrer's study, "Religious Intermarriage in the United States," also suggests that the increase may not apply to fundamental denominations. Waite and Sheps, "The Impact of Religious Upbringing and Marriage Markets on Jewish Intermarriage," is one of several papers documenting increasing rates of Jewish intermarriage from other datasets.

48. The major families of denominations used here were Baptist, Methodist, Lutheran, Presbyterian, and Episcopalian. Note that a chart using the religions that respondents and their spouses were *raised* in shows a similar trend line elevated about ten percentage points.

49. Poll cited by Musleah, "Jewish Jeopardy."

50. For overviews, see, for example, Marty, *Pilgrims in Their Own Land*; Butler, *Awash in a Sea of Faith*, and "Protestant Success in the New American City"; and Finke and Stark, *Churching of America*.

51. There are many more points at the end of each series because published Gallup reports provided data for a few polls in each of the later years and just annual averages for the earlier years. We show those points to give the reader a sense of how much month-to-month variation there can be. The Gallup data are from "Gallup Poll Topics A-Z" at the Gallup website (http://www.gallup.com) and from several early

points reported in Putnam, *Bowling Alone*, figure 12. The Roper data on attendance were provided by Henry Brady. GSS results point to a steeper downward slope since the 1970s, but the item there is not the same; it concerns frequency of attendance (see analysis later in the chapter).

52. On the debate over measuring attendance, see note 15. On cautions about early polls, see Glenn, "Review of Greeley."

53. Lynd and Lynd, *Middletown*, 358. The Lynds make a point about declining attendance from 1890 to 1924, but the 1890 data are retrospective reports. In 1977 Theodore Caplow and his colleagues (*Middletown Families*) did not replicate the census method but did replicate the interviews conducted by the Lynds. That replication showed an increase in respondents' reports of going to church (ch. 11; table A-11.2). Some of the other fragments include: surveys done in New York City in 1900, which reported that half of Protestants, 80 percent of Catholics, and 10 percent of Jews regularly attended services (Butler, "Protestant Success in the New American City," 307); a newspaper in Providence that reported in 1902 that 87 percent of Catholics and 69 percent of Protestants "claimed to attend church" (Sterne, "Bringing Religion into Working-Class History," 152); the fact that in 1930 only 20 percent of American Jews belonged to a synagogue (by 1960, 60 percent did; Shapiro, *A Time for Healing*, 159); a 1935 survey that found that almost 80 percent of Jewish men had *not* attended services for a year (Feingold, *A Time for Searching*, 93); and community studies of rural towns around 1940 that reported low attendance rates (for example, Moe and Taylor, "Culture of a Contemporary Rural Community: Irwin, Iowa," 61ff; MacLeish and Young, "Culture of a Contemporary Rural Community: Landaff, New Hampshire," 71ff). See also estimates in Finke and Stark, *Churching of America*. However partial these numbers are, they do not fit the image of universal religiosity many people hold for the early twentieth century.

54. We pooled 1957 and 1965 Gallup polls with the 1972 through 2000 General Social Surveys. The Gallup polls specifically asked about attendance in the last week. The GSS asked respondents how often they attended in the course of a year, so we converted those answers into an estimated probability that a person had attended services in the previous week. Respondents who answered that they attended two to three times a month, nearly every week, every week, or more than once a week were coded as having attended. We chose the cut-point for the GSS (two to three times a month) so that the resulting "yes" answer had a distribution in 1994-1996-1998 as close as possible (.407) to the Gallup poll result for 1996 (.435), thereby minimizing house effects.

In the GSS, looking only at twenty-five- to seventy-four-year-olds, the zero-order effect of birth year is to reduce the probability of attending by −.000438 per year. Controlling for age, marital status, and having a child at home reduces that coefficient by 77 percent to −.000135.

55. About two-thirds of Catholics born before 1930 reported weekly attendance, but about one-third of those born after 1960 did.

56. The pattern of reported attendance at age twelve for Protestants and Catholics is a little more complex. This table summarizes the key periods and the differential reports of attending at least two or three times a month during the middle of each period:

Percentage Reporting Attendance Two or Three Times a Month at Age Twelve

Religion	1920s	Depression	1946 to 1960	1990s
Raised Protestant	72%	85%	79%	67%
Raised Catholic	93	83	93	69

Source: Authors' compilation.

The Depression (and World War II) seemed to boost Protestant kids' attendance; Protestant attendance dropped about twelve points from the 1950s to the 1980s, while Catholic attendance dropped twenty-four points. (The number of other respondents was too small for accurate estimates.) These numbers are based on the 1991 and 1998 GSS surveys and eleven-year moving averages.

57. Hout and Greeley, "The Center Doesn't Hold."

58. We regressed the probability of attending (recoded from the multiple responses noted in note 54) on year of birth, age, sex, race, size of community (four categories), region of the country (four categories), education (three categories), and whether the respondent had a child at home. Birth year was no longer significant for the base population, but five interaction effects with birth year were significant: blacks, women, southerners (negatively), westerners, and respondents with children at home (positively). All but the latter interaction effects suggested a convergence in attendance patterns across lines of cleavage.

59. "The Center Doesn't Hold," 341.

60. Putnam, Bowling Alone, 72.

61. And ones tainted by technical problems—the most obvious being a total lack of respondents who expressed a preference for no religion.

62. We also analyzed answers to the survey question, "How often do you pray?" Unfortunately, we have that data for only a seventeen-year window, 1983 to 2000. The proportion of Americans who prayed at least

daily stayed between 50 and 60 percent. But generations differed. Eighty percent of respondents born around 1900 said they prayed at least daily, but only 42 percent of those born around 1970 reported doing so. Age and year of birth correlate at -.94 across the GSS samples in this short span, and the former accounts for most of the cohort effect, perhaps all but a small residual. Over the seventeen-year window, rural Americans, southerners, Protestants, and parents increased their praying relative to the comparison group. Latinos decreased theirs. Importantly, the college-educated raised their rates of praying to nearly the level of high school graduates.

63. The decline from the 1960s onward was true only for whites.

64. We dichotomized the GSS measure as "have no doubts" versus other answers in a regression model. There is a small positive year effect and a small negative cohort effect and a significant interaction of year by college graduate. Generational differences became sharper, most especially for Catholics.

65. From Bishop, "Americans' Belief in God."

66. The 1981 result, 63 percent, is on the low side of the GSS percentages, locating the change between 1964 and 1981.

67. This is the National Election Survey, and the question was, "Which of the following statements comes closest to describing your views about the Bible—the Bible is the actual word of God and is to be taken literally, word for word; the Bible is the inspired word of God but not everything in it should be taken literally; or the Bible is an ancient book of fables, legends, history, and moral precepts recorded by man?" The NES asked a different version of the question in 1996.

68. Within both periods, there was little net change. The data are from the Gallup poll (available by subscription at "Gallup Brain," www.gallup.com; accessed November 5, 2004) for 1976 to 1998 and the GSS for 1984 to 2000. The common question was: "Which of these statements comes closest to describing your feelings about the Bible? (a) The Bible is the actual word of God and is to be taken literally, word for word; (b) The Bible is the inspired word of God but not everything in it should be taken literally, word for word; (c) The Bible is an ancient book of fables, legends, history, and moral precepts recorded by men." Although the early years of this series are Gallup only, the three overlap years in the 1990s show virtually identical results. We are excluding a published Gallup data point, for 1963, with a 65 percent "literal" reply. Although occasionally cited, this fugitive report is probably an error; see Duncan, "Facile Reporting."

69. In regression analyses, controlling for many background characteristics and year effects, changing educational attainments accounts for about six points of the fifteen-point drop in literalness between the

entire 1910 and 1940 cohorts. The interaction effect of year of birth by not graduating from high school accounts for six more points of the fifteen-point drop.

70. This summary is based on replies to the Gallup and GSS questions, "Do you believe in life after death?" In 1995 and 2000, the percentages were 80 and 82 (1998 was 72 percent).

71. Using the GSS sample, the percentage believing in life after death ranged from a low of 77 percent for those born about 1913 to highs of 81 percent for those born around 1900, 1960, and 1980.

72. Generational patterns are similar to the period patterns, but the latter are more robust. These interaction effects hold up in large regression equations with one notable exception: when main effects and other interaction effects are held constant, the trend line for Catholics is negative—they become *less* believing than Protestants.

73. To assess these patterns systematically and simply we ran the following simple regression models. The dependent variables were dichotomies for frequent attendance, frequent prayer, certainty about God, literalism, and belief in the afterlife. The predictors were year and dummies for Protestant, Catholic, high school graduate, some college, and college graduate, plus interaction terms for Catholic by year and college graduate by year. The results indicate that Catholics' attendance and prayer declined over time relative to others and that college graduates' attendance, prayer, literalism, and belief in the afterlife increased over time relative to others. We ran the same models replacing year of survey with year of the respondent's birth. The Catholic by birth year interaction was (negatively) significant only for attendance. The college graduate by birth year interaction was (positively) significant for all five measures.

74. See Skocpol, "Civic Transformation and Inequality."

75. A vivid example is the conflict between Italian immigrants and the Irish hierarchy in New York; see Orsi, *Madonna of 115th Street*.

76. See Morris, *American Catholic*, and Massa, *Catholics and American Culture*.

77. Nevertheless, the United States remained a special case in the Vatican's eyes. Not accustomed to pluralism, the Roman hierarchy tried to comprehend the situation of the American church. For example, they struggled for over a century with Catholic bishops to find divorce policies that would work in the American context. Americans have won exceptions and some adaptations (see Wilde, "Marketing Divorce Through Annulments"), but the prohibition on remarriage following divorce is the single largest reason contemporary Catholics leave the Church (see Hout, "Angry and Alienated").

78. See Yang and Ebaugh, "Transformations in New Immigrant Religions"; Chaves, "Religious Congregations and Welfare Reform."

CHAPTER 9

1. See Hunter, *Culture Wars*; Schlesinger, *The Disuniting of America*; Hollinger, *Postethnic America*; Glazer, *We are All Multiculturalists Now*; Wolfe, *One Nation, After All*; Brooks, "One Nation, Slightly Divisible." On the elections, see Langer and Cohen, "Voters and Values in the 2004 Election."

In 1993 and 1994 the GSS asked respondents the UNITED question: "There is a lot of discussion today about whether Americans are divided or united. Some say that Americans are united and in agreement about the most important values. Others think that Americans are greatly divided when it comes to the most important values. What is your view about this?" Sixty-two percent said "divided." The Gallup poll continued to ask this question through at least 2004. Except for a brief period following the attacks of September 11, 2001, "divided" answers remained in the 60 to 65 percent range; Winseman, "Public Thinks Americans Divided." Americans showed some concern about ethnic divisions in particular. To the GSS MELTPOT question (asked in 1994 and 2000), "Some people say that it is better for America if different racial and ethnic groups maintain their distinct cultures. Others say that it is better if groups change so that they blend into the larger society as in the idea of a melting pot. . . . What score between 1 [maintain] and 7 [blend] comes closest to the way you feel?" 32 percent picked the "maintain" side of the scale. Ninety percent opposed the government helping groups maintain their cultures (GVTAPART, 1994), and 70 percent thought that ethnic organizations promoted separatism (ETHORGS, 1994).

On the moral correlates of the 2000 vote, see Edsall, "Blue Movie"; Brooks, "One Nation, Slightly Divisible." The sequel in 2004 led to even more cultural accounting. One losing Democratic candidate for senator in Oklahoma wrote, "The culture war is real, and it is a conflict not merely about some particular policy or legislative item, but about modernity itself. . . . Most voters in a state like Oklahoma—and I venture to say most other Southern and Midwestern states—reject the general direction of American culture and celebrate the political party that promises to reform or revise it"; Carson, "Vote Righteously!"

2. These were the debates over immigration that led, effectively, to the closing of America's borders in 1924. On violence, Graham and

Gurr, *The History of Violence in America*, is a general (and numbing) source. In Georgia alone, over two hundred men were lynched between 1890 and 1909; Tolnay and Beck, "Black Flight," 360. On the book-banning battles, see Kemeny, "Power, Ridicule, and the Destruction of Religious Moral Reform Politics in the 1920s," as well as other contributions on the moral conflicts in Smith, *The Secular Revolution*.

3. See Whyte, *The Organization Man*; Riesman, *The Lonely Crowd*; Fromm, *Escape from Freedom*; and Bell, *End of Ideology*. The novelist-playwright Thornton Wilder includes the *Time* quote in his essay "A Silent Generation," in which he defends the generation as not silent but ruminating; see also "A Generation on Trial," *New York Times*, August 28, 1954, 14; "Yale Head Holds Liberty Menaced," *New York Times*, June 8, 1953, 27.

4. See, for example, Galambos, "Technology, Political Economy, and Professionalization"; Ross, "The New and Newer Histories."

5. Zinn, *A People's History*, ch. 16.

6. Brooks, "Superiority Complex."

7. Buchanan, "Republican National Convention Speech," and "Why We Can't Quit the Culture War."

8. See, for example, Thornton and Young-Demarco, "Four Decades of Trends in Attitudes Toward Family Issues"; Astin, "The Changing American College Student"; Davis, "Patterns of Attitude Change in the USA." On changes in racial views, see Schuman et al., *Racial Attitudes in America*. Periodic reports of the Gallup poll, among other survey organizations, show such liberalizing trends. The premarital sex question asked by Gallup in 1969 had simple response categories: 68 percent said it was wrong. The categories of the GSS question asked later were more complex; in 2000, 35 percent said premarital sex was "always" or "almost always" wrong, and 22 percent said it was "sometimes wrong." Splitting the "sometimes" group in half yields the summary statement in the text; see also Harding and Jencks, "Changing Attitudes Toward Premarital Sex." Clearly, the big change was in the first few years. Actual sexual practice may not have shifted so abruptly; net of age, the proportion of never-marrieds who were sexually active between 1998 and 2000 increased linearly from 33 percent for the oldest cohort to 53 percent for the youngest; Davis, "Age, Birth Cohort, Monotony, and Sex Frequency," figure 7.

9. The key study is DiMaggio, Evans, and Bryson, "Have Americans' Social Attitudes Become More Polarized?" The many others include Evans, "Have Americans' Attitudes Become More Polarized?" and "Worldviews or Social Groups as the Source of Moral Value Attitudes"; Hoffman and Miller, "Denominational Influences on Socially Divisive

Issues"; Jelen, "Culture Wars and the Party System"; McConkey, "Whither Hunter's Culture War?"; Smith, "The Myth of Culture Wars"; Wolfe, *One Nation, After All*; Fiorina, *Culture War?*; and Baker, *America's Crisis of Values,* ch. 3. The abortion issue may be an exception; see, for example, Hout, "Abortion Politics in the United States"; Adams, "Abortion: Evidence of an Issues Evolution."

10. Hout, "Abortion Politics in the United States."

11. Smith, "The Myth of Culture Wars," 175. Republican and Democratic officeholders diverged after the 1970s, when congressional votes often had bipartisan mixes on both sides. By 2000, votes were more commonly along party lines; see, for example, David Broder, "Don't Bet on Bipartisan Niceties," *Washington Post,* January 1, 2003, A19; see also Fiorina, *Culture War?* The very labels "Republican" and "Democrat" acquired darker colorations of conservative and liberal, respectively, and the terms "conservative" and "liberal" increasingly signaled positions on cultural issues, losing some of their earlier associations with economic issues; Miller and Hoffmann, "The Growing Divisiveness." Concurrently, religious influence in national politics itself became a divisive matter; Bolce and de Majo, "The Anti-Christian Fundamentalist Factor." In addition to the citations in note 9, see Dimaggio, "The Myth of Culture War"; Layman and Carsey, "Party Polarization and 'Conflict Extension' in the American Electorate"; Hetherington, "Resurgent Mass Partisanship"; Rieder, "Getting a Fix on Fragmentation"; Brooks and Manza, "A Great Divide"; and Stonecash, Brewer, and Mariani, *Diverging Parties.* By 2004 the explanation that the culture war was a matter specific to the political class had reached the general press; see Rauch, "Bipolar Disorder"; see also John Tierney, "A Nation Divided? Who Says?" *New York Times,* June 13, 2004.

12. Hahrie and Brady, "An Extended Historical View of Congressional Party Polarization."

13. Norval Glenn ("Recent Intercategory Differences in Attitudes") did go back to the survey data from before the 1950s and concluded that there had been little convergence or divergence in attitudes by the mid-1960s. But Glenn pooled all sorts of disparate items together and did not track, as we do later, the trajectories of specific issues.

14. Specifically, we searched for survey items in the realm of gender roles, sexual mores, racial attitudes, drugs and alcohol, abortion, and the death penalty. We stipulated that the questions were asked at least a half-dozen times, two of which were before 1970. Relatively few of today's commonly surveyed topics met these criteria. For example, the standard question on premarital sex (see chapter 4) was asked in its current form only once before 1970; see Harding and Jencks, "Changing Attitudes Toward Premarital Sex." When a question had

been asked often before the GSS, we obtained a subset of the surveys to analyze, trying to find representative points across the century. Sandra Moog and Aliya Saperstein conducted this canvass.

15. The classic source on diffusion and population differences in the pace of diffusion is Rogers, *Diffusion of Innovations*. For earlier applications of these ideas to poll and social data, see Fischer, "Urban-to-Rural Diffusion of Opinions," and "The Spread of Violent Crime from City to Countryside." Diffusion modeling has become much more mathematically nuanced than our use here, but given the roughness of survey data, a simple version suffices. Note that we do not, in this report, try to separate out which population attribute associated with uptake of innovations best explains the patterns. (For example, do educational or age differences, which are highly correlated, best account for where people stand on issues of race?) Our purpose here is essentially descriptive, that is, to answer the question of whether and when Americans became more or less divided.

Some scholars study the culture wars by measuring the extent to which the distribution of answers to a question varies over time: for example, do replies to abortion questions tend to become bimodal—that is, polarized—over time? We do not conduct this sort of analysis here, for a few reasons. The statistical burdens, especially when dealing with single survey items, get exceedingly complex and the resolutions unpersuasive. Also, many of our items are, effectively, dichotomies, for which measures like bimodality and kurtosis mean little. We have relatively few items to analyze as we extend the historical horizon back to the 1930s. Finally, our focus is on the issue of social cleavages among Americans.

16. With this question and others, we dichotomized the responses to simplify the analysis. In this particular case, the 1945 survey included a qualified response category, which we divided into "yes" and "no" proportional to the rest of the sample. We are sensitive to possible house effects, particularly because often the Gallup and GSS surveys cover different eras. After exploratory work, we decided not to include a house effect variable in the equations, but where visual examination reveals a clear house effect (as in the case of drinking), we made adjustments.

17. For example, the difference in the estimated percentage of eighteen- to thirty-four-year-old Americans who approved of working wives (that is, using the smoothed lines) and fifty-one- to sixty-four-year-olds was eleven points in 1940, reached a maximum of seventeen points around 1970, and shrank to two points by 2000. The difference between city residents and town ones (rural residents were similar to town ones) was under two points in 1940, nine points around 1971,

and three points in 2000. Statistically, the higher-order coefficients were significantly different (for example, the coefficient for year-squared by age eighteen to thirty-four differed from the one for year-squared by age sixty-five plus).

18. Karin Brewster and Irene Padavic ("Change in Gender Ideology") analyze the GSS and report that during the 1970s and 1980s, there was much change *within* cohorts (implying that people changed their minds on gender issues), but that later change was increasingly a result of cohort replacement instead. Our analysis of a much longer run shows, in harmony with their findings, strong within-cohort liberalization until about 1985, and then little change within cohorts afterwards. Clem Brooks and Catherine Bolzendahl ("The Transformation of U.S. Gender Role Attitudes") present a more technically sophisticated analysis of these trends from 1985 on. They find that cohort effects predominated and that much of the change in views of gender roles may have been rooted in a broader movement toward a "rights" ideology.

    Other findings of note from our analysis are that small gender differences declined and small racial differences reversed over the decades. Religious differences—by faith, Protestant denomination, and church attendance, available only since 1972—were small and did not change.

19. Some complexities were specific to this item. Age differences showed up in 1945, narrowed in the 1950s, widened in the early 1980s, and then closed again. (Cohort differences were negligible until the 1970s and then became apparent.) The South's relative conservatism vis-à-vis the East and West was greatest in the 1960s. The difference between rural and city residents was greatest in 1969. The gap between high school graduates and dropouts peaked around 1982; the gap between college graduates and others shrank steadily after 1945, because the college-educated had already reached the level of 57 percent approval by 1945. We also looked at responses to this question from men only; the results are similar but much weaker, largely because the sample size is half as great.

20. Schuman et al., *Racial Attitudes in America*, is the standard citation, but the trend has been documented in numerous studies. What is sometimes debated is to what extent these statements are heartfelt or hypocritical (consciously or unconsciously). At minimum, trends in answers to questions about race issues reflect respondents' changing understandings of what is proper to say, and thus they index changing social norms.

21. After adjusting the reported percentages to exclude members of the group in question; see David W. Moore, "Little Prejudice Against a

Woman, Jewish, Black, or Catholic Presidential Candidate," Gallup News Service (June 10, 2003), available at: http://poll.gallup.com/content/default.aspx?ci=8611 (accessed May 24, 2006).

22. The widest (smoothed) East-South gap was in 1958 (twenty-seven points), as was the difference by age groups. The gap between eighteen- to thirty-four-year-olds and fifty-one- to sixty-four-year-olds was twelve points in 1958; between thirty-five- to fifty-year-olds and those sixty-five and older it was fifteen points, although the interaction effects were statistically marginal. There are hints of convergence as well with regard to education, but the interaction terms are not significant.

23. We see similar narrowing of differences by gender (from 1935 on), by race and age (both from 1958), and by region (which presents a complex pattern similar to the one for Jews shown in the top-right graph of figure 9.3, although the maximum gap between the South and other regions was in 1958). It is worth noting that even in 1965, after the election and assassination of a Catholic president, fewer than 80 percent of rural (non-Catholic) Americans said they would vote for an otherwise qualified Catholic.

24. Statistically, this pattern is best described by an equation that combines linear, quadratic, and cubic functions of year. Another way to see what happened is to calculate linear slopes (answering "yes" regressed on year) for segments of the total trend. From the 1958 through 1978 *observed* data (that is, the raw, unsmoothed percentages), the change was +2 points per year for all groups except college graduates (+1); from 1982 through 1989, it was −1 for all groups; and for 1990 through 1999, the slopes were +3 for high school dropouts, +2 for high school graduates, +1 for those with some college, and +½ for those with a BA degree—showing the convergence of all groups at the end.

25. Regression analyses using just the GSS from 1972 on reveal that the age, educational, regional, and religious interaction effects are all independently significant.

26. A similar but shallower inverted-U also describes the contrast between baby boomers and the generation of their parents.

27. We found that frequent church attenders and members of fundamentalist denominations had become more accepting of premarital sex in the 1980s, but a little more resistant to it in the 1990s. Bolzendahl and Brooks ("Polarization, Secularization, or Differences as Usual?") find, in multivariate analysis, that Catholics and mainline Protestants drifted toward the permissive side of the issue after the 1970s.

28. Alito quoted in "The Judge's Only Obligation Is to the Rule of Law," *New York Times,* January 9, 2006 (online); Arlyck quoted in "Leah Garchik," *San Francisco Chronicle*, January 9, 2006, E-8.

29. Gallup has asked a variety of questions regarding homosexuality since 1977, although not this question. Most of its items show increasing acceptance of homosexuals during the 1990s, especially of gays' legal rights. This trend was interrupted in 2003, Gallup suggests, because of a Supreme Court decision striking down sodomy laws; Gallup Poll, "2003 Gallup Poll Social Series: Moral Views and Values," 19ff, available to subscribers at: http://www.gallup.com; see also Gallup Poll, "Poll Topics and Trends: Homosexual Relations," available to subscribers at: http://www.gallup.com/poll/topics (accessed November 23, 2003). Approval of gay marriage seemed to grow around 1990 but did not increase afterwards; see Brewer and Wilcox, "Trends: Same-Sex Marriage and Civil Unions."

30. This claim is based on cross-tabulations in the GSS, 1973 to 2004. For example, before the 1990s, eighteen- to thirty-four-year-olds were thirteen points likelier than those sixty-five and older to say that homosexuality was "not wrong at all" (19 percent versus 6 percent from 1973 to 1989); in the 2000 to 2004 period, the young were twenty-six points likelier to say this (40 percent versus 14 percent). In the 1970s, easterners were nine points likelier than southerners to say homosexuality was "not wrong at all" (18 percent versus 9 percent); in the 2000s, they were eighteen points likelier to say this (39 percent versus 21 percent). In the 1970s, college graduates were twenty-one points likelier than high school dropouts to hold this view (28 percent versus 7 percent); in the 2000s, they were twenty-six points likelier (42 percent versus 16 percent). (The gap between postgraduates and holders of a BA degree, age thirty and older, grew from three to nine points.) Between 1973 and 2000, the percentage difference between conservative Protestants and mainline Protestants widened from four to twelve points; the difference between Catholics and mainliners grew from one to four points; and the difference between Jews and Catholics grew from twenty-three to thirty-one points. The gap between rare and frequent church attenders opened up from fifteen to twenty-six points. Although there were big differences by size of place, those gaps changed little.

31. See Loftus, "America's Liberalization in Attitudes Toward Homosexuality," for a closer look at changes in opinions toward homosexuality.

32. The abortion questions in the GSS we used are: "Please tell me whether or not you think it should be possible for a pregnant woman to obtain a legal abortion . . . (a) If there is a strong chance of serious defect in the baby? . . . (c) If the woman's own health is seriously endangered by the pregnancy? (d) If the family has a very low income and cannot afford any more children?" On the woman's life being in danger, Americans moved from 83 percent "yes" answers in 1962 to 91

percent in 1973, then down to 84 percent in 2000. On there being a defect in the baby, opinion shifted from 64 percent "yes" in 1962 to 83 percent in 1974 and 75 percent in 2000.

On another question—whether respondents approved of a woman having an abortion for any reason—the trend was 15 percent "yes" in 1969 to 43 percent in 1993 and 38 percent in 2000. Because it was first asked in 1969, the "any reason" question is not part of our abortion scale.

33. This pattern is evident in significant effects for interaction terms of education and region by year and year-squared. It also shows up simply looking at the linear slopes for the observed, unsmoothed *points* regressed on year. (That is, we did the regressions reported in this table on the observed means, not the underlying individual data.) So, for example, from 1962 to 1977, the slopes for the more-educated are upwardly steeper than those for the less-educated, and from 1977 to 2000, their slopes are steeper downwardly. In the second period, the slope for easterners is steeper, negatively, than that for southerners and midwesterners; only the westerners fail to fit this pattern, by having essentially zero change.

The Linear Slope for Average, Observed Mean Score on the Abortion Scale, Regressed on Year, by Category

Slope	No High School Diploma	High School Graduate	Some College	College Graduate	East	Midwest	South	West
1962 to 1977	.037	.045	.059	.051	.063	.046	.033	.063
1977 to 2000	−.006	−.007	−.008	−.014	−.010	−.005	−.003	−.003

Source: Authors' compilation.
Note: Positive slopes mean increasing support for abortion; negative ones mean declining support.

34. One important exception to this pattern is religion: from 1962 on, Catholics became more similar to Protestants (more pro-choice), so that the religion gap narrowed all along, from a half-point difference on our four-point scale to virtually no difference.

Among the specific items composing the scale, the question on economic hardship as an acceptable reason for abortion best fits the cycle described here, probably because change in the item was so wide, from 15 percent agreement up to 45 percent and down to 39 percent. Overall approval levels for abortions to protect the health of the mother or because of a defect in the child were much higher, and the variation from 1962 to 2000 was more limited (see note 32). If we restrict our analysis to the GSS, from 1972 on, we miss much of the first cycle, but we can expand the scale by adding three questions about whether abortion is justified: in cases of rape, for unwed mothers, or for any reason. A simple linear fit for this six-item scale shows a slight decline over the years, although a fourth-order fit better captures two peaks of liberalism, around 1975 and again around 1995. More important, regression analysis suggests that after 1972 the differences between blacks and whites, Catholics and others, and young and old (or more- versus less-educated) shrank a bit as blacks and Catholics became more liberal and the young more conservative.

35. Death penalty approval roughly followed the national homicide cycle with a lag of five to ten years. There were major differences in opinion by race and gender, but those did not change much over time.

36. Westerners were unusually supportive of capital punishment throughout. They seemed to be exceptionally and consistently pro-capital punishment, many other factors held constant; Jacobs and Carmichael, "The Political Sociology of the Death Penalty."

37. In 1960 city people were five points likelier to support capital punishment than rural people, but in 2000 the difference was minus-four points; in 1960 college graduates endorsed the death penalty by four points more than high school graduates, but in 2000 the reverse was true by about six points.

38. These are smoothed estimates from both GSS and Gallup data (and only Gallup before 1972). They also correct for a "house" effect: an average six-point difference in Gallup and GSS results from the same years. We split the difference between the two organizations. The raw, uncorrected percentages range from a low of 58 percent in 1968 to a high of 74 percent in 1981, but the trend line is still effectively zero.

39. Church attendance is available only in the GSS. Differences between frequent and rare attenders widened significantly only on the issues of premarital sex, homosexuality, and capital punishment, and in the last instance, frequent attenders became increasingly more *opposed* to capital punishment than did rare attenders. Differences narrowed on other topics, notably belief in life after death.

40. One might suspect that the 1960s culture war we document in the survey data is an artifact of polling, the arbitrary result of the kinds of topics that poll-takers of the 1960s and 1970s picked to ask about. But other, clear social changes of the era in law and behavior regarding race, civil liberties, and youth culture reinforce our conclusion.

41. Wuthnow, *Loose Connections*; Rieder, *The Fractious Nation*. It also underlies some late-century writings about the "fragmented self"—the

claim that people develop multiple personas to face the diverse social worlds they encounter (see, for example, Gergen, *The Saturated Self*).

42. The illustrative market segments are from the Claritas website in 2005. By 2006, the Mayberry-ville vehicle of choice was a Chevy Silverado (http://www.claritas.com/MyBestSegments; click on "Segment Look-up"; accessed May 25, 2006). On the sixty-seven types of Americans, see Weiss, *The Clustered World*, 10–11; for quotes, see 25 ("you are like your neighbors") and 10 ("Forget the melting pot"). See also Tharp, *Marketing and Consumer Identity in Multicultural America*; and Goss, "'We Know Who You Are and We Know Where You Live.'"

43. The theoretical literature on lifestyles includes works such as Bourdieu, *Distinction*; Giddens, *Modernity and Self-Identity*; and Featherstone, *Consumer Culture and Postmodernism*. The "cultural tribes" quote is from Katz-Gerro, "Cultural Consumption Research," 11. Examples of empirical research include Katz-Gerro, "Highbrow Cultural Consumption and Class Distinction," and Tomlinson, "Lifestyle and Social Class." On political applications, see Waldman and Green, "Tribal Relations," and Franke-Ruta, "Remapping the Culture Debate."

44. We used relatively crude categories, such as South versus non-South, to facilitate the statistical analysis and presentation of results. We tried more detailed categorizations and then eliminated those categories that did not seem to clearly distinguish or identify clusters. We did not use gender because it did not add information.

45. We ran another LCA analysis using only the attitude items and excluding the demographic background variables and came up with different results: four clusters in the 1970s and seven each in the 1980s and 1990s. However, the results presented here are preferable, in the end, because the clusters they describe are more coherent, stable, and interpretable.

46. Statistical power goes up with sample size, even if the same underlying population generates the data. P-valued tests, such as a likelihood ratio, are sensitive to sample size. However, we used the Bayesian information criterion (BIC) as our test, and it has a sample size correction. Nonetheless, the BIC too is affected by sample size, although the extent to which that is so has yet to be fully explored.

47. Another way to look at this issue is kurtosis (the degree to which the distribution is peaked versus flat) in cluster sizes in each decade: it fell from 3.2 to 1.7 from the 1970s to the 1980s and was 1.9 in the 1990s. Skewness (lack of symmetry) also fell, from .8 to .4 to .1. These estimates reinforce the impression of more even distribution later than earlier.

48. We draw this conclusion from inspection of the clusters and the following statistical exercise. For each cluster, we assembled an array of

scores that formed a "profile": the percentage of the cluster that was white, black, southern, and so on, through the percentage that opposed prayer in the schools, liked small families, and liked large families. (That is, the profiles were the distributions of respondents on each category of each item—minus one category to avoid redundancy.) We then correlated the profiles of each of the nine 1970s clusters with the ten 1990s profiles, the correlation coefficient being our indicator of similarity. The correlations for the pairs of clusters lined up in table 9.1—excepting 1990s cluster X—range from r = .86 (the profile of 1970s cluster I with the profile of the 1990s version of the cluster; 1970s cluster IX's profile with 1990s cluster IX profile) to r = .97 (the 1970s profile of cluster V with its 1990s profile). And the correlations for the pairings as we aligned them in table 9.1 are greater than the correlations of other 1970s profiles with 1990s profiles. The profile of cluster X, found in the 1990s, correlates r = .88 with the profile of 1970s cluster I and r = .87 with 1970s cluster IV.

49.   People in the new 1990s cluster X were clearly liberal on social issues such as abortion and premarital sex, while those in 1990s cluster III were considerably more conservative on these issues and more churchgoing than were people in its 1970s predecessor, suggesting that more liberal, non-attending Americans who would have otherwise been in cluster III appeared instead in 1990s cluster X. Cluster I, like III, also became slightly more conservative and churchgoing between the decades. These and a few similar indicators suggest that the number of Americans who were liberal, suburban, and secular (and also younger and wealthier) and who were subsumed in 1970s clusters I and III were sufficiently numerous by the 1990s to constitute their own cluster. (Recall, from chapter 8, that this is the era when "no religion" replies increased notably in the population. In the 1990s, cluster X was second only to cluster IV in the percentage of those claiming "other" or "no religion," implying that cluster X's emergence may have been part of that process.) While 1990s clusters IV and X were relatively similar to one another, those in cluster X were not as socially liberal as those in IV—for example, cluster X members supported the death penalty—and they were not as likely to self-label as politically liberal (and were much less urban and highly educated), implying that cluster X was not simply made up of cluster IV types but was, as we suggest, partly composed of would-have-been IIIs.

CHAPTER 10

1.   Actually, it was possible in 1990 to detect Italian neighborhoods in the largest metropolitan area, New York, but that concentration was a

shadow of its 1890 character; Alba, Logan, and Crowder, "White Ethnic Neighborhoods and Assimilation."

2. Replacement requires an average of slightly more than two births per woman—one to replace her, one to replace the father, and a few extra births to some women to replace any who die in childhood. The U.S. population has continued to grow despite below-replacement fertility because, on average, people replace themselves fifty or sixty years before they die and because immigration supplements the excess of births over deaths as a factor in population growth.

3. Seniors in 1900 were at substantial risk of poverty. In 1940, the first year that comprehensive income data were available, roughly two of every five seniors were living in poverty, and another two of the five were avoiding poverty by living with relatives in a household with at least one adult breadwinner. By 2000, only one in twelve was poor, and only one in eight was living with relatives. Most seniors today have some private pension income, nearly all have Social Security, and half have significant equity in the home they own. Together these factors added years of self-sufficiency to the lives of retired Americans.

4. Hout et al., "Inequality by Design."

5. Hout and Fischer, "Explaining the Rise of Americans with No Religious Preference."

6. There are very many such studies, but three are illustrative: Borch and Weakliem, "The Growth of Alienation in America"; Easterlin, "Life Cycle Welfare"; and Sampson, and Bartusch, "Legal Cynicism and (Subcultural?) Tolerance of Deviance." The Gallup Organization regularly presents poll results on racial differences in "The Racial Divide" (part of its weekly online bulletin); typically, black respondents give more negative responses than white respondents.

7. A language of "ascribed" and "achieved" status, common in midcentury sociology, captures much of the essence of this shift. We avoid using those terms here, however, because they invoke a kind of social science that seeks out universal laws and empirical regularities that transcend time and space. As our attention to history throughout this volume attests, we are skeptical of that project, in large part because its proponents all too often gloss over important variation and differences.

8. Wilson, *Declining Significance of Race*, 1.

9. We think here of classics like the Lynds' *Middletown*, Warner's *Yankee City* and *Jonesville*, and less well-known offshoots, which made much of discovering that the towns—iconic sites of American democracy—had pecking orders that were recognized, if not openly acknowledged.

10. Borch and Weakliem, "The Growth of Alienation in America."

11. See, for example, our own contribution to those debates: Fischer et al., *Inequality by Design*.

12. See Lucas, "Effectively Maintained Inequality"; Kane, "College-Going and Inequality."
13. Cutler and Miller, "The Role of Public Health Improvements in Health Advances."
14. Hochschild and Scovronick, *The American Dream and the Public Schools*.
15. We draw here from our discussion of higher education in Fischer et al., *Inequality by Design*, 152–55.

APPENDIX A

1. Cleveland, "Robust Locally Weighted Regression"; Cleveland and Devlin, "Locally Weighted Regression."
2. Yatchew, *Semiparametric Regression for the Applied Econometrician*; DiNardo and Tobias, "Nonparametric Density and Regression Estimation."
3. We do not have panel data, so each individual is observed at only one time.
4. Fitting curves instead of lines has a number of advantages, most notably the ability to constrain expected probabilities to the range from 0 to 1. But the inability to impose a simple "parallel lines" constraint for the expected probabilities rules out these popular models for our purposes.
5. Firebaugh and Davis, "Trends in Antiblack Prejudice."

APPENDIX B

1. We thank Sheldon Danziger and Frank Levy for discussing these concerns with us.
2. On household income measures, see U.S. Bureau of the Census, "Historical Income Tables—Income Inequality," table IE-6.
3. The average wage for the high school graduate and the consumer price conversion for 2000 are drawn from the Economic Policy Institute's "Datazone" on its website (http://www.epinet.org/content.cfm/datazone_dznational).
4. We can arithmetically express the change in the eightieth- versus twentieth-percentile differences shown in figure 6.2, left-hand side, and calculate that in 1949 an American at the twentieth percentile (and his or her family) would have had to work an additional 1,300 hours in a production manufacturing job to close the eightieth-minus-twentieth difference. For the twentieth-percentile person to do the same in 2000 would have required roughly 2,400 hours of work. By this measure, inequality widened from 1960 on, with virtually all that widening occurring between 1970 and 1990. These calculations are based on average hourly earnings for all employees in manufacturing. The 1950 to 1970 figures are drawn from annual earnings in manufacturing reported in

U.S. Bureau of the Census, *Historical Statistics of the United States*, 166, divided by 2,000 annual hours. We drew the 1980 through 1998—proxy for 2000—figures from the weekly earnings in manufacturing reported in U.S. Bureau of the Census, *Statistical Abstract of the United States, 2002*, table 682, divided by forty weekly hours. The intermediate estimates are 1960: 1,260; 1970: 1,310; 1980: 1,700; 1990: 2,200.

5. For discussions along these lines, see, for example, Sen, *On Economic Inequality*; Allison, "Measures of Inequality"; and Cowell, "Measurement of Inequality." One dissent is Kelley and Klein, "Revolution and the Rebirth of Inequality," 80, n. 3. Frank Cowell ("Measurement of Inequality," 121–22) considers two different ways of linking income growth to inequality. Under one conception, the same level of inequality would be sustained if parties all received the same absolute increase in income ("translation independence"); under the other conception, it would be sustained if they received the same proportional increase in income ("scale independence"). But Cowell essentially ignores the choice and pursues proportional models.

6. Amiel and Cowell, *Thinking About Inequality*.

7. On declining marginal returns to income, see, for example, Diener, "Individualism and Income"; Argyle, "Causes and Correlates of Happiness"; Frey and Stutzer, *Happiness and Economics*; and Frank, *Luxury Fever*, ch. 5. Key sources on measuring equality seem to take declining returns for granted—for example, Amartya Sen (*On Economic Inequality*, 28) writes: "It is possible to argue that the impact [of a transfer from someone with more money to someone with less] should be greater if the transfer takes place at a lower income level, and a transfer from a person with an income of £1,000 to one with £900 should be greater than a similar transfer from a man with £1,000,100 to one with £1,000,000." On how laypeople judge these matters, see, for example, Jasso, "On the Justice of Earnings"; and Rainwater, *What Money Buys*.

8. In the latter part of chapter 6, when we compare groups by measures of consumption, which are ratios to start with (for example, the proportion who own a car), we use *differences* in ratios rather than ratios of ratios.

APPENDIX C

1. A notable exception is the number and exclusivity of cultural clusters for racial minorities. Under certain combinations of questions and codings, the urban black cluster identified in the 1970s disappeared in the 1980s and reappeared in the 1990s. Furthermore, a distinct Latino cluster appeared in the 1980s, only to merge back into a relatively liberal Catholic cluster in the 1990s. We attribute this sensitivity to the small sample sizes for racial minorities.

2. An alternative we considered was to somehow estimate missing data. But any such procedure would build in associations between variables.

3. Answers to the question asking whether the courts are too harsh or lenient (COURTS) were highly associated with views on capital punishment (CAPPUN), and including or excluding COURTS did not change the classifications. Favoring or opposing gun permits (GUNLAW) did not discriminate between classes; its distribution tended to be similar across classes. Respondents' occupations (OCC) were redundant with education and income. COURTS, GUNLAW, and OCC were dropped from the analysis.

4. Magidson and Vermunt, "Latent Class Models for Clustering."

5. McCutcheon, "Basic Concepts and Procedures in Single and Multiple Group Latent Class Analysis," 58–61.

6. Magidson and Vermunt, "Technical Appendix for Latent Gold 3.0," 5.

7. Ibid., 5, 11–12.

8. Raftery, "Bayesian Model Selection."

REFERENCES

Abbott, Andrew. 1991. *The System of the Professions*. Chicago: University of Chicago Press.

Abma, J., A. Chandra, W. Mosher, L. Peterson, and L. Piccinino. 1997. "Fertility, Family Planning, and Women's Health." National Center for Health Statistics. *Vital Health Statistics* 23(19).

Adams, Greg D. 1997. "Abortion: Evidence of An Issues Evolution." *American Journal of Political Science* 3(July): 718–37.

Advocates for Youth. 2002. "Adolescent Sexual Behavior" (November). Available at: http://www.advocatesforyouth.org/publications/factsheet/fsbehdem.htm.

Alba, Richard D., John R. Logan, and Kyle Crowder. 1997. "White Ethnic Neighborhoods and Assimilation: The Greater New York Region, 1980–1990." *Social Forces* 75(March): 883–912.

Alba, Richard, John Logan, Wenquan Zhang, and Brian J. Stults. 1999. "Strangers Next Door: Immigrant Groups and Suburbs in Los Angeles and New York." In *A Nation Divided: Diversity, Inequality, and Community in American Society*, edited by Phyllis Moen, Donna Dempster-McClain, and Henry A. Walker. Ithaca, N.Y.: Cornell University Press.

Allen, Frederick Lewis. 1931. *Only Yesterday: An Informal History of the Nineteen-Twenties*. New York: Harper & Bros.

Allison, Paul. 1978. "Measures of Inequality." *American Sociological Review* 43(December): 865–80.

Alwin, Duane F. 1996. "Coresidence Beliefs in American Society, 1973 to 1991." *Journal of Marriage and the Family* 58(May): 393–403.

———. 2002. "Generations X, Y, and Z: Are They Really Changing America?" *Contexts* 1(Winter): 42–49.

American Sociological Association. 2003. *The Importance of Collecting Data and Doing Social Scientific Research on Race*. Washington, D.C.: American Sociological Association.

Amiel, Yoram, and Frank A. Cowell. 1999. *Thinking About Inequality: Personal Judgments and Income Distributions*. Cambridge: Cambridge University Press.

Anderson, Margo J. 1988. *The American Census: A Social History*. New Haven, Conn.: Yale University Press.

Anderson, Margo J., and Stephen E. Fienberg. 1999. *Who Counts? The Politics of Census-Taking in Contemporary America*. New York: Russell Sage Foundation.

Anderson, Michael. 1975. "Family, Household, and the Industrial Revolution." In *The American Family in Historical Perspective*, edited by Michael Gordon. New York: St. Martin's Press.

Argyle, Michael. 1999. "Causes and Correlates of Happiness." In *Well-being: The Foundations of Hedonic Psychology*, edited by Daniel Kahneman, Ed Diener, and Norberto Schwartz. New York: Russell Sage Foundation.

Arias, Elizabeth. 2004. "United States Life Tables, 2002." *National Vital Statistics Reports* 53(6). Hyattsville, Md.: National Center for Health Statistics.

Astin, Alexander W. 1998. "The Changing American College Student: Thirty-Year Trends, 1966-1996." *The Review of Higher Education* 21 (Winter): 115–35.

Atkinson, Anthony B., Lee Rainwater, and Timothy Smeeding. 1995. *Income Distributions in OECD Countries: Evidence from the Luxembourg Income Study*. Washington, D.C.: OECD Publications and Information Center

Axinn, William, and Arland Thornton. 2000. "The Transformation in the Meaning of Marriage." In *The Ties That Bind: Perspectives on Marriage and Cohabitation*, edited by Linda J. Waite. New York: Aldine de Gruyter.

Bachu, Amara. 1998. "Trends in Marital Status of U.S. Women at First Birth: 1930 to 1994." *Current Population Reports*, special studies P23-19. Washington: U.S. Bureau of the Census.

Bachu, Amara, and Martin O'Connell. 2001. "Fertility of American Women: June 2000." *Current Population Reports*, P20-543RV. Washington: U.S. Bureau of the Census.

Bahr, Howard M., Colter Mitchell, Xiaomin Li, Alison Walker, and Kristen Sucher. 2004. "Trends in Family Space/Time, Conflict, and Solidarity: Middletown 1924–1999." *City and Community* 3(September): 263–91.

Baker, Paula. 1991. *The Moral Frameworks of Public Life: Gender, Politics, and the State in Rural New York, 1870–1930*. New York: Oxford University Press.

Baker, Wayne. 2005. *America's Crisis of Values: Reality and Perception*. Princeton, N.J.: Princeton University Press.

Barkan, Elliott R. 2003. "Return of the Nativists? California Public Opinion and Immigration in the 1980s and 1990s." *Social Science History* 27(Summer): 229–83.

Barron, Hal S. 1997. *Mixed Harvest: The Second Great Transformation in the*

Rural North, 1870–1930. Chapel Hill: University of North Carolina Press.

Bauman, Kurt J. 1999. "Extended Measures of Well-being: Meeting Basic Needs." *Current Population Reports* P70-67 (June). Washington: U.S. Bureau of the Census.

Bean, Frank D., Jennifer Lee, Jeanne Batalova, and Mark Leach. 2005. "Immigration and Fading Color Lines in America." In *The American People: Census 2000*, edited by Reynolds Farley and John Haaga. New York: Russell Sage Foundation.

Becker, Gary. 1975. *Human Capital: Second Edition*. New York: National Bureau of Economic Research.

Beckfield, Jason. 2004. "Does Inequality Harm Health? New Cross-National Evidence." *Journal of Health and Social Behavior* 45(September): 231–48.

Bell, Daniel. 1960. *The End of Ideology: On the Exhaustion of Political Ideas in the Fifties*. Glencoe, Ill.: Free Press.

Beller, Emily, and Michael Hout. 2006. "Intergenerational Social Mobility: The United States in Comparative Perspective." *Future of Children* 16(Fall): 1–18.

Bender, Thomas. 1988. "New York in Theory." In *America in Theory*, edited by Leslie Berlowitz, Denis Donoghue, and Louis Menand. New York: Oxford University Press.

Bennett, Neil G., David E. Bloom, and Patricia H. Craig. 1989. "The Divergence of African-American and White Marriage Patterns." *American Journal of Sociology* 95(November): 629–722.

Berube, Alan, and Benjamin Foreman. 2003. "Racial Change in the Nation's Largest Cities: Evidence from the 2000 Census." In *Redefining Urban and Suburban America*, vol. 1, edited by Bruce Katz and Robert E. Lang. Washington, D.C.: Brookings Institution Press.

Bianchi, Suzanne M., Melissa A. Milkie, Liana C. Sayer, and John P. Robinson. 2000. "Is Anyone Doing the Housework? Trends in the Gender Division of Household Labor." *Social Forces* 79(September): 191–228.

Biblarz, Timothy J., and Adrian E. Raftery. 1999. "Family Structure, Educational Attainment, and Socioeconomic Success: Rethinking the 'Pathology of Matriarchy.'" *American Journal of Sociology* 105(2, September): 321–65.

Binford, Henry C. 1985. *The First Suburbs: Residential Communities on the Boston Periphery 1815–1860*. Chicago: University of Chicago Press.

Birch, Eugenie L. 2006. "Who Lives Downtown." Living Cities Census Series. Washington, D.C.: Brookings Institution (November).

Bishop, George. 1999. "Americans' Belief in God." *Public Opinion Quarterly* 63: 421–34.

Blakely, Edward J., and Mary Gail Snyder. 1997. *Fortress America: Gated Communities in the United States.* Washington, D.C.: Brookings Institution Press.

Blau, Peter M., and Otis Dudley Duncan. 1967. *The American Occupational Structure.* New York: Wiley.

Bleakley, Hoyt. 2003. "Language Skills and Earnings: Evidence from Childhood Immigrants." Center for Comparative Immigration Studies working paper 87. San Diego: University of California at San Diego.

Bluestone, Barry, and Bennett Harrison. 1982. *The Deindustrialization of America: Plant Closings, Community Abandonment, and the Dismantling of Basic Industry.* New York: Basic Books.

Bogue, Donald. 1953. "Population Growth in Standard Metropolitan Areas 1900–1950, with an Exploratory Analysis of Urbanized Areas." Washington: U.S. Government Printing Office for the Housing and Home Finance Agency.

Bolce, Louis, and Gerald de Majo. 1999. "The Anti-Christian Fundamentalist Factor in Contemporary Politics." *Public Opinion Quarterly* 63(Winter): 508–42.

Bolzendahl, Catherine, and Clem Brooks. 2005. "Polarization, Secularization, or Differences as Usual? The Denominational Cleavage in U.S. Social Attitudes Since the 1970s." *Sociological Quarterly* 46(1): 47–78.

Borch, Casey A., and David L. Weakliem. 2003. "The Growth of Alienation in America, 1966–2000." Unpublished paper. University of Connecticut.

Borjas, George. 1999. *Heaven's Door: Immigration Policy and the American Economy.* Princeton, N.J.: Princeton University Press.

Bourdieu, Pierre. 1984. *Distinction: A Social Critique of the Judgment of Taste.* Translated by Richard Nice. Cambridge, Mass.: Harvard University Press.

Bowles, Samuel, and Herbert Gintis. 1976. *Schooling in Capitalist America: Educational Reforms and the Contradictions of Economic Life.* New York: Basic Books.

Bradbury, Katherine, and Jane Katz. 2002. "Issues in Economics: Are Lifetime Incomes Growing More Unequal?" *Regional Review* (Federal Reserve Bank of Boston) Q4: 3–5.

Bramlett, Matthew D., and William D. Mosher. 2002. "Cohabitation, Marriage, Divorce, and Remarriage in the United States." *Vital Health Statistics* 23(22). Hyattsville, Md.: National Center for Health Statistics.

Brewer, Paul R., and Clyde Wilcox. 2005. "Trends: Same-Sex Marriage and Civil Unions." *Public Opinion Quarterly* 69(Winter): 599–616.

Brewster, Karin L., and Irene Padavic. 2000. "Change in Gender Ideology, 1977–1996: The Contributions of Intracohort Change and Population Turnover." *Journal of Marriage and the Family* 62(May): 477–87.

Briffault, Richard. 1990. "Our Localism: Part 2: Localism and Legal Theory." *Columbia Law Review* 90(March): 346–454.

Brittingham, Angela, and G. Patricia de la Cruz. 2004. "Ancestry: 2000." Census 2000 Brief (June). U.S. Bureau of the Census. Washington: U.S. Government Printing Office. Available at: http://www.census.gov/prod/2004pubs/c2kbr-35.pdf.

Brody, David. 1960. *Steelworkers in America: The Nonunion Era*. Cambridge, Mass.: Harvard University Press.

Brooks, Clem, and Catherine Bolzendahl. 2004. "The Transformation of U.S. Gender Role Attitudes: Cohort Replacement, Social-Structural Change, and Ideological Learning." *Social Science Research* 33(March): 106–30.

Brooks, Clem, and Jeff Manza. 2004. "A Great Divide: Religion and Political Change in U.S. National Elections, 1972–2000." *Sociological Quarterly* 45(3): 421–50.

Brooks, David S. 2002a. "Superiority Complex." *Atlantic Monthly* (November): 32.

———. 2002b. "One Nation, Slightly Divisible." *Atlantic Monthly* (December): 53–65.

Brown, Claire. 1994. *American Standards of Living, 1918–1988*. Cambridge, Mass.: Blackwell.

Bryce, Viscount James Bryce. 1995. *The American Commonwealth*, vol. 2. Indianapolis, Ind.: Liberty Fund. (Orig. pub. in 1888.)

Buchanan, Patrick J. 1992. "Republican National Convention Speech" (August 17). Available at: http://www.buchanan.org/pa-92-0817-rnc.html (accessed December 22, 2003).

———. 1999. "Why We Can't Quit the Culture War" (February 19). Available at: http://www.buchanan.org/pa-99-0219.html (accessed December 22, 2003).

Buchman, Marlis. 1989. *The Script of Life in Modern Society*. Chicago: University of Chicago Press.

Bumpass, Larry, and Hsien-Hen Lu. 2000. "Trends in Cohabitation and Implications for Children's Family Contexts in the United States." *Population Studies* 54(March): 29–41.

Burr, Jeffrey A., and Jan E. Mutchler. 1999. "Race and Ethnic Variation in Norms of Filial Responsibility Among Older Persons." *Journal of Marriage and the Family* 61(August): 674–87.

Burtless, Gary, and Christopher Jencks. 2003. "American Inequality and Its Consequences." Luxembourg Income Study Working Paper Series, working paper 339. Syracuse, N.Y.: Syracuse University, Maxwell School of Citizenship and Public Affairs.

Butler, Jon. 1979. "Magic, Astrology, and the Early American Religious Heritage, 1600–1760." *American Historical Review* 84(April): 317–46.

———. 1990. *Awash in a Sea of Faith: Christianizing the American People*. Cambridge, Mass.: Harvard University Press.

———. 1997. "Protestant Success in the New American City, 1870–1920." In *New Directions in American Religious History*, edited by Harry S. Stout and D. G. Hart. New York: Oxford University Press.

———. 2000. *Becoming America: The Revolution Before 1776*. Cambridge, Mass.: Harvard University Press.

Cain, Glen. 1966. *Married Women in the Labor Force*. Chicago: University of Chicago Press.

Campbell, John L., and Michael Patrick Allen. 2001. "Identifying Shifts in Policy Regimes: Cluster and Interrupted Time-Series Analyses of U.S. Income Taxes." *Social Science History* 25(Summer): 187–216.

Caplow, Theodore. 1985. "Contrasting Trends in European and American Religion." *Sociological Analysis* 46(Summer): 101–8.

Caplow, Theodore, and Howard M. Bahr. 1979. "Half a Century of Change in Adolescent Attitudes: Replication of a Middletown Survey by the Lynds." *Public Opinion Quarterly* 43(Spring): 1–17.

Caplow, Theodore, Howard M. Bahr, Bruce A. Chadwick, Rueben Hill, and Margaret Holmes Williamson. 1982. *Middletown Families: Fifty Years of Change and Continuity*. Minneapolis: University of Minnesota Press.

Caplow, Theodore, Howard M. Bahr, Bruce A. Chadwick, and Dwight W. Hoover. 1983. *All Faithful People: Change and Continuity in Middletown's Religion*. Minneapolis: University of Minnesota Press.

Caplow, Theodore, Louis Hicks, and Ben J. Wattenberg. 2001. *The First Measured Century*. Washington, D.C.: American Enterprise Institute.

Card, David, and John E. DiNardo. 2002. "Skill-Biased Technological Change and Rising Wage Inequality: Some Problems and Puzzles." Working paper 8769. Cambridge, Mass.: National Bureau of Economic Research.

Card, David, and Alan B. Krueger. 1995. *Myth and Measurement: The New Economics of the Minimum Wage*. Princeton, N.J.: Princeton University Press.

Carson, Brad. 2004. "Vote Righteously!" *The New Republic* 22(November 22): 34.

Carter, Susan B. 1988. "The Changing Importance of Lifetime Jobs, 1892–1978." *Industrial Relations* 27(Fall): 287–300.

Casper, Lynne M., Philip N. Cohen, and Tavia Simmons. 1999. "How Does POSSLQ Measure Up? Historical Estimates of Cohabitation." Population Division working paper 36. Washington: U.S. Bureau of the Census (May).

Castles, Stephen, and Mark J. Miller. 2003. *The Age of Migration: International Population Movements in the Modern World*. New York: Guilford Press. (Orig. pub. in 1993.)

Charles, Camille Zubrinsky. 2003. "The Dynamics of Racial Residential Segregation." *Annual Review of Sociology* 29: 167–207.

Chaves, Mark. 1999. "Religious Congregations and Welfare Reform." *American Sociological Review* 64(December): 836–46.

Cherlin, Andrew J. 1992. *Marriage, Divorce, Remarriage*, rev. ed. Cambridge, Mass.: Harvard University Press.

Cherlin, Andrew J., and Frank F. Furstenberg Jr. 1994. "Stepfamilies in the United States: A Reconsideration." *Annual Review of Sociology* 20: 359–81.

Chevan, Albert. 1989. "The Growth of Home Ownership: 1940–1980." *Demography* 26(May): 249–66.

Chevan, Albert, and Randall Stokes. 2000. "Growth in Family Income Inequality, 1979–1990: Industrial Restructuring and Demographic Change." *Demography* 36(August): 365–80.

Chudacoff, Howard. 1989. *How Old Are You? Age Consciousness in American Culture*. Princeton, N.J.: Princeton University Press.

Church, Robert L. 1993. "Collegiate Education." In *Encyclopedia of American Social History*, vol. 3, edited by Mary Kupiec Cayton, Elliott J. Gorn, and Peter W. Williams. New York: Scribner's.

Citro, Constance F., Daniel L. Cork, and Janet L. Norwood, eds. 2001. *The 2000 Census: Interim Assessment*. Washington, D.C.: National Academy Press for the National Research Council, Committee on National Statistics, Panel to Review the 2000 Census.

Cleveland, William S. 1979. "Robust Locally Weighted Regression and Smoothing Scatterplots." *Journal of the American Statistical Association* 74(December): 829–36.

————. 1984. *Elements of Graphing Data*. Summit, N.J.: Hobart Press.

Cleveland, William S., and Susan J. Devlin. 1988. "Locally Weighted Regression: An Approach to Regression Analysis by Local Fitting." *Journal of the American Statistical Association* 83(September): 596–610.

Cohen, Lizabeth. 2003. *A Consumer's Republic: The Politics of Consumption in Postwar America*. New York: Alfred A. Knopf.

Collins, William J., and Robert A. Margo. 2001. "Race and Home Ownership: A Century-Long View." *Explorations in Economic History* 38(January): 68–92.

Conley, Dalton. 1999. *Being Black, Living in the Red: Race, Wealth, and Social Policy in America*. Berkeley: University of California Press.

————. 2001. "Capital for College: Parental Assets and Postsecondary Schooling." *Sociology of Education* 74(January): 59–72.

Cookingham, Mary E. 1984. "Working After Childbearing in Modern America." *Journal of Interdisciplinary History* 14(Spring): 773–92.

Coontz, Stephanie. 1992. *The Way We Never Were: American Families and the Nostalgia Trap*. New York: Basic Books.

Costa, Dora. 1999. "American Living Standards: Evidence from Recreational Expenditures." Working paper 7148. Cambridge, Mass.: National Bureau of Economic Research.

————. 2000. "The Wage and the Length of the Workday." *Journal of Labor Economics* 18(January): 156–68.

————. 2001. *The Evolution of Retirement*. Chicago: University of Chicago Press.

Costa, Dora L., and Matthew E. Kahn. 2003. "Civic Engagement and Community Heterogeneity: An Economist's Perspective." *Perspectives on Politics* 1(March): 103–11.

Cott, Nancy F. 2000. *Public Vows: A History of Marriage and the Nation*. Cambridge, Mass.: Harvard University Press.

Cowan, Ruth Schwartz. 1983. *More Work for Mother*. New York: Basic Books.

Cowell, Frank A. 2000. "Measurement of Inequality." In *Handbook of Income Distribution*, vol. 1, edited by Anthony B. Atkinson and Francois Bourguignon. New York: Elsevier.

Cox, W. Michael, and Richard Alm. 1997. "Time Well Spent: The Declining Real Cost of Living in America." Annual Report of the Federal Reserve Bank of Dallas. Dallas: Federal Reserve.

————. 1999. *Myths of Rich and Poor: Why We're Better Off Than We Think*. New York: Basic Books.

Cutler, David M. 2001. "The Economics of Better Health." Paper presented to the Bay Area Colloquium on Population. Berkeley, Calif. (April).

Cutler, David M., Edward L. Glaeser, and Jacob L. Vigdor. 1999. "The Rise and Decline of the American Ghetto." *Journal of Political Economy* 107(3): 455–506.

Cutler, David M., and Lawrence F. Katz. 1992. "Rising Inequality? Changes in the Distribution of Income and Consumption in the 1980s." *American Economic Review* 82(May): 546–51.

Cutler, David M., and Grant Miller. 2005. "The Role of Public Health Improvements in Health Advances: The Twentieth-Century United States." *Demography* 42(February): 1–22.

Danziger, Sheldon, and Peter Gottschalk, eds. 1994. *Uneven Tides: Rising Inequality in America*. New York: Russell Sage Foundation.

————. 1995. *America Unequal*. Cambridge, Mass.: Harvard University Press.

Darden, Joseph, Linda Jones, and Julianne Price. 1998. "Ethnographic Evaluation of the Behavioral Causes of Undercount in a Black Ghetto of Flint, Michigan." Ethnographic Evaluation of the 1990 Decennial Census, report 24. Washington: U.S. Bureau of the Census, Statistical Research Division. Available at: http://www.census.gov/srd/papers/pdf/ev92-94.pdf, accessed May 25, 2006.

Davies, James B., and Anthony F. Shorroks. 2000. "The Distribution of Wealth." In *Handbook of Income Distribution*, vol. 1, edited by Anthony B. Atkinson and Francois Bourguignon. New York: Elsevier.

Davis, James A. 1982. "Achievement Variables and Class Cultures: Family, Schooling, Job, and Forty-nine Dependent Variables in the Cumulative GSS." *American Sociological Review* 47(October): 569–86.

————. 1996. "Patterns of Attitude Change in the USA: 1972–1994." In *Understanding Change in Social Attitudes*, edited by Bridget Taylor and Katarina Thomson. Aldershot, Eng: Dartmouth.

————. 2003. "Age, Birth Cohort, Monotony, and Sex Frequency Among U.S. Adults." Unpublished paper. University of Chicago, National Opinion Research Center.

Day, Jennifer Cheeseman, and Eric C. Newburger. 2002. "The Big Payoff: Educational Attainment and Synthetic Estimates of Work-Life Earnings." *Current Population Reports* P23-210 (July). Washington: U.S. Bureau of the Census.

DeNavas, Carmen, and Robert I. Cleveland. 2001. "Money Income in the United States: 2000." *Current Population Reports* P60-213 (September). Washington: U.S. Bureau of the Census.

Denton, Nancy A. 2001. "Housing as a Means of Asset Accumulation: A Good Strategy for the Poor?" In *Assets for the Poor*, edited by Thomas M. Shapiro and Edward N. Wolff. New York: Russell Sage Foundation.

Dickens, William T. 2003. "Comments [on Massey and Fischer]." *Brookings-Wharton Papers in Urban Affairs* 2003: 30–38.

Diener, Ed. 1994. "Individualism and Income as Correlates of Subjective Well-being Across Cultures." Paper presented to the International Sociological Association, Bielefeld, Germany (July).

Dimaggio, Paul. 2003. "The Myth of Culture War: The Disparity Between Private Opinion and Public Policies." In *The Fractious Nation: Unity and Division in Contemporary American Life*, edited by Jonathan Rieder. Berkeley: University of California Press.

Dimaggio, Paul, John Evans, and Bethany Bryson. 1996. "Have Americans' Social Attitudes Become More Polarized?" *American Journal of Sociology* 102(November): 690–755.

DiNardo, John E., Nicole Fortin, and Thomas Lemieux. 1996. "Labor Market Institutions and the Distribution of Wages, 1973–1992: A Semi-Parametric Approach." *Econometrica* 64(September): 1001–44.

DiNardo, John, and Justin L. Tobias. 2001. "Nonparametric Density and Regression Estimation." *Journal of Economic Perspectives* 15(Autumn): 11–28.

DiPrete, Thomas A., and Claudia Buchmann. 2006. "Gender-Specific Trends in the Value of Education and the Emerging Gender Gap in College Completion." *Demography* 43(February): 1–24.

Dolan, Jay P. 1992. *The American Catholic Experience from Colonial Times to the Present*. South Bend, Ind.: University of Notre Dame Press.

Donaldson, Scott. 1969. *The Suburban Myth*. New York: Columbia University Press.

Douglas, Mary, and Baron Isherwood. 1996. *The World of Goods: Towards an Anthropology of Consumption*. London: Routledge. (Orig. pub. in 1979.)

Doyle, Don Harrison. 1983. *The Social Order of a Frontier Community: Jacksonville, Illinois, 1825–1870*. Urbana: University of Illinois Press.

DQNews.com. 2002. "Bay Area Home Sales Down, Prices Up in December" (January 24). Available at: http://www.dqnews.com/RRBay0102 .shtm (accessed December 13, 2004).

Duncan, Greg J., and Ken R. Smith. 1989. "The Rising Affluence of the Elderly: How Far, How Fair, How Frail?" *Annual Review of Sociology* 15: 261–89.

Duncan, Otis Dudley. 2003. "Facile Reporting: The Supposed Decline in Biblical Literalism." *Public Perspectives* (May–June): 40–43.

Easterlin, Richard A. 1961. "Regional Income Trends." In *American Economic History*, edited by Seymour E. Harris. New York: McGraw-Hill.

———. 2001. "Life Cycle Welfare: Trends and Differences." *Journal of Happiness Studies* 2(1): 1–12.

Economist. 2005. "Ever Higher Society, Ever Harder to Ascend." Special Report: Meritocracy in America. U.S. Edition. January 1.

Edin, Kathryn, and Maria Kefalas. 2005. *Promises I Can Keep: Why Poor Women Put Motherhood Before Marriage*. Berkeley: University of California Press.

Edin, Kathryn, and Laura Lein. 1997. *Making Ends Meet: How Single Mothers Survive Welfare and Low-Wage Work*. New York: Russell Sage Foundation.

Edmonston, Barry, and Charles Schultze, eds. 1995. *Modernizing the U.S. Census*. Washington, D.C.: National Academy Press for the National Research Council, Commission on Behavioral Sciences and Education.

Edsall, Thomas Byrne. 2003. "Blue Movie: The Morality Gap Is Becoming the Key Variable in American Politics." *Atlantic Monthly* (January): 36–37.

Elman, Cheryl. 1996. "Old Age, Economic Activity, and Living Arrangements in Early Twentieth-Century United States." *Social Science History* 20(Fall): 439–68.

———. 1998. "Intergenerational Household Structure and Economic Change at the Turn of the Twentieth Century." *Journal of Family History* 23: 417–40.

Erikson, Robert, and John H. Goldthorpe. 2002. "Intergenerational Inequality: A Sociological Perspective." *Journal of Economic Perspectives* 16(Summer): 31–45.

Evans, John H. 1997. "Worldviews or Social Groups as the Source of Moral Value Attitudes: Implications for the Culture Wars Thesis." *Sociological Forum* 12(3): 371–404.

———. 2003. "Have Americans' Attitudes Become More Polarized? An Update." *Social Science Quarterly* 84(March): 71–90.

Fantasia, Rick, and Kim Voss. 2004. *Hard Work: Remaking the American Labor Movement*. Berkeley: University of California Press.

Farley, Reynolds. 1996. *The New American Reality: Who We Are, How We Got Here, Where We Are Going*. New York: Russell Sage Foundation.

————. 2002. "Racial Identities in 2000: The Response to the Multiple-Race Response Option." In *The New Race Question: How the Census Counts Multiracial Individuals*, edited by Joel Perlmann and Mary C. Waters. New York: Russell Sage Foundation.

Featherman, David L., and Robert M. Hauser. 1978. *Opportunity and Change*. New York: Academic Press.

Featherstone, Mike. 1991. *Consumer Culture and Postmodernism*. Newbury Park, Calif.: Sage Publications.

Federman, Maya, Thesia I. Garner, Kathleen Short, W. Bowman Cutter IV, John Kiely, David Levine, Duane McDough, and Marilyn McMillen. 1996. "What Does It Mean to Be Poor in America?" *Monthly Labor Review* 119(May): 3–17.

Feingold, Henry L. 1992. *A Time for Searching: Entering the Mainstream, 1920–1945*. Baltimore: Johns Hopkins University Press.

Fernandez, Roberto. 2001. "Skill-Biased Technological Change and Wage Inequality: Evidence from a Plant Retooling." *American Journal of Sociology* 107(September): 273–320.

Fields, Jason. 2003. "Children's Living Arrangements and Characteristics: March 2002." *Current Population Reports*, P20–547. Washington: U.S. Bureau of the Census.

Finke, Roger, and Rodney Stark. 1992. *The Churching of America, 1776–1990: Winners and Losers in Our Religious Economy*. New Brunswick, N.J.: Rutgers University Press.

Fiorina, Morris P. 2005. *Culture War? The Myth of a Polarized America*. New York: Pearson Longman.

Firebaugh, Glenn, and Kenneth E. Davis, 1988. "Trends in Antiblack Prejudice, 1972–1984: Region and Cohort Effects." *American Journal of Sociology* 94(September): 251–72.

Fischer, Claude S. 1978. "Urban-to-Rural Diffusion of Opinions in Contemporary America." *American Journal of Sociology* 84(July): 151–59.

————. 1980. "The Spread of Violent Crime from City to Countryside, 1955 to 1975." *Rural Sociology* 45(Fall): 416–34.

————. 1984. *The Urban Experience*, 2nd ed. San Diego: Harcourt Brace World.

————. 1992. *America Calling: A Social History of the Telephone to 1940*. Berkeley: University of California Press.

————. 2002. "Ever More Rooted Americans." *City and Community* 1(June): 175–94.

Fischer, Claude S., Michael Hout, Martin Sanchez Jankowski, Samuel R. Lucas, Ann Swidler, and Kim Voss. 1996. *Inequality by Design: Cracking the Bell Curve Myth*. Princeton, N.J.: Princeton University Press.

Fischer, Claude S., and Susan Phillips. 1982. "Who Is Alone?: Social Characteristics of People with Small Networks." In *Loneliness: A Sourcebook of Cur-*

rent Theory, Research, and Therapy, edited by Letitia Anne Peplau and Daniel Perlman. New York: Wiley.

Fischer, Claude S., Gretchen Stockmayer [Donehower], Jon Stiles, and Michael Hout. 2004. "Distinguishing the Levels and Dimensions of U.S. Metropolitan Segregation, 1960–2000." *Demography* 41(February): 37–59.

Fitch, Catherine, Ron Goeken, and Steven Ruggles. 2005. "The Rise of Cohabitation in the United States: New Historical Estimates." Working paper 2005-03. Minneapolis: University of Minnesota, Minnesota Population Center (March).

Fitch, Catherine A., and Steven Ruggles. 2000. "Historical Trends in Marriage Formation: The United States 1850–1990." In *The Ties That Bind: Perspectives on Marriage and Cohabitation*, edited by Linda J. Waite. New York: Aldine de Gruyter.

Fix, Michael, and Jeffrey S. Passel. 2001. "U.S. Immigration at the Beginning of the Twenty-first Century: Testimony Before the Committee on the Judiciary, U.S. House of Representatives" (August 2, 2001). Washington, D.C.: Urban Institute.

Fligstein, Neil. 2001. *The Architecture of Markets: An Economic Sociology of Twenty-first-Century Capitalist Societies*. Princeton, N.J.: Princeton University Press.

Fligstein, Neil, and Ofer Sharone. 2002. "Work in the Post-industrial Economy in California." Social Inequality Working Paper. New York: Russell Sage Foundation.

Fligstein, Neil, and Taekjin Shin. 2004. "The Shareholder Value Society." In *Social Inequality*, edited by Kathryn Neckerman. New York: Russell Sage Foundation.

Fogel, Robert William. 2000. *The Fourth Great Awakening & The Future of Egalitarianism*. Chicago: University of Chicago Press.

Folbre, Nancy. 1993. "Women's Informal Market Work in Massachusetts, 1875–1920." *Social Science History* 17(Spring): 135–60.

Frank, Robert H. 1999. *Luxury Fever: Why Money Fails to Satisfy in an Era of Excess*. New York: Free Press.

Frank, Robert L., and Phillip J. Cook. 1995. *The Winner-Take-All Society: Why the Few at the Top Get So Much More than the Rest of Us*. New York: Penguin.

Franke-Ruta, Garance. 2006. "Remapping the Culture Debate." *The American Prospect* 17(February): 38–44.

Fredrickson, George M. 1981. *White Supremacy: A Comparative Study in American and South African History*. New York: Oxford University Press.

———. 2002. *Racism: A Short History*. Princeton, N.J.: Princeton University Press.

Frey, Bruno S., and Alois Stutzer. 2002. *Happiness and Economics: How the Economy and Institutions Affect Well-being*. Princeton, N.J.: Princeton University Press.

Frey, William. 2001. "Melting Pot Suburbs: A Study of Suburban Diversity." In *Redefining Urban and Suburban America: Evidence from Census 2000*, vol. 1, edited by Bruce Katz and Robert E. Lang. Washington, D.C.: Brookings Institution Press.

Frey, William H., and Francis E. Kobrin. 1982. "Changing Families and Changing Mobility: Their Impact on the Central City." *Demography* 19(August): 261–77.

Friedberg, Leora. 1998. "Did Unilateral Divorce Raise Divorce Rates? Evidence from Panel Data." *American Economic Review* 88(June): 608–27.

Fromm, Erich. 1964. *Escape from Freedom*. New York: Holt, Rinehart and Winston. (Orig. pub. in 1941.)

Furstenberg, Frank F., Jr. 1999. "Family Change and Family Diversity." In *Diversity and Its Discontents*, edited by Neil J. Smelser and Jeffrey C. Alexander. Princeton, N.J.: Princeton University Press.

Furstenberg, Frank F., Sheela Kennedy, Vonnie C. Mcloyd, Rubén G. Rumbaut, and Richard A. Settersten Jr. 2004. "Growing Up Is Harder to Do." *Contexts* 3(Summer): 33–41.

Gabin, Nancy F. 1993. "Women and Work." In *Encyclopedia of American Social History*, vol. 2, edited by Mary Kupiec Cayton, Elliott J. Gorn, and Peter W. Williams. New York: Scribner's.

Galambos, Louis. 1983. "Technology, Political Economy, and Professionalization: Central Themes of the Organizational Synthesis." *Business History Review* 57(Winter): 471–93.

Gans, Herbert J. 1967. *The Levittowners: Ways of Life and Politics in a New Suburban Community*. New York: Pantheon Books.

———. 1988. *Middle American Individualism: The Future of Liberal Democracy*. New York: Free Press.

———. 1999. "The Possibility of a New Racial Hierarchy in the Twenty-first-Century United States." In *The Cultural Territories of Race: Black and White Boundaries*, edited by Michele Lamont. Chicago: University of Chicago Press.

Ganzeboom, Harry B. G., Donald J. Treiman, and Wout C. Ultee. 1991. "Comparative Intergenerational Stratification Research." *Annual Review of Sociology* 17: 277–302.

Gardner, Todd Kelly. 1998. "The Metropolitan Fringe: Suburbanization in the United States Before World War II." PhD diss., University of Minnesota. Available to subscribers at: http://www.lib.umi.com/dissertations/fullcit/9826827.

———. 2001. "The Slow Wave: The Changing Residential Status of Cities and Suburbs in the United States, 1850–1940." *Journal of Urban History* 27(March): 293–312.

General Accounting Office. 2004. *Census 2000: Design Choices Contributed to Inaccuracy of Coverage Evaluation Estimates*. GAO-05-71. Washington: U.S. Government Printing Office.

Gergen, Kenneth J. 2000. *The Saturated Self: Dilemmas of Identity in Contemporary Life*. New York: Basic Books. (Orig. pub. in 1991.)

Gerson, Kathleen. 1985. *Hard Choices: How Women Decide About Work, Career, and Motherhood*. Berkeley: University of California Press.

Gibson, Campbell, and Kay Jung. 2005. "Historical Census Statistics on Population Totals by Race, 1790 to 1990, and by Hispanic Origin, 1970 to 1990, for Large Cities and Other Urban Places in the United States." Population Division working paper 76. Washington: U.S. Bureau of the Census (February).

Gibson, Christina, Kathryn Edin, and Sara McLanahan. 2003. "High Hopes but Even Higher Expectations: The Retreat from Marriage Among Low-Income Couples." Working paper 03-06-FF. Princeton, N.J.: Princeton University, Center for Research on Child Well-being (June).

Giddens, Anthony. 1991. *Modernity and Self-Identity: Self and Society in the Late Modern Age*. Palo Alto, Calif.: Stanford University Press.

Glazer, Nathan. 1997. *We Are All Multiculturalists Now*. Cambridge, Mass.: Harvard University Press.

Glenn, Norval D. 1974. "Recent Trends in Intercategory Differences in Attitudes in the United States." *Social Forces* (March): 395–401.

———. 1990. "Review of Greeley, *Religious Change in America*." *Public Opinion Quarterly* 54(Fall): 444–47.

Glenn, Susan A. 1990. *Daughters of the Shtetl: Life and Labor in the Immigrant Generation*. Ithaca, N.Y.: Cornell University Press.

Glick, Jennifer E., Frank D. Bean, and Jennifer V. W. Van Hook. 1997. "Immigration and Changing Patterns of Extended Family Household Structure in the United States." *Journal of Marriage and the Family* 59(February): 177–91.

Goldin, Claudia. 1983. "Life-Cycle Labor Force Participation of American Women, 1900–1980." Paper presented to the Social Science History Association. Washington (October).

———. 2000. "Labor Markets in the Twentieth Century." In *The Cambridge Economic History of the United States*, vol. 3, edited by Stanley L. Engerman and Robert E. Gallman. New York: Cambridge University Press.

Goldin, Claudia, and Lawrence F. Katz. 1999. "The Returns to Skill in the United States Across the Twentieth Century." Working paper 7126. Cambridge, Mass.: National Bureau of Economic Research.

———. 2000. "Education and Income in the Early Twentieth Century: Evidence from the Prairies." *Journal of Economic History* 60(September): 782–819.

———. 2001. "Decreasing (and Then Increasing) Inequality in America: A Tale of Two Half-Centuries." In *The Causes and Consequences of Increasing Inequality*, edited by Finis Welch. Chicago: University of Chicago Press.

Goldin, Claudia, and Robert A. Margo. 1992. "The Great Compression: The Wage Structure in the United States at Midcentury." *Quarterly Journal of Economics* 107(February): 1–34.

Goldscheider, Frances K., and Regina M. Bures. 2003. "The Racial Crossover in Family Complexity in the United States." *Demography* 40(August): 569–87.

Goldscheider, Frances K., Dennis Hogan, Susan Short, and Berna Mille. 2002. "The Growing Isolation of Parenthood in the Life Course and in the Family, 1880–1990." Paper presented to the American Sociological Association. Chicago (August).

Goldscheider, Frances K., and Leora Lawton. 1998. "Family Experiences and the Erosion of Support for Intergenerational Residence." *Journal of Marriage and the Family* 60(August): 623–32.

Goldstein, Joshua R., and Catherine T. Kenny. 2001. "Marriage Delayed or Marriage Forgone? New Cohort Forecasts of First Marriage for U.S. Women." *American Sociological Review* 66(August): 506–19.

Goldstein, Joshua R., and John Robert Warren. 2000. "Socioeconomic Reach and Heterogeneity in the Extended Family: Contours and Consequences." *Social Science Research* 29(September): 382–402.

Goodman, Leo. 1991. "Measures, Models, and Graphical Displays in Cross-Classified Data." *Journal of the American Statistical Association* 86: 1085–1111.

Gorski, Philip S. 2003. *The Disciplinary Revolution: Calvinism and the Rise of the State in Early Modern Europe*. Chicago: University of Chicago Press.

Goss, Jon. 1995. "'We Know Who You Are and We Know Where You Live': The Instrumental Rationality of Geodemographic Systems." *Economic Geography* 71(April): 171–98.

Gossett, Thomas. 1997. *Race: The History of an Idea in America*. New York: Oxford University Press. (Orig. pub. in 1963.)

Gottschalk, Peter, and Timothy M. Smeeding. 2000. "Empirical Evidence on Income Inequality in Industrialized Countries." In *Handbook of Income Distribution*, vol. 1, edited by Anthony B. Atkinson and Francois Bourguignon. New York: Elsevier.

Graefe, Deborah Roempke, and Daniel T. Lichter. 1999. "Life Course Transitions of American Children: Parental Cohabitation, Marriage, and Single Motherhood." *Demography* 36(May): 205–17.

Graham, Hugh Davis, and Ted Robert Gurr, eds. 1970. *The History of Violence in America: A Report to the National Commission on the Causes and Prevention of Violence*. New York: Bantam.

Greeley, Andrew. 1991. "American Exceptionalism: The Religious Phenomenon." In *Is America Different? A New Look at American Exceptionalism*, edited by Byron E. Shafer. Oxford: Clarendon.

————. 2001. *Religion in Europe at the End of the Second Millennium: A Sociological Profile*. New Brunswick, N.J.: Transaction Press.

Greeley, Andrew M., and Paul Sheatsley. 1971. "Attitudes Toward Racial Integration." *Scientific American* 238: 42–49.

Greenwood, Jeremy, Ananth Seshadri, and Guilliame Vandenbroucke. 2005. "The Baby Boom and Baby Bust." *American Economic Review* 95(March): 183–207.

Gutmann, Myron P., Sara M. Pullum-Pinon, and Thomas W. Pullum. 2002. "Three Eras of Young Adult Home Leaving in Twentieth-Century America." *Journal of Social History* 35(Spring): 533–76.

Hadaway, C. Kirk, Penny Marler, and Mark Chaves. 1993. "What the Polls Don't Show: A Closer Look at U.S. Church Attendance." *American Sociological Review* 58(December): 741–52.

Hagan, John, and Ruth D. Peterson, eds. 1995. *Crime and Inequality*. Palo Alto, Calif.: Stanford University Press.

Hagerty, Michael. 2000. "Social Comparisons of Income in One's Community: Evidence from National Surveys of Income and Happiness." *Journal of Personality and Social Psychology* 78(April): 764–71.

Hahrie, Han, and David W. Brady. 2005. "An Extended Historical View of Congressional Party Polarization." Unpublished paper. Wellesley College, Department of Political Science (August).

Hall, Patricia Kelly, and Steven Ruggles. 2004. " 'Restless in the Midst of Their Prosperity': New Evidence on the Internal Migration of Americans, 1850–2000." *Journal of American History* 91(December): 829–46.

Halman, Loek, and Ruud de Moor. 1993. "Religion, Churches, and Moral Values." In *The Individualizing Society: Value Change in Europe and North America*, edited by Peter Ester, Loek Halman, and Ruud de Moor. Tilburg, Neth.: Tilburg University Press.

Handlin, Oscar, and Lillian Handlin, eds. 1997. *From the Outer World*. Cambridge, Mass.: Harvard University Press.

Harding, David J., and Christopher Jencks. 2003. "Changing Attitudes Toward Premarital Sex: Cohort, Period, and Aging Effects." *Public Opinion Quarterly* 67(Summer): 211–26.

Hareven, Tamara K. 1978. "Historical Changes in the Life Course and the Family: Policy Implications." In *Major Social Issues: A Multidisciplinary View*, edited by J. Milton Yinger and Steven J. Cutler. New York: Free Press.

————. 1986. *Family Time and Industrial Time: The Relationship Between the Family and Work in a New England Industrial Community*. New York: Cambridge University Press.

————. 1991. "The History of the Family and the Complexity of Social Change." *American Historical Review* 96(February): 95–124.

————. 1994. "Aging and Generational Relations: A Historical and Life Course Perspective." *Annual Review of Sociology* 20: 437–61.

Harper, Miles D., and Darrell Steffensmeier. 1992. "The Differing Effects of Economic Inequality and Black and White Rates of Violence." *Social Forces* 70(June): 1035–54.

Harris, Ed, and John Sabelhaus. 2000. "Consumer Expenditure Survey Family-Level Extracts—1980:1, 1998:2" (computer files). Washington: Congressional Budget Office.

Harris, Richard. 1990. "Working-Class Homeownership in the American Metropolis." *Journal of Urban History* 17(November): 46–69.

Hartog, Henrik. 2000. *Man and Wife in America: A History*. Cambridge, Mass.: Harvard University Press.

Hawkins, Daniel N., and Alan Booth. 2005. "Unhappily Ever After: Effects of Long-term, Low-quality Marriages on Well-being." *Social Forces* 84(September): 451–71.

Hayes, Timothy, and Matthew Lee. 2005. "The Southern Culture of Honor and Violent Attitudes." *Sociological Spectrum* 25(September): 593–617.

Heaton, Tim B. 2002. "Factors Contributing to Increasing Marital Stability in the United States." *Journal of Family Issues* 23(April): 392–409.

Heaton, Tim B., and Caroline Hoppe. 1987. "Widowed and Married: Comparative Change in Living Arrangements, 1900 and 1980." *Social Science History* 11(Fall): 261–80.

Helliwell, John F., and Robert D. Putnam. 1999. "Education and Social Capital." Working paper W7121. Cambridge, Mass.: National Bureau of Economic Research.

Herberg, Will. 1983. *Protestant, Catholic, Jew: An Essay in American Religious Sociology*. Chicago: University of Chicago Press. (Orig. pub. in 1960.)

Hetherington, Marc J. 2001. "Resurgent Mass Partisanship: The Role of Elite Polarization." *American Political Science Review* 95(September): 619–31.

Heuser, Robert L. 1974. "U.S. Cohort and Fertility Tables, 1917–1980." Washington: National Center for Health Statistics. Available at: http://opr.princeton.edu/Archive/cpft.

Hitt, Jack. 2004. "Neo-Secessionism." *New York Times Magazine*, December 12, 84.

Hobbs, Frank, and Nicole Stoops. 2002. *Census 2000 Special Reports*. Series CENSR-4: Demographic Trends in the Twentieth Century. Washington: U.S. Government Printing Office for the U.S. Bureau of the Census.

Hochschild, Arlie. 1989. *The Second Shift*. New York: Viking.

————. 1997. *The Time Bind*. New York: Metropolitan.

Hochschild, Jennifer L. 1981. *What's Fair: American Beliefs About Distributive Justice.* Cambridge, Mass.: Harvard University Press.

Hochschild, Jennifer, and Nathan Scovronick. 2003. *The American Dream and the Public Schools.* New York: Oxford University Press.

Hofferth, Sandra L., Joan R. Kahn, and Wendy Baldwin. 1987. "Premarital Sexual Activity Among American Teenage Women over the Past Three Decades." *Family Planning Perspectives* 19(March): 46–53.

Hoffmann, John, and Alan Miller. 1998. "Denominational Influences on Socially Divisive Issues: Polarization or Continuity?" *Journal for the Scientific Study of Religion* 37(September): 528–47.

Hogan, Howard, and Gregg Robinson. 1993. "What the Census Bureau's Coverage Evaluation Programs Tell Us About Differential Undercount." Proceedings of the "Research Conference on Undercounted Ethnic Populations." Richmond, Va. (May 5–7). Available at: http://www.census.gov/population/www/documentation/1993/conference.html.

Hollinger, David A. 1995. *Postethnic America: Beyond Multiculturalism.* New York : Basic Books.

Hout, Michael. 2004. "How Trends Differ Among Subpopulations." Working paper. Berkeley: Survey Research Center.

Hout, Michael. 1988. "More Universalism, Less Structural Mobility: The American Occupational Structure in the 1980s." *American Journal of Sociology* 9(3, May): 1358–1400.

———. 1995. "The Politics of Mobility." In *Generating Stratification Research*, edited by Alan Kerckhoff. Boulder, Colo.: Westview Press.

———. 1997. "Inequality at the Margins: The Effects of Welfare, the Minimum Wage, and Tax Credits on Low-Wage Labor Markets." *Politics and Society* 25(4): 513–24.

———. 1999. "Abortion Politics in the United States, 1972–1994: From Single Issue to Ideology." *Gender Issues* 17(Spring): 3–31.

———. 2000. "Angry and Alienated: Divorced and Remarried Catholics in the United States." *America* (December 16): 10ff.

———. 2005a. "Money and Morale: How Growing Inequality Affects How Americans View Themselves and Their Place in Society." Social Inequality Working Paper. New York: Russell Sage Foundation.

———. 2005b. "Educational Progress for African Americans and Latinos Since the 1950s." In *Ethnicity and Social Mobility in Comparative Perspective*, edited by Glenn Loury, Tariq Madood, and Steve Teles. Cambridge: Cambridge University Press.

Hout, Michael, Richard Arum, and Kim Voss. 1996. "The Political Economy of Inequality in the Age of Extremes." *Demography* 33(November): 421–25.

Hout, Michael, and Claude S. Fischer. 2002. "Explaining the Rise of Americans with No Religious Preference: Politics and Generation." *American Sociological Review* 67(April): 165–90.

Hout, Michael, with Claude S. Fischer, Martín Sánchez Jankowski, Samuel R. Lucas, Ann Swidler, and Kim Voss. 1997. "Inequality by Design: Data, Myths, and Politics." Working paper. New York: Russell Sage Foundation.

Hout, Michael, and Joshua R. Goldstein. 1994. "How 4.5 Million Irish Immigrants Became 40 Million Irish Americans." *American Sociological Review* 59(February): 64–82.

Hout, Michael, and Andrew Greeley. 1987. "The Center Doesn't Hold: Church Attendance in the United States, 1940–1984." *American Sociological Review* 52(June): 325–45.

Hout, Michael, Andrew Greeley, and Melissa J. Wilde. 2001. "The Demographic Imperative in Religious Change: The Case of American Protestants." *American Journal of Sociology* 107: 468–500.

Hout, Michael, and Caroline Hanley. 2002. "The Overworked American Family." Social Inequality Working Paper. New York: Russell Sage Foundation.

Hout, Michael, Jeff Manza, and Clem Brooks. 1999. "Classes, Unions, and the Realignment of U.S. Presidential Voting, 1952–1992." In *The End of Class Politics?* edited by Geoff Evans. Oxford: Clarendon.

Hunter, James Davison. 1987. *American Evangelicalism: The Coming Generation.* Chicago: University of Chicago Press.

———. 1991. *Culture Wars: The Struggle to Define America.* New York: Basic Books.

Iceland, John, Daniel H. Weinberg, and Erika Steinmetz. 2002. "Racial and Ethnic Residential Segregation in the United States: 1980–2000." Series CENSR-3. Washington: U.S. Government Printing Office for the U.S. Bureau of the Census.

Immigration and Naturalization Service. 1998. *1997 Statistical Yearbook of the United States.* Washington: U.S. Department of Justice.

———. 2001. *2000 Statistical Yearbook of the United States.* Washington: U.S. Department of Justice.

Ioannides, Yannis M. 2004. "Neighborhood Income Distributions." *Journal of Urban Economics* 56(November): 435–57.

Jackson, Kenneth T. 1985. *Crabgrass Frontier: The Suburbanization United States.* New York: Oxford University Press.

Jacobs, David, and Jason T. Carmichael. 2002. "The Political Sociology of the Death Penalty: A Pooled Time-Series Analysis." *American Sociological Review* 67(February): 109–32.

Jacobs, Eva, and Stephanie Shipp. 1990. "How Family Spending Has Changed in the United States." *Monthly Labor Review* 113(March): 20–27.

Jacobs, Jerry A., and Kathleen Gerson. 2001. "Overworked Individuals or Overworked Families? Explaining Trends in Work, Leisure, and Family Time." *Work and Occupations* 28(1): 40–63.

Jacobson, Matthew Frye. 1998. *Whiteness of a Different Color: European Immigrants and the Alchemy of Race.* Cambridge, Mass.: Harvard University Press.

Jacoby, Sanford M., and Sunil Sharma. 1992. "Employment Duration and Industrial Labor Mobility in the United States, 1880–1980." *Journal of Economic History* 52(March): 161–79.

Jacoby, Tamar. 2004. *Reinventing the Melting Pot: The New Immigrants and What It Means to Be an American.* New York: Basic Books.

James, David R. 1989. "City Limits on Racial Equality: The Effects of City-Suburb Boundaries on Public-School Desegregation, 1968–1976." *American Sociological Review* 54(December): 963–85.

James, David R., and Karl E. Taeuber. 1985. "Measures of Segregation." *Sociological Methodology* 13: 1–32.

Jargowsky, Paul A. 2003. "Stunning Progress, Hidden Problems: The Dramatic Decline of Concentrated Poverty in the 1990s." Living Cities Census Series Report. Washington, D.C.: Brookings Institution (May).

Jasso, Guillermina. 1978. "On the Justice of Earnings: A New Specification of the Justice Evaluation Function." *American Journal of Sociology* 83(May): 1398–1419.

Jelen, Ted G. 1997. "Culture Wars and the Party System: Religion and Realignment, 1972–1993." In *Cultural Wars in American Politics: Critical Reviews of a Popular Myth*, edited by Rhys H. Williams. New York: Aldine de Gruyter.

Jencks, Christopher. 2002. "Does Inequality Matter?" *Daedalus* 131: 49–65.

Jencks, Christopher, and Susan E. Mayer. 1996. "Do Official Poverty Rates Provide Useful Information About Trends in Children's Economic Welfare?" Unpublished paper. Northwestern University, Center for Urban Affairs (May 30).

Jencks, Christopher, and David Riesman, 1968. *The Academic Revolution.* New York: Doubleday.

Jensen, Richard. 1989. "The Causes and Cures of Unemployment in the Great Depression." *Journal of Interdisciplinary History* 19(Spring): 553–83.

Johnson, David S., Timothy M. Smeeding, and Barbara Boyle Torrey. 2004. "United States Inequality Through the Prisms of Income and Consumption." Paper presented to the conference "The Link Between Income and Consumption Inequality." Madrid, Spain (March 26–27).

Jones, Jeffrey. 2002. "Public Divided on Benefits of Living Together Before Marriage" (August 16). Available at Gallup News Service, http://www.gallup.com.

Jorgenson, Dale W. 1998. "Did We Lose the War on Poverty?" *Journal of Economic Perspectives* 12(Winter): 79–96.

Kaestle, Carl F. 1993. "Public Education." In *Encyclopedia of American Social History*, vol. 3, edited by Mary Kupiec Cayton, Elliott J. Gorn, and Peter W. Williams. New York: Scribner's.

Kalleberg, Arne L., Barbara Reskin, and Ken Hudson. 2000. "Bad Jobs in America." *American Sociological Review* 65(April): 256–78.

Kalmijn, Matthijs. 1991. "Shifting Boundaries: Trends in Religious and Educational Homogamy." *American Sociological Review* 56(December): 786–800.

———. 1998. "Intermarriage and Homogamy: Causes, Patterns, Trends." *Annual Review of Sociology* 24: 395–421.

Kane, Thomas J. 2004. "College-Going and Inequality." In *Social Inequality*, edited by Kathryn M. Neckerman. New York: Russell Sage Foundation.

Kaplan, David L., and M. C. Casey. 1958. "Occupational Trends." Washington: U.S. Government Printing Office for the U.S. Bureau of the Census.

Karoly, Lynn A., and Gary Burtless. 1995. "Demographic Change, Rising Earnings Inequality, and the Distribution of Well-being, 1959–1989." *Demography* 32(August): 479–505.

Katz, Michael B., Mark J. Stern, and James J. Fader. 2005. "The New African American Inequality." *Journal of American History* 92(June): 75–108.

Katz-Gerro, Tally. 2002. "Highbrow Cultural Consumption and Class Distinction in Italy, Israel, West Germany, Sweden, and the United States." *Social Forces* 81(September): 207–29.

———. 2004. "Cultural Consumption Research: Review of Methodology, Theory, and Consequence." *International Review of Sociology* 14(1): 11–29.

Katzman, David. 1978. *Seven Days a Week: Women and Domestic Service in Industrializing America*. New York: Oxford University Press.

Keating, Michael. 1991. *Comparative Urban Politics: Power and the City in the United States, Canada, Britain, and France*. Brookfield, Vt.: Edward Elgar.

Keister, Lisa A. 2000. *Wealth in America: Trends in Wealth Inequality*. New York: Cambridge University Press.

———. 2001. "Family Background and the Racial Wealth Gap: How Childhood Resources and Family Structure Contribute to Racial Inequality in Adult Wealth." Unpublished paper. Ohio State University, Department of Sociology.

Keister, Lisa A., and Stephanie Moller. 2000. "Wealth Inequality in the United States." *Annual Review of Sociology* 26: 63–81.

Kelley, Jonathan, and M. D. R. Evans. 1993. "The Legitimation of Inequality: Occupational Earnings in Nine Nations." *American Journal of Sociology* 99(July): 75–125.

Kelley, Jonathan, and Herbert S. Klein. 1977. "Revolution and the Rebirth of Inequality: A Theory of Stratification in Postrevolutionary Society." *American Journal of Sociology* 83(July): 78–99.

Kemeny, P. C. 2003. "Power, Ridicule, and the Destruction of Religious Moral Reform Politics in the 1920s." In *The Secular Revolution*, edited by Christian Smith. Berkeley: University of California Press.

Kenworthy, Lane. 1999. "Do Social-Welfare Policies Reduce Poverty? A Cross-National Assessment." *Social Forces* 77(March): 1119–39.

————. 2004. *Egalitarian Capitalism*. New York: Russell Sage Foundation.

Keyssar, Alexander. 1986. *Out of Work: The First Century of Unemployment in Massachusetts*. New York: Cambridge University Press.

Kim, Sukkoo. 1998. "Economic Integration and Convergence: U.S. Regions, 1840–1987." *Journal of Economic History* 58(3): 659–83.

Kirschner, Don S. 1970. *City and Country: Rural Responses to Urbanization in the 1920s*. Westport, Conn.: Greenwood.

Klein, Herbert S. 2004. *A Population History of the United States*. New York: Cambridge University Press.

Kleinberg, S. J. 1989. *The Shadow of the Mills: Working-Class Families in Pittsburgh, 1870–1907*. Pittsburgh: University of Pittsburgh Press.

Kline, Ronald R. 2000. *Consumers in the Country: Technology and Social Change in Rural America*. Baltimore: Johns Hopkins University Press.

Kobrin [Goldscheider], Francis E. 1978. "The Fall in Household Size and the Rise of the Primary Individual in the United States." In *The American Family in Social-Historical Perspective*, 2nd ed., edited by Michael Gordon. New York: St. Martin's Press.

Kramarow, Ellen A. 1995. "The Elderly Who Live Alone in the United States: Historical Perspectives on Household Change." *Demography* 32(August): 335–52.

Krueger, Dirk, and Fabrizio Perri. 2002. "Does Income Inequality Lead to Consumption Inequality? Evidence and Theory." Working paper 9202. Cambridge, Mass.: National Bureau of Economic Research. Available at: http://www.nber.org/papers/w9202.

Ladd, Everett, and Karlyn H. Bowman. 1998. *Attitudes Toward Economic Inequality*. Washington, D.C.: American Enterprise Institute Press.

Lane, Robert E. 2000. *The Loss of Happiness in Market Democracies*. New Haven, Conn.: Yale University Press.

Langer, Gary, and Jon Cohen. 2005. "Voters and Values in the 2004 Election." *Public Opinion Quarterly* 69(special issue): 744–59.

Larson, O. F., and T. B. Jones. 1976. "The Unpublished Data from Roosevelt's Commission on Country Life." *Agricultural History* 50(October): 583–99.

Lassonde, Stephen. 1996. "Learning and Earning: Schooling, Juvenile Employment, and the Early Life Course in Late-Nineteenth-Century New Haven." *Journal of Social History* 29(Summer): 839–70.

Laumann, Edward, John H. Gagnon, Robert T. Michael, and Stuart Michaels. 1994. *The Social Organization of Sexuality: Sexual Practices in the United States*. Chicago: University of Chicago Press.

Laumann, Edward O., Jenna Mahay, and Yoosik Youm. 2002. "Sex, Intimacy, and Family Life in the United States." Paper presented to the annual meeting of the International Sociological Association, XV World Congress of Sociology. Brisbane, Aust. (July 8-13).

Layman, Geoffrey C., and Thomas M. Carsey. 2002. "Party Polarization and 'Conflict Extension' in the American Electorate." *American Journal of Political Science* 46(October): 786–803.

Lebergott, Stanley. 1971. "Changes in Unemployment 1800–1960." In *The Reinterpretation of American Economic History*, edited by Robert W. Fogel and Stanley L. Engerman. New York: Harper & Row.

———. 1976. *The American Economy: Income, Wealth, and Want*. Princeton, N.J.: Princeton University Press.

———. 1996. *Consumer Expenditures: New Measures and Old Motives*. Princeton, N.J.: Princeton University Press.

Lee, Jennifer, and Frank D. Bean. 2003. "Beyond Black and White: Remaking Race in America." *Contexts* 2(Fall): 26–33.

Lehrer, Evelyn L. 1998. "Religious Intermarriage in the United States: Determinants and Trends." *Social Science Research* 27(September): 245–63.

Leibowitz, Arleen, and Jacob Alex Klerman. 1995. "Explaining Changes in Married Mothers' Employment over Time." *Demography* 32(August): 365–78.

Levy, Frank. 1987. *Dollars and Dreams: The Changing American Income Distribution*. New York: Russell Sage Foundation.

Licht, Walter. 1992. *Getting Work: Philadelphia, 1840–1950*. Cambridge, Mass.: Harvard University Press.

Lichter, Daniel T. 1997. "Poverty and Inequality Among Children." *Annual Review of Sociology* 23: 121–45.

Lichter, Daniel T., and Zhenchao Qian. 2004. *Marriage and Family in a Multiracial Society*. New York: Russell Sage Foundation and Population Reference Bureau.

Lieberson, Stanley. 1969. "Measuring Population Diversity." *American Sociological Review* 34: 850–62.

———. 1980. *A Piece of the Pie: Blacks and White Immigrants Since 1880*. Berkeley: University of California Press.

Lieberson, Stanley, and Mary C. Waters. 1989. "The Rise of a New Ethnic Group: The 'Unhyphenated Americans.'" *Social Science Research Council Items* 43(March): 7–10.

———. 1990. *From Many Strands: Ethnic and Racial Groups in Contemporary America*. New York: Russell Sage Foundation.

———. 1993. "The Ethnic Responses of Whites: What Causes Their Instability, Simplification, and Inconsistency." *Social Forces* 72(2): 421–50.

Lindberg, Laura Duberstein, Scott Boggess, Laura Porter, and Sean Williams. 2000. *Teen Risk-Taking: A Statistical Portrait*. Washington, D.C.: Urban Institute.

Lindert, Peter H. "Three Centuries of Inequality in Britain and America." In *Handbook of Income Distribution*, vol. 1, edited by Anthony B. Atkinson and Francois Bourguignon. New York: Elsevier.

Litwak, Eugene. 1960. "Geographic Mobility and Extended Family Cohesion." *American Sociological Review* 25(June): 385–94.

Loftus, Jeni. 2001. "America's Liberalization in Attitudes Toward Homosexuality, 1973 to 1998." *American Sociological Review* 66(October): 762–82.

Logan, John R., and Mark Schneider. 1984. "Racial Segregation and Racial Change in American Suburbs, 1970–1980." *American Journal of Sociology* 89(January): 874–88.

Lucas, Samuel R., 2001. "Effectively Maintained Inequality: Education Transitions, Track Mobility, and Social Background Effects." *American Journal of Sociology* 106: 1642–90.

Ludwig, Jack. 2003. "Is America Divided into Haves and Have Nots?" The Gallup Poll. Available at: http://www.gallup.com (accessed September 8, 2004).

Luria, Daniel D. 1976. "Wealth, Capital, and Power: The Social Meaning of Homeownership." *Journal of Interdisciplinary History* 7(Autumn): 261–82.

Luxembourg Income Study. 2001. "Income Inequality Measures." Available at: http://lisproject.org/keyfigures/ineqtable.htm (accessed May 25, 2006).

Lynd, Robert, and Helen Lynd. 1929. *Middletown: A Study in Modern American Culture*. New York: Harcourt, Brace and World.

MacLeish, Kenneth, and Kimball Young. 1942. "Culture of a Contemporary Rural Community: Landaff, New Hampshire." Rural Life Studies 3. Washington: U.S. Department of Agriculture, Bureau of Agricultural Economics.

Macunovich, Diane J. 2002. *Birth Quake: The Baby Boom and Its Aftershocks*. Chicago: University of Chicago Press.

Magidson, Jay, and Jeroen Vermunt. 2002. "Latent Class Models for Clustering: A Comparison with K-Means." *Canadian Journal of Marketing Research* 20: 37–44.

———. 2003. "Technical Appendix for Latent Gold 3.0." Available at Statistical Innovations website, http://www.statisticalinnovations.com.

Manza, Jeff, and Clem Brooks. 1999. *Social Cleavages and Political Change: Voter Alignments and U.S. Party Coalitions*. New York: Oxford University Press.

Margo, Robert. 1999. "The History of Wage Inequality in America, 1820 to 1970." Working paper 286. Annandale-on-Hudson, N.Y.: Bard College, Jerome Levy Institute.

Marsh, Margaret. 1989. "From Separation to Togetherness: The Social Construction of Domestic Space in American Suburbs, 1840–1915." *Journal of American History* 76(September): 506–27.

Martin, Philip, and Elizabeth Midgley. 2003. "Immigration: Shaping America." *Population Bulletin* 58(June): entire issue.

Martin, Steven P. 2004. "Growing Evidence for a 'Divorce Divide'?" Social Inequality Working Paper. New York: Russell Sage Foundation (July).

Martin, Steven P., and Sangeeta Parashar. 2003. "An Education Crossover in

Divorce Attitudes." College Park: University of Maryland, Department of Sociology and Maryland Population Research Center (July).

Marty, Martin. 1984. *Pilgrims in Their Own Land: Five Hundred Years of American Religion*. Boston: Little, Brown.

Massa, Mark S. 1999. *Catholics and American Culture: Fulton Sheen, Dorothy Day, and the Notre Dame Football Team*. New York: Crossroad.

Massey, Douglas S., and Nancy A. Denton. 1988. "Suburbanization and Segregation in U.S. Metropolitan Areas." *American Journal of Sociology* 94(November): 592–626.

———. 1993. *American Apartheid: Segregation and the Making of the Underclass*. Cambridge, Mass.: Harvard University Press.

Massey, Douglas S., Jorge Durand, and Nolan J. Malone. 2002. *Beyond Smoke and Mirrors: Mexican Immigration in an Era of Economic Integration*. New York: Russell Sage Foundation.

Massey, Douglas S., and Mary J. Fischer. 2003. "The Geography of Inequality in the United States 1950–2000." Brooks-Wharton Papers on Urban Affairs. Washington, D.C.: Brookings Institution.

Massey, Douglas S., and Zoltan L. Hajnal. 1995. "The Changing Geographic Structure of Black-White Segregation in the United States." *Social Science Quarterly* 76(September): 527–42.

Matthaei, Julie A. 1982. *An Economic History of Women in America*. New York: Schocken Books.

May, Elaine Tyler. 1980. *Great Expectations: Marriage and Divorce in Post-Victorian America*. Chicago: University of Chicago Press.

McConkey, Dale. 2001. "Whither Hunter's Culture War? Shifts in Evangelical Morality, 1988–1998." *Sociology of Religion* 62(2): 149–74.

McCracken, Grant. 1990. *Culture and Consumption*. Bloomington: Indiana University Press.

McCutcheon, Allan. 2002. "Basic Concepts and Procedures in Single and Multiple Group Latent Class Analysis." In *Applied Latent Class Analysis Models*, edited by Jay Hagenaars and Allan McCutcheon. New York: Cambridge University Press.

McFalls, Joseph A. 1990. "Risks of Reproductive Impairment in the Later Years of Childbearing." *Annual Review of Sociology* 16: 491–519.

McGarry, Kathleen, and Robert F. Schoeni. 2000. "Social Security, Economic Growth, and the Rise in Elderly Widows' Independence in the Twentieth Century." *Demography* 37(May): 221–36.

McLanahan, Sara. 2002. "Life Without Father: What Happens to the Children?" *Contexts* 1(Spring): 35–44.

———. 2004. "Diverging Destinies: How Children Are Faring Under the Second Demographic Transition." *Demography* 41(November): 607–27.

Mencken, Jane. 1988. "Age and Fertility: How Late Can You Wait?" *Demography* 22: 469–84.

Michael, Robert T., Victor R. Fuchs, and Sharon R. Scott. 1980. "Changes in the Propensity to Live Alone, 1950–1976." *Demography* 17(February): 39–56.

Miller, Alan S., and John P. Hoffmann. 1999. "The Growing Divisiveness: Culture Wars or a War of Words?" *Social Forces* 78(December): 721–45.

Mintz, Steven. 2004. *Huck's Raft: A History of American Children*. Cambridge, Mass.: Harvard University Press.

Modell, John. 1979. "Changing Risks, Changing Adaptations: American Families in the Nineteenth and Twentieth Centuries." In *Kin and Communities: Families in America*, edited by Allan J. Lichtman and Joan R. Challenor. Washington, D.C.: Smithsonian Institution Press.

————. 1989. *Into One's Own: From Youth to Adulthood in the United States, 1920–1975*. Berkeley: University of California Press.

Moe, Edward O., and Carl C. Taylor. 1942. "Culture of a Contemporary Rural Community: Irwin, Iowa." Rural Life Studies 5. Washington: U.S. Department of Agriculture, Bureau of Agricultural Economics.

Moehling, Carolyn M. 2002. "Broken Homes: The 'Missing' Children of the 1910 Census." *Journal of Interdisciplinary History* 33(Autumn): 205–33.

Monkonnen, Erik H. 1988. *America Becomes Urban: The Development of U.S. Cities and Towns, 1780–1980*. Berkeley: University of California Press.

Moon, Dawne. 2004. *God, Sex, and Politics: Homosexuality and Everyday Theologies*. Chicago: University of Chicago Press.

Morgan, S. Philip. 1991. "Late-Nineteenth- and Early-Twentieth-Century Childlessness." *American Journal of Sociology* 97(3): 779–807.

Morgan, S. Philip, Antonio McDaniel, Andrew T. Miller, and Samuel H. Preston. 1993. "Racial Differences in Households and Family Structure at the Turn of the Century." *American Journal of Sociology* 98(4): 799–828.

Morris, Charles. 1997. *American Catholic*. New York: Times Books.

Mosher, William D., and Christine A. Bachrach. 1996. "Understanding U.S. Fertility: Continuity and Change." *Family Planning Perspectives* 28(January–February): 4–12.

Muller, Edward N. 1998. "Democracy, Economic Development, and Income Inequality." *American Sociological Review* 53(February): 50–68.

Musleah, Rahel. 2001. "Jewish Jeopardy." *Reform Judaism* (Fall): 18–22.

National Center for Educational Statistics. 2004. "Trends in International Mathematics and Science Study." Available at: http://nces.ed.gov/timss (accessed March 27, 2006).

National Center for Health Statistics. 2005. *Health United States 2005*. Washington, D.C.: National Center for Health Statistics.

Neckerman, Kathryn M., ed. 2004. *Social Inequality*. New York: Russell Sage Foundation.

Nie, Norman H., Jane Junn, and Kenneth Stehlik-Barry. 1996. *Education and Democratic Citizenship in America*. Chicago: University of Chicago Press.

Nobles, Gregory H. 1989. "Breaking into the Backcountry: New Approaches to the Early American Frontier, 1750–1800." *William and Mary Quarterly*, 3rd ser. (46, October): 641–70.

Nobles, Melissa. 2000. *Shades of Citizenship: Race and the Census in Modern Politics*. Palo Alto, Calif.: Stanford University Press.

Nugent, Walter T. 1981. *Structures of American Social History*. Bloomington: Indiana University Press.

Office of Management and Budget. 1997. "Revisions to the Standards for the Classification of Federal Data on Race and Ethnicity." Washington: Federal Register Notice (October).

Omi, Michael, and Howard Winant. 1994. *Racial Formation in the United States: From the 1960s to the 1990s*. New York: Routledge & Kegan Paul.

Ono, Hiromi. 1999. "Historical Time and U.S. Marital Dissolution." *Social Forces* 77(March): 969–97.

Oppenheimer, Valerie Kincaid. 1973. "Demographic Influences on Female Employment and the Status of Women." *American Journal of Sociology* 78(January): 946–61.

———. 1988. "A Theory of Marriage Timing." *American Journal of Sociology* 94(November): 563–91.

———. 2000. "The Continuing Importance of Men's Economic Position in Marriage Formation." In *The Ties That Bind: Perspectives on Marriage and Cohabitation*, edited by Linda J. Waite. New York: Aldine de Gruyter.

Oppenheimer, Valerie Kincaid, Matthijs Kalmijn, and Nelson Lim. 1997. "Men's Career Development and Marriage Timing During a Period of Rising Inequality." *Demography* 34(August): 311–29.

Orfield, Gary, Dan Losen, and Johanna Weld. 2004. "Losing Our Future: How Minority Youth Are Being Left Behind in the Graduation Rate Crisis." Civil Rights Project final report. Cambridge, Mass.: Harvard University.

Orsi, Robert A. 1985. *Madonna of 115th Street*. New Haven, Conn.: Yale University Press.

Owen, Carolyn A., Howard Eisner, and Thomas R. McFaul. 1981. "A Half-Century of Social Distance Research: National Replication of the Bogardus Studies." *Sociology and Social Research* 66(October): 80–98.

Pagnini, Deanna L., and S. Philip Morgan. 1990. "Intermarriage and Social Distance Among U.S. Immigrants at the Turn of the Century." *American Journal of Sociology* 96(September): 405–32.

———. 1996. "Racial Differences in Marriage and Childbearing: Oral History Evidence from the South in the Early Twentieth Century." *American Journal of Sociology* 101(May): 1694–1718.

Parsons, Talcott. 1943. "The Kinship System of the Contemporary United States." *American Anthropologist*, new series 45 (January): 22–38.

Passel, Jeffrey S. 2005. "Unauthorized Migrants: Numbers and Characteris-

tics." Washington: Pew Hispanic Center. Available at: http://www
.pewhispanic.org (accessed June 15, 2005).

Perlmann, Joel. 2005. *Italians Then, Mexicans Now: Immigrant Origins and Second-Generation Progress, 1890–2000*. New York: Russell Sage Foundation.

Petersen, Trond, and Laurie A. Morgan. 1995. "Separate and Unequal: Occupation-Establishment Sex Segregation and the Gender Gap in Wages." *American Journal of Sociology* 101(September): 329–65.

Pettit, Becky, and Bruce Western. 2004. "Mass Imprisonment and the Life Course: Race and Class Inequality in U.S. Incarceration." *American Sociological Review* 69(April): 151–69.

Pew Internet and American Life Project. 2003. "Internet Use by Region" (August 27). Available at: http://www.pewinternet.org/pdfs/PIP_ Regional_Report_Aug_2003.pdf.

Pew Research Center. 2001. "Economic Inequality Seen as Rising, Boom Bypasses Poor" (June 21). Available at: http://people-press.org/ reports/display.php3?ReportID=8 (accessed September 22, 2004).

———. 2002. "Americans Struggle with Religion's Role at Home and Abroad." Report of the Pew Research Center for the People and the Press. Available at: http://www.people-press.org (accessed October 11, 2004).

Piketty, Thomas, and Emmanuel Saez. 2001. "Income Inequality in the United States, 1913–1998." Working paper 8467. Cambridge, Mass.: National Bureau of Economic Research (September).

Plotnick, Robert D., Eugene Smolensky, Erik Evenhouse, and Siobhan Reilly. 2000. "The Twentieth-Century Record of Inequality and Poverty in the United States." In *The Cambridge Economic History of the United States*, vol. 3, edited by Stanley L. Engerman and Robert E. Gallman. New York: Cambridge University Press.

Popenoe, David. 1988. *Disturbing the Nest: Family Change and Decline in Modern Societies*. New York: Aldine de Gruyter.

Portes, Alejandro. 2002. "English-Only Triumphs, but the Costs Are High." *Contexts* 1(Winter): 10–15.

Presser, Harriet B. 2004. *Working in a 24/7 Economy*. New York: Russell Sage Foundation.

Preston, Samuel H. 1977. "Mortality Trends." *Annual Review of Sociology* 3: 163–78.

Prewitt, Kenneth. 2003. "Ethno-Racial Classification in Public Policy: Does It Have a Future?" Presentation to the ninth annual Aaron Wildavsky Forum for Public Policy. University of California, Berkeley (April 10).

Public Agenda. 2003. "For Goodness' Sake: Why So Many Americans Want Religion to Play a Greater Role in Public Life." Available at: http://www .publicagenda.org/specials/religion/religion.htm (accessed August 21, 2003).

Putnam, Robert D. 2000. *Bowling Alone: The Collapse and Revival of American Community*. New York: Simon & Schuster.

Qian, Zhenchao, and Samuel H. Preston. 1993. "Changes in American Marriage, 1972 to 1987: Availability and Forces of Attraction by Age and Education." *American Sociological Review* 58(August): 482–95.

Rabin, Jonathan. 1991. *Hunting Mister Heartbreak*. New York: Burlingame Books.

Raftery, Adrian E. 1995. "Bayesian Model Selection in Social Research." *Sociological Methodology* 25: 111–96.

Rahn, Wendy M., and Thomas J. Rudolph. 2005. "A Tale of Political Trust in American Cities." *Public Opinion Quarterly* 69(Winter): 508–29.

Rainwater, Lee. 1974. *What Money Buys: Inequality and the Social Meanings of Income*. New York: Basic Books.

Raley, R. Kelly. 2000. "Recent Trends and Differentials in Marriage and Cohabitation: The United States." In *The Ties That Bind: Perspectives on Marriage and Cohabitation*, edited by Linda J. Waite. New York: Aldine de Gruyter.

Rauch, Jonathan. 2005. "Bipolar Disorder: A Funny Thing Happened to Many of the Scholars Who Went into the Country to Investigate the Red-Blue Divide. They Couldn't Find It." *Atlantic Monthly* (January–February): 102–10.

Reardon, Sean F., and John T. Yun. 2000. "The Changing Structure of School Segregation." *Demography* 37(August): 351–64.

Reskin, Barbara, and Irene Padavic. 1994. *Women and Men at Work*. Thousand Oaks, Calif.: Pine Forge.

Rieder, Jonathan. 2003. "Getting a Fix on Fragmentation." In *The Fractious Nation: Unity and Division in Contemporary American Life*, edited by Jonathan Rieder. Berkeley: University of California Press.

———, ed. 2003. *The Fractious Nation: Unity and Division in Contemporary American Life*. Berkeley: University of California Press.

Riesman, David. 1950. *The Lonely Crowd: A Study of the Changing American Character*. New Haven, Conn.: Yale University Press.

Rindfuss, Ronald R. 1991. "The Young Adult Years: Diversity, Structural Change, and Fertility." *Demography* 28(November): 493–512.

Roediger, David, and Phillip Foner. 1989. *Our Own Time: A History of the American Labor Movement*. London: Verso.

Rogers, Everett. 2003. *Diffusion of Innovations*, 5th ed. New York: Free Press.

Romer, Christina. 1986. "New Estimates of Prewar Gross National Product and Unemployment." *Journal of Economic History* 46(June): 341–52.

———. 1999. "Changes in Business Cycles: Evidence and Explanations." *Journal of Economic Perspectives* 13(Spring): 23–44.

Roof, Wade Clark. 1999. *Spiritual Marketplace*. Princeton, N.J.: Princeton University Press.

Rosenbloom, Joshua L. 1996. "The Extent of the Labor Market in the

United States, 1850–1914." Historical Working Paper 78. Cambridge, Mass.: National Bureau of Economic Research (January).

Rosenbloom, Joshua L., and William A. Sundstrom. 2003. "The Decline and Rise of Interstate Migration in the United States: Evidence from the IPUMS, 1850–1990." Working paper W9857. Cambridge, Mass.: National Bureau of Economic Research (July).

Rosenfield, Geraldine. 1982. "The Polls: Attitudes Toward American Jews." *Public Opinion Quarterly* 46(Fall): 431–43.

Ross, Dorothy. 1998. "The New and Newer Histories: Social Theory and Historiography in an American Key." In *Imagined Histories: American Historians Interpret the Past*, edited by Anthony Molho and Gordon S. Wood. Princeton, N.J.: Princeton University Press.

Ross, Edward A. 1901. "The Causes of Race Superiority." *Annals of the American Academy of Political and Social Science* 18(July): 67–89.

Roth, Philip. 2005. "I Got a Scheme." *The New Yorker*, April 25, 72–85.

Rothman, Ellen. 1984. *Hands and Hearts: A History of Courtship in America*. New York: Basic Books.

Ruggles, Steven. 1988. "The Demography of the Unrelated Individual: 1900–1950." *Demography* 25(November): 521–46.

———. 1994a. "The Transformation of American Family Structure." *American Historical Review* 99(February): 103–28.

———. 1994b. "The Origins of African-American Family Structure." *American Sociological Review* 59(February): 136–51.

———. 1997. "The Rise of Divorce and Separation in the United States, 1880–1990." *Demography* 34(November): 455–66.

———. 2003. "Multigenerational Families in Nineteenth-Century America." *Continuity and Change* 18(1): 139–65.

Ruggles, Steven, and Susan Brower. 2003. "Measurement of Household and Family Composition in the United States, 1850–2000." *Population and Development Review* 29(1): 73–101.

Ruggles, Steven, Matthew Sobek, Trent Alexander, Catherine A. Fitch, Ronald Goeken, Patricia Kelly Hall, Miriam King, and Chad Ronnander. 2004. *Integrated Public Use Microdata Series: Version 3.0* (machine-readable database). Minneapolis: Minnesota Population Center (http://www.ipums.org).

Rytina, Steven. 2000. "Is Occupational Mobility Declining in the United States?" *Social Forces* 78(June): 1227–76.

Sampson, Robert J., and Dawn Jeglum Bartusch. 1998. "Legal Cynicism and (Subcultural?) Tolerance of Deviance: The Neighborhood Context of Racial Differences." *Law and Society Review* 32(December): 777–804.

Schlesinger, Arthur Meier. 1992. *The Disuniting of America*. New York: Norton.

Schneider, Barbara, and Yongsook Lee. 1990. "A Model for Academic Success: The School and Home Environment of East Asian Students." *Anthropology and Education Quarterly* 21(December): 358–77.

Schoeni, Robert F. 1988. "Reassessing the Decline in Parent-Child Old-Age Coresidence During the Twentieth Century." *Demography* 35(August): 307–14.

Scholz, John Karl, and Kara Levine. 2004. "U.S. Black-White Wealth Inequality." In *Social Inequality*, edited by Kathryn Neckerman. New York: Russell Sage Foundation.

Schuman, Howard, Charlotte Steeh, and Lawrence Bobo. 1997. *Racial Attitudes in America: Trends and Interpretations*, 2nd ed. Cambridge, Mass.: Harvard University Press.

Schwartz, Christine R., and Robert D. Mare. 2005. "Trends in Educational Assortative Marriage from 1940 to 2003." *Demography* 42(November): 621–46.

Schwirian, Kent P., F. Martin Hankins, and Carol A. Ventresca. 1990. "The Residential Decentralization of Social Status Groups in American Metropolitan Communities, 1950–1980." *Social Forces* 68(June): 1143–63.

Seidman, Stuart N., and Ronald O. Rieder. 1994. "A Review of Sexual Behavior in the United States." *American Journal of Psychiatry* 151(March): 330–41.

Sellers, Charles. 1991. *The Market Revolution: Jacksonian America, 1815–1846*. New York: Oxford University Press.

Sen, Amartya. 1997. *On Economic Inequality*, enlarged edition. Oxford: Clarendon.

Shammas, Carole. 1993. "A New Look at Long-Term Trends in Wealth Inequality in the United States." *American Historical Review* 98(April): 412–31.

———. 2002. *A History of Household Governance in America*. Charlottesville: University Press of Virginia.

Shanahan, Michael J. 2000. "Pathways to Adulthood in Changing Societies: Variability and Mechanisms in Life Course Perspective." *Annual Review of Sociology* 26: 667–92.

Shanahan, Suzanne, and Susan Olzak. 1999. "The Effects of Immigrant Diversity and Ethnic Competition on Collective Conflict in Urban America: An Assessment of Two Moments of Mass Migration, 1869–1924 and 1965–1993." *Journal of American Ethnic History* 18(3): 40–54.

Shapiro, Edward S. 1992. *A Time for Healing: American Jewry Since World War II*. Baltimore: Johns Hopkins University Press.

Shavit, Yossi, and Hans-Peter Blossfeld. 1993. "Persisting Barriers: Changes in Educational Opportunities in Thirteen Countries." In *Persistent Inequality: Changing Educational Attainment in Thirteen Countries*, edited by Yossi Shavit and Hans-Peter Blossfeld. Boulder, Colo.: Westview Press.

Sherkat, Darren. 1999. "Tracking the 'Other': Dynamics and Composition of 'Other' Religions in the General Social Survey, 1973–1996." *Journal for the Scientific Study of Religion* 38(December): 551–60.

Sherkat, Darren, and John Wilson. 1999. "Preferences, Constraints, and Choices in Religious Markets: An Examination of Religious Switching and Apostasy." *Social Forces* 73(March): 993–1026.

Short, Susan, Frances K. Goldscheider, and Berna Miller Torr. 2004. "Less Help for Mother: The Decline in Adult Support for the Mothers of Small Children, 1880–2000." Unpublished paper. Brown University, Department of Sociology (March).

Sigelman, Lee, Steven A. Tuch, and Jack K. Martin. 2005. "What's in a Name? Preference for 'Black' Versus 'African American' Among Americans of African Descent." *Public Opinion Quarterly* 69(3): 429–38.

Simmons, James C. 2000. *Star-Spangled Eden*. New York: Carroll & Graf.

Skocpol, Theda. 2004. "Civic Transformation and Inequality in the Contemporary United States." In *Social Inequality*, edited by Kathryn Neckerman. New York: Russell Sage Foundation.

Skolnick, Arlene S. 1991. *Embattled Paradise: The American Family in an Age of Uncertainty*. New York: Basic Books.

Slesnick, Daniel T. 1994. "Consumption, Needs, and Inequality." *International Economic Review* 35(August): 677–703.

———. 2001. *Consumption and Social Welfare: Living Standards and Their Distribution in the United States*. New York: Cambridge University Press.

Smeeding, Timothy M. 2000. "Changing Income Inequality in OECD Countries: Updated Results from the Luxembourg Income Study (LIS)." Working paper 252. Luxembourg: Luxembourg Income Study.

Smeeding, Timothy M., and Lee Rainwater. 2001. "Comparing Living Standards Across Nations: Real Incomes at the Top, the Bottom, and the Middle." Working paper 266. Luxembourg: Luxembourg Income Study.

Smith, Christian. 1997. "The Myth of Culture Wars: The Case of American Protestantism." In *Cultural Wars in American Politics: Critical Reviews of a Popular Myth*, edited by Rhys H. Williams. New York: Aldine de Gruyter.

———. 2003. *The Secular Revolution: Power, Interests, and Conflict in the Secularization of American Public Life*. Berkeley: University of California Press.

Smith, Daniel Scott. 1978. "The Dating of the American Sexual Revolution." In *The American Family in Social-Historical Perspective*, 2nd ed., edited by Michael Gordon. New York: St. Martin's Press.

Smith, James P. 1999. "Why Is Wealth Inequality Rising?" Paper presented to the conference "Increasing Income Inequality in America." Texas A&M University (March 12–13).

Smith, Tom W. 1990a. "Classifying Protestant Denominations." *Review of Religious Research* 31(March): 225–45.

———. 1990b. "Social Inequality in Cross-National Perspective." In *Attitudes to Inequality and the Role of Government*, edited by Duane F. Alwin et al. Rijswijk: Sociaal en Cultureel Planbureua; Samsom, Neth.: Alphen aan des Rijn.

———. 1990c. "Timely Artifacts: A Review of Measurement Variation in the 1972–1989 General Social Survey." GSS Methodological Report 56. Chicago: National Opinion Research Center.

———. 1992. "Changing Racial Labels: From 'Colored' to 'Negro' to 'Black' to 'African American.'" *Public Opinion Quarterly* 56(Winter): 496–514.

———. 2002. "Religious Diversity in America: The Emergence of Muslims, Buddhists, Hindus, and Others." *Journal for the Scientific Study of Religion* 41(3): 577–85.

———. 2003. "American Sexual Behavior: Trends, Sociodemographic Differences, and Risk Behavior." GSS Topical Report 25 (updated). Chicago: National Opinion Research Center.

Smith, Tom W., and Seokho Kim. 2004. "The Vanishing Protestant Majority." GSS Social Change Report 49. Chicago: National Opinion Research Center (April).

Smock, Pamela J. 2000. "Cohabitation in the United States." *Annual Review of Sociology* 26: 1–20.

Sollors, Werner. 2002. "What Race Are You?" In *The New Race Question: How the Census Counts Multiracial Individuals*, edited by Joel Perlmann and Mary C. Waters. New York: Russell Sage Foundation.

Solon, Gary. 2002. "Cross-Country Differences in Intergenerational Earnings Mobility." *Journal of Economic Perspectives* 16(Summer): 59–67.

Soltow, Lee. 1993. "Wealth and Income Distribution." In *Encyclopedia of American Social History*, vol. 2, edited by Mary Kupiec Cayton, Elliott J. Gorn, and Peter W. Williams. New York: Scribner's.

South, Scott J. 2001. "Time-Dependent Effects of Wives' Employment on Marital Dissolution." *American Sociological Review* 66(April): 226–45.

Spilerman, Seymour. 2000. "Wealth and Stratification Processes." *Annual Review of Sociology* 26: 497–24.

Stahura, John M. 1987. "Suburban Socioeconomic Status Change: A Comparison of Models, 1950–1980." *American Sociological Review* 52(April): 268–77.

Stanger-Ross, Jordan, Christina Collins, and Mark J. Stern. 2005. "Falling Far from the Tree: Transitions to Adulthood and the Social History of Twentieth-Century America." *Social Science History* 29(Winter): 625–48.

Sterne, Evelyn Savidge. 2000. "Bringing Religion into Working-Class History." *Social Science History* 24(Spring): 149–82.

Stevens, David A. 1990. "New Evidence on the Timing of Early Life Transitions: The United States 1900–1980." *Journal of Family History* 15(2): 163–78.

Stevenson, Harold W., Chuansheng Chen, and Sing-Ying Lee. 1993. "Mathematics Achievement of Chinese, Japanese, and American Children: Ten Years Later." *Science* 259(1, January): 53–58.

Stier, Haya, Noah Lewin-Epstein, and Michael Braun. 2001. "Welfare Regimes, Family-Supportive Policies, and Women's Employment Along the Life-Course." *American Journal of Sociology* 106(May): 1731–60.

Stiles, Jon. 2002. "Education: Comparison of Absolute Versus Relative Measures." Century of Difference Project working paper. Available at: http://ucdata.berkeley.edu:7101/rsfcensus/Papers/Relative Education.pdf.

Stockmayer [Donehower], Gretchen. 2004. "The Demographic Foundations of Change in U.S. Households in the Twentieth Century." PhD diss., University of California, Berkeley (May).

Stonecash, Jeffrey M., Mark D. Brewer, and Mack D. Mariani. 2003. *Diverging Parties: Social Change, Realignment, and Party Polarization*. Boulder, Colo.: Westview Press.

Sullivan, Teresa A., Elizabeth Warren, and Jay Lawrence Westbrook. 2000. *The Fragile Middle Class: Americans in Debt*. New Haven, Conn.: Yale University Press.

Sussman, Marvin B. 1959. "The Isolated Nuclear Family: Fact or Fiction." *Social Problems* 6(Spring): 333–40.

Sutton, John R., and Mark Chaves. 2004. "Explaining Schism in American Protestant Denominations, 1890–1990." *Journal for the Scientific Study of Religion* 43(June): 171–90.

Takaki, Ronald, ed. 2002. *Debating Diversity: Clashing Perspectives on Race and Ethnicity in America*. New York: Oxford University Press.

Taylor, D. Garth, Paul Sheatsley, and Andrew M. Greeley. 1978. "Attitudes Toward Racial Integration." *Scientific American* 238(June): 42–49.

Taylor, Quintard, Jr. 1993. "Postbellum African American Culture." In *Encyclopedia of American Social History*, vol. 2, edited by Mary Kupiec Cayton, Elliott J. Gorn, and Peter W. Williams. New York: Scribner's.

Tharp, Marye C. 2001. *Marketing and Consumer Identity in Multicultural America*. Thousand Oaks, Calif.: Sage Publications.

Thernstrom, Stephan. 1973. *The Other Bostonians: Poverty and Progress in the American Metropolis, 1880–1970*. Cambridge, Mass.: Harvard University Press.

Thornton, Arland. 1985. "Changing Attitudes Toward Separation and Divorce: Causes and Consequences." *American Journal of Sociology* 90(January): 856–72.

———. 1989. "Changing Attitudes Toward Family Issues in the United States." *Journal of Marriage and the Family* 51(4): 873–93.

Thornton, Arland, and Willard L. Rodgers. 1987. "The Influence of Individual and Historical Time on Marriage Dissolution." *Demography* 24(February): 1–22.

Thornton, Arland, and Linda Young-Demarco. 2001. "Four Decades of Trends in Attitudes Toward Family Issues in the United States: The 1960s Through the 1990s." *Journal of Marriage and the Family* 63(November): 1009–38.

Thurow, Lester. 1975. *Generating Inequality*. New York: Basic Books.

Tindall, George B. 1993. "Regionalism." In *Encyclopedia of American Social History*, vol. 1, edited by Mary Kupiec Cayton, Elliott J. Gorn, and Peter W. Williams. New York: Scribner's.

Tobey, Ronald C. 1996. *Technology as Freedom: The New Deal and the Electrical Modernization of the American Home*. Berkeley: University of California Press.

Tobey, Ronald C., Charles Wetherell, and Jay Brigham. 1990. "Moving Out and Settling In: Residential Mobility, Home Owning, and the Public Enframing of Citizenship, 1921–1950." *American Historical Review* 95(December): 1395–1423.

Tolnay, Stewart E. 2003. "The African American 'Great Migration' and Beyond." *Annual Review of Sociology* 29: 209–32.

———. 2004. "The Living Arrangements of African American and Immigrant Children, 1880–2000." *Journal of Family History* 29(4): 421–45.

Tolnay, Stewart E., and E. M. Beck. 1990. "Black Flight: Lethal Violence and the Great Migration, 1900–1930." *Social Science History* 14(Autumn): 347–70.

Tomlinson, Mark. 2003. "Lifestyle and Social Class." *European Sociological Review* 19(1): 97–111.

Tyack, David. 1996. "Preserving the Republic by Educating Republicans." In *Diversity and Its Discontents: Cultural Conflict and Common Ground in Contemporary American Society*, edited by Neil Smelser and Jeffrey Alexander. Berkeley: University of California Press.

Uhlenberg, Peter R. 1969. "A Study of Cohort Life Cycles: Cohorts of Native-Born Massachusetts Women, 1830–1920." *Population Studies* 23(November): 407–20.

———. 1985. "Death and the Family." In *Growing Up in America: Children in Historical Perspective*, edited by N. Ray Hiner and Joseph M. Hawes. Urbana: University of Illinois Press.

United States Bureau of the Census. 1959. *Occupational Trends, 1900–1950*. Washington: U.S. Government Printing Office.

———. 1977. *Historical Statistics of the United States, 1790–1970*. Washington: U.S. Government Printing Office.

———. 1999. "Money Income in the United States, 1998." *Current Population Reports*, series P60–206. Washington: U.S. Bureau of the Census. Available at: http://www.census.gov/prod/99pubs/p60-206.pdf.

———. 2001a. *Annual Housing Survey, 1999: National Microdata* (computer file). Washington: U.S. Department of Commerce, Bureau of the Census.

Distributed by Inter-University Consortium for Political and Social Research, Ann Arbor, Mich.

————. 2001b. *Statistical Abstract of the United States, 2000* (CD-ROM). Washington: U.S. Government Printing Office.

————. 2001c. *Mapping Census 2000: The Geography of U.S. Diversity.* Washington: U.S. Government Printing Office.

————. 2002. *Supplemental Survey Data Report,* "2002." Available at: http://www.census.gov/acs/www/Downloads/ACS/Paper41.pdf.

————. 2003. *Statistical Abstract of the United States, 2002* (CD-ROM). Washington: U.S. Government Printing Office.

————. 2004a. *Statistical Abstract of the United States, 2003* (CD-ROM). Washington: U.S. Government Printing Office.

————. 2004b. "Historical Income Tables—Households." Available at: http://www.census.gov/hhes/income/histinc/h02.html (last revised July 8, 2004).

————. 2004c. "Population by Race and Hispanic or Latino Origin." Available at: http://www.census.gov/population/www/cen2000/phc-t1.html (last revised September 29, 2004).

————. 2005a. *Income, Poverty, and Health Insurance Coverage in the United States, 2003.* Washington: U.S. Government Printing Office.

————. 2005b. "Geographical Mobility/Migration." Available at: http://www.census.gov/population/www/socdemo/migrate.html (last revised June 22, 2005; accessed January 9, 2006).

————. 2005c. "Historical Income Tables—Income Inequality," table IE-6. Available at: http://www.census.gov/hhes/www/income/histinc/ie6.html (last revised May 13, 2005; accessed 2001).

————. 2005d. "Families and Living Arrangements." Table HH-4, Households by Size: 1960 to Present. Available at: http://www.census.gov/population/socdemo/hh-fam/hh4.pdf (release date June 29, 2005).

————. N.d. "State and County QuickFacts: Metropolitan Statistical Area," available at: http://quickfacts.census.gov/qfd/meta/long_metro.htm.

————. N.d. "Population and Ranking Tables of the Older Population: Table 6, Counties Ranked." Available at: http://www.census.gov/population/cen2000/phc-t13/tab06.pdf (accessed May 25, 2006).

U.S. Citizenship and Immigration Services. 2004. *Fiscal Year 2003 Yearbook of Immigration Statistics.* Available at: http://uscis.gov/graphics/shared/aboutus/statistics/IMM03yrbk/IMM2003list.htm (last modified September 24, 2004; accessed July 27, 2005).

U.S. Department of Health and Human Services. 1999. *National Vital Statistics Reports* 47(26, October).

U.S. Immigration and Naturalization Service. 1998. *1997 Statistical Yearbook of the United States.* Washington: U.S. Government Printing Office.

U.S. Senate. 1909. *Report of the Country Life Commission*. U.S. Senate document 705. Washington: U.S. Government Printing Office.

Venkatesh, Sudhir Alladi. 2000. *American Project: The Rise and Fall of a Modern Ghetto*. Cambridge, Mass.: Harvard University Press.

Verba, Sidney, and Gary R. Orren. 1985. *Equality in America: The View from the Top*. Cambridge, Mass.: Harvard University Press.

Waite, Linda J., and Judith Sheps. 1994. "The Impact of Religious Upbringing and Marriage Markets on Jewish Intermarriage." Unpublished paper. University of Chicago, Population Research Center (April).

Waldman, Steven, and John C. Green. 2006. "Tribal Relations: How Americans Really Sort Out on Cultural and Religious Issues—and What It Means for Our Politics." *Atlantic Monthly* 297(January–February): 136–42.

Ward, Florence. 1920. "The Farm Woman's Problem." Department of Agriculture circular 148. Washington: U.S. Government Printing Office.

Waters, Mary C. 1990. *Ethnic Options: Choosing Identities in America*. Berkeley: University of California Press.

———. 1999. *Black Identities: West Indian Immigrant Dreams and American Realities*. New York: Russell Sage Foundation.

Watkins, Susan Cotts, Jane A. Mencken, and John Bongaarts. 1987. "Demographic Foundations of Family Change." *American Sociological Review* 52(June): 346–58.

Weiss, Marc A. 1987. "Planning Subdivisions: Community Builders and Urban Planners in the Early Twentieth Century." In *Planning and Financing Public Works*, edited by Howard Rosen. Chicago: Public Works Historical Society.

Weiss, Michael J. 2000. *The Clustered World: How We Live, What We Buy, and What It All Means About Who We Are*. Boston: Little, Brown.

Wells, Robert V. 1995. "The Mortality Transition in Schenectady, New York, 1880–1930." *Social Science History* 19(Fall): 399–423.

West, Kirsten K., and J. Gregory Robinson. 1999. "What Do We Know About the Undercount of Children?" Working paper 39. Washington: U.S. Bureau of the Census, Population Division (August). Available at: http://www.census.gov/population/www/documentation/twps0039/twps0039.html.

Western, Bruce. 2006. *Prisons and Inequality*. New York: Russell Sage Foundation.

Western, Bruce, and Becky Pettit. 2002. "Beyond Crime and Punishment: Prisons and Inequality." *Contexts* 1(Fall): 37–43.

Westoff, Charles. 1977. "Marriage and Fertility in Developed Countries." *Scientific American* 239(December): 51–57.

Westoff, Charles F., and Norman B. Ryder. 1977. *The Contraceptive Revolution*. Princeton, N.J.: Princeton University Press.

Westoff, Leslie Aldridge, and Charles Westoff. 1971. *From Now to Zero: Fertility, Contraception, and Abortion in America*. Boston: Little, Brown.

Whaples, Robert. 2001. "Hours of Work in U.S. History." EH.Net Encyclopedia. Available at: http://www.eh.net/encyclopedia/contents/whaples.work.hours.us.php (accessed March 25, 2003).

White, Kevin, and Samuel H. Preston. 1996. "How Many Americans Are Alive Because of Twentieth-Century Improvements in Mortality?" *Population and Development Review* 22(September): 415–29.

Whyte, William Hollingsworth. 1956. *The Organization Man*. New York: Simon & Schuster.

Wilder, Thornton. 1953. "A Silent Generation." *Harper's* 206(April): 34–36.

Wildsmith, Elizabeth. 2004. "Race-Ethnic Differences in Female Headship: Exploring the Assumptions of Assimilation Theory." *Social Science Quarterly* 85(March): 89–106.

Williams, David R., and Chiquita Collins. 1995. "U.S. Socioeconomic and Racial Differences in Health: Patterns and Explanations." *Annual Review of Sociology* 21: 349–86.

Williamson, Jeffery G., and Peter Lindert. 1980. *American Inequality*. New York: Academic Press.

Williamson, Joel. 1995. *The New People: Miscegenation and Mulattoes in the United States*. Baton Rouge: Louisiana State University Press. (Orig. pub. in 1980.)

Wilson, William Julius. 1978. *The Declining Significance of Race: Blacks and Changing American Institutions*. Chicago: University of Chicago Press.

———. 1987. *The Truly Disadvantaged: The Inner City, the Underclass, and Public Policy*. Chicago: University of Chicago Press.

———. 1996. *When Work Disappears: The World of the New Urban Poor*. New York: Alfred A. Knopf.

Winseman, Albert L. 2004a. "Eternal Destinations: Americans Believe in Heaven, Hell." Gallup Poll, available to subscribers at: http://www.gallup.com (accessed May 25, 2004).

———. 2004b. "Public Thinks Americans Divided." Gallup Poll, available to subscribers at: hhtp://www.gallup.com (accessed December 28, 2004).

Witter, Robert A., Morris A. Okun, William A. Stock, and Marilyn J. Haring. 1984. "Education and Subjective Well-being: A Meta-Analysis." *Educational Evaluation and Policy Analysis* 6(Summer): 165–73.

Wolfe, Alan. 1998. *One Nation, After All: How Middle-Class Americans Really Think About God, Country, Family, Racism, Welfare, Immigration, Homosexuality, Work, the Right, the Left, and Each Other*. New York: Viking.

Wolff, Edward N. 2000. "Recent Trends in Wealth Ownership, 1983–1998." Working paper 300. Annandale-on-Hudson, N.Y.: Bard College, Jerome Levy Economics Institute.

———. 2001. "Racial Wealth Disparities: Is the Gap Closing?" Public Policy Brief 66. Annandale-on-Hudson, N.Y.: Bard College, Jerome Levy Economics Institute.

———. 2003. "Inheritances and Wealth Inequality, 1989–1998." *American Economic Review* 92(May): 260–64.

Wolff, Edward N., Ajit Zacharias, and Asena Caner. 2003. "Household Wealth, Public Consumption, and Economic Well-being in the United States." Working paper 386. Annandale-on-Hudson, N.Y.: Bard College, Jerome Levy Economics Institute.

Woodward, C. Vann. 1991. *The Old World's New World*. New York: Oxford University Press.

World Health Organization. 2001. *World Health Report 2000* (statistical annex). Available at: http://www.who.int/whr (accessed October 17, 2001).

Wuthnow, Robert. 1988. *The Restructuring of American Religion*. Princeton, N.J.: Princeton University Press.

———. 1998. *Loose Connections: Joining Together in America's Fragmented Communities*. Cambridge, Mass.: Harvard University Press.

Yang, Fenggang, and Helen Rose Ebaugh. 2001. "Transformations in New Immigrant Religions and Their Global Implications." *American Sociological Review* 66(April): 269–88.

Yatchew, Adonis. 1998. "Nonparametric Regression Techniques in Economics." *Journal of Economic Literature* 36(June): 669–721.

———. 2003. *Semiparametric Regression for the Applied Econometrician*. Cambridge: Cambridge University Press.

You, Jong-Sung, and Sanjeev Khagram. 2005. "A Comparative Study of Inequality and Corruption." *American Sociological Review* 70(February): 136–57.

Zhou, Min. 2004. "Are Asian Americans Becoming 'White'?" *Contexts* 3(Winter): 29–37.

Zinn, Howard. 1980. *A People's History of the United States*. New York: Harper & Row.

Zunz, Olivier. 1990. *Making America Corporate, 1879–1920*. Chicago: University of Chicago Press.